Rethinking Copyright for Sustainable Human Development

This book explores the interfaces between copyright and higher education, and their complementarities for the advancement of sustainable human development. In its broader sense, the concept of human development is noted as a set of freedoms and human capabilities that are essential for human flourishing. Adopting a rights-based human development and capability approach (HDCA), this book primarily examines the relevant policy and legal flexibilities under the existing international copyright system, and their implications for access to knowledge required for creative innovation and higher education.

Exploring the interfaces between copyright and higher education, this book argues that an unbalanced and restrictive copyright system impedes reasonable access to knowledge, and stifles creative and learning freedoms or capabilities. In effect, a restrictive copyright system results in serious ramifications for sustainable human development. In view of its findings, this book underscores the need for rethinking copyright and reframing its relevant flexibilities as users' rights that are vital for promoting creative and learning capabilities towards sustainable human development. Further, the book emphasizes the complementarities between copyright and higher education, and their joint roles for sustainable human development.

Given its application of the HDCA to explore ranges of interlinked topics, this book will be of a great interest to researchers across the fields of intellectual property law, innovation, global development, human rights, and higher education.

Dr. Sileshi Bedasie Hirko is a *Queen Elizabeth II Diamond Jubilee Advanced Scholar* and a Postdoctoral Fellow affiliated with University of Ottawa and Open African Innovation Research Organization (Open AIR) in Canada. For several years, he had worked as an Assistant Professor at Haramaya University in Ethiopia. In addition to holding a PhD in Law from University of Ottawa in Canada, the author has earned an LL.M from Munich Intellectual Property Law Center (MIPLC) in Germany and an LL.B from Haramaya University in Ethiopia. Apart from his areas of specialization—intellectual property and competition laws, the author's major research interests include, among others, international trade and investment laws, digital technologies and innovation, international human rights law, and sustainable human development. Besides this book, the author has made several publications, including peer-reviewed articles in reputable national and international journals.

Routledge Explorations in Development Studies

This Development Studies series features innovative and original research at the regional and global scale. It promotes interdisciplinary scholarly works drawing on a wide spectrum of subject areas, in particular politics, health, economics, rural and urban studies, sociology, environment, anthropology, and conflict studies.

Topics of particular interest are globalization; emerging powers; children and youth; cities; education; media and communication; technology development; and climate change.

In terms of theory and method, rather than basing itself on any orthodoxy, the series draws broadly on the tool kit of the social sciences in general, emphasizing comparison, the analysis of the structure and processes, and the application of qualitative and quantitative methods.

Foreign Aid and Development in South Korea and Africa
A Comparative Analysis of Economic Growth
Kelechi A. Kalu and Jiyoung Kim

Women and the UN
A New History of Women's International Human Rights
Edited by Rebecca Adami and Dan Plesch

Youth Civic Engagement and Local Peacebuilding in the Middle East and North Africa
Prospects and Challenges for Community Development
Edited by Ibrahim Natil

Women-Owned SMEs in Emerging Markets
The Missing Link in Global Supply Chains
Shabnam Shalizi

Rethinking Copyright for Sustainable Human Development
Higher Education and Access to Knowledge
Sileshi Bedasie Hirko

For more information about this series, please visit: www.routledge.com/Routledge-Explorations-in-Development-Studies/book-series/REDS

Rethinking Copyright for Sustainable Human Development

Higher Education and Access to Knowledge

Sileshi Bedasie Hirko

Routledge
Taylor & Francis Group
LONDON AND NEW YORK

First published 2022
by Routledge
2 Park Square, Milton Park, Abingdon, Oxon OX14 4RN

and by Routledge
605 Third Avenue, New York, NY 10158

Routledge is an imprint of the Taylor & Francis Group, an informa business

British Library Cataloguing-in-Publication Data
A catalogue record for this book is available from the British Library

Library of Congress Cataloging-in-Publication Data
A catalog record has been requested for this book

ISBN: 978-1-032-10222-1 (hbk)
ISBN: 978-1-032-10224-5 (pbk)
ISBN: 978-1-003-21429-8 (ebk)

DOI: 10.4324/9781003214298

Typeset in Bembo
by MPS Limited, Dehradun

In loving memory of my father, Bedasie Hirko Boka and my younger sibling, Kebede Bedasie Hirko.

Contents

Preface

In its human-centered approach, the notion of sustainable human development is understood as a framework for an equitable and intergenerational pursuit of valuable beings and doings. From among others, higher education and creative innovation are both constitutive and instrumental components of sustainable human development. For most people across the globe, education is thus valued not for its own sake alone, but also for its vital roles to achieve human development. In a similar vein, a copyright system that promotes creative innovation is instrumental for human development. In its fullest human-centered sense, human development is thus regarded as an essential freedom all human beings aspire to achieve and need to enjoy meaningful lives. To this end, the increasing role of advanced education has become crucial for fostering human development—both at individual and collective levels.

Nevertheless, the indispensable role of higher education is undermined without sufficient and affordable access to learning materials. Yet, access to copyrighted learning materials depends upon the existence of appropriate access-oriented flexibilities. Absent the flexibilities, a limited access to knowledge remains a critical problem for future creators, learners and educators. Indeed, the profound implications of this challenge for sustainable human development underpin the interfaces between copyright and higher education. As a matter of global concern, the issue of the interfaces has garnered an increasing traction among several scholars and stakeholders. Nonetheless, it seems that a scant attention is accorded to the human development perspective to inform the debates. Noting its potential to enrich the debates, this author has thus drawn on the perspective in exploring the interfaces in this book.

From human development perspective, this book explores an interplay between copyright and higher education, and their joint contributions for sustainable human development. An overarching and multidimensional context of interfaces, access to knowledge is essential for a robust copyright and quality higher education. Further, access to knowledge is vital for both regimes to advance sustainable human development through respective contributions—creative innovation and human capabilities. Critiquing the narrow lens of economic development, this book goes further to underscore the richer notion of sustainable human development as an intergenerational enlargement or expansion of human capabilities.

Exploring the interfaces in this sense, the book appraises the potential roles and limitations of the various international copyright-related flexibilities. Stifling creative and learning capabilities, the existing restrictive international copyright has serious ramifications for sustainable human development. Emphasizing their complementarities, this book thus underlines the need for rethinking both copyright and higher education in the light of human capabilities. In effect, embracing such an integrative and inclusive approach will enhance their roles for sustainable human development.

Given its multidisciplinary content, this book will be of a great interest to learners, educators, researchers, and policy makers in the fields of international IP law, higher education, innovation, human rights, and development studies.

Sileshi Bedasie Hirko

Foreword

Intellectual Property has conflicting and complementary relations with humanity's perennial aspirations to development and the promotion of the 'public interest'. This is so even though development and public interest are subjects of contested, even if elastic, framings. The ironic convergence of the fraught and complementary effects of intellectual property in the promotion of multiple interests that drive human progress is part of the constantly animating factors in the evolution of intellectual property jurisprudence. As an ongoing matter, that dynamic in intellectual property is the catalyst for negotiations in policy and academic circles at national and international levels for the balancing of complex interests at various sites where intellectual property or knowledge production intersects with the exigencies of development.

Rethinking Copyright for Sustainable Human Development: Higher Education and Access to Knowledge focuses on the copyright regime of intellectual property and its complex intersection with human rights, and with special consideration for the right to education. Using the human rights framework, this refreshing work spotlights the right to higher education. It offers a compelling case for a departure from the discriminatory appeal to the right to education in which higher education is relegated to tertiary or residual consideration, no pun intended, under the 'progressive' latitude for realization of human rights. The author takes a bold and holistic approach to the right to education which integrates and entrenches, without equivocation, the right to higher education. Education at all levels is interdependent even as higher education serves as a direct incentive for development generally and for sustainable human development more so. Human right to higher education resonates with some urgency for developing regions of the world. For example, Africa's desperate need to bridge development gaps commends the continent for an urgent and immediate access to higher education in a rights-based approach. Not only do the urgency and appetite for higher education find support in African regional human rights architecture, but they are also consistent with human development and capability approach as a shared aspiration of human rights and the intellectual property system.

Based on the shared interest between human rights and intellectual property, specifically copyright, in the pursuit of optimal human capability, development and progress, this book places the copyright system on trial. Through stimulating analytical insights, it engages, contributes and builds on the tensed debate at international level over the jurisprudence of limitations and exceptions or flexibilities in copyright law, and the overall dynamic of access to knowledge debate. It associates copyright with access to knowledge and to learning materials. Those are critical elements for the advancement of education, especially higher education, which fuels humanity's capability for optimum realization of potential for sustainable development. Notwithstanding elaborate jurisprudence around copyright limitations and exceptions or flexibilities, Hirko insists that based on the urgency of access to knowledge and learning materials in the higher education context, there is opportunity to deliberately orient or evaluate the jurisprudence on copyright flexibilities towards sustainable development outcomes as a deliberate matter. An aspect of that project is to align copyright jurisprudence to a robust human-centred capability approach which mainstreams the integration of the right to higher education. To further human-centred capability approach, the book makes a case for a bold, creative and imaginative effort to open the space for exploring flexibilities in the copyright system including, most notably, the open access domain which is a pragmatic mechanism for advancing access to knowledge, especially learning materials in the higher education context.

This book is exceptionally distinguished for its boldness in offering a very refreshing perspective on the ever-animated debate around intellectual property, human rights and development. Its ability to shine light on the right to higher education as a human right and in making the link to human-centred capability approach offers an inspirational insight to intellectual property and development scholars, students, jurists, including copyright experts and policy makers, educationists and administrators as well as rights holders and users of copyright materials in various settings. The author has done a commendable work of illuminating less explored and foggy areas of intersection of intellectual property and human rights with noticeable boldness, and provocation for new priorities and new direction in the exploration of copyright flexibilities.

Professor Chidi Oguamanam
Faculty of Law (Common Law)
University of Ottawa
Fall, 2021

Select List of Abbreviations

ACHPR	African Charter on Human and Peoples' Rights
ACRWC	African Charter on the Rights and Welfare of the Child
Art.	Article
AU	African Union
CA	Capabilities Approach
CC	Creative Commons
CESCR	Committee on Economic, Social, and Cultural Rights
CMOs	Collective Management Organizations
CRPD	Convention on the Rights of Persons with Disabilities
DA	Development Agenda
DRD	Declaration on the Right to Development
ECL	Extended Collective Licensing
EU	European Union
GPL	General Public Licensing
HDCA	Human Development and Capability Approach
ICESCR	International Covenant on Economic, Social and Cultural Rights
L&Es	Limitations and Exceptions
MDGs	Millennium Development Goals
OA	Open Access
RTD	Right to Development
TPMs	Technological protection measures
TRIPs	Trade-Related Aspects of Intellectual Property Rights
UCC	Universal Copyright Convention
UDHR	Universal Declaration on Human Rights
UNCPD	UN Convention on Persons with Disabilities
UNCRC	United Nations Convention on the Rights of the Child
UNESCO	United Nations Educational, Scientific and Cultural Organization
UN SDGs	United Nations Sustainable Development Goals
UNTS	United Nations Treaty Series
WCT	WIPO Copyright Treaty
WIPO	World Intellectual Property Organization
WPPT	WIPO Performances and Phonograms Treaty
WTO	World Trade Organization

Acknowledgement

First of all, I praise God for His enabling grace in bringing this book to full fruition after years of rigorous research. Next, I am grateful to Professors Jeremy de Beer and Chidi Oguamanam for their invaluable comments, unreserved support, and continuous guidance on the research that culminated in this book. Without their generous assistance of all kinds and unabated mentorship, the completion of the research work would have been inconceivable. Moreover, I am thankful to Professors Ruth Okediji, Michael Geist, Teresa Scassa, and Obiora Okafor for their insightful and detailed comments on the research. From among several others, I am also indebted to the Open African Innovation Research (Open AIR) and the Centre for International Governance Innovation (CIGI) for their financial support in the course of the same research. In this respect, worth mentioning is Mrs. Victoria Schorr for her facilitative assistance during the period of research fellowship I spent at Open AIR.

Last but not least, a special heartfelt gratitude goes to my beloved wife, Mozart Tadesse Belachew, for her selfless support, unfailing love, and moral encouragement throughout this book project. In shouldering all the burdens, she devoted herself to look after our wonderful children. As a caring mother and woman of wisdom, she has been gracious enough to offer me her unreserved and loving support without interruption. In the same vein, I remain grateful to my mother, Mamme Tullu Fita, for her unrivaled love and dedication. Further, all brothers, sisters, relatives, colleagues, and friends of mine from near and afar deserve heartfelt thanks for their encouragements. For their editorial support, I am thankful to Helena Hurd, Rosie Anderson, and other editors.

1 The conceptual framework of the book

1.1 Copyright, education, and development: introduction

For all segments of societies—individuals, communities, and nations, the issue of development remains an ultimate objective of life all human beings endeavor to achieve. Despite its multifaceted nature with, *inter alia*, social, cultural, and economic dimensions, the economic dimension of development often gets undue emphasis. More often than not, the economic dimension permeates various policy documents and market-driven research. In effect, economic growth—the more truncated notion of development—drives and guides the objectives and operation of copyright and education systems. In fact, the more rich and human-centered notion of the multifaceted development remains underemphasized despite its potential to serve as an all-encompassing policy objective. As a result, human beings and their desired valuable ends are either neglected or used as a *mere means* for economic growth.

Noting such inadequate and narrow goals, scholars and development organizations have drawn a significant attention to the human-centered notion of human development. Framed as a set of freedoms, human development is understood as the expansion of human capabilities for the attainment of valuable achievements. Further, the notion is infused with the inclusive, equitable and intergenerational principle of sustainable development. Construed both *as a process and an end of human welfare,* sustainable human development is thus constituted of and intertwined with several elements. From various areas of interlinkages, copyright, education and development are interlinked in the context of human capital, human capabilities, and access to knowledge. In their interdependence, sustainable human development remains the ultimate objective and an inclusive context. Suffice for introduction, the notion of human development is noted to denote the expansion of human capabilities or freedoms.[1]

As defined in the *Human Development Report (1990)*, human development is "a process of enlarging people's choices or opportunities."[2] In essence, what constitute human development are people's actual abilities or freedoms *to do* and *to be* in order to lead worthwhile lives.[3] From among others, access to knowledge is essential for the realization of human development.[4] Subject to

DOI: 10.4324/9781003214298-1

copyright system that serves as a model for its governance, access to knowledge is thus a crucial point of nexus between copyright and education, and their joint roles for human development. In this regard, human rights and constitutional dimensions are useful to inform and channel the interfaces towards human development.

Central to the broader domain of access to knowledge, access to learning materials is vital for the knowledge-intensive higher education, scientific research, and innovation. From among the major knowledge governance mechanisms, the relevant learning materials depend upon copyright for their creation, utilization and dissemination. Within the broader context of access to knowledge, access to learning materials constitutes a more focused and specific context for the multidimensional interfaces this book undertakes to examine. Taking this as a useful context, the book seeks to examine the interplay between higher education and the protection of copyright, and their roles for human development. To this end, the book adopts the combined human development and capability approach (HDCA) as an overarching theoretical and normative framework. As explained further in the subsequent chapter, the framework emphasizes the expansion or advancement of human capabilities for valuable achievements. That said, this chapter is limited to highlighting the normative dimensions of education, copyright and development.

1.2 Education in the context of access to learning materials

1.2.1 Education as a human right

As a matter of fact, education is of a fundamental significance for human beings. According to John Dewey, a leading philosopher of modern education, education is essential both for transformative lives and continued existence of human beings as a social group.[5] Given its inherent and central role for human beings to develop and live dignified lives, education is recognized as one of the various human rights. Framed as a basic human right, the right to education is a multifaceted right. In its manifold dimensions, the right cuts across civil, political, social, economic and cultural rights.[6] Along with other socio-economic rights, the right has been incorporated in major human rights instruments.[7] It bears noting that the embodiment of the right to education in legal regimes at various levels affirms the fundamental importance of education.

For instance, the right to education has been enshrined in the relevant provisions of the Universal Declaration on Human Rights (UDHR),[8] the International Covenant on Economic, Social and Cultural Rights (ICESCR),[9] and the UN Convention on the Rights of the Child (UNCRC).[10] Serving as a blueprint for subsequent human rights instruments, art. 26(1) of the UDHR states that "everyone has the right to education." In the same vein, art.13(1) of the ICESCR—a binding international human rights instrument—reiterates an explicit recognition of "the right of everyone to education."

At a regional level, the African Charter on Human and Peoples' Rights (African Charter) is the major regional human rights instrument that enshrines every individual's right to education.[11] In contrast to its international counterparts, the African Charter makes a generic reference to the right to education without a distinction among its various levels. Further, the African Charter on the Rights and Welfare of the Child (ACRWC) is another important regional human rights instrument that recognizes the right to education.[12] Given its distinctive approach, the African Charter places all categories of human rights, including the right to education, on a par with each other to command an immediate application.

In its detailed treatment of the various levels, the ICESCR underscores the importance of the right to education.[13] In fact, the realization of education at all levels will be critical for the fullest enjoyment of the right to education. In principle, education must be made available at all levels.[14] As opposed to the approach under the African Charter, the ICESCR embodies a significant variance in terms of the weight attached to each level of education. For example, the Covenant obligates members to ensure an *immediate* provision of free and *compulsory* primary education.[15] The immediate and non-optional requirements of the education underline the fundamental, unfettered, unconditional and urgent attributes of the human right to basic education. As such, the right to basic education is affirmed as the minimum essential or core level of education. In contrast, secondary education is required to be made *generally* available and accessible to all by *progressive* introduction of free education.[16] As elaborated below, this variance is even more pronounced for higher education.

1.2.2 Higher education as an integral element of right to education

As mentioned previously, the realization of education as a human right is classified into three levels. Based on the levels, degrees of prioritization and conditions are provided for their respective realization. Given the variance among the levels, scholars often dismiss the human rights status of higher education. Cognizant of its limitations that militate against its status, this author however disagrees with the outright denial of its human rights dimension. In view of the values and purpose of education, higher education can be regarded as an integral element of the human right to education in its fullest remit and content. It is argued that the variance attached to the levels of education and necessitated for their realization would not single out higher education and divest it of its human right status. Rather, the human right to education is constituted of all the levels built into an interdependent and a coherent whole. As a human being, an individual is thus entitled to the right, the enjoyment of which spans human's life from childhood to adulthood. Yet, the levels of the right to education and the time for their enjoyment would often correspond with the respective life stages of human beings.

Given the emphasis upon the basic level and the issue of resource constraints, human rights instruments and scholars tend to neglect such a holistic understanding of the levels of education. Taking a holistic view affirms their interdependence as interlinked elements of the human right to education. Despite the conditions attached to its enjoyment, it leaves no doubt that "education as a human right includes higher education."[17] As Klaus Beiter correctly notes, "international human rights law deals with higher education as a right and requires such education to be made progressively free."[18]

Indeed, various human rights instruments have enshrined higher education as one of the levels of human right to education. Known for its differential treatment of the levels of education, the ICESCR was the first binding human rights instrument to include higher education under its provision. Although its *immediate* and *unconditional* realization is not required, art.13(2)(c) of the Covenant recognizes the right of equal access to higher education. For a practical reason, the right to higher education is however not as absolute as the right to basic education. Nor is it required to be *generally* available and accessible like that of secondary education. Rather, the enjoyment of the right to higher education is contingent upon the requirements of *capacity* and *merit.*[19]

Notwithstanding the above-mentioned conditions, the right to higher education should still be noted as an integral element of the right to education in its fullest sense. In this regard, it is useful to bear in mind art.17(1) of the African Charter's generic reference to the right to education without similar conditions and a distinction among the levels of education. In a stark departure from the African Charter, the ACRWC rather follows the differential approach of the ICESCR to mirror the above requirements. In so doing, the ACRWC requires states to take "all appropriate measures" in order to "make higher education accessible to all on the basis of capacity and ability by every appropriate means."[20] In contrast to the ICESCR, the ACRWC adds a specific emphasis on states' obligation to take *"all appropriate measures"* to make higher education accessible to all.

In spite of the slight variance among the wordings of the relevant human rights instruments, it is incumbent upon the member states to take a more progressive approach to ensure a better implementation of the right to education. Taking an opposite measure is tantamount to a regressive action that requires an adequate justification to remain lawful. In African context, higher education is integral to the human right recognized under the African Charter on the same footing with other rights. The equitable provision of higher education is thus required to be of an immediate application as the Charter avoids the notion of progressive realization animating the ICESCR.[21]

Given their obligation under the more context-based Charter, African countries should take this approach to ensure an equal and immediate access to higher education. Due to their urgent development imperatives, Africans are in a greater need of better and an immediate access to higher education in order to harness development opportunities. In this respect, a state's resort to the resource-contingent principle of progressive realization entrenched in the ICESCR remains a significant clawback.

Embodied in the Covenant, the principles of non-discrimination and progressive realization are the governing rules for the required access. Despite the need for its immediate application, the operation of the principle of equal access depends upon objective criteria nations might set to determine capacities for admission.[22] For the resource-and-time-contingent rule of progressive realization, *concrete* and *progressive measures* are required to achieve the full enjoyment of all the rights enshrined in the ICESCR.[23] From among levels of education, higher education is subject to even a more flexible degree of progressive realization.[24]

In effect, all the foregoing pragmatic qualifications and disparities might militate against the claimed human rights status of higher education. In part, this is attributed to both past and current trends. In its traditional evolution, higher education was treated as a privilege reserved for the elites.[25] In the present context of globalization, it is regarded as a tradable commodity or service that is subject to the global trade regime.[26] In both situations, the proponents of commodification contend that access to education is not within the reach of the public at large to be claimed as a right. In effect, the human right status is often disputed for, *inter alia*, lack of a universal recognition as such.[27] In the positivist international law, the reluctance on the status seems to indicate the nature of human rights instruments as embodiments of global norms recognized or developed through consensus.[28]

Lacking a clear legal recognition, a norm remains a mere moral standard or entitlement short of an enforceable legal obligation. As argued above, states should take a purposive interpretation and a holistic understanding of human right to education that encompasses higher education as its integral element. This approach will both require and encourage states to integrate right to higher education into its national laws in force within their respective jurisdiction. For instance, Venezuela has taken this approach to recognize a constitutional right to higher education.[29] In the same vein, South Africa's constitution enshrines the right to education, including "further education" that appears to embrace higher education.[30]

Critical of the conceptual deficit in the global norms, some scholars construe higher education as an integral part of the general right to education.[31] For instance, Tristan McCowan criticizes the distinction among levels of education for its arbitrariness and considers higher education as a component of the right to education.[32] Likewise, the late human rights scholar Katrina Tomasevski—the first Special Rapporteur on the right to education—appeared to suggest this view. For her, "the right to education may be defined in terms of access to free-of-charge schooling at all levels—from the nursery to postgraduate studies."[33] Nonetheless, both take note of the cumbersome financial implication for its realization.[34]

Further, seen through a lifelong learning process as a continuum, the conceptual distinction might run counter to the progressive, continuing, nurturing nature and objective of education.[35] The conceptual conundrum aside, the existing human rights instruments tend to be pragmatic in their approach to reflect the variance among the levels of education. This is evident from the readings of the provisions and the conditions attached to each level of education. In line with the distinctive approach in the African Charter and the concomitant progressive jurisprudence of the African Human Rights Commission, the variance under the ICESCR and the ACRWC should wane for human development to flourish in its fullest extent.

1.2.3 Purpose and significance of education

Given its fundamental importance, the purpose of education irrespective of its levels is articulated in all the major international human rights instruments—the UDHR, the ICESCR, and the UNCRC. A clear articulation of the objective of education is relevant to determine the nature, content and scope of education at all levels. As a precursor to the subsequent binding instruments, the UDHR under its art.26 (2) states that "[e]ducation shall be directed to the full development of the human personality and to the strengthening of respect for human rights and fundamental freedoms." In the same vein, art. 13(1) of the ICESCR, while echoing the same purpose in verbatim, intertwines the development of human personalities with the "sense of dignity" as an intrinsic purpose of education.[36]

In respect of its instrumental role, education advances other human rights values that, in turn, further the respect for human rights and fundamental freedoms.[37] In particular, education promotes an effective and informed participation in a free society. To this end, it nurtures a democratic culture of understanding, tolerance and friendship among all nations, racial, ethnic, and religious groups.[38] In effect, education fosters the maintenance of national, regional, and global peace. Further, education is a catalyst for, and a driver of, socio-economic development. In view of its holistic purpose, the effectiveness of the intrinsic and instrumental roles of education should be measured by the successful realization of its fundamental purpose—the fullest development of the human personalities.[39] In this regard, Martha Nussbaum reminds us of the critical role of "a higher education [as] a part of every human being's self-realization."[40]

In furtherance of the same core objective it shares with other levels,[41] higher education is thus notable for its role in the progressive realization of other human rights and human development.[42] Sharing the 4-A features of the right to education, higher education must also be available, accessible, acceptable, and adaptable.[43] As can be noted from the ICESCR, the significance of higher education is implicit in the need for its *accessibility to all on equal basis.* To this effect, states are encouraged to ensure a progressive introduction of free education.[44] As emphasized in the *General Comment No. 13,* member states are expected to embrace the *progressive realization* approach that requires them to "*move … towards the full realization of art. 13.*"[45] Given its empowering potential, education is considered to have a multiplier effect.[46]

Over a period of time, the *progressive steps* towards the *full realization of education at all levels* will facilitate the progressive realization of other human rights, including the right to development.[47] From a lifelong learning perspective, the progressive realization of higher education and its significance are noted as an integral part of lifelong learning opportunities.[48] Further, higher education is often considered a vital tool for development through advanced human capital. As argued in this book, this role should rather be reframed and understood in the context of more-inclusive human capabilities.

1.2.4 Education's essential input: access to learning materials

Whether noted as a human right or an instrument for development, or a combination thereof, the realization of education at all levels depends, *inter alia*, upon access to learning materials.[49] In particular, a quality education at a higher level requires an adequate access to relevant and advanced learning materials. As articulated in Tomasevski's 4-A scheme,[50] the availability, accessibility, and acceptability (quality) of education are linked to an adequate availability of the relevant learning materials. For instance, a human rights-based report of the United Nations Educational, Scientific and Cultural Organization (UNESCO) highlights the provision of books and equipment as a fundamental prerequisite for education and its quality.[51] Likewise, the Committee on Economic, Social, and Cultural Rights (CESCR) underlines an access to learning materials as one of the essential inputs required for the realization of the right to education in its relevant general comments.[52]

It should thus be noted that access to learning materials is an essential resource for the realization of higher education that remains instrumental for the achievement of a holistic development with its economic, social, and cultural dimensions.[53] As Ruth Okediji observes, both education and access to basic scientific knowledge are essential to create an enabling environment for "domestic initiatives and development policies to take root."[54] In sum, the realization of higher education and its role depend, *inter alia*, upon the availability of or access to relevant learning materials.

1.3 Copyright and education: a shared function of advancing public interests

1.3.1 Copyright: an instrument of public interest

In principle, copyright protection is premised on the desire to promote the production and dissemination of creative works for the purpose of public interest. Integral to the notion of public interest are the twin-interests of authors and users. That is, copyright system is *a means* devised to promote both the protection of, and access to, the creative works.[55] In fact, the dual aspects of the public interest are inextricably interlinked that one aspect cannot be considered in isolation from the other. As Rebecca Tushnet notes, both rights and limitations are designed to serve public interests by providing the authors the necessary incentive for creative innovation and the users (the public) the freedom of access to the creative works.[56] Enshrined in the U.S Constitution, the protection of intellectual property (IP) is justified in order to promote the progress of science and useful arts.[57] Confirming such an instrumental role, the WIPO Copyright Treaty (WCT) "[emphasizes] the outstanding significance of copyright protection as an incentive for literary and artistic creation."[58]

In practice, there is a disproportionate emphasis on authors' aspect of public interest to promote the production of knowledge without a due attention for users' access to the knowledge—another essential aspect of public interest.[59] Further, various nations adopt slightly different approaches towards the intended public interest. For instance, the Anglo-American utilitarian objective of promoting "the progress of useful arts" underlines the primacy of the interest of the public at large.[60] In contrast, the continental copyright system emphasizes the natural-right-based individual and creative autonomy of the authors with an indirect contribution to the interest of the society.[61]

Outside IP's legal regime, the overriding importance of public interest for regulating IP is embodied in various human rights instruments. For instance, the EU Charter on Fundamental Rights enshrines the general public interest as a guiding parameter for regulating the use of property.[62] Interpreted to be applicable for IP including copyright,[63] art.17(1) of the Charter makes clear that "[t]he use of property may be regulated by law *in so far is necessary for the general interest.*"[64] In the same provision, the Charter states that "[n]o one may be deprived of his or her possessions, except *in the public interest.*"[65] In so doing, the Charter underscores the overriding importance of public interest both for regulation and limitations of private property rights.[66]

In its protection of creative works within the internal market to promote "*learning and culture,*" the EU Directive 2001/29/EC reiterates the significance of the principle for "permitting exceptions or limitations *in the public interest* for the purpose of *education and teaching.*"[67] Despite the existence of different degrees of emphasis, the legal protection underpinning both systems is driven by legally recognized public and private interests. Indeed, both conceptions of copyright protection are instrumental for their direct or indirect role of advancing public interest for socio-economic development.[68] In this sense, the hitherto conceptual distinction in the copyright traditions has almost waned in the global copyright system.[69] That said, the instrumentalist purpose of copyright is embedded in the rights and limitations intended to advance the interest of the society at large. An issue of a protracted debate is however the extent to which the existing copyright system serves its intended purpose as an instrument of public interest. The issue is even more pressing at national levels.

1.3.2 Education: an element of public interests

From among various societal interests, education is one of the vital public interests that interact with copyright protection in the context of access to learning materials. In this context, the preamble to the WCT—recognizing the need to maintain a balance—makes an explicit reference to *education, research, and access to information* as illustrative elements of *the larger public interest.*[70] In placing education within the ambit of *the larger public interest,* the Treaty underlines the need to maintain a fair balance between the rights of authors and education. At this juncture, it is useful to note the double-sided interactions between copyright and education. First, most learning materials required for education are subject to copyright protection.[71] Second, the protected materials are an essential input for education to advance societal goals. In particular, learning materials constitute a vital prerequisite for quality higher education and scientific research.

It is this context that brings to the fore the relationship between copyright and higher education. From copyright perspective, the production and dissemination of creative works including learning materials are integral to the purpose of copyright protection. Indeed, promoting learning was one of the early intended objectives of the Statute of Anne (1710).[72] Despite its increasing marginalization, revitalizing this age-old public interest aspect of copyright is instrumental for access to copyrighted learning materials. Education is thus one of the public interests that can be served through different mechanisms.

For example, both international and national copyright regimes allow various flexibilities that serve to facilitate access to copyrighted learning materials for educational purposes. In the international trade regime, members states might invoke education as one of the vital public interests integral to their development objectives. In this regard, art.8(1) of the TRIPs Agreement can be construed to embrace education as a public interest in "sectors of vital importance" for socio-economic and technological development.[73] In view of its crucial role, Margaret Chon contends that "the key term 'development' in the TRIPs preamble and objectives should include the provision of basic education."[74]

Despite the absence of an explicit reference to education or other aspects of the public interest in the provisions of the TRIPs Agreement or its negotiation record, this assertion can be inferred from the incorporation of the Berne Convention into the TRIPs Agreement. In addition to the TRIPs Agreement's flexible notion of public interests in "sectors of vital importance," this inference ensues from the Convention's unequivocal recognition of education from among the various public interest aspects of copyright. In line with this understanding, Okediji notes educational purpose as one of the "enduring aspects of public interest in access to protected works."[75]

As mentioned above, the WIPO Internet Treaties—special agreements adopted in accord with the Berne Convention—recognize education as a component of the larger public interest. In effect, an education is an element of public interest that needs to be considered in determining the necessary balance the Berne Convention seeks to maintain. Commenting on the WIPO Treaties, Okediji points out the significance of the Treaties for the interpretation of the TRIPs Agreement that has embraced the Berne Convention.[76] Further, art.10 (2) of the Berne Convention and its Appendix are the major instances of the relevant pre-TRIPs development-oriented copyright flexibilities designed to promote an access to learning materials. Due to the Berne Convention's integration into the TRIPs Agreement, all the aforementioned instances of access to protected works indicate the existence of an implicit substantive link between access to learning materials and the copyright provisions of the TRIPs Agreement.[77] However, the access prong of copyright is quite inadequate as its actual extent lies within the constrained content and scope of the flexibilities.[78]

Given their role to facilitate access to learning materials, it is thus imperative to explore the relevant flexibilities and the need to rethink or reintegrate them for the advancement of sustainable human development. Framed within the broad context of access to knowledge that might be regarded as a human right,[79] access to learning materials is also treated as users' right which, in turn, is deemed integral to copyright system.[80] In particular, the notion of users' right marks an emerging right-based approach towards an enhanced access to learning materials required for higher education. It is a useful approach as it allows the exploration of the relevant flexibilities through a right-based and development lens.

1.4 Copyright and education for development: an overview of the nexus

As indicated previously, both copyright and education share common objectives of promoting development. Copyright contributes to development by promoting creative innovation and scientific progress. In the same vein, education fosters development through the development of human personalities, human capital/advanced skills, and human capabilities. Thus, development is the ultimate end of both regimes. Indeed, development is an important issue at global, regional, and local levels. In African countries that have ratified the African Charter, the issue of development is not a mere aspirational or policy objective. It is rather a binding human right and, in some countries, a constitutional right that demands concrete and progressive measures for its realization. For instance, the right to development that is central to the African Charter has been enshrined in Ethiopia's national constitution.[81]

Within the broader development context, the instrumental functions of copyright and higher education are pivotal to facilitate the realization of sustainable human development. Concerning copyright's instrumental role for sustainable human development, an inference of the role can be gathered from the WCT's objective to resolve issues of "new economic, social, cultural and technological developments."[82] Further, the TRIPs Agreement recognizes "developmental and technological objectives" as the underlying public policy objectives of IP protection.[83] To this end, the TRIPs Agreement reiterates the objectives of IP protection and enforcement to advance "the mutual advantage of producers and users (..) in a manner conducive to social and economic welfare."[84]

In contrast, various instruments are more explicit to highlight the crucial role of education for sustainable development. For instance, as stated in the Agenda 21, "[e]ducation is critical for promoting sustainable development and improving the capacity of the people to address environment and development issues."[85] In the same vein, the United Nations Economic Commission for Europe (UNECE)[86] is worth quoting in this regard for its elaboration of the role of education for sustainable development as follows:

> Education for sustainable development develops and strengthens the capacity of individuals, groups, communities, organizations and countries to make judgments and choices in favour of sustainable development. It can promote a shift in people's mindsets and in so doing enable them to make our world safer, healthier and more prosperous, thereby improving the quality of life. Education for sustainable development can provide critical reflection and greater awareness and empowerment so that new visions and concepts can be explored and new methods and tools developed.

Relevant for all educational sectors, this elaboration applies also to higher education and underscores the latter's role for sustainable development.[87] Promoting the expansion of human capabilities that in turn advance human well-being, higher education is thus vital for sustainable human development.

As noted above, the linkage between the instrumental roles of copyright and higher education for development converges upon access to learning materials within the broader domain of knowledge goods. In other words, the creation and dissemination of knowledge are the common domains of both copyright and education. The knowledge created and disseminated through copyright is an essential input for education. In the same vein, the knowledge and skills developed through education are important inputs for sustainable creative works in a robust copyright system. In their joint contribution, both copyright and education are vital to enrich a vibrant store of knowledge required for human flourishing.

In consequence, the interaction between the regimes requires a careful examination in the light of their intended common goals towards human development. In particular, the issue of access to copyrighted learning materials underpins the interplay between the legal protection of copyright and higher education.[88] For their interface, an access to copyrighted learning materials constitutes their immediate context of linkages. That is, the competing interests of the users/learners and that of the creators subsisting in the copyrighted learning materials underline the linkage between education and copyright system.[89]

In the context of their joint roles for development, an implicit recognition of the interface, and the need for maintaining a balance between the regimes are embedded, *inter alia*, in the TRIPs Agreement and the WIPO Internet Treaties.[90] In fact, the WIPO Internet Treaties make the interface and the consequent need for the balance more explicit in its reference to education as an element of the larger public interest that should be factored into the balance between the rights of authors and the public interest.[91] It is useful to note that art.8(1) of the TRIPs Agreement contemplates the existence of the public interest "in sectors of vital importance to [members] socio-economic and technological development." From supranational legal regimes, the *InfoSoc Directive* is worth mentioning for its due recognition of *the public interest* as a guiding principle in setting limitations and exceptions (L&Es) for the purpose of *education and teaching.*[92]

Further, their substantive nexus is grounded in the human rights and human capabilities dimensions of copyright protection and the right to education. In guiding their joint roles towards their shared goals, both dimensions are vital for the realization of the right to sustainable human development. Given their potential to complement human capabilities, the various human rights documents "form the legal basis for a human capability approach to the question of copyright on educational materials."[93]

As regards the human rights' attributes of copyright, both arts. 27(2) of the UDHR and 15(1) (c) of the ICESCR provide for an authoritative legal and normative basis to ensure the protection of authors' material and moral interests over their literary, scientific, and artistic works.[94] As the CESCR pointed out in its general comment, copyright is however neither a human right in itself nor the sole means to secure the required legal protection.[95] Yet members are required to guarantee the legal protection of the authors' interests at national levels. It is noted that the legal protection of the material interests is essential to ensure the authors an adequate standard of living.[96] In this regard, the linkage between authors' "adequate living standard" and their materials interests can be used to determine the core minimum human rights threshold for the required protection.[97]

In so doing, setting the required level of protection can free up more space to strike the necessary balance between copyright and other fundamental rights such as the right to education in the ICESCR.[98] In particular, the *General Comment No. 17* states that members "have a duty to prevent unreasonably high costs for (…) schoolbooks and learning materials from undermining the rights of large segments of the population to (….) education."[99] Furthermore, the issue of interface would arise in respect of access to learning materials within the broad context of access to knowledge as the latter is considered to involve a human rights dimension.[100] Although it is not as urgent and essential as an access to medicines that carries a stronger ethical force, an access to knowledge is critical to implicate an issue of human rights.[101] In particular, its significance is evident in the context of the foundational role of education for a decent life.[102] As James Nickel notes, "[s]aving people's lives will often have special priority, but life loses much of its value if the other requirements of making it decent are not met."[103]

Emphasizing the instrumental role of IP, the CESCR highlights IP's goal to serve a "social function" of balancing the competing individual and public interests.[104] Like that of IP, it bears noting the role of education to advance, *inter alia*, social function.[105] That is, both IP and education share a common social function of promoting knowledge creation and dissemination. In affirming their possible interaction, the CESCR thus underscores the direct interface between the protection of a copyright and the right to education in the context of access to learning materials. To this effect, the Committee stresses the need to strike a balance between the human rights aspects of copyright protection and the right to education.[106]

In this respect, it is essential to direct both copyright and higher education towards human development as their shared objective. Further, both regimes are supposed to advance the general public interests that fit into a holistic framework for human development and welfare. This shared objective constitutes a compelling ground to carve out the necessary flexibilities for a reasonable access to the relevant copyrighted materials required for higher education. Nonetheless, this requires a holistic exploration of the linkages between the higher education and copyright regimes. In particular, the analysis and reframing of the flexibilities should emphasize the need to direct the complementary objectives of the regimes towards human development. To this end, this book undertakes to examine, *inter alia*, the aforesaid core issues from a right-based human development perspective.

1.5 Exploring flexibilities in the context of access to learning materials

1.5.1 A brief exposition of key concepts

A Delineating learning materials

As mentioned earlier, learning materials are one of the essential inputs required for education in general and higher education in particular. At this juncture, it is important to elaborate what constitutes or comprises learning materials. Indeed, there is no standard definition of learning materials with a delineated scope. From the existing literature, one often observes an interchangeable reference to learning materials to mean teaching materials or educational materials. Further, in the international documents and major reports such as the *General Comment No. 17* and the report prepared under the auspices of UNESCO, the term "learning materials" is used along with terms such as schoolbooks or textbooks.[107] In general, there is a variance in the meaning, scope, and usage of the terms across literature and documents.

Despite the lack of their consistent usage, the terms essentially refer to educational resources that are required for a formal education. In fact, the meaning of the term "education" itself varies depending upon how broad or narrow one construes it. Defined in its narrow sense of promoting learning as its primary objective, education refers to a learning process within formal educational settings.[108] It is argued that this narrow construction of education is envisaged in the human right to education.[109] In contrast, learning—an ongoing lifelong process—is a broader notion that applies to both formal and informal settings. This holds true for learning materials that are produced and used both within and outside a formal educational environment. Nonetheless, the term "learning materials" is used in this book in its narrow sense as a notion that encompasses educational resources such as textbooks, reference books, journal articles, software products, research reports, and course packs used in a formal educational environment. These learning materials may exist in either digital or non-digital, or in both formats. Irrespective of their formats, this book focuses on those learning materials that are both relevant for higher education and often subject to copyright protection.

As such, various educational resources that can be regarded as learning materials such as laboratory equipment, technological devices and similar physical objects lie outside its scope. Hence, the *educational relevance* of the materials and the *potential or actual involvement of copyright as the primary legal protection* will be used as the major criteria in delineating the content and scope of learning materials in this book. This purposive delineation of the scope of learning materials is intended to maintain the objective of this book to explore the interaction between copyright and higher education in depth. To this end, the notion of "learning materials" is not only important in the context of the right to education.[110] But, it is also more consistent with the development and objective of copyright law.[111] From the broader domain of access to knowledge, a more focused notion of access to learning materials is adopted as a useful context for exploring the relationship among copyright, higher education, and the human development.

B The notion of flexibilities

Despite the wide use of the term "flexibilities" both in scholarly literature and various international instruments, the existing literature and international instruments do not provide for a working definition. Nonetheless, the notion of flexibilities can be gleaned from its various usages in the existing literature as well as in binding and non-binding documents. Given the central significance of the notion in this book, it is essential to elaborate on its normative scope and its instrumental role based on its usage in select IP-related literature and documents. In spite of the frequent reference to the term "limitations and exceptions" (L&Es) to mean flexibilities, such a reference is not indicative of their conceptual equivalence and normative scope. Hence, this section intends to delineate the notion of flexibilities used in this book while highlighting its inconsistent usage in literature.

To begin with, some scholars refer to the L&Es provided or permitted by copyright regimes as the core elements of flexibilities. For instance, Ruth Okediji makes a frequent use of the term in her an in-depth exploration of copyright-related flexibilities under the international copyright system.[112] It is noted that Okediji's persistent reference to L&Es in that aforesaid work reflects her comprehensive approach to underscore the need for a set of minimum international L&Es under the international copyright system.[113] As is evident from her recent work, she points out the deficit in the system and argues for a broader reformulation of copyright flexibilities as development tools designed to address national development needs.[114] In their joint work on the promise of the U.S fair-use doctrine for Europe, Bernt Hugenholtz and Martin Senftleben refer to flexibilities as a "policy or breathing space" that includes the statutory L&Es as well as the flexibilities inherent in the requirement of originality.[115]

In another seminal work, Sam Ricketson prefers using the term L&Es to "flexibilities" in his extensive exploration of the various copyright flexibilities under the major copyright-related treaties.[116] In contrast, Paul Goldstein and Bernt Hugenholtz make a generic reference to the copyright flexibilities as "limitations" on exclusive rights that are designed to "accommodate a variety of cultural, social, technological, economic, and political needs and objects."[117] In terms of their interpretative significance, "flexibilities" are referred to as "constructive ambiguities"[118] or "normative elasticities"[119] inherent in a treaty.

In this respect, Peter Yu argues that these constructive ambiguities "can be strategically interpreted and deployed to provide less-developed countries with an additional "wiggle room" to implement their obligations under the TRIPS Agreement."[120] The content and extent of such flexibilities are thus determined subject to the appropriate customary rules of treaty interpretation that primarily take into account the context, purpose and object of the treaty.[121] Taking a comprehensive approach, other scholars construct the notion of flexibilities quite broadly as a combination of rights, safeguards, and options. For instance, Carolyn Deere refers to "flexibilities" as a set of rights, safeguards, and options that can be exploited by the WTO members in their implementation of the TRIPs Agreement.[122]

At a multilateral level, given its instrumental role of socio-economic development of the state parties, the language of flexibilities has been used both in the preamble and provisions of the TRIPs Agreement.[123] For instance, the objectives and principles laid down under arts.7 and 8 of the TRIPs Agreement along with its preamble provide for a broad picture of IP-related flexibilities that are equally applicable for the major IPRs including copyright.[124] Further, the three-step test is another general rule of flexibilities within the purview of the objectives and the principles of the TRIPs Agreement. At this juncture, it is important to note that the three-step test is now applicable to almost all exclusive rights that have been further integrated into the TRIPs Agreement along with other emerging rights.[125]

Indeed, the three-step test itself is a binding and blanket rule of circumscription. Yet, the test is regarded to have a potential to offer members "considerable" flexibilities in relation to designing the appropriate L&Es at a national level.[126] As embodied in the TRIPs Agreement, member states are allowed to devise L&Es that shall conform to the three steps of the test.[127] First, the permitted L&Es to exclusive rights are required to be confined to *certain special cases*. Second, the L&Es shall *not conflict with a normal exploitation* of the work. Third, the L&Es shall *not unreasonably prejudice the legitimate interests of the right holder*. As will be discussed in this book, the three-step test is considered to have both constraining and accommodative aspects. Embracing the Berne Convention, the TRIPs Agreement envisages flexibilities that comprise rights, safeguards, measures, substantive L&Es, and policy options subject to the requirement of compliance with its provisions and principles.[128]

As the foregoing discussion reveals, it is evident that the precise meaning and the scope of flexibilities are not fully developed. Leaving aside the disparities, the broad notion of flexibilities and the essential elements thereof can be gathered from both binding and non-binding instruments. From among the non-binding documents, the notion is also at the heart of both Doha Declaration on Public Health[129] and the WIPO Development Agenda.[130] Further, the notion has the tendency to embrace the various licensing models such open access. If integrated well, OA has the potential to augment the existing copyright flexibilities and enhance access to knowledge required for education and creative innovation. In this context, OA licensing scheme can be considered an emerging aspect of flexibilities that is worth exploring to address development needs.

Indeed, an integrative approach to the existing and emerging flexibilities has the potential to offer an added layer of policy space needed for sustainable human development. Yet, this integration will require appropriate policy and legal measures within the broad domains of the existing global copyright system. In this respect, the guiding elements of the notion of flexibilities should be their instrumental role and the public interests or goals the relevant legal regimes seek to advance. As a result, the meaning and scope of "public interests" and "sectors of vital importance," and the flexibilities they justify at a domestic level depend upon the particular socio-economic needs and priorities of the concerned nation.[131] In this sense, the WIPO secretariat has also noted the inevitable variance in the copyright flexibilities across nations based on the socio-economic contexts of each nation.[132] Therefore, the notion of flexibilities is used in this book in its broadest possible sense as long as the flexibilities are relevant and applicable to copyright. Further, the exploration of the flexibilities is kept to be consistent with the existing international legal regimes that serve as a standard framework.

1.5.2 The instrumental role of flexibilities for education and development

A The role of copyright flexibilities for higher education

In view of the interfaces explored in this book, the significance of copyright flexibilities for higher education is two-fold. First, the flexibilities facilitate users' access to existing copyrighted learning materials. Second, they allow prospective authors an access to the copyrighted content for future production of relevant knowledge including learning materials. In so doing, the flexibilities promote a sustainable access to learning materials required for a quality higher education. As noted in her recent work, Pamela Samuelson articulates the various justifications underpinning copyright L&Es. From among several rationales, worth mentioning are: (a) promotion of authorial interests and ongoing authorship, (b) recognition of users' rights and ownership interests of consumers, and (c) the advancement of broader set of public interests such as public access to information and education.[133] In relation to the potential of scientific opportunities in the digital environment, both Ruth Okediji and Jerome Reichmann underscore the essential role of copyright flexibilities to foster creative innovation and trade for production, and dissemination of knowledge goods.[134]

Despite their potential instrumental roles, the actual significance of the flexibilities for higher education is subject to the existing restrictive and right-holders-oriented copyright system. For instance, Margaret Chon has undertaken a critical exploration of the relevant copyright flexibilities for education from capability perspective. In her conclusion, Chon laments the restrictive impact of the contemporary international copyright system on access to knowledge required for education.[135] Noting its resonance with development needs, she recommends the adoption of a bottom-up and development-oriented reform approach at a national level for an optimal utilization of the existing flexibilities under the international copyright regimes.[136]

Exploring the flexibilities from the WIPO DA's perspective, Andrew Rens also underlines the role of the international flexibilities for education in developing countries. Further, Rens highlights the need for adopting multilateral treaty provisions on minimum L&Es that can facilitate access to learning materials for education.[137] Given the slow move towards the anticipated negotiation on a comprehensive L&Es, such a proposal might be regarded as a strategic move with uncertain success. In the meantime, it is wise to make an effective use of the existing policy and legal space in manner that suits development needs.

From among a number of relevant works, the aforementioned works explore the instrumental role of the flexibilities and the need for their optimal utilization in various contexts. In their respective explorations, a comprehensive approach is however not taken to examine the roles of copyright and higher education for the sustainable human development. Building upon the existing works, this book endeavors to fill in the gap in undertaking an in-depth exploration of the issues from the perspective of human development with human rights dimensions.

B The role of flexibilities for development

In her recent study, Okediji notes the lack of adequate alignment between the design of copyright system and the requirements for socio-economic development.[138] For instance, she deplores the limited capacity of the existing flexibilities to facilitate access to copyrighted materials.[139] In particular, Okediji stresses the significance of development-oriented copyright flexibilities for educational institutions and libraries in order to promote the formation of human capital.[140] To this effect, she underscores the need to reframe copyright L&Es as development policy tools so as to allow developing countries more policy spaces for their domestic development needs.[141] In exposing the limits of L&Es and calling for a reform, Okediji underlines the development-inducing roles of copyright flexibilities for human development.[142] In the same vein, several scholars affirm the role of the flexibilities while noting their inadequate incorporation into the international copyright regime.[143]

In the international legal regime, the role of flexibilities for development is evident in the increasing reference to the term "development." Despite its inadequacy, the TRIPs Agreement mentions the issue of development in its preamble. Further, it recognizes the significance of a policy space for members to "adopt measures necessary (…) to promote the public interest in sectors of vital importance to their socio-economic and technological development."[144] In other words, the recognition of members' discretion to adopt the necessary measures or flexibilities underlines the significance of the flexibilities to offer a policy space for promoting sustainable development.

Moreover, the instrumental role of flexibilities to promote development is central to the WIPO DA and the Doha Declaration. Both initiatives have attempted to integrate development policy considerations intended to facilitate development.[145] In relation to the WIPO DA, Okediji notes that "the Development Agenda is an institution-wide mandate dedicated to the integration of development considerations into its substantial normative and capacity-building activities."[146] In this regard, Jeremy de Beer, examining the prospects of the practical implementation of the WIPO DA, highlights the relevant development-related flexibilities integrated into the WIPO DA and their linkages with those of pertinent UN agencies.[147] It is also important to bear in mind that the implementation of the WIPO DA is expected to promote the interpretation and application of the flexibilities in the context of sustainable development goals.[148]

In the development-oriented interaction between copyright and education, it must be emphasized that the copyright flexibilities such as the various L&Es along with the three-step test are integral to this general framework of flexibilities.[149] Yet, what remains questionable is the extent to which these flexibilities are fully and appropriately tailored to reflect the development needs of a nation. Important as it is, the scrutiny of this issue is central to one of the core questions this book seeks to address in its subsequent chapters. In sum, the relevant flexibilities in general and copyright flexibilities in particular are quite instrumental to promote human development.

1.6 Contribution of the book and overviews of its contents

1.6.1 Scope and contribution of the book

As noted from the existing literature, there exists a bourgeoning scholarship on copyright, higher education and sustainable development as separate topics of research. Likewise, there is a significant corpus of literature that deals with their linkages and their mutual roles to reinforce each other. To this end, various perspectives are used to examine the linkages and their respective roles. Nonetheless, there is a dearth of scholarship exploring the interfaces from a human development perspective. Indeed, there are few emerging works that take capabilities approach as a normative and analytical framework to rethink the roles of copyright for human development.

In contrast, an overwhelming stock of the relevant scholarship emphasizes the utilitarian approach to examine copyright flexibilities for economic growth. In effect, the more robust human-centered CA is not used to guide and reframe copyright towards a holistic and inclusive sustainable human development. Further, the framework is not deployed in its fullest to examine the multifaceted interfaces between copyright and higher education, and their roles for sustainable human development. In this regard, access to knowledge constitutes both a common factor and an appropriate context to map and explore the linkages or interfaces between copyright and higher education. Building upon the relevant works for their insights and development-oriented perspectives, this book seeks to fill in the gap and explore the unaddressed issues.

Adopting the HDCA, this book examines the interplay between copyright and higher education, and their instrumental roles for development in the broader context of access to knowledge. In order to make a more focused analysis, access to copyrighted learning materials is emphasized within the broader context. Further, the reference to higher education in this book is understood as a postsecondary education offered by higher educational institutions. In most countries, higher educational institutions are often constituted of universities, colleges and research institutes. Noting its potentials for reform measures, this book calls for the appropriate deployment of the HDCA for policy and legal reforms in a manner that promotes sustainable human development.

1.6.2 Overviews of this book's contents

As noted above, the present chapter lays down the conceptual framework of this book. As such, it introduces the core topics of interfaces—copyright, higher education, and development—this book seeks to deal with while situating the topics within the framework. Within the domain of access to knowledge, access to learning materials required for higher education is depicted as a useful context. Further, it makes a brief delineation of the key concepts as used in the relevant literature. In sum, this chapter lays down a conceptual foundation for the core issues this book explores in its subsequent chapters.

In Chapter Two, this book highlights the major theoretical justifications of copyright, human rights, education, and development. In so doing, a brief exposition of pertinent philosophical underpinnings is made to reflect the importance and objectives of the subject matters under consideration. The insights from the theoretical justifications are important to inform and guide the objectives of copyright and higher education, and their complementarities for sustainable human development. Further, the theoretical and analytical framework adopted in this book is also explained, along with its limitations.

Intended to map the global development context, Chapter Three examines the international copyright and human rights system in the context of development. A contextual exploration of the interfaces between copyright and higher education, and their roles for human development cannot be made in isolation from their global development contexts. As such, this chapter makes a general overview of the international copyright and human rights systems from the perspective of development.

Building upon the normative objectives of copyright and higher education and the in-built legal strategies, Chapter Four looks into the relevant international copyright flexibilities that can be used to facilitate access to knowledge for higher education. In examining the existence and normative extent of the flexibilities, both human development and human rights perspectives are infused and deployed to make a critical analysis of the linkage between the flexibilities and the underlying objectives to advance human development.

In Chapter Five, this book explores the various copyright-related flexibilities that bridge the linkage between copyright and higher education, and their complementing roles for sustainable human development. In particular, taking the inclusive framework of HDCA, the discussion underlines the need to rethink and re-orient policy and legal frameworks of copyright and higher education towards a sustainable human development. Further, it explores the appropriate (re)integration of the relevant international flexibilities that are instrumental for sustainable human development. To this end, this chapter highlights the possible options or strategies for rethinking and making a coherent and comprehensive (re)integration of the relevant copyright-related flexibilities to facilitate access to learning materials.

An extension of the preceding chapter, Chapter Six both highlights and explores the integration of open access (OA) licensing models as an emerging copyright-related flexibilities. Given its increasing significance in the digital environment, the prospects and challenges of the models are thus examined for their possible integration into the framework of flexibilities. To this end, the HDCA is suggested as an appropriate framework to direct the flexibilities towards enhanced access to knowledge for sustainable human development.

As a concluding chapter, Chapter Seven offers a concise synopsis of the major findings of this book that have emerged from the preceding chapters. In so doing, the chapter attempts to present a succinct set of concluding remarks and recommendations. In particular, it underscores the roles of copyright-related flexibilities for human development while figuring out the gaps in the existing copyright regime of flexibilities. For appropriate reforms, it reitrates the potential of the HDCA to rethink the interfaces between copyright and higher education in a manner that channels their complementarities towards sustainable human development.

Notes

1 Amartya Sen, *Development as Freedom* (New York: Anchor Books, 1999) at 3 & 8 [Sen, *Development as Freedom*].
2 UNDP, *Human Development Report 1990* (New York and Oxford: UNDP & Oxford University Press, 1990) at 1 & 10.
3 Sen, *Development as Freedom*, *supra* note 1 at 75; see Martha C. Nussbaum, *Women and Human Development: The Capability Approach* (Cambridge: Cambridge University Press, 2000) at 84–85 [Nussbaum, *Women and Human Development*].
4 Yochai Benkler, *The Wealth of Networks: How Social Production Transforms Markets and Freedom* (New Haven, CT: Yale University Press, 2006) at 1 [Benkler, *The Wealth of Networks*].
5 John Dewey, *Democracy & Education: An Introduction to the Philosophy of Education* (New York: The Free Press, 1916) at 1–22.
6 Katarina Tomasevski, "Has the Right to Education a Future in the United Nations?: A Behind-the-Scene Account by the Special Rapporteur on the Right to Education 1998–2004" (2005) 5:2 Hum Rights L Rev 205 at 224; Katrina Tomasevski, *Human Rights Obligations: Making Education Available, Accessible, Acceptable and Adaptable, Right to Education Premiers No. 3* (Gothenburg: Novum Grafiska AB, 2001) at 8–9 [Tomasevski, *Human Rights Obligations*].
7 See Fon Coomans, "Exploring the Normative Content of the Right to Education as a Human Right: Recent Approaches" (2004) 50 Persona & Derecho 61 at 61.
8 *See Universal Declaration of Human Rights*, GA Res 217A (III), UNGAOR, 3d Sess, 1st plen mtg, UN Doc A/810 (December 12, 1948) at art. 26 [UDHR].
9 *International Covenant on Economic, Social and Cultural Rights,* 16 December 1966, 993 UNTS No 3 (entered into force on January 3, 1976) at art. 13 [ICESCR].
10 *UN Convention on the Rights of the Child*, 20 November 1989, 1577 UNTS 3 (entered into force on 2 September 1990) at art. 28 & 29 [UNCRC]. In particular, in the recognition and progressive realization of the right of the child to education on the basis of equal opportunity, State parties are required to "make higher education accessible to all on the basis of capacity by every appropriate means." See *ibid* at art. 28(1)(c).
11 *African Charter on Human and Peoples' Rights*, 27 June 1981, 21 ILM 58 (entered into force on 21 October 1986) at art. 17(1) [African *Charter*].
12 *African Charter on the Rights and Welfare of the Child,* 01 July 1990, OAU Doc. CAB/LEG/24.9/49 (entered into force on 29 November 1999). Ethiopia has been a party to the Charter since its ratification of the charter in 2002.
13 See ICESCR, *supra* note 9 at arts. 13(2)(a)–(c). As one can readily observe from the articles of the Covenant, the article on human right to education (art. 13) is the longest provision in the Covenant. The inclusion of such a lengthy provision in the Covenant is neither accidental nor insignificant. Rather, it is an indicative of the weight attached to the significance of the right and its detailed treatment. See generally Committee on Economic, Social and Cultural Rights, *General Comment No. 13: The Right to Education,* UN Doc. E/C 12/1999/10 (8 December 1999) [*CESCR General Comment No. 13*].

14 ICESCR, *supra* note 9 at art. 13; See *General Comment No. 13, supra* note 13 at para 6; Klaus Beiter, *The Protection of the Right to Education by International Law: Including a Systematic Analysis of Article 13 of the International Covenant on Economic, Social and Cultural Rights* (Leiden and Boston: Martinus Nijhoff, 2006) at 478 [Beiter, *The Protection of the Right to Education*].

15 ICESCR, *supra* note 9 at art. 13(2)(a); *General Comment No. 13, supra* note 13 at paras 8–10; Beiter, *The Protection of the Right to Education, supra* note 14 at 510–516.

16 ICESCR, *supra* note 9 at art. 13(2)(b); *General Comment No. 13, supra* note 13 at paras 11–14; Beiter, *The Protection of the Right to Education, supra* note 14 at 516–521.

17 Klaus D. Beiter, "Is the Age of Human Rights Really Over?: The Right to Education in Africa—Domesticization, Human Rights-Based Development and Extraterritorial State Obligations" (2018) 49 Georget J Int Law 9 at 47.

18 *Ibid.*

19 ICESCR, *supra* note 9 at art. 13(2)(c); *General Comment No. 13, supra* note 13 at paras 17–20; Beiter, *The Protection of the Right to Education, supra* note 14 at 521–526.

20 ACRWC, *supra* note 11 at art. 11(3)(c). For the realization of higher education, the emphasis added to the provision under the ACRWC can be noted from its usage of words such as "all appropriate measures" & "every appropriate means."

21 Chidi Anselm Odinkalu, "Analysis of Paralysis or Paralysis by Analysis? Implementing Economic, Social, and Cultural Rights Under the African Charter on Human and People's Rights" (2001) 23:2 Hum Rts Q 327 at 349–350. As Odinkalu points out, given their equal status under the Charter, obligations assumed for implementation of economic, cultural and social rights are "*clearly stated as of immediate application.*" (emphasis added). *Ibid* at 349.

22 Beiter, *The Protection of the Right to Education, supra* note 14 at 403–406, 457 & 522–526; Beiter notes the equal access to tertiary education as an issue of substantive equality that requires equal opportunities and equal treatment. *Ibid* at 404. As noted in the *General comment No. 13*, capacities of individuals "should be assessed by reference to all their relevant expertise and experience." *General Comment No. 13, supra* note at 13 para 19.

23 See ICESCR, *supra* note 9 art. 2(1); *CESCR General Comment No. 3: The Nature of States Parties Obligations (Article 2(1))*, UN Doc. E/1991/23 (14 December 1990) at paras 1, 2 & 9 [*CESCR General Comment No. 3*]; *General Comment No. 13, supra* note 13 at paras 43–48; Beiter, *The Protection of the Right to Education, supra* note 14 at 374–391; Katrina Tomasevski, *Education Denied: Costs and Remedies* (New York: Zed Books, 2003) at 53 [Tomasevski, *Education Denied*]. Tomasevski points out that "'progressive realization' was the key phrase used for the right to education in international human rights treaties." *Ibid.*

24 Beiter, *The Protection of the Right to Education, supra* note 14 at 390–391.

25 Tristan McCowan, *Education as a Human Right: Principles for a Universal Entitlement to Learning* (London, UK: Bloomsbury, 2013) at 122–124.

26 Katrina Tomasevski, "Globalizing What: Education as a Human Right or as a Traded Service?" (2005) 12:1 Ind J Global Leg Stud 1 at 8–15 [Tomasevski, "Globalizing What"]; Tomasevski, *Human Rights Obligations, supra* note 6 at 9; Tomasevski, *Education Denied, supra* note 23 at 2. In noting the implication of other laws such as trade law, Tomasveski pointed out how "the advent of trade in education services challenged the very notion that education is a human right." Tomaseveski, "Has the Right to Education a Future Within the United Nations?" *supra* note 6 at 224 & 229.

27 See generally Tomasevski, "Globalizing What" *supra* note 26. The major grounds of the criticism against the assertion of a tertiary education as a right relate to: Its resource-intensive and specialized nature, its historical restriction to the elites, lack of universal desire or capacity to pursue the study at this level, and the inability of states to ensure its universal access. See McCowan, *supra* note 25 at 122.

28 See Tomasevski, "Has the Right to Education a Future?" *supra* note 6 at 212 (pointing out how states' consensus matters even for adoption of resolutions related to the right to education). This is not to suggest that human rights are creations of treaties. Rather, "[i]nternational treaties are meant to be tools to vindicate human rights." *Ibid* at 229.

29 See Venezuela's (Bolivarian Republic of) Constitution of 1999 with Amendments through 2009, art. 103. The relevant part of art. 103 reads: "*Every person has the right to a full, high-quality, ongoing education* under conditions and circumstances of equality (......) Education is obligatory at all levels from maternal to the diversified secondary level. *Education offered at State institutions is free of charge up to the undergraduate university level.*" Emphasis added.

30 See Eric Berger, "The Right to Education Under the South African Constitution," (2003) 103 Columbia Law Review 614–661.

31 McCowan, *supra* note 25 at 119–126. Defined by its overarching purpose, the right to education can be regarded as a unitary right with multiple levels of enjoyment or implementation. Beiter also tends to treat tertiary education as an element of the right to education. See generally Beiter, *The Protection of the Right to Education, supra* note 14.

32 McCowan, *supra* note 25 at 118–122. McCowan contends that "[a]ny threshold of educational development established to mark the ending of the entitlement would be arbitrary. (........) The right to education—if it is a right at all—must apply in some way through life." *Ibid* at 119.

33 Tomasevski, *Human Rights Obligations, supra* note 6 at 17. Elsewhere, Tomasevski also cites an early jurisprudence of African Commission on the art. 17 of the African Charter, wherein the Commission held the closure of universities and secondary schools in Zaire to be in violation of the Charter. *Ibid* at 19. See *African Commission on Human and Peoples' Rights–Free Legal Assistance Group, Lawyers Committee for Human Rights, Union Interafricaine des Droits del'Homme, Les Témoins de Jehovah v. Zaire, Communications 25/89, 47/90, 56/91 and100/93* (joined), Decision of the Commission adopted at its 18th ordinary session at Prais (Cape Verde), *Ninth Annual Activity Report of the African Commission on Human and Peoples' Rights 1995/96, Assembly of Heads of State and Government,* Thirty-second Ordinary Session, 7–10 July 1996, Yaounde, Cameroon.

34 Tomasevski, *Human Rights Obligations, supra* note 6 at 17. McCowan, *supra* note 25 at 127.

35 McCowan, *supra* note 25 at 119–120; David N. Aspin & Judith D. Chapman, "Lifelong Learning: Concepts and Conceptions" in Aspin, ed, *Philosophical Perspectives on Lifelong Learning* (The Netherlands: Springer, 2007) 19 at 34–35.

36 ICESCR, *supra* note 9 at art. 13(1); *General Comment No. 13, supra* note 13 at para 4. Beiter, *The Protection of the Right to Education, supra* note 14 at 463–475.

37 Laurence R. Helfer & Graeme W. Austin, *Human Rights and Intellectual Property: Mapping the Global Interface* (Cambridge & New York: Cambridge University Press, 2011) at 321 [Helfer & Austin, *Human Right and Intellectual Property*].

38 *See* ICESCR, *supra* note 9 at art. 13(1); UDHR, *supra* note 8 at art. 26(2).

39 UDHR, *supra* note 8 at art. 26(2); ICESCR, *supra* note 9 at art. 13(1). See also *CESCR General Comment No. 13, supra* note 13 at para 4.

40 Martha Nussbaum, *Cultivating Humanity: A Classical Defense of Reform in Liberal Education* (Cambridge, MA: Harvard University Press, 1997) at 30 [Nussbaum, *Cultivating Humanity*].

41 ICESCR, *supra* note 9 art. 13(1); *General Comment No. 13, supra* note 13 at para 4; Beiter, *The Protection of the Right to Education, supra* note 14 at 463–475.

42 *See CESCR General Comment No. 13, supra* note 13 at para 1. Despite its textual omission, the notion of progressive realization has been introduced via the jurisprudence of African Commission on the interpretation of the African Charter in the light of the ICESCR. See Abdi Jibril Ali, "Interpretation of Economic, Social and

Cultural Rights Under the African Charter on Human and People's Rights" (2018) 30 Journal of Ethiopian Law 1 at 3–12 & 17–26 [Ali, "Interpretation"].

43 *General Comment No. 13*, *supra* note 13 at paras 6–7;

44 ICESCR, *supra* note 9 at art. 13(2)(c). The provision reads: Higher education shall be made equally accessible to all, on the basis of capacity, *by every appropriate means*, and in particular *by the progressive introduction of free education. General Comment No. 13*, *supra* note 13 at para 20.

45 *General Comment No. 13*, *supra* note 13 para 44. Drawn from *General Comment No. 3*, "[p]rogressive realization means that States parties have a specific and continuing obligation "to move as expeditiously and effectively as possible" towards the full realization of article 13." *Ibid*.

46 Tomasevski, *Human Rights Obligations, supra* note 6 at 10.

47 *Ibid*. As Tomasevski notes, "[e]ducation operates as a multiplier, enhancing the enjoyment of all individual rights and freedoms where the right to education is effectively guaranteed, while depriving people of the enjoyment of many rights and freedoms where the right to education is denied or violated." *Ibid*.

48 See generally Christopher Knapper & Arthur Cropley, *Lifelong Learning in Higher Education,* 3rd ed (London: Kogan Page, 2000). Lifelong education is important to promote equal educational opportunities, democratization and self-actualization. *Ibid* at 9 & 10. The core features of life learning include universal access to learning opportunities, learning throughout lifespan, a stronger emphasis upon the intrinsic value of education, due recognition of learning in diverse settings, a focus on interactive learning process, etc.

49 *CESCR General Comment No. 13*, *supra* note 13 at para 6; see Sharon E. Foster, "The Conflict Between the Human Right to Education and Copyright" in Paul Torremans, ed, *Intellectual Property and Human Rights: Enhanced Edition of Copyright and Human Rights* (The Netherlands: Kluwer Law International, 2008) 287 at 288.

50 Developed by the first special rapporteur on the human right to education, the essential elements of the right to education comprises the availability, accessibility, acceptability and adaptability of an education. The scheme is very important as it offers an important substantive and evaluative framework for the domestic implementation of the right. See generally Tomasevski, *Human Rights Obligations, supra* note 6.

51 UNESCO, *A Human Rights-Based Approach to Education for All*, 56 & 77 (2007), online: UNESCO <http://unesdoc.unesco.org/images/0015/001548/154861E.pdf>.

52 See *CESCR General Comment No. 13*, *supra* note 13 at para 6; *CESCR General Comment No. 17: The Right of Everyone to Benefit from the Protection of the Moral and Material Interests Resulting from Any scientific, Literary or Artistic Production of Which He or She Is the Author* (Art. 15 (1)(c) of the Covenant), UN Doc. E/C12/GC/17 (12 January 2006) at para 35 [*CESCR General Comment No. 17*].

53 Margaret Chon, "Intellectual Property 'from Below': Copyright and Capability for Education" (2007) 3 UC Davis L Rev 805 at 819 [Chon, "Intellectual Property from Below"].

54 Ruth L. Okediji, "The International Copyright System: Limitations, Exceptions and Public Interest Considerations for Developing Countries" (2006) UNCTAD-ICTSD Issue Paper No. 15 [Okediji, *The International Copyright System*].

55 *Ibid* at ix.

56 Rebecca Tushnet, "Intellectual Property as a Public Interest Mechanism," in Rochelle C. Dreyfuss & Justine Pila, eds, *The Oxford Handbook of Intellectual Property Law* (Oxford: Oxford University Press, 2018) 95 at 99. Tushnet also notes the notion of public interest as "the aggregated interest of the people who may be affected by some private action, as opposed to the concentrated interest of that private actor." *Ibid* at 95.

57 *U.S. Constitution* (1787), Article 1, Section 8, Clause 8.

58 *WIPO Copyright Treaty (WCT)*, 20 December 1996, 2186 U.N.T.S 121; 36 I.L.M 65 (1997), Preamble, para 4 [WCT].
59 *Ibid.*
60 See Paul Goldstein, *International Copyright: Principles, Law and Practice* (New York: Oxford University Press, 2001) at 3 [Goldstein, *International Copyright*].
61 *Ibid* at 4.
62 Christophe Geiger, "Implementing Intellectual Property Provisions in Human Rights Instruments: Towards a New Social Contract for the Protection of Intangibles" in Geiger, ed, *Research Handbook on Human Rights and Intellectual Property* (Cheltenham, UK: Edward Elgar, 2015) 661 at 678–679 [Geiger, "Implementing Intellectual Property"].
63 *Ibid* at 680–682.
64 *Charter of Fundamental Rights of the European Union 2012/C 326/02, Official Journal of the European Union* 326, Oct 26/2012, at 391–407; see also *Council of Europe, European Convention for the Protection of Human Rights and Fundamental Freedoms*, as amended by Protocols Nos. 11 and 14, 4 November 1950, ETS 5, Protocol, art. 1.
65 *Charter of Fundamental Rights*, *supra* note 64 at art. 17(1); see *Protocol to ECHR*, *supra* note 64 at art. 1, para 1.
66 Geiger, "Implementing Intellectual Property," *supra* note 62 at 668–671 & 678–681.
67 *Directive 2001/29/EC of the European Parliament and of the Council of 22 May 2001 on the Harmonization of Certain Aspects of Copyright and Related Rights in the Information Society* [InfoSoc Directive], Recital 14, Official Journal L 167, 22/06/2001.
68 Goldstein, *International Copyright, supra* note 60 at 4.
69 See generally Gillian Davis, "The Convergence of Copyright and Authors' Rights—Reality or Chimera?" (1995) 26 IIC 964 [Davis, "The Convergence"].
70 WCT, *supra* note 58, Preamble, para 5.
71 See Okediji, "The International Copyright System," *supra* note 54 at 8 & 31–32.
72 Helfer & Austin, *Human Right and Intellectual Property, supra* note 37 at 316. The Statute of Anne is the first copyright statute that marked the beginning of the statutory copyright system.
73 Chon, "Intellectual Property from Below," *supra* note 53 at 820. See *Agreement on Trade-Related Aspects of Intellectual Property Rights,* 15 April 1994, Marrakesh Agreement Establishing the World Trade Organization, Annex 1C, 33 ILM1125 (1994) at art. 8 [TRIPS Agreement].
74 *Ibid.* Margaret Chon, "Intellectual Property and the Development Divide" (2006) 27:6 Cardozo L Rev 2813 at 2893–2908 [Chon, "IP and Development Divide"].
75 Okediji, "International Copyright System," *supra* note 54 at 8.
76 See Ruth L. Okediji, "Regulation of Creativity under the WIPO Treaties" (2009) 77 Fordham L Rev 2379 at 2394 [Okediji, "Regulation of Creativity"]. For detailed analysis of the relationship between the WIPO Internet Treaties and the TRIPs Agreement, see generally WIPO, Implications of the TRIPS Agreement on Treaties Administered by WIPO, at 164, WIPO Publ'n No. 464(E) (1996); Neil W. Netanel, "The Next Round: The Impact of the WIPO Copyright Treaty on TRIPS Dispute Settlement" (1997) 37 Va J Int'l L 441 (1997) [Netanel, "The Next Round"].
77 See Chon, "Intellectual Property from Below," *supra* note 53 at 827–846.
78 See Okediji, "The International Copyright System," *supra* note 54 at 10–19.
79 See Marcelo Thompson, "Property Enforcement or Retrogressive Measure? Copyright Reform in Canada and the Human Right of Access to Knowledge" (2007) 4:1&2 UOLTJ 163 at 212–241.
80 See David Vaver, "Copyright Defenses as User Rights" (2013) 60:4 Journal of the Copyright Society of the USA 661 at 672 [Vaver, "Copyright Defenses"]. Having underscored the solid judicial recognition of user's right, Vaver argues that "equating users rights with human rights would certainly help transform user rights beyond mere defenses and give them substantive content." *Ibid.*

81 African Charter, *supra* note 11 at art. 22; *Proclamation on the Constitution of the Federal Democratic Republic of Ethiopia, Proc. No. 1/1995*, Fed. Negarit Gazetta, 1st Year No. 1, Addis Ababa, 21 August 1995, art. 43 [*FDRE Constitution*].
82 *WCT, supra* note 58, Preamble, para 2.
83 *TRIPs Agreement, supra* note 73, Preamble, para 5.
84 *Ibid* at art. 7.
85 United Nations Division for Sustainable Development, *United Nations Conference on Environment & Development,* Rio de Janerio, Brazil, 3–14 June 1992, Agenda 21, Chap 36.3.
86 United Nations Economic Commission for Europe (UNECE), *UNECE Strategy for Education for Sustainable Development*, 2005, at 1, online: <http://www.unece.org/env/documents/2005/cep/ac.13/cep.ac.13.2005.3.rev.1.e.pdf>
87 Gerd Michelsen, "Policy, Politics and Polity in Higher Education for Sustainable Development," in Matthias Barth et al., eds, *Routledge Handbook of Higher Education for Sustainable Development* (London: Routledge, 2015) 40 at 45–53.
88 See Helfer & Austin, *Human Right and Intellectual Property, supra* note 37 at 318.
89 *Ibid.*
90 *TRIPs Agreement, supra* note 73, arts. 7 & 8(1); *WCT, supra* note 58, Preamble, para 5; WIPO Performances and Phonograms Treaty, Preamble, para 4, 20 December 1996, 36 I.L.M. 76 (entered into force 20 May 2002) [WPPT]. Under art. 7 of the TRIPs Agreement, the reference to the open-ended "vital sectors of public interests" is inclusive of education). This assertion is more evident from the explicit reference of the WIPO Treaties to education within the domain of *the larger public interests.*
91 *WCT, supra* note 58, Preamble, para 5; WPPT, *supra* note 90, Preamble, para 4.
92 *InfoSoc Directive 2001/29/EC, supra* note 67, Recital 14.
93 Chon, "Intellectual Property from Below," *supra* note 53 at 818.
94 *Helfer & Austin, Human Rights and Intellectual Property, supra* note 37 at 173.
95 *See CESCR General Comment No. 17, supra* note 52 at paras 3 & 16.
96 Helfer & Austin, *Human Right and Intellectual Property, supra* note 37 at 189; *CESCR General Comment No. 17, supra* note 52 at para 3.
97 Despite the lack of a specific definition, the notion of "*adequacy*," as noted by the CESCR in relation to the right to food, is a dynamic and flexible notion the precise meaning of which is determined by the prevailing social, economic and cultural conditions. See *CESCR General Comment No. 12: The Right to Adequate Food* (Art. 11 of the Covenant) (12 May 1999) at para 7 [*CESCR General Comment No. 12*].
98 *CESCR General Comment No. 17, supra* note 52 at para 35. Given the human rights aspects of copyright and education, it is important to consider the possible human rights implications of the interaction between the regimes. Nonetheless, it is noted that the human rights implication of the interplay between copyright and education is less compelling at a tertiary level than at a basic level.
99 *Ibid.* Likewise, the *General Comment No. 13* on the right to education includes access to "teaching materials" among the illustrative list of determining factors for the availability and quality of education, both of which constitute the essential elements of the core of the right. See *CESCR General Comment No. 13, supra* note 13 at para 50; see also Helfer & Austin, *Human Right and Intellectual Property, supra* note 37 at 332.
100 See Thompson, *supra* note 79; Peter K. Yu, "Ten Common Questions About Intellectual Property and Human Rights" (2007) 23:4 Ga St U L Rev 709 at 719–720 [Yu, "Ten Common Question"]; Jeremy de Beer et al., "Copyright and Education: Lessons on African Copyright and Access to Knowledge" (2009/10) 10 African Journal of Information and Communication 37 at 38 [de Beer et al, "Copyright and Education"].
101 Yu, "Ten Common Questions," *supra* note 100 at 719–720.

102 *Ibid.* James Nickel, *Making Sense of Human Rights*, 2nd ed (Malden, MA: Blackwell Publishing, 2007) at 67 [Nickel, *Making Sense of Human Rights*]; Chon, "Intellectual Property from Below" *supra* note 53 at 819.

103 *Ibid* at 67.

104 *CESCR General Comment No. 17, supra* note 52 at para 35; see Christophe Geiger, "Reconceptualizing the Constitutional Dimension of Intellectual Property," in Paul L.C. Torremans, ed, *Intellectual Property and Human Rights,* 3rd ed (The Netherlands: Kluwer Law International, 2015) 115 at 119–124 & 128–129 [Geiger, "Reconceptualizing"]; see generally Christophe Geiger, "The Social Function of intellectual Property Rights, Or How Ethics Can Influence the Shape and Use of IP Law" in Graeme B. Dinwoodie (ed), *Methods and Perspectives in Intellectual Property* (Cheltenham, UK: Edward Elgar, 2013) 153–176. While entitling creators to rewards for their creation, the social function of copyright should be understood in terms of its contribution to "intellectual, cultural and economic progress." *Ibid* at 168.

105 Dewey, *Democracy and Education, supra* note 5 at 11–22 (see the chapter on "education as social function").

106 See the joint reading of *CESCR General Comment No. 13, supra* note 13 at paras 6 & 50 *cum CESCR General Comment No. 17, supra* note 52 at para 35.

107 See *CESCR General Comment No. 17, supra* note 52; see also Ian Montagnes, *Textbooks and Learning Materials 1990-99*, 2000, online: UNESCO <http://unesdoc.unesco.org/images/0012/001234/123487e.pdf.> (last visited 22 September 2019).

108 The term "education," in its wider sense, refers to "the process by which a society endeavors to transmit beliefs, culture, and other values." Heller and Austin, *Human Rights and Intellectual Property, supra* note 37 at 319.

109 See Beiter, *The Protection of the Right to Education, supra* note 14 at 19.

110 See Helfer and Austin, *Human Right and Intellectual Property, supra* note 37 at 332–336.

111 *Ibid* at 39.

112 See generally Okediji, "International Copyright System," *supra* note 54.

113 *Ibid* at 23.

114 Ruth Okediji, "Reframing International Copyright Limitations and Exceptions as Development Policy," in *Copyright Law in an Age of Limitations and Exceptions* (Cambridge: Cambridge University, 2017) 429 [Okediji, "Refarming International Copyright"].

115 See generally Bernt Hugenholtz and Martin Senftleben, "Fair Use in Europe: In Search of Flexibilities," (2012) Amsterdam Law School Research Paper No. 2012-39; Institute for Information Law Research Paper No. 2012-33, online: SSRN <https://ssrn.com/abstract=2013239> (last visited 10 April 2021).

116 *See* Sam Ricketson, WIPO Study on Limitations and Exceptions of Copyright and Related Rights in the Digital Environment, Standing Committee on Copyright and Related Rights, Ninth session, Geneva, 23–27 June 2003, online: <www.wipo.int/edocs/mdocs/copyright/en/sccr_9/sccr_9_7.pdf> (last visited on 10 April 2021) [Ricketson, "WIPO Study on L&Es"].

117 Paul Goldstein and P. Bernt Hugenholtz, *International Copyright: Principles, Law and Practice,* 3rd ed (New York: Oxford University Press, 2013) at 371–375 [Goldstein & Hugenhotz, *International Copyright*].

118 Jayashree Watal, *Intellectual Property Rights in the WTO and Developing Countries* (Oxford: Oxford University Press, 2001) at 7; see also Peter K. Yu, "TRIPS and Its Discontents," (2006) 10 Marq Intell Prop L Rev 369 at 387 [Yu, "TRIPS and Its Discontents"].

119 Daniel Gervais, "IP, Trade and Development: The State of Play" (2005) 74 Fordham L Rev 505 at 528–534 [Gervais, "IP, Trade and Development"] (highlighting the potential use of the "normative elasticity" of TRIPS by developing countries to design a policy suited to their needs).

120 See Peter K. Yu, "The Objectives and Principles of the TRIPS Agreement" (2009) 46 Hous L Rev 979 at 1023 [Yu, "The Objectives and Principles"].

121 See *Vienna Convention on the Law of Treaties*, 23 May 1969, 1155 UNTS 331, 8 ILM 679 (entered into force 27 January 1980) at art. 31 [Vienna Convention].

122 See Carolyn Deere, *The Implementation Game: The TRIPs Agreement and the Global Politics of Intellectual Property reform in Developing Countries* (Oxford: Oxford University Press, 2009) at 68 [Deere, *The Implementation Guide*].

123 See e.g. *TRIPs Agreement, supra* note 73, Preamble, para 6 and art. 66.1 [Read in light of paragraph 6 of the Preamble of the TRIPs Agreement, art. 66.1 states: "In view of the special needs and requirements of the least-developed country members, their economic, financial and administrative constraints, and their need for *flexibility* to create a viable technological base, such members shall not be required to apply the provisions of this Agreement, other than art. 3, 4 and 5, for a period of…" (emphasis added).

124 *See* Yu, "The Objectives and Principles," *supra* note 120 at 1020–1046.

125 It is argued that the three-step test under art. 9 (2) of the Berne Convention is not applicable for the self-contained exceptions such as the exceptions for news reporting and teaching purpose and under arts. 10(1) & (2), compulsory licensing under its art. 11 bis (2) and sound recordings under art. 13 (1). See Christophe Geiger, Daniel Gervais & Martin Senftleben, "The Three-Step Test Revisited: How to Use the Test's Flexibility in National Copyright Law" (2014) 29:3 Am U Int'l L Rev 581 at 583–588 [Geiger, Gervais & Senftleben, "The Three-Step Test Revisited"]; *see also* Chon, *Intellectual Property from Below, supra* note 53 at 842–844.

126 *See* Geiger, Gervais and Senftleben, "The Three-Step Test Revisited," *supra* note 125 at 617 & 625.

127 *TRIPs Agreement, supra* note 73, art. 13.

128 Carlos M. Correa, *Trade Related Aspects of Intellectual Property Rights: A Commentary on the TRIPS Agreement* (Oxford: Oxford University Press, 2007) at 103–106 [Correa, *Trade Related Aspects*]; see also *TRIPs Agreement, supra* note 73 at art. 8(2).

129 See *World Trade Organization, Declaration on the TRIPS Agreement and Public Health*, WT/MIN (01)/DEC/2, 41 ILM 755 (2002) [Doha Declaration].

130 The Doha Declaration was one of the official attempts to identify and clarify the various flexibilities available under the TRIPs Agreement in relation to patent protection and in order to promote access to medicines for health concerns in the developing and least developed countries. *See* Yu, "The Objectives and Principles," *supra* note 120 at 995.

131 See Correa, *Trade Related Aspects, supra* note 128 at 105–106.

132 The WIPO Secretariat states:

> Flexibilities regarding the scope and exercise of copyright and related rights vary from one country to another. Being based on the particular social or economic needs of each country, the diversity of exceptions to copyright has been permitted, and even promoted at [the] international level, notably by the standards provided under the Berne and Rome Conventions and, more recently, the WCT [WIPO Copyright Treaty] and the WPPT [WIPO Performances and Phonograms Treaty]. WIPO Comm. on Dev. & Intellectual Prop. [CDIP], *Initial Working Document for the Committee on Development and Intellectual Property*, Annex III at 26, WIPO Doc CDIP/1/3 (3 March 2008) [hereinafter, *CDIP Working Document*].

133 Pamela Samuelson, "Justifications for Copyright Limitations and Exceptions," in Okediji, *Copyright Law in an Age of Limitations and Exceptions, supra* note 114 at 25–53 [Samuelson, "Justifications"]. Samuelson also makes a detailed discussion of other justifications such as advancing economic goals such as fostering competition and innovation, serving politically expedient ends, and providing flexibility and adaptability to accommodate future developments. *Ibid.* See also Okediji, "International Copyright System," *supra* note 54 at 29–34.

134 See Jerome H. Reichmann & Ruth L. Okediji, Empowered Digital Integrated Scientific Research: The Pivotal Role of Copyright Law's Limitations and Exceptions (2009) online:

<http://policydialogue.org/files/events/Reichman_Okediji_Empowering_Digitally_Integrated_Scientific_Research.pdf> (last visited on 20 April 2021). [Reichman & Okediji, " Empowered Digital"].

135 See generally Chon, "Intellectual Property from Below," *supra* note 53.

136 *Ibid.*

137 See generally Andrew Rens, "Implementing WIPO's Development Agenda: Treaty Provisions on Minimum Exceptions and Limitations for Education" in Jeremey de Beer, ed, *Implementing WIPO's Development Agenda* (Ottawa: Wilfred University Press, 2009) 158.

138 See generally Okediji, "Reframing International Copyright," *supra* note 114.

139 *Ibid* at 475.

140 *Ibid.*

141 *Ibid.*

142 Ruth L. Okediji, "The Limits of International Copyright Exceptions for Developing Countries" (2019) 21:3 Vand J Ent & Tech L 689 [Okediji, "The Limits of International Copyright"].

143 See, e. g, Annette Kur, "Of Oceans, Islands, and Inland Water – How Much Room for Exceptions and Limitations Under the Three-Step Test?" (2009) 8 Rich. J. Global L. & Bus. 287; Geiger, Gervais and Senftleben, "The Three-Step Test Revisited," *supra* note 125.

144 *See* TRIPs Agreement, *supra* note 73, Preamble at paras 6 & 7 and art. 8; Correa, *Trade Related Aspects, supra* note 128 at 104–107.

145 Chon, "Intellectual Property and Development," *supra* note 53 at 35–41.

146 Okediji, "Reframing International Copyright," *supra* note 114 at 439.

147 de Beer, "Defining WIPO's Development Agenda" in de Beer, ed, *Implementing WIPO's Development Agenda, supra* note 137 at 4–6 [de Beer, "Defining WIPO's Development Agenda"].

148 See Chon, "IP and Development Divide," *supra* note 74 at 2838.

149 See Geiger, Gervais & Senftleben, "The Three-Step Revisited," *supra* note 125 at 3, 16–19, & 44.

2 Copyright, education, and human development: theoretical frameworks

2.1 Introduction

The emergence and development of copyright, education and human development are grounded in their respective philosophical foundations. The theoretical foundations are useful to offer insights into the purpose, significance and attributes of each of the subject matters under consideration. As such, highlighting the major theories underpinning copyright and education is important to inform the analysis of the interaction between the copyright and higher education to advance human development. In the same vein, it is important to shed a light on theories of human rights and development. As an in-depth treatment of the theories is outside the ambit and purpose of this book, the discussion is limited to a brief account of the major theories. In the end, the theoretical framework adopted in this book will also be elaborated. Except for the sake of completeness, it is admitted that not all theories discussed in this chapter are of a direct relevance to the issues in this book.

2.2 Theories of copyright protection

Despite the inevitable philosophical debates related to each of the theories, the legal protection of copyright is justified on the basis of various theories. A concise exposition of the relevant theories is thus offered to reflect the conception, role and purpose of copyright protection. From the broad economic theories and theories of rights used to justify IP's protection,[1] below are the major theories applicable to copyright protection.

2.2.1 The utilitarian theory

Entrenched in IP system, the utilitarian theory is one of the major theoretical justifications for the legal protection of a copyright. This theory traces its roots back to Bentham's classic principle of utility. Drawing on its classic version, the central tenet of the theory is the promotion of the "greatest good for the greatest number."[2] In its consequentialist approach, the utilitarian theory justifies an action or a measure in terms of its consequence as long as the action

DOI: 10.4324/9781003214298-2

or measure maximizes the happiness or welfare of the majority.[3] Considered a dominant economic theory of IP, the utilitarian justification is invoked to underpin the legal protection of IP in order to promote welfare maximization or optimal efficiencies.[4]

In a copyright system, the legal protection of a copyright is thus justified both as a recoupment for the creator and a necessary incentive for further creative innovation contemplated to advance a social welfare. In so doing, the overriding objective is to benefit the society as a whole.[5] Adopted in the Anglo-American legal systems, the theory underlies a statutory right granted to creators primarily for the benefit of the society.[6] For instance, the theory is believed to be embodied in the U.S Constitution's purpose of IP "to promote the progress of science and useful arts."[7] In contrast, the continental authors' right is anchored in the natural rights tradition. Given their growing convergence, both economic and natural rights theories underpin the international copyright system.[8] Nonetheless, the utilitarian justification has been the driver of the global copyright system since the latter's integration into the global trade regime.[9] In the trade regime, utilitarianism serves to underpin wealth maximization.

The utilitarian theory has long been critiqued for its obsession with utility and economic efficiency. Its wealth-maximization and efficiency criteria are both incommensurable and narrow in their conception of social welfare.[10] Further, the theory is instrumental and aggregative in its orientation. In a copyright system, this orientation overlooks the intrinsic values of individual creativities integral to copyright objectives.[11] In the same vein, the theory tends to entrench an exclusive monopoly over creative works without a due consideration for distributive issues. In effect, an excessive monopolization of, and a limited access to, creative works would hamper further creative innovation and affect other vital public interests such as education.

2.2.2 The labor theory

Grounded in the natural law, the labor theory is attributed to the British classical philosopher John Locke. Often referred to as Lockean, the theory's initial development was made to support a justification for the protection of physical property. Central to the tenets of the theory are the interlinkages among labor, natural commons and the owner of the labor. For its appropriation, a property is considered to be a product of individual's labor mixed with the natural commons.[12] This assertion is premised upon the fact that a labor belongs to one's own body over which the person has a natural control.[13] According to the justification, the owner of a labor is thus entitled to the ownership of the property acquired through the labor.[14]

Given the value added through the labor mixed with commons,[15] Justin Hughes notes the appropriateness of the theory for protection of intellectual property over intangible objects.[16] In a copyright system, the labor theory is often invoked to justify the legal protection of creative works as the product of intellectual labor mixed with ideas—an intellectual commons for the intangibles.[17] That is, the legal protection of an author's right over a creative expression of ideas is a reward for the creative labor of the author.[18] In practice, it is quite difficult to measure the amount of the labor invested in a creative work. To reward an author for his/her creative labor, a minimum level of creativities suffices to merit a legal protection.[19] Once met, an author is thus justified to assert a natural right of ownership over the creative work. In this context, the author is entitled to the right upon a mere creation.

Nevertheless, as the theory is operative subject to the provisos of "enough and as good for others" and "the non-waste conditions,"[20] the protection of a copyright so justified is subject to the necessary limitations. In particular, the condition inherent in the first proviso reflects a public interest-driven limitation against the exclusive legal protection of a copyright.[21] In effect, this limitation reflects the non-absolute character of the authorial rights. From among other reasons, the theory is still disputed for want of an authoritative interpretation and the conceptual misfit between "commons" and ideas.[22]

2.2.3 The personality theory

As a natural-law-driven justification, the personality theory is used to justify the legal protection of copyright over creative works. Credited to Frederick Hegel and Immanuel Kant for their respective contributions to its development, this deontological justification underpins the legal protection of property as "a mechanism for self-actualization, for personal expression, and for dignity and recognition as an individual person."[23] In other words, the protection of a property is considered to reflect an expression or embodiment of the self.[24] According to this justification, the ownership of things is essential for the manifestation and actualization of human will and personal freedom as the core values of individual's existence.[25] From author's perspective, the ownership of a creative work is an expressive embodiment of human will and creative freedom.[26]

In his analysis of Kant's theory, Merges notes a "legal ownership central to human freedom."[27] In this sense, it is argued that a legal protection of creative works serves as an essential instrument for self-actualization and human development.[28] In other words, the legal protection is considered vital in order to "promote human flourishing by protecting or fostering fundamental human needs or interests."[29] As the manifestation of an individual's autonomy/liberty[30] and the creative freedom of an author,[31] the author's right is viewed to subsist in a creative work by virtue of the creator's personality.[32] In this context, the justification has a stronger relevance for artistic and literary works as the creative expressions of the creator's personal freedom.

Nonetheless, there are contrasting views on the appropriateness of the theory for functional objects. For instance, in Justin Hughes' observation, the personality theory is a weak justification for the copyright protection of scientific works such as a computer software.[33] In contrast, Peter Drahos disagrees with this view. In Drahos' functional view of the subject matters, the theory is rather well-suited for both artistic and utilitarian objects.[34] One of the critiques leveled against the personality theory lies in its abstract conceptions of the personhood or the individual self.[35] Given its historical roots in the continental legal tradition, the theory remains a solid normative justification for the protection of author's moral rights. As elements of moral rights, an author's right to the integrity, paternity, and divulgation are often justified on this ground.

2.2.4 The contractarian/social contract theory

Rooted in the works of Thomas Hobbes, John Locke, and Jean-Jacques Rousseau, the contractarian theory was developed to justify the formation of the government and people's voluntary submission to its acquired sovereign power.[36] In Rousseau's view, an implicit social contract underpins individuals' exchange of natural liberties for civil liberties and proprietorship.[37] In so doing, individuals admit a reasonable restraint upon their liberties. Individuals' contractual freedom was also integral to Locke's conception of men as "equal, free and independent beings" that are subject only to political authority by their consent.[38] Later, in his work on justice, John Rawls further developed the social contract theory by elaborating the principles of distributive justice to underlie the basic structure of a fair and rational society.[39] According to Rawls, the "principles of justice for the basic structure of a society are the object of the original agreement."[40]

Drawing on the Rawlsian conception of justice, Robert Merges articulates a distributive justice as a justification for IP rights. Further, Merges conceives IP right as a primary right integral to the "total system of basic liberties" due to IP's benefits to the society with a "net positive distributional effect."[41] Noting the problem of distributional concerns associated with IP system, Merges contends that these concerns can be addressed through appropriate L&Es to a copyright such as a fair-use doctrine.[42] In this contractarian justification, the creators are granted a legal protection in return for their creative contributions for the benefit of the society.[43] In other words, the protection of IP is justified in order to promote its social function.[44] Central to the justification is thus an exchange of a limited legal right for a promised access to creative works after a specified duration.[45]

In this context, the social contract theory attempts to strike a balance between the interests of authors and that of the public. Balancing the interests is achieved through granting the authors a just reward and the public a reasonable access to the works.[46] For instance, the public interests might be served through reasonable term limits to the protection and eventual enrichment of the public domain after its expiration. In the same vein, other L&Es allow a reasonable access to the protected creative works for both transformative and non-transformative uses. In contrast to patent regime, the theory is less evident in copyright due to its longer terms of protection and for want of disclosure requirements in its protection.[47] Seen in the light of the social contract justification, the current expansive international copyright system falls short of delivering on its promises to advance public interest. Often critiqued for its imbalance, the system thus needs to be revisited or rethought to restore the balance required for the copyright to serve its intended social function.[48]

2.2.5 Social planning theory

The social planning theory is an emerging approach that is still under construction. Yet, it is important to offer a valuable insight into the purpose and role of copyright. For its inspiration and development, the theory draws on the works of "an eclectic cluster of political and legal theorists"[49] that underpin all forms of IP. As its central tenet, the theory holds that IP "can and should be shaped so as to foster the achievement of a just and attractive culture."[50] In William Fisher's observation, an attractive intellectual culture "would be one in which citizens [have] access to a wide array of information, ideas and forms of entertainment" vital for the attainment of self-determination and self-expression.[51] Emphasizing the criterion of distributive justice as its core element, Fisher highlights the equitable access of all persons to informational and artistic resources.[52] While it shares the utilitarian objective of advancing a net social welfare, the social planning theory takes a wider perspective to accommodate a broader visions of a desirable society.[53]

In his seminal contribution to a "democratic paradigm," Neil Netanel underlines the role of a copyright law to foster creative expressions and support a sector of creative activities needed for a democratic culture.[54] In particular, he argues that copyright "promotes the creation and distribution of information and educational resources."[55] In Netanel's view, copyright is thus instrumental to serve "robust, participatory and pluralist civil society."[56] Maintaining "careful balance between exclusivity and access," the writer posits, "copyright seeks to foster widespread citizen participation in public deliberation."[57] To this end, he suggests promoting public domain through a reduction of both copyright term and control over derivative works.[58] Fisher claims that social planning arguments are useful to inform the debates on the appropriate scope of copyright on Internet, commentary, and education.[59] Nonetheless, the social planning justification has its own drawbacks. For example, the theory is critiqued for (a) its emphasis on "the amorphous concept of culture" and (b) the *indeterminate* character of the desired social vision it seeks to advance.[60]

In sum, subject to their respective limitations,[61] the aforementioned major theories of copyright are useful to enrich valuable conversations in policy reforms and law-making process.[62] The theories are also valuable to "catalyze useful conversations among the various people and institutions responsible for shaping the law."[63] In particular, Netanel's insightful democratic approach "would build on traditional incentive theory to support a richer vision of public domain."[64] In contrast to the dominant economic-centered theories, this approach emphasizes the "copyright's democratic purpose" of advancing valuable and pluralistic socio-economic and cultural freedoms.[65] In this regard, this pluralistic and democratic approach aligns with the various objectives of sustainable human development. In this book, the discussion of the theories is thus intended to highlight the purposes and justifications of the copyright from human development perspective. In highlighting its goals, the theoretical justifications are relevant to rethink the existing copyright and inform the necessary reforms towards sustainable human development.

2.3 Theories of human rights

2.3.1 Overview of the major theories

In the human rights regime, there are several theories or schools of thought. From among the theories, the four major schools of human rights are the natural, deliberative/social justice, protest/redressal and discourse schools of thought. For the natural rights school, human nature forms the foundation of human rights. In consequence, the natural school conceives of human rights as universal and natural entitlements inherent in all human beings. In contrast, the social justice/deliberative school that tends to reject the natural character of human rights emphasizes liberal and democratic political values.[66] For the proponents of the school, "human rights come into existence through societal agreement."[67]

In its departure from the deliberative school, the protest school of thought draws closer to the natural school due to its recognition of the natural conception of human rights. The protest school however cautions the possible perversion of human rights to become "a tool of power" for imposition.[68] Redressal of injustice being its prime concern, the school still regards human rights as "claims and aspirations that allow the status quo to be contested in favor of the oppressed."[69] Confined to the works of few academics, the discourse school is the least popular school of thought with no faith in the potentials of human rights. Skeptical of human rights' actual existence more than a mere rights talk, the discourse school however acknowledges the "powerful language" of human rights to assert political claims.[70]

Central to the variance among the schools of thought, both the nature and the philosophical underpinnings of human rights are still debatable.[71] For instance, there lacks a consensus on the notions of "rationality, sentience or artifacts of state action" claimed as the foundation of human rights.[72] In the same vein, contested is whether or not rights are necessarily correlated to duties.[73] Further, the disagreement among scholars on the universal character of human rights manifests itself in the debate of moral universalism and cultural relativism.

In short, there are several unsettled philosophical issues that permeate the notions, attributes and foundations of human rights. Despite the lack of a consensus on the normative foundations of human rights, there appears to be a little doubt about the normative and practical significance of human rights. It is thus useful to make a brief discussion of the major theories that are often reflected in the international human rights regime. In this sense, the natural and deliberative/social justice theories are selected for further discussion due to their global dominance and general relevance to the issues in this book.

2.3.2 The natural rights theory of human rights

As noted from its historical evolution, the modern natural rights school is rooted in the general principles of natural law. According to John Locke—a leading proponent of natural law, people are endowed with certain natural rights by virtue of their creation by the Creator.[74] For the natural law theorists, human nature/dignity serves as the foundation of human rights.[75] In this sense, the theorists assert the ontological existence of human rights irrespective of social recognition and positive law.[76] Yet, the roles of social recognition and positive law—human rights and constitutional laws—are acknowledged.[77] Nonetheless, the notion of human dignity/nature itself is unsettled issue of philosophical debate.[78] Noting the disputed metaphysical foundation, most natural law scholars tend to emphasize the global legal consensus underpinning the concrete manifestation of human rights in international law.[79] According to Jack Donnelly, "[h]uman rights are at once a utopian ideal and a realistic practice for implementing that ideal."[80]

Despite the growing prominence of the deliberative school, the natural rights school is the dominant philosophical justification that underlies the contemporary human rights.[81] Its central tenet lies in its justification of the notion of human rights as natural rights inherent in the human dignity.[82] The proponents of the natural rights school assert the unconditional existence of human rights, their universal nature, and the rights' equal inherence in human beings by virtue of human dignity.[83] Derivatives of the natural character of the rights, these features are all considered the basic attributes of human rights.

Nevertheless, the basic attributes and the inherent features deriving thereof are often contested. As mentioned above, the debate stems from the disputed notion of human nature itself as a normative basis for human rights.[84] Critics argue that its contested foundation would expose the subjectmatter of human rights to a "philosophical insecurity" for its international protection.[85] Further, a critique is leveled against the theory due to its roots in the "Western" liberalism and its consequent individualistic conception.[86] In this context, the theory is often considered ill-suited for the protection of the more collective social, economic and cultural rights.[87]

2.3.3 Social justice theory of human rights

Given the disputed normative basis of the natural rights school, the deliberative/social justice school has emerged as an alternative to the natural rights theory of human rights. Considering societal agreement as the source of human rights, the deliberative scholars are more concerned with the justification than the foundation of human rights.[88] Designed to advance liberal and democratic values often embodied in the constitutional principles of deliberation,[89] human rights are thus not inherent in human beings but developed through democratic and fair process.[90] For the proponents of the school, "there are no human rights beyond human rights law."[91]

According to Charles Beitz, the social justice school emphasizes the principles of social justice as a normative basis for human rights instead of a human nature.[92] As David Miller notes "social justice" itself is a broad notion that deals with "the distribution of benefits and burdens throughout a society as it results from social institutions."[93] Thus, the principle of social justice includes the possession and protection of persons' rights as well as the allocation of welfare benefits.[94] For John Rawls, the objective of social justice is to guide "the way in which the major social institutions distribute fundamental rights and duties and determine the division of advantages from social cooperation."[95] In his contribution to the deliberative school with a greater emphasis on social justice theory, Beitz regards human rights as "entitlements to the satisfaction of various human interests guaranteed to members of a group by principles of social justice."[96]

In drawing on Rawls's conception of social cooperation, the social justice theory of human rights treats human rights as a subset of social justice and products of social cooperation.[97] To this end, the idea of international concern that calls for a concrete action is central to this theory of human rights in order to distinguish the latter from the broad conception of social justice.[98] In Beitz's opinion, "a satisfactory theory of human rights is better conceived as an aspect of a more general theory of global justice."[99] For the deliberative scholars, constitutional law is thus an important instrument to enshrine human rights values that in turn serve to guide policy and legal reforms for good governance.[100]

Given its collective orientation and emphasis upon democratic process of deliberation, the deliberative/social justice school might offer a solid basis to accommodate factors such as culture and socio-economic development, in particular, for the protection of social, economic, and cultural rights.[101] Emphasizing their roots in the claims of basic human needs, Miller observes the strong relation between this category of human rights and the social justice as the latter guides the distribution of benefits on the basis of entitlements and needs.[102] The social justice theory of human rights is however critiqued both for its rejection of the universality of human rights and the reduction of human rights to the "dictates of social justice."[103] For the scholars of the deliberative school, the universal attribute of human rights is not a given, but a desirable goal to be achieved through a global consensus and adoption of the liberal values.[104]

2.4 Theories of education

Like copyright and human rights, the protection and promotion of education as a fundamental entitlement are based on various philosophical foundations.

Elucidating the nature, purpose, and functions of education, the theoretical justifications are often used to underline the intrinsic and instrumental significance of education. From among the theories, three major theories or approaches are selected here to highlight the fundamental importance of education.

2.4.1 "Liberal" theory of education

From among several variants of theories of education, the reference to the "liberal" theory is noted here to mean the general theory of education embedded in the modern conception of liberal and democratic education.[105] Traced to ancient Greek philosophers and developed during an era of Enlightenment, the modern notion of liberal education is primarily attributed to Jean-Jacques Rousseau from among the liberal thinkers of the era.[106] According to Rousseau's philosophical thought, the purpose of education is to develop the "general will" of citizens while preserving their freedom.[107] In his observation, a liberal education is useful to transform the egoistic nature of human beings.[108] Despite his contested notion of "will," Rousseau's conception of liberal education underscores the intrinsic and instrumental values of education to develop individuals' freedom and their collective common good.

From among the contemporary philosophers, John Dewey is credited for further development and alignment of the liberal thought of education infused with the modern conception of democracy. For Dewey, democracy is the most important element of social and political life that enables human beings to flourish.[109] In its alignment with democracy, education is considered to be a necessary cause for a free or democratic society and a vital instrument for promoting social freedom.[110] In this regard, both Rousseau and Dewey share the view that learning is essential for human beings to survive and flourish with a freedom.[111] As an instrument of both personal development and social function,[112] education is thus noted as "a fostering, a nurturing, and a cultivating process."[113] Further, education is valued for its instrumental roles of promoting growth and democracy.[114] In addition to its instrumental values, the learning process that remains central to education is regarded as the latter's intrinsic value.[115] According to Dewey, an education should aim to enable individuals' pursuit of life-long learning as a social process that caters to a continued capacity for growth both as its object and reward.[116]

Given its emphasis of a democratic individual freedom and social interaction, this theory resonates well with the conception of human rights that shares similar philosophical foundations. In fact, this philosophical thought appears to have made its way into the human rights instruments. For instance, both the UDHR and ICESCR underline the fundamental purpose of education for "the full development of the human personality and its sense of dignity."[117] In particular, Dewey's view on the aim of education in a democratic society is embedded within the provisions of the ICESCR. For instance, art. 13(1) of the Covenant emphasizes the purpose of education to "enable all persons to participate effectively in a free society, promote understanding, tolerance and friendship among all nations and all racial, ethnic or religious groups."[118] As will be discussed below, liberal education is also central to "a richer, more humanistic, multifaceted approach to development" through expansion of human capabilities.[119]

2.4.2 Human capital theory of education

Emerging from the works of Gary Becker and Theodore Schultz in the 1960s, human capital is a prevailing economic justification for the roles of education. In this context, the human capital theory offers a justification for an investment in the development of human capital as a means of an increased productivity.[120] Functionalist in its orientation, the theory emphasizes the instrumental roles of education in the production of skilled manpower required for an economic growth.[121] Thus, an investment in a quality education is often justified due to its functional significance to enhance an economic return in the long-run.

In this era of knowledge-based economy, higher education is instrumental for the production and diffusion of advanced knowledge and skilled labor that are essential inputs for economic and technological development.[122] In this respect, advanced knowledge and innovation are both interdependent and the drivers of a knowledge-driven development.[123] Underscoring, *inter alia*, the roles of education, Paul Romer concludes that "the stock of human capital determines the rate of growth."[124] In particular, higher education is becoming a crucial tool for a faster economic growth through technological catch-up and poverty reduction.[125]

In its General Comment No. 13, the CESCR has affirmed the instrumental roles of education for an economic growth. For instance, the General Comment notes the increasing recognition of education as "one of the best financial investments states can make."[126] In this sense, the proponents of the human capital approach thus underline the instrumental importance of education for its contribution to an economic development.[127] Despite his critique of its narrow end, Amartya Sen acknowledges the significance of the approach to underline the instrumental role of education for economic growth through the enhancement of human capital.[128] Nonetheless, the major critique is leveled against the theory due to: (a) its neglect of the non-economic dimensions of education, and (b) its treatment of human beings as a mere means for an economic growth.[129]

In his critique, Sen, while noting the theory as inadequate, goes further to suggest the integration of the theory into the more inclusive human capabilities approach that encompasses "both the direct and indirect consequences of human abilities."[130] As such, the human capital theory of education can be used to complement other theories of education and emphasize the intrinsic values of education. Further, it can also be aligned with the economic aspects of the theories of copyright and the right to development.

2.4.3 The capability approach to education

Conceived as a framework for human development, the capability approach (CA) has attracted the attention of scholars in various fields such as health and education.[131] In fact, education has been one of the components of CA-driven human development index since its formulation in the 1990s. Given the limitation of the human capital theory, the CA is increasingly adapted to the field of education to highlight both the intrinsic and instrumental values of education.[132] According to the basic tenets of the approach, the central functions of education are: (a) expansion or enhancement of human capabilities and opportunities, and (b) the development of the capacity to make reasoned and valuable choices in the exercise of the capabilities.[133] From the two major functions, the latter represents the agency aspect of human freedom. In this respect, Nussbaum highlights the role of higher education to cultivate critical and self-reflective human capabilities.[134]

In its departure from other theories, the CA underscores the significance of a quality education for the expansion of individual's capabilities or freedoms through development of specific abilities and skills.[135] In this context, higher education is "understood as a capability in itself, and constitutive of other capabilities now and in the future."[136] In turn, the enhanced capabilities or freedoms will empower learners to make reasoned and effective choices of valuable achievements for meaningful and dignified lives.[137]In underscoring the intrinsic and instrumental roles of higher education,[138] the CA offers "a method to evaluate real educational advantage."[139] According to this approach, higher education should be evaluated in terms of learners' expanded capabilities or opportunities for "valued beings and doings."[140] In the process of expansion, resources such as learning materials are considered important inputs for the development of the human capabilities.[141]

For the effective realization of the right to education, the approach surpasses a mere formal entitlement to underline the need for combined human capabilities that encompass both internal abilities and external conditions.[142] In support of a right-based approach to education that specifies duty-bearers, the CA offers a vital normative tool for evaluating real opportunities for the full realization of higher education and its contribution to sustainable human development. In this sense, CA is considered useful to fill in the gaps in, and complement, the state-focused limitations of the rights-based approach.[143] To this end, this human-centered approach can highlight the importance of a moral imperative for human development-oriented education at all levels and the need for concerted actions towards its realization.[144]

In sum, the above major theories of education highlight the objectives, instrumental roles and intrinsic values of education that hold true for an education at all levels. Although the general liberal approach emphasizes the free will of the learners, it is quite related to the CA that underscores the values of education for the expansion of individual and collective freedoms. Indeed, the constitutive and instrumental aspects of the CA have the potential to accommodate and reflect the central tenets of the other two approaches. As such, this book affirms this human development-oriented approach as a better perspective for possible reforms towards sustainable human development.

2.5 Theories of development

Over the last several decades, various modern theories of economic development have evolved to guide and shape economic systems both at national and global levels. Despite the gradual refinement of some of the theories to embrace non-economic aspects, an economic growth has remained the central focus of most of the theories. An attempt is made here to highlight the salient features of the major theories. Although the discussion is made for the sake of completeness, not all theories are of a direct and an equal relevance for the subsequent analysis in this book.

2.5.1 Neoliberal theory of development

Since its emergence in the 1980s, the neoliberal theory of economic development has attained a predominance over its predecessors. Central to the principles of neoliberalism are private ownership of rights and market freedoms. According to this theory, the persistent underdevelopment in the less developed nations is attributable to an inefficient allocation of resources and the distorting effect of an excessive action of state intervention.[145] Drawing on the classical economic theories, the neoliberal theory thus underlines the need for liberalization of the national economy and the instrumental role of a free market. For the proponents of the theory, both dynamic economic efficiency and growth require free and competitive markets, trade liberalization, foreign direct investment, privatization of state-owned enterprises, deregulation of financial sectors, etc.[146] Given its emphasis upon private ownership of property rights as one of its pillars, the neoliberal theory underpins the contemporary IP system.

From among its variants, the three major ones are the free-market approach, the public choice approach and the market-friendly approach. As its core tenet, the free-market approach considers market as an efficient mechanism for resource allocation, investment and effective competition. Dubbed as "market fundamentalism" by its critics, the approach views a government action as a distorting and counterproductive one.[147] Sharing the same tenets, the public choice approach goes further to assume politicians and bureaucrats to be self-interested actors who use public resources to serve their selfish political ends. Due to its distortive effect, the proponents of the free-market approach hold that a government intervention must be kept to a minimum.[148]

In contrast, the market-friendly approach is a recent variant that recognizes the facilitative role of government intervention and the existence of market failures in the less developed nations.[149] In effect, an appropriate government intervention is considered vital to create an enabling environment for investment and free markets through its investment in the physical and social infrastructure such as education.[150]

Despite the respective contributions of its variants, general criticisms are directed at the neoliberal theory of development. First, it is critiqued for its neglect of the deep-seated realties in the less developed nations. Second, it is disputed for its emphasis on the GDP/GNP as a sole measure of development. Third, the theory's aggregative measure is inattentive to the consequent distributive inequalities. In the context of market, its over-reliance on a free market mechanism overlooks the inevitable realities of a market failure. For instance, this is an issue for copyright and higher education in less developed nations with an inefficient market. For want of purchasing power due to low income, the market is ineffective to address the issue of access to learning materials in those nations. Further, the theory tends to entrench an expansive copyright protection.[151] In effect, the public interests are often undermined due to lack of a reasonable access to creative works relevant for quality higher education. As recognized in one of its variants, the role of reasonable state intervention is thus critical to address the socio-economic realities in the less developed nations.

2.5.2 Contemporary theories of development

For their emergence, the contemporary theories draw on the insights and principles of the classical theories of development. From among the modern theories of economic development, the new (endogenous) growth and the coordination failure models are the major variants. In drawing on Solow's model of technological change,[152] the new growth model underscores the instrumental roles of knowledge accumulation and technology for a sustained economic growth.[153] From among the leading proponents of the new growth model, Paul Romer considers "ideas as the source of economic progress" and "technological progress as the product of economic activity."[154] In contrast to Solow's model, the technological progress is noted to be endogenous and market-driven.[155] As such, the new growth model highlights the shift from the traditional physical resource-based economies to the current knowledge-based economies.[156]

Thus, central to the new growth model are knowledge creation, investment in human capital and innovation through education, research and development as the drivers of economic growth.[157] That is, an economic growth is a function of investment in human capital and technological progress. In the context of copyright and higher education for development, the endogenous growth model is thus useful to underscore their respective roles for knowledge production and human capital. In particular, the theory underlines the importance of human capital and knowledge creation for innovation and technological progress.[158]

The coordination failure is another variant of the contemporary theories of economic development. Noting the inevitable limitation of a free market, the coordination failure model indicates a scenario where the market might fail to coordinate among complementary activities.[159] In its holistic view, the model describes the economy as an ecosystem wherein economic activities are interdependent and subject to general economic conditions.[160] According to the proponents, the coordination problem stems from the interdependence between individual investors for production and investment decisions.[161] Since market mechanism is not effective enough to coordinate all economic activities, the model holds that such a market failure will result in multiple and inefficient equilibria with sub-optimal allocation of resources.[162] In order to mitigate the effect of the market failure, the model highlights the role of a strategic government intervention to coordinate complementary economic activities and guide them towards the desirable equilibria and optimal resource allocation.[163] Hence, the model calls for complementarities between market mechanism and government action.[164]

Given its coordinative function to facilitate complementarities, this model is useful to justify an appropriate government measure to channel copyright protection and higher education towards sustainable human development. Such a coordinative measure is vital for less developed countries where market mechanism is less effective to facilitate efficient allocation of resources. In its recognition of government's positive roles for economic growth, the model is related to the developmental state model. Credited for the stated-led economic success in Southeast Asian countries such as Japan, China and Korea,[165] the developmental state model is premised on the crucial role of state-led industrialization for an economic growth in the long-run.[166] Noting the coordination problems and the need for developmental strategies designed in an international context,[167] the model underscores the leading roles of the government to coordinate economic activities in the development process.[168] Yet, the success of the industrialization sought depends upon the existence of effective institutional arrangements.[169]

In sum, each of the previous theories of economic development offers relevant insights to inform, guide and rethink development policies and objectives. For instance, it is crucial to note the instrumental roles of capital and investment, the need for an appropriate structural economic transformation, the negative impact of unequal and exploitative relationship between nations and the importance of liberalization. From among the contemporary theories the new growth model is more important to highlight the significance of an investment in a human capital, knowledge creation, and innovation for development. Also, crucial is the issue of technological progress. Important for its emphasis on state's coordinative function is the coordination failure model.

Given its justification of extensive state intervention and for its success story elsewhere, knowledge-driven developmental state model could be appealing to less developed countries in Africa for a state led-development. For instance, for its emulation of China and recording state-driven economic growth, Ethiopia has been regarded a developmental state in Africa.[170] Despite their positive contributions, the failure of the economic growth models to address distributive issues and their overemphasis on an economic aspect are few of the common limitations that necessitate an alternative holistic approach to development.

2.5.3 The human development approach: an emerging framework for development

In the 1990s, the human development (HD) approach emerged as an alternative framework to the existing and predominant neoliberal theory of development.[171] In the emergence of HD approach, the pioneers of the CA such as Amartya Sen and Martha Nussbaum have played a key role through their monumental contributions to the conceptual and philosophical foundations of the approach.[172] As is evident from their extensive works, both have been critical of the dominant neoliberal/utilitarian development theory for its emphasis on GNP (wealth or income) as a measure of development.[173] Further, they often lament the theory's undue emphasis on the narrow economic growth and its neglect of other dimensions of development.[174] Sen also notes the limitations of the dominant neoliberal theory for its exclusive focus on market mechanisms and calls for an integrated approach to market and other relevant institutions.[175] Operating within the framework of political liberalism, both proponents have developed a robust and an inclusive approach that conceptualizes development as an expansion of freedoms or capabilities.[176] Indeed, this is one of the basic points of departure from the neoliberal theory that underpins economic growth or wealth as an overriding measure of development.

While noting the importance of economic growth, Sen goes further to articulate development as "a process of expanding the real freedoms that people enjoy."[177] Placing human beings at its epicenter, the advancement of freedoms or expansion of capabilities is thus regarded as the overarching objective of human development.[178] As a comprehensive normative and analytical approach to human development, the human development and capability approach (HDCA) is founded upon the core concepts of human capabilities and functionings developed within the broader framework of capability approach.[179] In simple terms, capabilities are noted as an alternative combination of what a person is *able* to achieve while functionings refer to the *actual* achievements.[180]

In the HDCA, human development is measured in terms of the expansion of people's capabilities and functionings. As noted in the HDCA-inspired *Human Development Reports* (1990), human development refers to both "the process of enlarging people's choices" and "the level of their achieved well-being."[181] In Ul Haq's observation, "the objective of development is to create an enabling environment for people to enjoy long, healthy and creative lives."[182]

In dealing with people and their development, central to HDCA are the fundamental notions of evaluative and agency aspects. According to the proponents, an evaluative aspect underscores the assessment of progress in terms of the expansion of people's freedoms.[183] In the approach's agency aspect, people are considered free and active agents of their valuable choices that entail policy changes for development.[184] As "the real wealth of a nation," people's active roles are thus crucial for social and economic development.[185]

In stressing human capabilities as a better measure of human well-being, the HDCA deviates from its predecessors, including the basic needs approach—its precursor—that prioritizes meeting the basic needs of all people.[186] In view of its significance for the human development index (HDI) and its holistic perspective, the HDCA is comprehensive enough to embrace sustainable development.[187] In the same vein, the HDCA also embraces the recognition and promotion of human rights due to the latter's intrinsic and instrumental values for human development.[188]

In addition to its holistic feature, the HDCA is distinctive, *inter alia*, for its: (a) conception of development as an expansion of human capabilities, (b) treatment of a person as an *end* and central focus of development, and (c) pluralistic approach to values.[189] In general, as Richard Jolly observes, the HDCA departs from its predecessors in "[its] objectives, assumptions, constraints, and in the main areas for policy and in the indicators for assessing results."[190] Nonetheless, the HDCA is critiqued for want of operationalization.[191] Yet its increasing application to diverse studies seems to counter the critique. In this regard, more evidence is emerging in support of the practical significance of the HDCA.

2.6 The HDCA as the normative and analytical framework

2.6.1 The notion of development and capability approach

As noted previously, development is an elusive notion that is less understood, theorized, and applied in various perspectives and contexts.[192] For instance, from the perspective of the dominant neoliberal theories of development, the notion is often construed to mean an economic growth.[193] For instance, the dominant metrics of development such as GDP/GNP, wealth, and utility are primarily framed in economic terms.[194] In effect, the socio-cultural and ecological aspects of development are often neglected. In fact, these hitherto marginalized aspects of development have been embraced in the now-popular and inclusive notion of sustainable development.

In its articulation, sustainable development is defined to mean "a development that meets the needs of the present without compromising the ability of future generations to meet their own needs."[195] Underscoring both the intergenerational equity and the comprehensive nature of development, the notion of sustainable development is built upon three major pillars: economic, social, and ecological development.[196] It is this holistic conception of sustainable development that resonates well with the CA. Having human beings as the central focus of their common concern, both emphasize the intrinsic and instrumental roles of human beings and their overall well-being.[197]

As developed by the pioneers, Sen and Nussbaum, the CA rejects the narrow economic conception of development. To reiterate what is mentioned above, the CA is founded upon two core concepts—the human capabilities and functionings. Conceptualized as the *ability to do or to be*, human capabilities are a kind of the substantive freedom or real opportunities required for a set of valuable achievements or functionings.[198] It follows that functionings are "beings or doings" that a person has a reason to value, such as being educated or healthy.[199] As essential constitutive elements of human development, both concepts are thus interlinked in such a manner that human capabilities are vital for valuable achievements. Despite the slight variance in their versions of the CA,[200] both Sen and Nussbaum stress the expansion of human capabilities as the basis for human development.

As an alternative framework, the CA disputes the dominant welfare approach confined to an economic growth and welfare maximization. In so doing, the CA reframes development as "a process of expanding the real freedoms that people enjoy."[201] It bears noting that the CA does recognize economic growth as an important means for human development. It, however, critiques the overemphasis on the economic growth and considers indicators such as economic efficiency, wealth, and income as a poor set of measures for human well-being.[202]

Noting the advancement of individuals' freedoms as the core objective of development, Sen emphasizes the expansion of freedoms both as "the *primary end and the principal means* of development."[203] From the CA's perspective, development is thus understood as "an expansion of human capabilities" or "expansion of freedom."[204] Embracing both the intrinsic and instrumental elements of freedoms, the CA underscores the instrumental roles of rights, opportunities, and entitlements to promote human development. In this sense, the CA places a human development at the center of its normative and analytical remit. Indeed, the CA is a normative framework well-suited to conceptualize and measure individual and collective well-being as well as evaluate the impact of legal norms, policies, and practices upon human development.[205]

2.6.2 The HDCA as a normative framework for copyright, education, and development

Given the evolving notion of development as a right anchored in the dignity and freedom of human beings,[206] central to the HDCA are thus both human beings and human development as its focal points of development analysis. In its recognition of the right to development as a human right, the Declaration on the Right to Development (DRD)[207] defines the right as "a comprehensive economic, social, cultural and political process, which aims at the constant improvement of the well-being of the entire population and of all individuals."[208] Aiming at the constant improvement of the well-being of human beings, the DRD seems to draw on the feature of HDCA to underline development as a process for enhanced capabilities to achieve human development. In this respect, a higher education can be regarded both as a capability in itself and a crucial means for enhancing other human capabilities required for a sustainable human development.

Indeed, "[e]ducation is critical for promoting sustainable development."[209] In particular, the instrumental roles of quality and inclusive education for sustainable development is underlined by its treatment as one of the UN SDGs.[210] As an important level of education, a quality higher education is thus instrumental for sustainable human development. In the same vein, copyright protection can be a useful tool for promoting human development through enhanced creative and learning human capabilities.[211] Given their crucial roles for expansion of human capabilities, both copyright and higher education contribute to foster human development.

Nonetheless, their effective roles for expansion of human capabilities depends, *inter alia*, upon the existence of an adequate access to relevant knowledge or access to learning materials.[212] In this respect, the HDCA offers a useful normative and analytical tool to explore and evaluate the material conditions, policies and legal frameworks, and their roles for sustainable human development. Thus, the HDCA is more suitable to rethink and redirect the objectives of the protection of copyright and the promotion of education towards their intended intrinsic and instrumental goals of fostering sustainable human development.

As a theoretical framework underpinning the human development, the HDCA embraces both the instrumental and intrinsic aspects of copyright, education and development. In fact, the approach recognizes the roles of human beings as individuals and collective agents of development. In contrast to the narrow instrumental view of the human capital approach, the HDCA however goes further to emphasize the freedoms or enhanced capabilities of human beings as the primary objective of development.[213] As integral elements of the human development, copyright protection and higher education must thus be treated in a complementary manner. In this sense, human development undergirds their reinforcing roles.

In the light of their respective central objectives, the promotion of creative innovation and scientific progress, and the fullest development of human personalities reinforce each other to advance human development. Thus, the HDCA treats both copyright and higher education as important capabilities for human development. In this regard, Nussbaum asserts that "all rights are understood as entitlements to capabilities."[214] In accordance with this view, rights attached to copyright and higher education can be noted as entitlements to capabilities.[215] As noted above, the actual realization of rights or the enhancement of capabilities depends upon material and institutional support through government action.[216]

To this effect, the HDCA offers a common normative framework to examine the constitutive and functional aspects of copyright protection and higher education towards the realization of sustainable human development. As Nussbaum notes "capabilities, like human rights, supply a moral and humanly rich set of goals for development."[217] In relation to human rights framework, she articulates that "capabilities are complementary to, and augment, rather than compete with, human rights."[218] As noted earlier, framing socio-economic rights such as education in terms of human capabilities can also strengthen the rationale for allocating resources for the effective realization of the rights.[219] In spite of its disputed human rights status, the HDCA is also useful to enrich the content, the role, and actual realization of higher education for human development. In so doing, HDCA can have a remedial function to augment and advance the status of higher education in the human rights regime.[220] In sum, the HDCA reinforces the complementarities between copyright and higher education for sustainable human development.

2.6.3 The potential and limits of the HDCA as an analytical framework

As noted above, the HDCA is a useful analytical framework to examine the interplay between copyright and higher education, and their roles for sustainable human development. Further, relevant constitutional and human rights dimensions can be drawn into the discussion to enrich the analysis. In interrogating these multiple dimensions, the HDCA offers a broad perspective to evaluate the effective realization of relevant rights or capabilities for sustainable human development. In this respect, the HDCA is regarded a useful normative framework suited to reframing rights as entitlements to capabilities. In a national context, the approach is also important to examine the interaction between the relevant policies, legal regimes, and practices. In stressing access to learning materials as a direct context for the interaction, the HDCA is thus helpful to explore and rethink the existing copyright flexibilities. Further, the approach can also guide appropriate reforms in the existing regimes of copyright and higher education.

From among the essential resources, the HDCA recognizes the instrumental value of access to learning materials for the enhancement of human capabilities through a quality higher education. In the same vein, the approach goes further to acknowledge the acquisition of the education both as a functioning in itself and an instrumental capability for related functionings.[221] For example, the human capabilities cultivated through education are vital for a robust creative innovation. In this context, the deployment of the HDCA is thus more suited to explore the linkages and direct copyright and higher education towards human development. Furthermore, the conceptual affiliation between human capabilities and human rights, and their complementing roles are other reasons that make the approach a useful analytical tool to examine the human rights dimensions in a development context.[222]

In fact, the analytical relevance of the HDCA for development-related studies has been confirmed in various contexts and studies.[223] In view of its potential to offer a multivariate metrics of development, the HDCA is used in a wide range of fields of studies, including education, IP and international development. From its inception, its contribution has been quite evident in the UN Human Development Index since 1990. In IP and development-related research, the approach has drawn a significant interest from leading scholars such as Yochai Benkler,[224] Jeremy de Beer,[225] and Margaret Chon[226] for their respective works on the treatment of linkages between information policy, information markets, implementation of the WIPO Development Agenda (DA), and intellectual property and development. Several other studies are emerging to evidence its increasing relevance. In particular, Chon's adoption of the approach for the subsequent work on copyright and education in the context of development is a specific instance of the analytical relevance of the HDCA for the issues explored in this book. Emphasizing the expansion of freedoms in terms of development of human capabilities, the approach helps underline the contingency of the realization of the human development upon access to essential resources and the availability of real opportunities.[227]

Nevertheless, like every approach or theory, the HDCA's analytical significance is not immune to limitations and criticisms. For instance, its incompleteness, the difficulty for its operationalization and other related issues are considered major limitations.[228] Further, it is critiqued for its weakness to make inter-personal comparisons of well-being where there arise disagreements on the valuation of capabilities.[229] Despite the limitations of the HDCA, it has managed to draw an increasing acceptance among scholars in various areas of studies. In particular, the combination of Sen's and Nussbaum's perspectives of the HDCA attenuates limitations. That said, the HDCA offers a better framework to examine the interfaces among copyright, higher education and sustainable human development. Furthermore, the analysis in this book may also draw on other appropriate theories to augment the theoretical framework.

2.7 Conclusion

As can be noted from the brief exposition of relevant theories or approaches, the notion and significance of copyright, education, human rights, and human development are each grounded in different philosophical foundations. Although some of them are somehow related, each theoretical justification has evolved to advance different or related values and interests. Nonetheless, all the theoretical justifications share one basic objective—economic growth or development.

Granted as an incentive mechanism for creative works, copyright protection is justified on a utilitarian ground to advance an aggregate welfare of the society. To this end, a legal protection is considered a necessary incentive to ensure the continued production of creative works. Central values of the theory are thus efficient resource allocation and maximization of utilities. In contrast, the labor theory is used to justify copyright protection as a product of an author's labor mixed with commons. The protection is deemed a legal guarantee offered to the author as a reward for the transformative creative labor added to the intellectual or creative commons. Grounded in a similar natural rights tradition, the personality theory justifies the protection of author's right, *inter alia,* for the purpose of self-actualization. In contrast, the contractarian theory underpins copyright protection on the basis of an implicit social contract that serves to guide the mutual interests of the public and the authors. Intended to fill in the gaps in the existing theories, the social planning paradigm goes further to achieve a just and democratic culture. As such, it emphasizes the need to strike a reasonable balance and accommodate social goals. In short, one or more of these theories often underpin the existing legal protection of copyright.

From among several schools of thought, two major theories underlie the protection of human rights. Commanding a normative dominance, the natural rights theory grounds human rights in the human dignity or human nature of human beings. That is, a human person is entitled to human rights by virtue of humanity upon birth. In contrast, the social justice theory regards human rights as a subset of social justice and products of social cooperation. Although the philosophical grounds of both theories are disputed, the contrast is indicative of the distinction between the *inherency* and the *acquisition* of human rights. In addition to other schools of thought, each of these theories thus offers relevant perspectives.

In the same vein, the significance of education is justified both on intrinsic and instrumental grounds. For instance, the liberal (general) theory of education underscores the value of education for the development of a democratic individual freedoms and social interaction. That is, education is deemed essential for human beings to survive and flourish in a democratic society. Indeed, this understanding stands in a stark contrast to the human capital theory that emphasizes the instrumental role of education for an economic growth. In consequence, the latter has drawn a criticism for its treatment of human beings as a mere means for economic purposes. Drawn from other fields of studies to inform education, the CA fares better to embrace both intrinsic and instrumental values of education. As a robust approach, it regards education as one of the essential human capabilities that is vital both for its enhancement of individual freedoms and instrumental roles for a human development. It bears mentioning that the proponents of the approach tend to construe the right to education as an entitlement to human capabilities.

As noted in this chapter, a sustainable human development is central to the objectives of copyright, education at all levels and their respective human rights dimensions. Despite the recent shift in the notion and theoretical foundations of development, almost all the theories that have evolved over the last several decades emphasize an economic development. From among several other theories, an overemphasis on economic growth is at the core of neoliberal and the contemporary theories of economic development. Capital accumulation, technological progress, investment, and markets are all common to most of the theories. The extent of the roles of the market, and government intervention are the points of distinction among the theories and within their major variants. Further, most of the theories point out various endogenous factors as the causes for underdevelopment.

In its clear departure from most of the theories of economic development, the HDCA has emerged to be comprehensive enough to accommodate the hitherto neglected social aspects of development. Indeed, the approach has made a major shift both in the notion and the conventional metrics of development. Placing human beings at its center, the HDCA reframes development as the expansion or enlargement of individuals' freedom to lead worthwhile lives. The measure of human development is thus the expansion of the capabilities that are essential for valuable functionings. In line with this notion, the HDCA is adopted in this book both as a normative and analytical framework to explore the interplay between copyright and higher education, and their joint roles for sustainable human development. For exploring the interfaces under consideration, the relevance and appropriateness of the HDCA to the issues in this book are evident from its increasing application to the respective fields and their interlinkages.

Notes

1 Julie E. Cohen, "Creativity and Culture in Copyright Theory" (2007) 40 UC Davis L Rev 1151 at 1155–1158 [Cohen, "Creativity and Culture"]. Despite the emergence of other theories of copyright such as culture-related theory that do not squarely fit into the categories, both the rights and economic theories dominate the normative framework of copyright system. *Ibid* at 1156 & 1158.

2 Jeremy Bentham, "Of the Principle of Utility" in Jonathan Glower, ed, *Utilitarianism and Its Critics* (Macmillan, 1990) 9 at 10.

3 *Ibid.*

4 William Fisher, "Theories of Intellectual Property," in Stephen Munzer, ed, *New Essays in the Legal and Political Theory of Property* (Cambridge University Press, 2001) 168 at 177 [Fisher, "Theories of IP"].

5 Orit Fischman-Afori, "Human Rights and Copyright: The Introduction of Natural Law Considerations into American Copyright Law" (2004) 14:2 Fordham IP Media & Ent L J 498 at 498 [Fischman-Afori, "Human Rights and Copyright"].

6 *Ibid* at 502.

7 *U.S. Constitution,* art. I, §8, cl. 8; Paul Goldstein & P. Bernt Hugenholtz, *International Copyright: Principles, Law and Practice,* 3rd ed (New York: Oxford University Press, 2013) at 6 [Goldstein & Hugenholtz, *International Copyright*].

8 Goldstein & Hugenholtz, *International Copyright, supra* note 7 at 6 & 7.

9 *Ibid* at 8 & 9. Daniel Gervais, "Human Rights and the Philosophical Foundations of Intellectual Property," in Christophe Geiger, ed, *Research Handbook on Human Rights and Intellectual Property* (Cheltenham: Edward Elgar Publishing, 2015) at 92–93 [Gervais, "HRs & Philosophical Foundations"].

10 Fisher, "Theories of IP," *supra* note 4 at 177.

11 *Ibid* at 503–505.

12 See Justin Hughes, "The Philosophy of Intellectual Property" (1988) 77 Geo L J 287 at 297–298 [Hughes, *The Philosophy of IP*].

13 *Ibid.* Edwin C. Hettinger, "Justifying Intellectual Property" (1989) 18 Phil & Pub Aff 31 at 37 ("A person owns her body and hence she owns what it does, namely, its labor.

A person's labor and its product are inseparable, and so ownership of one can be secured only by owning the other.")

14 *Ibid.* As Hettinger argues, "if a person is to own her body and thus its labor, she must also own what she joins her labor with—namely, the product of her labor." *Ibid.*

15 *Ibid.*

16 *Ibid* at 297–300.

17 Peter Drahos, *A Philosophy of Intellectual Property* (Aldershot: Ashgate, 1996) at 47–50 [Drahos, *A Philosophy of IP*]; Hughes, *The Philosophy of IP, supra* note 12 at 314–316.

18 Gervais, "HRs & Philosophical Foundations," *supra* note 9 at 89. Thus, author's ownership of his creative works is based on a similar argument premised on the ownership of a body from which a labor is derived. The acquisition of the right is considered as a just reward for the author's creative contribution through his intellectual labor.

19 See Robert Merges, *Justifying Intellectual Property* (Cambridge: Harvard University Press, 2011) at 144 [Merges, *Justifying IP*].

20 Hughes, *supra* note 7 at 297–298.

21 *Ibid* at 319–325 & 329–330. As argued by Lockean theorists, reproduction or copying of a protected work is justified to the extent required by the proviso of 'enough and as good' for others' use. Further, the idea-expression dichotomy is considered to serve the purpose. *Ibid* at 313–319. See Wendy J. Gordon, "A Property Right in Self-Expression: Equality and Individualism in the Natural Law of Intellectual Property" (1993) 102 Yale LJ 1533 at 1581–1583 [Gordon, "A Property Right in Self-Expression"].

22 Fisher, "Theories of IP," *supra* note 4 at 184. For instance, what constitutes "intellectual labor" is not clear from the theory due to multiple lines of interpretation. In the same vein, it is difficult to determine and apply the conception of "commons" to the field of IP though it is often equated with "ideas." *Ibid* at 185–186.

23 Hughes, *The Philosophy of IP, supra* note 12 at 310–311; Jeremy Waldron, *The Right to Private Property* (Clarendon Press, 1988) at 352–378.

24 Hughes, *The Philosophy of IP, supra* note 12 at 330; Waldron, *supra* note 23 at 361–374.

25 *Ibid.*

26 *Ibid* at 331–333. *See also* Drahos, *A Philosophy of IP, supra* note 17 at 75–77; Waldron, *supra* note 23 at 361–365 & 371–377.

27 Merges, *Justifying IP, supra* note 19 at 17. Merges observes that "ownership confers both control and the prospect of compensation" that constitute the two important practical dimensions of Kantian notion of autonomy. In his view, Kantian conception of individual ownership also acknowledges a need for "a deep and true engagement with the interest of third parties." *Ibid* at 18.

28 Fishman-Afori, "Human Rights and Copyright," *supra* note 5 at 504.

29 Fisher, "Theories of IP," *supra* note 4 at 189.

30 Hettinger, *supra* note 13 at 45. As Hettinger notes, "Private property can be justified as a means to sovereignty. Dominion over certain objects is important for individual autonomy." *Ibid.*

31 Gervais, "HRs & Philosophical Foundations," *supra* note 9 at 90.

32 Drahos, *A Philosophy of IP, supra* note 17 at 80.

33 Hughes, *The Philosophy of IP, supra* note 12 at 341–342.

34 Drahos, *A Philosophy of IP, supra* note 17 at 80–81.

35 Fisher, "Theories of IP," *supra* note 204 at 191. Further, missing is a parameter to identify the various human needs or interests such as self-realization, identity and privacy that need to be promoted. See Neil Wilkof, Editorial, "Theories of Intellectual Property: Is It Worth the Effort?" (2014) 9:4 J. Intell. Prop. L. & Pract. 257 at 257.

36 Thomas Hobbes, *Leviathan* (Penguins Classics 1985) 1651 at 228–229.

37 John-Jacques Rousseau, *The Social Contract and Discourses* (1762) at 195.

38 Alina Ng, "The Social Contract and Authorship: Allocating Entitlements in the Copyright System" (2008) 19:2 Fordham IP Med & Ent L J 414 at 470.

39 John Rawls, *A Theory of Justice* (Cambridge: Harvard University Press, 1971) at 11.

40 *Ibid*. For Rawls, the principles of justice are "the principles that free and rational persons concerned to further their own interests would accept in an initial position of equality as defining the fundamental terms of their association." *Ibid*.

41 Merges, *Justifying IP*, *supra* note 19 at 136. Underscoring the significance of desert (individual's will to create being the core) as a ground for IP rights, Merges asserts that "creators truly deserve some sort of property right" and "it is appropriate to include well-deserved IP rights among the list of basic liberties that people are entitled to in a just society." *Ibid* at 127–128.

42 *Ibid* at 129.

43 *Ibid* at 122–123.

44 Christophe Geiger, "The Social Function of Intellectual Property Rights, Or How Ethics Can Influence the Shape and Use of IP Law" in Graeme B. Dinwoodie (ed), *Methods and Perspectives in Intellectual Property* (Cheltenham, UK: Edward Elgar, 2013) 153 at 165 & 170. As the author notes, "the social contract [underlies] the social function" of IP. *Ibid* at 170.

45 Chidi Oguamanam, "Beyond Theories: Intellectual Property Dynamics in the Global Knowledge Economy" (2009) 9:2 Wake Forest Intell Prop L J 105 at 116 [Oguamanam, "Beyond Theories"].

46 Ng, *supra* note 38 at 478–480. Based on this implicit social contract, authors are entitled to the legal protection of their creative works that guarantees them a fair and just reward for their contribution to the public interest through: (a) reasonable public access to the works during the legal protection, and (b) free access to the works upon their entry into and consequent enrichment of the public domain after the expiry of the protection. With an emphasis on distributive justice, the contractarian theory is thus considered to address the relationship between the interests of authors, users and distributors/publishers in their entitlements to the rights over creative works and their respective duties towards the society at large. *Ibid* at 479. See Oguamanam, "Beyond Theories," *supra* note 45 at 113–114.

47 Oguamanam, "Beyond Theories," *supra* note 45 at 112–114.

48 See generally Christophe Geiger, "Implementing Intellectual Property Provisions in Human Rights Instruments: Towards a New Social Contract for the Protection of Intangibles" in Geiger, ed, *Research Handbook on Human Rights and Intellectual Property* (Cheltenham, UK: Edward Elgar, 2015) 661–689.

49 Fisher, "Theories of IP," *supra* note 4 at 172–173.

50 *Ibid* at 172.

51 *Ibid* at 192.

52 *Ibid* at 193.

53 See Neil Netanel, "Copyright and a Democratic Civil Society" (1996) 106:2 The Yale L J 283 at 341–364 [Netanel, "Copyright"].

54 *Ibid* at 347–364; see also Fisher, "Theories of IP," *supra* note 4 at 172.

55 Netanel, "Copyright," *supra* note 53 at 363.

56 *Ibid* at 343. Among the list of his pluralist civil society are educational institutions. *Ibid*.

57 *Ibid* at 364.

58 *Ibid* at 366–385.

59 Fisher, "Theories of IP," *supra* note 4 at 175.

60 *Ibid* at 193–194. Fisher also points out the "paternalistic" nature of the theory as one of its limitations. That is, a prior determination of a particular social vision limits persons' freedom to hold their own conception of what is "good for them." *Ibid* at 194. Oguamanam, "Beyond Theories," *supra* note 45 at 130. As Oguamanam observes, "the social planning approach puts too much emphasis on the amorphous concept of culture as if it is the only intellectual property paradigm." *Ibid*.

61 Apart from the specific limitations applicable to each theory, both personality and social planning theories are critiqued due to their indeterminacy and the latter's "paternalistic" element with regard to what is "good" for people. In contrast, labor and utilitarian theory are considered to be free from indeterminacy. The utilitarian justification is rather considered to be neutral and objective. *Ibid* at 194.
62 *Ibid* at 194. For the detailed discussion on the value of theories, see *ibid* at 194–199.
63 *Ibid* at 198.
64 Netanel, "Copyright," *supra* note 53 at 368. For Netanel, "[c]opyright's fundamental purpose is to underwrite political competency, with allocative efficiency a secondary consideration." *Ibid* at 364.
65 *Ibid* at 363–364. In Netanel's view, "the democratic paradigm emphasizes that copyright represents a careful balance of owner right and user access designed to serve the public's paramount interest in self-reliant authorship and democratic discourse." *Ibid* at 385.
66 Marie-Benedicte Dembour, "What Are Human Rights?: Four Schools of Thought" (2010) 32 *Human Rights Quarterly* 1 at 3.
67 *Ibid.*
68 *Ibid* at 6. Neil Stammers, *Human Rights and Social Movements* (London: Pluto Press, 2009) at 3. "While [human rights] can still be used to challenge power, their origins and meanings as 'struggle concepts' can get lost or be switched in ways that result in human rights becoming a tool of power, not a challenge to it." *Ibid.*
69 Dembour, *supra* note 66 at 3.
70 *Ibid* at 4.
71 See generally Michael Freeman, "The Philosophical Foundations of Human Rights" (1994) 16:3 Hum Rts Q 491; Martha Nussbaum, "Capabilities and Human Rights" (1997) 66 Fordham L Rev 273 at 273–275 [Nussbaum, *Capabilities and Human Rights*].
72 *Ibid* at 273.
73 *Ibid* at 274.
74 John Locke, *The Second Treatise of Government*, Para 6, in Thomas P. Peardon (ed), The Liberal Arts, Inc., 1952 (1690).
75 Freeman, *supra* note 71 at 497–498. Freeman observes that classic claim about the foundation of natural rights as a grant from God is now substituted with the notion of "human dignity/nature" due to the ontological debate related to God. *Ibid.*
76 Dembour, *supra* note 63 at 3.
77 *Ibid.*
78 Freeman, *supra* note 71 at 501–502. See Rowan Cruft, S. Matthew Liao & Massimo Renzo, "The Philosophical Foundations of Human Rights: Overview" in Cruft, Liao & Renzo, eds, *Philosophical Foundations of Human Rights* (Oxford: Oxford University Press, 2015) at 1–40.
79 Dembour, *supra* note 63 at 6.
80 Jack Donnelly, *Universal Human Rights in Theory and Practice*, (2nd ed, 2003) at 15. For Donnelley, man's moral nature constitutes the source of human rights. *Ibid* at 14.
81 *Ibid* at 3; Jack Donnelly, "Human Rights as Natural Rights" (1982) 4:3 Hum Rts Q 391 at 391 [Donnelly, "Human Rights"].
82 *Ibid.* See generally Jean Porter, "From Natural Law to Human Rights: Or, Why Rights Talk Matters" (2000) 14:1 JL & Religion 77 at 77–96.
83 Donnelly, "Human Rights" *supra* note 81 at 397–401.
84 Freeman, *supra* note 71 at 501–502. Amartya Sen, "Elements of a Theory of Human Rights" 32:4 Philosophy and Public Affairs 315 at 315–316 [Sen, "Elements"]; Cruft, Lio & Renzo, *supra* note 78.
85 Charles Beitz, "Human Rights and Social Justice," in Peter G. Brown & Douglas Maclean, eds, *Human Rights and U.S Foreign Policy* (Massachusetts: Lexington Books, 1979) at 55 [Beitz, "Human Rights and Social Justice"].
86 Freeman, *supra* note 71 at 495.

87 *Ibid*. See generally Beitz, "Human Rights and Social Justice," *supra note* 85.
88 Dembour, *supra* note 63 at 7; see James W. Nickel, *Making Sense of Human Rights* (2nd ed, 2007).
89 Dembour, *supra* note 63 at 6 & 8.
90 *Ibid* at 8.
91 *Ibid* at 6.
92 Beitz, "Human Rights and Social Justice," *supra* note 85 at 59.
93 David Miller, *Social Justice* (Oxford: Clarendon Press, 1976) at 22.
94 *Ibid*.
95 See Rawls, *supra* note 39 at 6.
96 Beitz, "Human Rights and Social Justice," *supra* note 85 at 59. Although this conception of human rights is grounded in the general theory of social justice, Beitz emphasizes the idea of international concern as a constitutive element of his theory to distinguish human rights from social justice. *Ibid*.
97 Donnelly, "Human Rights," *supra* note 81 at 401.
98 Beitz, "Human Rights and Social Justice," *supra* note 85 at 59–60; Charles Beitz, The *Idea of Human Rights* (Oxford: Oxford University Press, 2009) at 136 [Beitz, *The Idea of Human Rights*]; Beitz regards human rights as "standards intended to play a regulative role for a range of actors in the political circumstances of the contemporary world." Charles Beitz, "Human Rights as Common Concern" (2001) 95:2 American Political Science Review 269 at 276–277 [Beitz, "Human Rights as Common Concern"].
99 Beitz, "Human Rights as Common Concern," *supra* note 98 at 281.
100 Dembour, *supra* note 63 at 3 & 8.
101 Beitz, "Human Rights and Social Justice," *supra* note 85 at 59–60.
102 Miller, *supra* note 93 at 79.
103 Donnelly, "Human Rights," *supra* note 81 at 403–404.
104 Dembour, *supra* note 63 at 9. Michael Ignatieff, "Human Rights as Politics and Idolatry," in Amy Gutmann, ed, *Human Rights* (Princeton: Princeton University Press, 2001) 3 at 73–83.
105 See generally Overton Taylor, "Liberal Education and Liberalism" (1945) 55:2 Ethics 88–109; Charles Bailey, *Beyond the Present and the Particular: Liberal Theory of Education,* Volume 2 (London & New York: Routledge, 2010).
106 Patrick Riley & Jennifer Welchman, "Dewey, Rousseau and Democracy," in Randall Curren, ed, *A Companion to the Philosophy of Education* (Oxford: Blackwell, 2003) 94 at 96. The liberal conception of education that traces its roots back to the philosophical thought of ancient Greek philosophers such as Plato. *Ibid*.
107 *Ibid*.
108 *Ibid*. For Rousseau, education is useful to transform the egoistic nature of human beings so as to make them 'what they out to be' in the pursuit of their 'general will'—the will a person has as a citizen. *Ibid*.
109 *Ibid* at 96. *See also* John Dewey, *Democracy and Education: An Introduction to Philosophy of Education* (New York and London: Free Press, 2009) (first published in 1916) at 94–108.
110 Riley & Welchman, *supra* note 106 at 96.
111 In particular, Dewey stresses the necessity of education as "the means of social continuity of life." Dewey, *supra* note 109 at 3.
112 *Ibid* at 10–22, 41–53 & 111–123.
113 *Ibid* at 10.
114 Riley & Welchman, *supra* note 106 at 104.
115 *Ibid* at 106–107. See also Dewey, *supra* note 109 at 54.
116 Dewey, *supra* note 109 at 117–121.
117 *See Universal Declaration of Human Rights*, GA Res 217A (III), UNGAOR, 3d Sess, 1st plen mtg, UN Doc A/810 (12 December 1948) at art. 26(2) [UDHR]; *International*

Covenant on Economic, Social and Cultural Rights, 16 December 1966, 993 UNTS No 3 (entered into force on 3 January 1976) at art. 13 [ICESCR].

118 See also UDHR, *supra* note 117 art. 26(2).

119 Martha Nussbaum, "Cultivating Humanity in Legal Education" (2003) 70 U Chicago L Rev 265 at 268 [Nussbaum, "Cultivating Humanity in Legal Education"]; see generally Martha Nussbaum, *Cultivating Humanity: A Classical Defense of Reform in Liberal Education* (Cambridge, MA: Harvard University Press, 1997) at 30 [Nussbaum, *Cultivating Humanity*]. For Nussbaum, education cultivates humanity through the development of the capacities for, *inter alia,* critical self-examination and thinking. *Ibid.*

120 See Ingrid Robeyns, "Three Models of Education: Rights, Capabilities and Human Capital" (2006) 4:1 Theory Res Educ 69 at 72 [Robeyns, "Three Models of Education"].

121 Gary Becker, Human Capital Revisited, in *Human Capital: A Theoretical Analysis with Special Reference to Education* (The University of Chicago Press, 1994) 15 at 17–25.

122 David Bloom et al., "Higher Education and Economic Growth in Africa" (2014) 1:1 Int J Afr High Educ 23 at 37–49.

123 See generally Paul Romer, "Endogenous Technological Change" (1990) 98:5 J Polit Econ 71 [Romer, "Endogenous Technological Change"]. See Kingsley C. Moghalu, *Emerging Africa: How the Global Economy's "Last Frontier" Can Prosper and Matter* (London: Penguin Books Ltd, 2014) at 202.

124 Romer, "Endogenous Technological Change" *supra* note 123 at 71.

125 Bloom et al., *supra* note 122 at 48–49.

126 Committee on Economic, Social and Cultural Rights, *General Comment No. 13: The Right to Education,* para 1, UN Doc E/C 12/1999/10 (8 December 1999) [*CESCR General Comment No. 13*].

127 Romer, "Endogenous Technological Change" *supra* note 123 at 72.

128 Amartya Sen, "Human Capital and Human Capability" (1997) 25:12 World Dev 1959 at 1959–1960 [Sen, "Human Capital and Human Capability"].

129 *Ibid* at 1959–1960. See also Robeyns, "Three Models of Education," *supra* note 120 at 72–73.

130 *Sen, "Human Capital and Human Capability," supra* note 128 at 1959–1960.

131 Madoka Saito, "Amartya Sen's Capability Approach to Education: A Critical Exploration" (2003) 37:1 J. Philos. Educ 17; Elaine Unterhalter, "The Capabilities Approach and Gendered Education: An Examination of South African Complexities" (2003) 1:1 Theory Res Educ 7 [Unterhalter, "The Capabilities Approach"]; Melanie Walker, Framing Social Justice: What Does the 'Capabilities' Approach Offer? (2003) 51:2 Br J Educ Stud 168 [Walker, "Framing Social Justice"].

132 See generally Melanie Walker, "Widening Participation in Higher Education: Lifelong Learning as Capability," in David N. Aspin, ed, *Philosophical Perspectives on Lifelong Learning* (The Netherlands: Springer, 2007) 131 [Walker, "Widening Participation in Higher Education"].

133 Tristan McCowan, *Education as a Human Right: Principles for a Universal Entitlement to Learning* (London, UK: Bloomsbury, 2013) at 145.

134 See generally Nussbaum, *Cultivating Humanity, supra* note 119.

135 McCowan, *supra* note 133 at 145.

136 Walker, "Widening Participation in Higher Education" *supra* note 132 at 132.

137 *Ibid* at 131–134 & 138–145.

138 *Ibid.*

139 *Ibid* at 135.

140 *Ibid* at 138.

141 *Ibid* at 134. As Walker points out, "[r]esources such as bursaries for students, teaching facilities, books and journals, computers, the staff-student ratio, academic scholarship, and so on, might be considered capability inputs." *Ibid.* Also important are other social

arrangements or external conditions, such as institutional and policy designs. *Ibid* at 135–137.

142 *Ibid*. See Marth C. Nussbaum, "Capabilities and Human Rights" (1997) 66 Fordham L Rev 273 at 289–297 [Nussbaum, "Capabilities and Human Rights"].

143 Robeyns, "Three Models of Education," *supra* note 120 at 76–77. See Amartya Sen, "Human Rights and Capabilities" (2005) 6:2 J Human Dev Capabil 151 at 152–157 [Sen, "Human Rights and Capabilities"].

144 Leon Tikly & Angeline Barret, "Social Justice, Capabilities and the Quality of Education in Low Income Countries" (2011) 31 Int J Educ Dev 3 at 7–10.

145 Michael P. Todaro & Stephen C. Smith, *Economic Development,* 11th ed (Boston: Addison-Wisely, 2012) at 128. The theory assumes the existence of efficient market, perfect competition, information symmetry and rational decision-making or expectations.

146 All these economic policy prescriptions are included in the so-called Washington Consensus adopted in 1989. The Bretton Woods Institutions (World Bank and International Monetary Fund (IMF) are considered to be proponents and agents of the Washington Consensus. See John Williamson, "A short History of the Washington Consensus" (2009) 15 Law & Business Review of the Americas 7. For a critique on the Washington Consensus, see generally Joseph Stiglitz, *More Instruments and Broader Goals: Moving Towards the Post-Washington Consensus* (Helsinki: World Institute for development Economics Research, 1998).

147 Todaro & Smith, *supra* note 145 at 129. The approach tends to assume the existence of an efficient market in the developing countries.

148 See Richard Peet & Elaine Hartwick, *Theories of Development: Contentions, Arguments and Alternatives*, 3rd ed (New York: Guilford Press, 2015) at 90–95.

149 *Ibid* at 96–97. See Ray Kiely, "Neoliberalism Revised?: A Critical Account of World Bank Concepts of Good Governance and Market Friendly Intervention" (1998) 28:4 Int J Health Serv 683 at 684–688.

150 Todaro & Smith, *supra* note 145 at 129. The approach acknowledges the information asymmetries, lack of absorptive capacity for technology and economies of scale in production in the less developed nations.

151 See Netanel, "Copyright," *supra* note 53 at 306–311 & 314–324 (making a critical analysis of the neoliberal approach to copyright).

152 Robert M. Solow, "Technical Change and the Aggregate Production Function" (1957) 39:3 The Review of Economics and Statistics 312–320. For Solow, a significant increase in gross output is attributable to technical progress. Nonetheless, the technical change is considered exogenous and neutral. In his conclusion drawn from data between 1909 and 1949, "[g]ross output per man hour doubled over the interval, with 87 1/2 per cent of the increase attributable to technical change and the remaining I2 1/2 per cent to increased use of capital." *Ibid* at 320.

153 See generally Paul Romer, "The Origins of Endogenous Growth" (1994) 8:1 J Econ Perspect 3–22 [Romer, "The Origins of Endogenous Growth"]; Robert E. Lucas, "Ideas and Growth" (2009) 76 Economica 1 [Lucas, "Ideas & Growth"] (underscoring the contribution of knowledge of individuals for economic growth).

154 *Ibid*; see generally Romer, "Endogenous Technological Change" *supra* note 123.

155 Romer, "Endogenous Technological Change," *supra* note 123 at 72–73. In Romer's view, "technological change arises in large part because of intentional actions taken by people who respond to market incentives. Thus, the model is one of endogenous rather than exogenous technological change." For him, "the stock of human capital determines the rate of growth." *Ibid* at 71.

156 *Ibid*.

157 *Ibid* at 74. Romer argues that capital, labor, human capital and technology are central to this model of growth. *Ibid* at 78–88. Robert E. Lucas, "On the Mechanics of

Economic Development" (1988) 22 J Monet Econ 3 at 17–41 [Lucas, "On the Mechanics"]. For Robert Lucas, human capital (accumulated both through schooling and learning by doing) is 'the engine of growth.' *Ibid* at 35.

158 See Linda Yueh, "Global Intellectual Property and Economic Growth" (2007) 5:3 Nw J Tech & Intell Prop 436 at 443–444.

159 Karla Hoff, "Beyond Rosentein-Rodan: The Modern Theory of Coordination Problem in Development," in Boris Pleskovich & Nicholas Stern, eds, *Annual World Bank Conference on Development Economics* (Washington, DC: The World Bank, 2001) 145 at 145–146 & 152–159. The modern coordination failure model draws on the insights of Rosentei-Rodan. In view of externalities or spillovers, the model identifies instances of coordination failures such as spillovers related to the technology of an agent, social or political interactions, information, and a search process. *Ibid* at 146.

160 *Ibid* at 151. The coordination failure occurs due to a complex economic ecosystem in which the action of an individual or a firm depends upon the behavior of others.

161 Dani Rodrick, "Getting Interventions Right: How South Korea and Taiwan Grew Rich" (1995) 10 Econ Policy 53 at 79–80.

162 Karla Hoff & Joseph Stiglitz, "Modern Economic Theory and Development," in Gerald Meier & Joseph Stiglitz, eds, *Frontiers of Development Economics: The Future in Perspective* (Washington, DC: World Bank, 2000) 389 at 390.

163 Hoff, *supra* note 159 at 165–168.

164 *Ibid* at 170.

165 See generally Chalmers Johnson, *Japan, Who Governs?: The Rise of Developmental State* (New York: Norton, 1995).

166 Stephan Haggard, *Developmental States* (Cambridge: Cambridge University Press, 2018) at 2–6 & 10–12.

167 *Ibid* at 4 & 28–34; Rodrick, *supra* note 161 at 79–80.

168 Haggard, *supra* note 166 at 13–14.

169 *Ibid* at 29–32.

170 See generally Christopher Clapham, "The Ethiopian Developmental State" (2018) 39:6 Third World L J 1151. Given its new economic reforms, Ethiopia seems to be embracing a liberal economic approach to promote private sectors.

171 Sakiko Fukuda-Parr, "Theory and Policy in the International Development: Human Development and Capability Approach and the Millennium Development Goals" (2011) 13 Int Stud Rev 122 at 125–126 [Fukuda-Parr, "Theory and Policy in International Development"].

172 Sakiko Fukuda-Parr, "The Human Development Paradigm: Operationalizing Sen's Ideas on Capabilities" (2003) 9:2/3 *Feminist Economics* 301 at 303–304 [Fukuda-Parr, "The Human Development Paradigm"].

173 See Amartya Sen, *Commodities and Capabilities* (New Delhi: Oxford University Press, 1999) at 1–16 [Sen, *Commodities and Capabilities*]; Martha Nussbaum, "Capabilities and Human Rights," *supra* note 142 at 276 & 281–283; Amartya Sen, *Development as Freedom* (New York: Anchor Books, 1999) at 5 & 57–62 [Sen, *Development as Freedom*]. In his critique of utilitarian conception of efficiency, Sen argued for the evaluation of efficiency in terms of people's capabilities. *Ibid* at 117–126 & 43.

174 Sen, *Development as Freedom, supra* note 173 at 117–126 & 43. Sen recognizes the role of industrialization, technological progress and social modernization for the expansion of human freedom. Nonetheless, he argues that there are many other factors that are important such as social and economic arrangements (e.g. facilities for education), and civil and political rights. *Ibid* at 3.

175 *Ibid* at 11–142. In particular, Sen points out the limitation to address social opportunities such as provision of education to the poor. *Ibid* at 127–133 & 42. In addition to markets, the HDA recognizes the role of institutions such as government, civil society,

and global institutions. Paul Streeten, "Human Development: Means and Ends" (1993) 21:4 Bangladesh Dev Stud 65 at 68.

176 Nussbaum defines the CA to human development as "an approach to comparative quality of life assessment and to theorizing about basic social justice." Martha Nussbaum, *Creating Capabilities: The Human Development Approach* (Cambridge: Harvard University Press, 2011) at 18 [Nussbaum, *Creating Capabilities*]. She observes that Sen and this collaborators regard "capability as the most pertinent space of comparison for purposes of quality of life assessment." *Ibid* at 19. Sen, *Development as Freedom, supra* note 173 at 74–86.

177 Sen, *Development as Freedom, supra* note 173 at 3 & 14.

178 *Ibid* at xii &3.

179 Both concepts constitute the conceptual foundations of the human development approach. Fukuda-Parr, "The Human Development Paradigm," *supra* note 172 at 303-04. Despite the interchangeable reference to both human development approach and the capability approach, the latter is a broader framework that is used in various disciplines and for a number of additional issues such as social justice, development, and ethical theory and practice. Ingrid Robeyns views the capability approach as "an umbrella, or a family, of normative theories." Ingrid Robeyns, "Capabilitarianism" (2016) 17:3 J Hum Dev Capab 397 at 403 [Robeyns, "Capabilitarianism"].

180 Sen, *Development as Freedom, supra* note 173 at 75. Sen defines capability as a kind of "substantive freedom to achieve alternative combination of functionings" and functionings "things a person may value doing or being." *Ibid.* Nussbaum, *Creating Capabilities, supra* note 176 at 20–25.

181 UNDP, *Human Development Report 1990* (New York and Oxford: UNDP & Oxford University Press, 1990) at 9–10. Started in 1990 and published annually since then, Human Development Reports (HDRs) is founded on the conceptual framework of Sen's capability approach for its analysis of contemporary development challenges. Fukuda-Parr, "The Human Development Paradigm," *supra* note 172 at 301–302. Inspired by Sen's capability approach, Mahbub Ul Haq in collaboration with Sen further developed the HDA to underpin both the Human Development Reports and Human Development Index (HDI). See Mahbub Ul Haq, *Reflections on Human Development* (New York: Oxford University Press, 1995) at 24–65 [ul Haq, *Reflections*].

182 Mahbub ul Haq, "The Human Development Paradigm" in Fukuda-Parr & Shiva Kumar, eds, *Readings in Human Development: Concepts, Measures and Policies for a Development Paradigm*, 2nd ed (New Delhi: Oxford University Press, 2005) at 17 & 18 [ul Haq, "The Human Development Paradigm"].

183 Fukuda-Parr, "The Human Development Paradigm," *supra* note 172 at 303–307. Sen, *Development as Freedom, supra* note 173 at 4.

184 Fukuda-Parr, "The Human Development Paradigm," *supra* note 172 at 303 & 308–309. Sen, *Development as Freedom, supra* note 173 at 53. From the perspective of the human development approach, human beings are autonomous to make their decisions and advance key social and economic objectives that promote development. Sabina Alkire & Severine Deneulin, "The Human Development and Capability Approach" in Severine Deneulin & Lila Shani, eds, *An Introduction to the Human Development and Capability Approach: Freedom and Agency* (London: Earthscan, 2009) at 27–28.

185 Fukuda-Parr, "The Human Development Paradigm," *supra* note 172 at 308–309. For instance, this justifies an investment in human resource development such as education for the people to play an instrumental role in the process of development. Fukuda-Parr notes that "the concept of human capital or human resource development is typically about individual agency for material production." *Ibid* at 309.

186 *Ibid* at 304. For the details regarding the basic needs approach to development, see Frances Stewart, *Panning to Meet Basic Needs* (London: Macmillan, 1985) at 1–13.

187 Ul Haq, *Reflections, supra* note 181 at 76–92. Ul Haq was forerunner of the concept of sustainable development through his integration of environmental concerns and development into a single concept. Paul Streeten, "Foreword," in Mahbub Ul Haq, *ibid* at ix.
188 Fukuda-Parr, "The Human Development Paradigm," *supra* note 172 at 310. See also Nussbaum, "Capabilities and Human Rights," *supra* note 142 at 277–279.
189 Nussbaum, *Creating Capabilities, supra* note 176 at 18–19. Nussbaum identifies five elements as the essential features of CA: respect for the principle of treating each person as an end; a focus on choice or freedom rather than on achievements; pluralism about value; a deep concern with entrenched social injustice and inequality; and a commitment to describe an urgent task to government and public policy. *Ibid.* In contrast, Robeyns points out many more core elements of the CA such as the difference in abilities (conversion functions), human diversity, structural constraints (e.g. effect of laws or norms), and human agency. See Robeyns, "Capabilitarianism," *supra* note 179 at 405–410.
190 Richard Jolly, "Human Development and Neoliberalism: Paradigms Compared" in Sakiko Fukuda-Parr and A. K. Shiva Kumar, eds, *Readings in Human Development: Concepts, Measures and Policies for a Development Paradigm* (New Delhi: Oxford University Press, 2003) at 106.
191 Robert Sugden, "Welfare, Resources and Capabilities: A Review of Inequality Examined by Amartya Sen" (1993) 31:4 J Econ Lit 1947 at 1953.
192 See Margaret Chon, "Global Intellectual Property Governance (Under Construction)" (2011) 12:1 *Theor Inq L* 349 at 368 [Chon, "Global Intellectual Property"].
193 Sen, *Development as Freedom, supra* note 173 at 3.
194 *Ibid.*
195 *See* Hans Bugge Christian, "1987–2007: 'Our Common Future' Revisited" *in* Hans Bugge Christian & Voigt Christina, eds, *Sustainable Development in International and National Law: What Did the Brundtland Report Do to Legal Thinking and Legal Development, and Where Can We Go from Here?* (Groningen: Europa Law Publishing, 2008) 3 at 7.
196 See United Nations World Commission on Environment and Development, *Our Common Future: World Commission on Environment and Development* (Oxford: Oxford University Press, 1987) at 43–66 [UNWCED, *Our Common Future*].
197 See generally Sudhir Anand and Amartya K. Sen, "Sustainable Human Development: Concepts and Priorities," at 46, online: UNDP <http://hdr.undp.org/sites/default/files/anand_sudhir_-_sustainable_human_development-_concepts_and_priorities.pdf> (last visited 15 April 2021) [Anand and Sen, *Sustainable Human Development*].
198 See Sen, *Development as Freedom, supra* note 173 at 75. Martha Nussbaum has developed basic, internal and combined capabilities as the categories of human capabilities. The basic capabilities are innate as compared to the internal and combined ones that are contingent on external conditions for their development. Martha C. Nussbaum, *Women and Human Development: The Capability Approach* (Cambridge: Cambridge University Press, 2000) at 84–85 [Nussbaum, *Women and Human Development*].
199 *Ibid.*
200 In her treatment of CA, Nussbaum has developed list of ten central human capabilities as a minimum set of capabilities required for a person to live a dignified and meaningful life. In contrast, Sen prefers leaving the formulation and determination of capabilities subject to public reasoning or deliberative dialogue. See Nussbaum, "Capabilities and Human Rights," *supra* note 142 at 285–288.
201 *Sen, Development as Freedom, supra* note 173 at 3.
202 Amartya Sen, "Development as Capability Expansion," in Sakiko Fukuda-Parr & A.K. Shiva Kumar, eds, *Readings in Human Development: Concepts, Measures and Policies for a Development Paradigm* (New Delhi: Oxford University Press, 2003) at 44–45 [Sen, "Development as Capability Expansion"].

203 *Sen, Development as Freedom, supra note* 173 at 36.
204 *Ibid* at 3 & 18.
205 Ingrid Robeyns, "The Capability Approach in Practice" (2006) 14:3 J Polit Philos 351 at 352 [Robeyns, "The Capability Approach in Practice"]. The CA is not a theory, but a framework for conceptualization and evaluation of well-being and inequality. *Ibid* at 353.
206 See generally Arjun K. Sengupta, "Conceptualizing the Right to Development for the Twenty-First Century: Situating the Right to Development," at 1, online: <http://www.ohchr.org/Documents/Issues/Development/RTDBook/PartIChapter4.pdf> (last visited 15 April 2021).
207 Declaration on the Right to Development, GA Res 41/128, Annex, UNGAOR, 41st Sess, No 53, UN Doc. A/4/53 (4 December 1986), Preamble at paras 1 & 5 [hereinafter DRD]. It worth mentioning that a consensus has been reached during the Vienna Declaration and Program of Action (1993) affirming the indivisible, interdependent and universal human right status of the right to development along other human rights. See World Conference on Human Rights, Vienna Declaration and Program of Action, 12 July 1993, GA A/CONF157/23 (Vienna: 14–25 June 1993) at para 5 [Vienna Declaration].
208 DRD, *supra* note 207, Preamble at para 2. See also Sengupta, *supra* note 206 at 68–69; James C. N. Paul, "The Human Right to Development: Its Meaning & Importance" (1992) 25 *John Marshall L Rev* 235.
209 Johannesburg Plan of Implementation, Report of the World Summit on Sustainable Development, UN Doc. A/CONF199/20 (Johannesburg: 26 August–4 September 2002) [World Submit on Sustainable Development (2002)].
210 See UN Sustainable Development Goals, Goal 4, online: UNDP <http://www.un.org/sustainabledevelopment/education/> [UNSDGs] (last visited 10 April 2021).
211 Ruth Okediji, "Reframing International Copyright Limitations and Exceptions as Development Policy," in *Copyright Law in an Age of Limitations and Exceptions* (Cambridge: Cambridge University, 2017) 429 at 494 [Okediji, "Reframing International Copyright"].
212 See Sen, *Development as Freedom*, *supra* note 173 at 4 & 39. Sen points out the instrumental role of social opportunities such as educational facilities (e.g. learning materials) for expansion of freedom through education. See *ibid.*
213 *Ibid* at 293–296. Nussbaum, *Women and Human Development, supra* note 198 at 78–79.
214 Martha Nussbaum, "Human Rights and Capabilities: Twentieth Anniversary Reflections" (2007) 20 *Harv Hum Rts J* 21 at 21 [Nussbaum, "Human Rights and Capabilities"].
215 For instance, McCowan argues that the right to education should be conceptualized in terms of capabilities. McCowan, *supra* note 133 at 144–148.
216 Nussbaum, "Human Rights and Capabilities," *supra* note 214 at 21. Understood as entitlements to capabilities, Nussbaum observes that all rights "have material and social preconditions" that require government action. *Ibid.*
217 Martha Nussbaum, "Capabilities as Fundamental Entitlements: Sen and Social Justice" (2003) 9:2/3 *Feminist Economics* 33 at 35–36 [Nussbaum, "Capabilities as Fundamental Entitlements"].
218 Martha Nussbaum, "Capabilities, Entitlements, Rights: Supplementation and Critique" (2011) 12:1 J Human Dev Capabil 23 at 23 [Nussbaum, "Capabilities"]. In Nussbaum's opinion, capabilities are important human entitlements, inherent in the idea of basic social justice, and can be viewed as one species of human rights approach." *Ibid.* Amartya Sen, "Human Rights and Capabilities" (2005) 6:2 J Human Dev Capabil 151 at 151. Sen notes the consonance between the concepts of human rights and capabilities as long as one concept is not subsumed within the confine of the other. *Ibid.*
219 Nussbaum, *Women and Human Development, supra* note 198 at 99.

220 See McCowan, *supra* note 133 at 135.
221 Sengupta, *supra* note 206 at 71.
222 See Nussbaum, "Capabilities and Human Rights," *supra* note 142 at 292–297. For instance, the intrinsic and instrumental aspects of the CA showcase the normative reach of the approach to explore the multifaceted roles of the human right to education. As is aptly elaborated by the CESCR, the human right to education is essential both for the development of human personality and the enjoyment of other fundamental human rights. See *CESCR General Comment No. 13*, *supra* note 126 at para 1.
223 See Robeyns, "The Capability Approach in Practice," *supra* note 205 at 360–370.
224 See generally Yochai Benkler, *The Wealth of Networks: How Social Production Transforms Markets and Freedom* (New Haven, CT: Yale University Press, 2006); Tzen Wong & Graham Dutfield, eds, *Intellectual Property and Human Development: Current Trends and Future Scenarios* (Cambridge: Cambridge University Press, 2011).
225 See Jeremy de Beer, "Defining WIPO's Development Agenda," in de Beer, ed, *Implementing WIPO's Development Agenda* (Ottawa: Wilfred University Press, 2009).
226 See generally Margaret Chon, "Intellectual Property and the Development Divide" (2006) 27:6 Cardozo L Rev 2813.
227 See Sen, *Development as Freedom*, *supra* note 173 at 70–85.
228 See Robert Sugden "Welfare, Resources and Capabilities: A Review of Inequality Re-examined by Amartya Sen" (1993) 31 J Econ Lit 1947 at 1953.
229 Charles C. Beitz, "Amartya Sen's Resources, Values and Development" (1986) 2:2 Econ Philos 282 [Beitz, "Amartya Sen's Resources"].

3 International copyright and human rights systems: development context

3.1 Introduction

The contemporary IP and human rights systems are the results of reformative evolutions since their inception. Each system has its own historical accounts and distinguishing features. The evolution of copyright as a major component of IP system was primarily driven by the need to promote an economic progress.[1] In addition to the Holocaust and the devastating effects of the World War II that prompted the adoption of international bill of rights, the issue of socio-economic development was one of the reasons behind the emergence of the socio-economic human rights. In this context, both copyright and human rights systems somehow share common development objectives. It is thus important to highlight the theoretical foundations and operation of the systems through the lens of a development context. In the subsequent chapters, the roles of copyright and higher education for sustainable human development will be examined against this backdrop.

To begin with the overall context, development has remained an important issue of a common concern at international, regional and national levels. It is central to the national policy agenda of all nations. In particular, the issue of development is at the top of the national policy objectives of developing nations. Both for states and non-state actors, development issue is often central to undergird or constitute the primary objective of most IP or human rights–related policy initiatives. Despite the variance in the scope and degree of emphasis, development is an overarching objective both for IP and human rights systems. At a specific level, this general objective, *a fortiori*, holds true for copyright protection and education. For example, both copyright and education contribute to human development through creative innovation and human capital.[2] As such, development has been one of the major driving forces behind the evolution of both systems at national and global levels. Nonetheless, there is a significant variation in the notion and scope of development that underpins copyright and human rights systems. For instance, despite its instrumental role to promote non-economic aspects of development such as socio-cultural developments,[3] the existing author-centered international copyright system is unduly skewed towards an economic growth.[4] In

DOI: 10.4324/9781003214298-3

contrast, a human rights system has been shaped by a broader notion of development encompassing political, social, economic, and cultural aspects. The variance in the scope and degree of emphasis on development in the systems might be attributed, *inter alia*, to the historical contexts of their evolution.

Yet, development constitutes a shared context for both systems. As mentioned in the preceding chapter, the notion of development context is noted in its broadest sense to mean a sustainable human development with its holistic approach. Given its transformative integration into the existing notion of development and its central emphasis on human beings, the objective of sustainable human development offers an important framework or context to examine copyright and human rights systems at international and national levels. In mapping the development context in the light of the objective of sustainable development, the rights-based human development approach is thus vital to keep in view.

3.2 International copyright system: development context

3.2.1 An overview of the international copyright system

Prior to exploring the development context, it is important to offer a brief account of the international copyright system. In terms of its evolution, the contemporary international copyright system is the product of long-time legal and institutional developments. Driven by economic imperatives and the desire to prevent copyright infringements in other jurisdictions, the international copyright system had emerged from the consolidation of the existing bilateral agreements between European countries.[5] In this context, the adoption of the Berne Convention[6] was the first step towards a multilateral legal regime to mark the emergence of the international copyright system. In underpinning the international system, the Convention had drawn on the basic principles of the existing bilateral agreements and national copyright systems. Anchored in an economic reason embedded in the one-sided and expansive minimum standards,[7] the international copyright system was designed to coordinate the protection of authors and right holders across national jurisdictions.[8] Setting an increasing trajectory in the standards and development of the system, the Berne Convention had thus served a coordinative function.[9] To serve the purpose, the principle of national treatment has been central to the Berne system as a rule of non-discrimination between foreigners and nationals with regard to protection of their copyright in a member-state's jurisdiction.[10]

Since its adoption in 1886, the Berne Convention has been revised several times in order to address the impact of the emerging media and technologies on the international copyright system.[11] In the opinion of learned scholars, the emergence and expansion of information technologies as well as the driving economic interest were the compelling impetus for the revision or adoption of major international treaties,[12] including the TRIPs Agreement.[13] Indeed, the TRIPs Agreement that embraces the Berne Convention is another significant legal regime to shape the substantive legal framework of the international copyright system.[14]

To date, the TRIPs Agreement has remained to be the most comprehensive and effective trade agreement devoted to protection of IPRs within the global trade regime. Of a particular significance is its injection of an enforcement aspect into the existing IP system. In the digital environment, the WIPO Copyright Treaty (WCT) and the WIPO Performances and Phonograms Treaty (WPPT)—jointly known as the WIPO Internet Treaties[15]—are the most important treaties adopted for the international protection of copyright and neighboring rights. Adopted within the framework of the Berne Convention, the WIPO Internet Treaties were designed to maintain and adapt the existing principles of the Berne Convention and its in-built expansive protection in the digital environment.[16]

In addition to the substantive frameworks, the need to ensure the international implementation of the Berne Convention and other treaties resulted in the establishment of a global institutional framework. As a successor to the previous institution vested with the power to oversee both the Berne and Paris Conventions,[17] the WIPO was established in 1967 to reform the existing institutional framework and promote the global protection of international IP.[18] Since its establishment, the organization has been the most dominant IP institution for the administration of the international copyright system. In the global trade regime, the WTO has emerged as a powerful trade institution with a significant role in the global protection of IPRs through the TRIPs Agreement.

In particular, the integration of the Berne and the Rome Conventions into the TRIPs Agreement has ushered the WTO into the existing copyright system as a global institution with an effective enforcement mechanism.[19] Thus, both the WTO and the WIPO play key roles in shaping the international copyright system.[20] Given their overlapping roles, both are expected to operate in cooperation towards their common objective of promoting global protection of copyright.[21] In general, since the inception of the international copyright system, both the substantive legal and institutional frameworks have been further strengthened, expanded and consolidated through series of legal and institutional reforms. In effect, relevant flexibilities are both neglected and constrained thereby restricting access to knowledge.

3.2.2 The encounter between development and international copyright system

A Copyright in development context: general overview

As mentioned above, an economic development has been central to the very objective and design of the IP system. In particular, copyright—one of the major forms of IP—has long been underpinned by the utilitarian assumption of economic development. In principle, the design and functioning of a copyright system are supposed to be guided by its roles to foster creative innovation and facilitate the dissemination of the creative works, both of which are essential for development. Nonetheless, due to its narrow focus on the economic aspect of development, the long-felt reform in its right holders-oriented system and its unabated globalization have all brought the IP system into the spotlight. For instance, the emerging notion of human development has underscored the need to revisit the very purpose and operation of IP in the light of the development needs and local contexts of nations.[22]

Given the expansive scope of IP and the exclusive nature of the rights with a global impact, the profound implication of IP for development has been an issue of a heated debate. From among several development issues, the debate has been spotlighted in the context of access to essential medicines for chronic diseases, affordable seeds for food security and access to knowledge or learning materials for education in the developing nations.[23] In general, the increasing globalization of the system and its impact on the ability of the developing nations to address their domestic development priorities such as education underpin the current encounter between copyright and development.

Though the encounter between IP and the concept of economic development has been more persistent since the early twenty-first century,[24] it is argued that development concerns are not adequately addressed in the contemporary IP system.[25] The issue of development has however remained a recurring concern ever since the evolution of a copyright system at national and international levels. This is evident from both national and international copyright regimes. For instance, the U.S. Constitution underlines the need to promote 'the progress of science and useful arts' through a legal protection of copyright for a limited duration.[26] In practice, this utilitarian-driven purpose often overemphasizes the role of copyright protection for economic growth. Hence, rethinking the practice and embracing a broader development objective are useful to underscore copyright's roles to promote learning and foster creative autonomy, cultural diversity and democracy.[27]

B Development context for Berne, Rome, and related conventions

At the international level, starting with the Berne Convention, various aspects of economic development feature in the international copyright regime either as a driving reason or an intended objective.[28] Shaped by the national copyright systems of developed nations,[29] all the major treaties comprising the international copyright system have embraced a similar utilitarian development objective.[30] This objective is embedded in most copyright treaties. Intended to advance the development objective, the Berne Convention and the TRIPs Agreement are the major treaties that constitute the bedrock of the international copyright system. In contrast to their marginal non-economic aspect, the economic aspect of copyright system is thus the major development context for all copyright treaties.

In this regard, adopted with the primary purpose of ensuring the effective and uniform protection of "the rights of authors in their literary and artistic works,"[31] the Berne Convention seeks to safeguard the economic and personal interests of the authors across member states.[32] In so doing, the Convention underscores the instrumental significance of copyright for the generation of advanced creative works that are prerequisites for economic, social and cultural development.[33] Indeed, the issue of development has been integral to the Berne Convention since its inception.[34] Nonetheless, the Berne Convention is critiqued for its undue emphasis on a narrow aspect of development—economic growth and the overriding interests of authors.[35]

In response to the critiques, some efforts, *albeit* insufficient, were made to reflect the development needs of member states. For instance, the adoption of the Berne Appendix was one such an effort made to address the development needs of developing countries.[36] Despite its limited practical significance, the Appendix was intended to facilitate a bulk access to copyrighted works for the purpose of education, scholarship, and scientific research.[37] Circumscribed in its scope, a similar purpose was embedded in the Berne Convention's structural design to allow member states a discretion to devise appropriate L&Es to the exclusive rights within their respective jurisdictions.[38] That is, acting within the permitted scope, the member states have the discretion to formulate and utilize appropriate flexibilities in order to address their socio-economic development needs.

Given the difference in the levels of development across nations, this cabined discretion may allow member states to consider their respective domestic development contexts. As Okediji notes, the discretion forms part of "the reserved powers of the state to protect the welfare of its citizens."[39] However, the exercise of this sovereign discretion has been subjected to the principle of the three-step test incorporated in the Berne Convention.[40] In addition to its structural design, a development element can be gleaned from the Convention's substantive provisions. For instance, the exception for educational purpose under art. 10(2) of the Berne Convention indicates the Convention's recognition of the instrumental role of education for socio-economic development.[41]

Although the adequacy and effective utilization of the permitted flexibilities are debatable, these instances of development imperatives and the very purpose of copyright protection can be considered to constitute the development context of the international copyright system. In other words, the collective combinations of the dominant economic and the limited socio-cultural aspects embedded in the Berne Convention reflect the breadth and depth of its development context. In the same vein, the Universal Copyright Convention (UCC)[42] also embodies similar elements integral to the development context for the international copyright system. In particular, the Convention recognizes "the temporary need[s] of some states to adjust their level of copyright protection in accordance with their stage of cultural, social and economic development."[43] Once regarded to be more flexible for and favorable to developing countries, the now-defunct UCC is of a little significance due to the TRIPs Agreement's embrace of the Berne Convention to bind all members.[44]

Moreover, the major copyright treaties adopted within the framework of the Berne Convention enshrine various development elements that form part of the overall development context for international copyright system. Following a similar approach, the Rome Convention (1961)[45]—adopted for the international protection of neighboring rights[46]—permits member states to design the appropriate L&Es to the exclusive rights.. Member states are thus allowed to provide a set of L&Es corresponding to those provided for copyright protection within their jurisdictions.[47]

Subject to the guiding principles of the Berne Convention, member states can exercise a similar sovereign discretion to design the appropriate L&Es. In the same vein, the Phonograms Convention (1971)[48]—dedicated to the exclusive rights. of producers of phonograms—allows member states to provide L&Es corresponding to those prescribed for authors of literary and artistic works.[49] Although it lacks a general rule of compulsory license, the Convention allows a compulsory license intended for the purpose of teaching or scientific research, subject to the prescribed conditions. As noted from both conventions, the flexibilities inherent in the discretion to design the appropriate L&Es, and the latter's instrumental role to address development needs are important elements integral to the development context.

C Development context for WIPO internet and Marrakesh treaties

As in the basic treaties, similar elements indicative of the development objective of the copyright system are enshrined in the most recent copyright treaties. Indeed, there is an increasing tendency to make an explicit mention of development aspects in the treaties. For instance, the WIPO Internet Treaties recognize the need to orient copyright protection in the digital environment towards their intended objectives. Adopted within the framework of the Berne Convention[50] and embracing its approach for devising the appropriate L&Es,[51] the WIPO Internet Treaties make an explicit reference to "development" and related terms in their preambles.

Viewed from the perspective of right holders, both Treaties recognize the need to introduce new rules "in order to provide adequate solutions to the questions raised by new economic, social, cultural and technological developments."[52] From users' perspective, the Treaties acknowledge "the need to maintain a *balance* between the rights of authors and the larger *public interest,* particularly *education*, *research* and *access to information*, as reflected in the Berne Convention."[53] In this respect, Pamela Samuelson notes the WCT's desire to maintain the traditional balance within the global digital copyright environment for the purpose of education as embedded within the Berne Convention.[54]

In theory, the WIPO Internet Treaties hint at the need for enhanced access to the protected works for the purposes of education and research as the basic aspects of public interest and vital prerequisites for development.[55] As such, the Treaties highlights their intended objectives to maintain a balance and address the emerging economic, social, cultural, and technological developments. Nonetheless, the actual scope of the permitted flexibilities under the WIPO Internet Treaties and their effective role to address development needs are subject to the combined restrictive effect of the existing copyright system and the introduction of technological protection measures (TPMs).[56] In this regard, Ruth Okediji observes that the treaties have so far delivered "too little too early" and would "serve a more technocratic and political—rather than substantive and legal—role in the future of digital copyright."[57]

In general, the (in)adequacy of the development policy space retained under the various copyright treaties remains debatable. In spite of its status as the UN agency and the consequent development mandate it assumes, the WIPO's explicit commitment to address development issues is an act of a recent phenomenon.[58] As articulated in its UN-driven development mandate in the aftermath of its establishment, the WIPO is still required to "facilitate the transfer of technology related to industrial property to the developing countries in order to accelerate economic, social and cultural development."[59] Further, the WIPO's development commitment is implicit in its establishment objectives and institutional mandate to assist developing countries in promoting their cultural, scientific and technological development through 'modernization' of, *inter alia*, copyright system.[60]

Long after several decades of reluctance and resistance, the WIPO has taken a reform initiative to enunciate its development mandate in its Development Agenda—an IP-related development policy objective that is supposed to embrace the UN development goals.[61] Hence, the relevant parts of both the WIPO DA and the UN SDGs are vital to complement each other and inform a broader development context for the international copyright system.[62] Indeed, the WIPO DA marks an explicit linkage between copyright and development. Should it succeed in its implementation, the WIPO DA will constitute a significant step in re-orienting the global copyright system towards broader development objectives.[63] Despite the promise, it remains incomplete without similar efforts from the WTO to match the WIPO's development initiatives.

From the recent copyright treaties adopted under the auspices of the WIPO, an important and visible development context has been reflected in the Marrakesh Treaty to Facilitate Access to Published Works for Persons Who Are Blind, Visually Impaired, or Otherwise Print Disabled (Marrakesh Treaty).[64] Although its scope is limited to specific categories of users, the adoption of the Marrakesh Treaty is both historic and a positive gesture for future steps towards a broader development context.[65] In affirming it as an important context, the Marrakesh Treaty itself mentions the significance of the WIPO DA for the integration of development considerations into WIPO's work.[66]

In contrast to its predecessors, the Marrakesh Treaty is the first multilateral treaty of its kind to provide *mandatory* L&Es to copyright.[67] Informed by the WIPO DA to address the development needs of member states,[68] the Treaty stresses the appropriate consideration of the broad aspects of public interest such as *education, research, and access to information* in maintaining a balance between the effective protection of rights of authors and the larger public interest.[69] It is also the first copyright treaty to make a reference to the relevant human rights instruments. Indeed, the Marrakesh Treaty is considered to signify the instrumental role of copyright to advance human rights ends.[70] Nonetheless, it remains unclear should this positive step lead to a much more comprehensive treaty on the long-neglected issue of international copyright L&Es in the near future. As it stands, it is hard to speculate the adoption of such a treaty at the moment.

D Development context for copyright under the TRIPs Agreement

Outside the WIPO-administered copyright treaties, the TRIPs Agreement forms an important part of the international copyright system due to its: (a) integration of the Berne Convention into the international trade regime, and (b) explicit embodiment of elements of a broader development context. As a result, the development elements enshrined both in the preamble and the relevant provisions of the TRIPs Agreement constitute a useful development context for the implementation of its copyright provisions at a national level.[71] In its affirmation of the development needs of member states, the TRIPs Agreement makes an explicit reference to development objectives both in its preamble and substantive provisions.[72] For the realization of their respective national development objectives, the Agreement allows member states to adopt measures necessary, *inter alia*, to promote "the public interest in sectors of vital importance to their *socio-economic and technological development*."[73] In the same vein, art. 7 of the TRIPs Agreement recognizes the expected contribution of the IPRs "to the promotion of technological innovation (…) in a manner conducive to social and economic welfare and, to a balance of rights and obligations."

It is noted that the notions of 'public interest' and 'sectors of vital importance' are left open to the determination of the member states in light of their development needs within the ambit of the TRIPs Agreement.[74] As regards the scope of the development context, Carlos Correa observes that "the concept of 'socio-economic and technological development' is broad enough to embrace any sector, socially, economically or technologically relevant."[75] In the light of this development context, Peter Yu underscores the significance of art. 8 of the TRIPs Agreement for less developed member states to promote the public interest in their respective sectors of socio-economic and technological development.[76] Nonetheless, Yu acknowledges the constrained scope of the provision due to the necessity and consistency requirements attached to its application.[77]

Despite the debate on their normative scope, the development principles and objectives set in the TRIPs Agreement will play an important role to guide the recalibration and interpretation of the Agreement. As re-affirmed in the Doha Ministerial Declaration, in its review of implementation-related issues, the TRIPs Council "shall be guided by the objectives and principles set out in Articles 7 & 8 of the TRIPs Agreement and shall fully take into account development dimension."[78] In particular, integral to the development context for copyright system are the interpretation and application of the infamous three-step test under Article 13 of the TRIPs Agreement in a manner that suits the development needs of a member state.[79]

3.2.3 Placing copyright within sustainable human development context

In all the major copyright treaties, the development instances or elements should be understood in the broader context of *sustainable human development.* As its title runs, this infused and inclusive notion represents the overall development context of this research. Despite the frequent emphasis of IP regime on the economic growth—a narrow lens of development, the notion of sustainable development has been enshrined in the international copyright system. Indeed, the preamble to the WTO Agreement recognizes the notion of sustainable development as a guiding objective for member states in their trade and economic endeavor.[80] Although it is sidelined in practice, such an inclusive and equitable normative guidance is useful for states to direct their trade and economic activities towards raising standards of living and optimal use of world's resources in a manner consistent with their respective needs and concerns at different levels of economic development.[81]

In addition to its embodiment in the binding instrument, the significance of the sustainable development objective was further affirmed in the Doha Declaration that underlined members "commitment to the objective of sustainable development, as stated in the Preamble to the Marrakesh Agreement."[82] Moreover, its practical importance was underscored as an overarching interpretative guidance of WTO agreements in the US-Shrimp case.[83] In the case, the WTO Appellate Body pointed out the significance of a reference to the objective of sustainable development for the interpretation of the agreements annexed to the WTO Agreement.[84] In concurring scholars' opinion, the TRIPs Agreement is one of the agreements that should lend itself to the objective and notion of sustainable development for its interpretation and implementation. As Henning Ruse-Khan correctly notes, the reference to the sustainable development objective in the WTO Agreement is meant to inform and guide the interpretation of all agreements annexed thereto, including the TRIPs Agreement.[85]

In this regard, Ruse-Khan observes the existence of an overlap between the WTO sustainable development objective and Articles 7 and 8.[86] In his opinion, both serve an equivalent interpretative function in the integration and reconciliation of economic, social and environmental issues in order to address the linkages between IP protection and other development goals.[87] Indeed, some scholars construe the reference to "sustainable development" and "socio-economic and technological development" in order to affirm the

WTO's mandate to accommodate "human rights norms or human development goals."[88] Hence, the WTO's theoretical embodiment of the overarching objective of sustainable development constitutes a useful and holistic development framework for the international copyright protection.

Further, the UN SDGs that form part of the national development objectives of the member states are important norms within the broad development context for copyright system. In this respect, both the WTO and WIPO are expected to integrate the SDGs into their respective administrative and norm-setting processes.[89] For instance, their respective development agenda should be aligned with the appropriate SDGs. In particular, as a special agency of the UN, the WIPO is expected to integrate the SDGs into its areas of competence that includes the international copyright system. It is imperative for the global copyright system to advance a sustainable human development through enhanced creative innovation and access to knowledge at national levels.[90] In order to achieve this end, the interpretation and implementation of copyright treaty provisions should be tailored towards the objective of sustainable human development.[91] Building upon the rich notion of human development, the objectives and operation of the copyright system should thus be seen through the prism of sustainable human development.

3.3 International human rights system: development text

3.3.1 An overview of the international human rights system

The inception of the international human rights system is traced back to the adoption of the UN Charter that underscored nations' commitment to promote respect for human rights.[92] In this regard, central to the UN Charter are: (a) the re-affirmation of nations' faith in fundamental human rights, and (b) the significance of international cooperation for the promotion of the rights without a discrimination.[93] Further, the UN Charter underlines the international commitment of the UN and all members to "promote universal respect for, and observance of, human rights and fundamental freedoms."[94] In this sense, the emergence of the international human rights system is integral to the foundation of the UN system itself. In particular, the adoption of the UDHR in 1948 was vital to set in motion the human rights system. In fact, the UDHR was instrumental to serve as a blue-print for the subsequent adoption of the International Covenants.[95]

Although the ICCPR and ICESCR deal with different but interdependent sets of human rights, both covenants stemmed from the UDHR. In the common parlance, the three basic human rights instruments are all together dubbed an "International Bill of Human Rights."[96] From the twin covenants, the ICCPR is dedicated to ensure the protection of civil and political rights such as the right to life, liberty, privacy, and freedom of expression.[97] In contrast, the ICESCR is committed to the realization of socio-economic rights such as the right to adequate standard of living, education, protection of material and moral interests of an author, and the right to benefit from scientific progress and applications.[98]

As noted in the opening chapter, more relevant to this book are the right to education and the authors' right to protection of their material interests. Both rights have been elaborated in-depth in the general comments issued on the respective provisions. Indeed, the intended analysis of the interaction between copyright and higher education might draw on pertinent human rights dimensions. For all the rights enshrined therein, the ICESCR obligates member states to ensure the progressive realization of the rights, subject to the available resources.[99] Given the socio-economic conditions of the continent, the blend of ICESCR and the African Charter constitutes a cornerstone for human rights regime in Africa.[100]

Despite the initial categorization, the demise of the once ideological-based bifurcation between the international covenants was heralded in the Vienna Declaration Program of Action.[101] To this end, the Declaration made an emphatic re-affirmation of the universal, indivisible, interrelated and interdependent attributes of all human rights as anchored in human dignity.[102] From the binding human rights instruments, the African Charter is the first instrument to reject the fictitious bifurcation and adopt a holistic approach to human rights. In addition to the international bill of human rights, there are several human rights instruments adopted both at international and regional levels. At a continental level outside Africa, prominent regional human rights instruments include the European Convention for the Protection of Human Rights and Fundamental Freedoms[103] and the American Convention on Human Rights.[104] Besides the UDHR and ICESCR, the human rights instruments of paramount relevance to the issues of interfaces in this book are the conventions on children's rights and the African Charter.

For instance, the African Charter is relevant both for its: (a) foundational significance to the African human rights system, (b) incorporation of binding rights to education, property (including copyright) and development, and (c) binding effect upon African nations. Further, it is the first regional human rights instrument to articulate both the individual and collective human rights in a manner that reflect African context and traditions.[105] In the same vein, both the UN Convention on the Rights of the Child (UNCRC) and its regional counterpart—the African Charter on the Rights and Welfare of the Child (ACRWC)—are quite significant for their incorporation of the right to education, including higher education.[106] In particular, the ACRWC obligates state parties to take "all appropriate measures" in order to "make higher education accessible to all on the basis of capacity and ability by every appropriate means."[107]

Common to all human rights instruments, the various international and regional human rights instruments enshrine three core obligations or duties: (a) the duty to respect, (b) the duty to protect, and the duty to fulfill. Given a state as the principal duty-bearer, the duty to respect requires states to refrain from encroaching upon the human rights of individuals.[108] In contrast, the duty to protect obligates states to protect individuals against the infringing acts of third parties.[109] On the other hand, the duty to fulfill requires the states to provide the available resources and take the appropriate measures to ensure the realization of the human rights.[110] Although the degree of the action required varies, an effective compliance with the triple obligations requires the states to take the necessary actions to ensure the respect for, protection and fulfillment of the human rights.[111]

As noted in the General Comment No. 3 on the nature of obligations under the ICESCR, the ultimate objective of the Covenant is the full realization of the rights.[112] To this end, a state is required to ensure the progressive realization of the rights to the maximum of its available resources.[113] Further, the progressive realization of the rights calls for other nations' effective compliance with their obligation of international cooperation and assistance as enshrined in the ICESCR.[114] An issue that still remains unsettled is the legal status of the international cooperation enshrined in the Covenant and other documents.[115] Furthermore, debatable is the extraterritorial effect of the international cooperation.

Although the various human rights instruments highlighted above are vital to provide the substantive content of the rights, their effective implementation depends, *inter alia* , upon the existence of appropriate institutional frameworks. In this regard, the Human Rights Council (HRC) is responsible for the promotion, and protection of human rights and fundamental freedoms.[116] In the execution of its mandate, the HRC depends upon the UNGA for the adoption of new treaties, declarations and resolutions pertaining to human rights. Also, the UNESCO is another important UN organ with an explicit mandate on the promotion and protection of human rights falling under its areas of competence in the fields of science, education, culture and information.[117] From among relevant subsidiaries, the CESCR is instrumental for the implementation and interpretation of the ICESCR through its general comments.

At a continental level, the African Human Rights Commission and the African Human Right Court have been the principal organs established for the implementation and interpretation of the African Charter and other supplementary human rights instruments. Entrusted with protective, interpretative and promotional functions,[118] and irrespective of its limitations,[119] the African Commission is the most important regional human rights institution in Africa.[120] Besides, the African Court of Justice and Human Rights (ACJHR)—replacing the African Court of Human Rights—is a judicial organ vested with a broader jurisdiction to decide on human rights violations, including international crimes committed in the continent.[121] Outside Africa, the European Court of Human Rights[122] and the Inter-American Court of Human Rights[123] are notable regional human rights institutions that have generated a rich corpus of human rights jurisprudence.

In sum, both the substantive and institutional frameworks constitute the human rights system both at global and regional levels. The human rights systems at both levels operate in tandem with the systems at the national levels.

As such, the development context for the international human rights system offers an important lens for the human rights dimensions of copyright, education, and development at national levels.

3.3.2 Development and human rights

In spite of the variation in the degree of emphasis and the approaches, the notion of development is central to the international human rights system as it is to copyright system. It is thus essential to frame human rights within the context of sustainable development as informed by the human development approach. Both human rights and development are among the pillars of the UN system that mutually reinforce each other for their realization. In this regard, the UN Charter lays down the basic legal framework that stresses "the importance of social justice and human rights as the foundation for a stable international order."[124] In the same vein, the objective of the UN Charter "to promote social progress and better standards of life in larger freedom" envisages the relations between human rights and development.[125] In so doing, the UN Charter highlights the fundamental relationship between human rights and development. The relationship was further underlined in the UNGA's affirmation of the contribution of "a balanced and integrated social and economic development (...) towards (...) social progress and better standards of living, and observance of, and respect for, human rights and fundamental freedoms for all."[126]

Further, the Vienna Declaration confirms the interdependent and reinforcing features of development, and the respect for human rights and fundamental freedoms.[127] As pointed out in the *2000 UN Human Development Reports*, both human development and human rights envision "to secure the freedom, well-being and dignity of all people everywhere."[128] Seen from the perspective of human development, the realization of human rights is thus considered vital for advancing human development.[129] Indeed, the proponents of the CA construe rights as entitlements to human capabilities.[130] In this context, both human rights and capabilities are apt to complement each other towards sustainable human development.[131] In particular, human rights are useful for their moral urgency, specification of duty-bearers and accountability mechanisms.[132] Hence, instrumental is the linkage between human rights and development. In this respect, the intrinsic value of human rights offers development actors suitable normative and analytical frameworks for the achievement of development objectives.

An important point worth highlighting is the affiliated evolution of human rights and development. The affiliation is in fact evident from the inception of the international human rights system. As mentioned above, there exists an early reference both to human rights and development in the UN Charter. Elements of development also appear in the UN human rights instruments such as the UDHR. Despite their concurrent mention, over two decades had elapsed before the articulation of their linkage and the conceptualization of development as a right in the post-World War II period.[133] For instance, an explicit recognition and articulation of the nexus between the two regimes started in the 1970s.[134] It is true that the human rights instruments consist of principles and rights that constitute essential components of development.

Nevertheless, even the most relevant rights—the socio-economic and cultural rights—as enshrined in the UDHR and the ICESCR were not explicitly framed in terms of development.[135] In subsequent normative developments, the process of framing development as a right drew on the principles incorporated in those instruments and occurred under a mounting pressure from the emerging independent states. For the first time, the notion of right to development emerged in the 1970s in the context of the New International Economic Order (NIEO).[136] Adopted to change the existing imbalanced international economic relations, the NIEO provisions are deemed to have shaped the development of the right to development.[137]

Further, the Charter of Economic Rights and Duties of States (CERDS) underlined the responsibility of every state to promote economic, social and cultural development.[138] Thus, the reference to the notion of development was quite recurrent in various human rights instruments. For instance, the DRD is important for its articulation of right to development as a soft norm. Enshrined in the African Charter, the notion is now ensconced as a binding human right with both individual and collective as well as intrinsic and instrumental dimensions.

3.3.3 Human rights approaches to development

In the analysis of human rights and development with a human development as their shared core objective, two major approaches are often used to elucidate the linkage between human rights and development. The first one is a right-based approach to development that underscores the *integration* of human rights into development efforts or initiatives for sustainable human development.[139] An important example of this strategic approach is "the human rights approach to development assistance."[140] In several development assistance projects, the human rights-based approach requires the integration of human rights standards and principles into all programs of development cooperation in order for the latter to further the realization of human rights.[141]

In this integrated approach, the principles of human rights are helpful to guide development policies towards the achievement of sustainable human development.[142] The second approach frames development as *a human right in and of itself.* In the 1970s and 1980s, the right to development emerged as one of the so-called "third generation" of human rights.[143] Since its conception as a right in the 1970s, the right to development is considered to be the right of individuals, peoples and states.[144] Conceptualizing both as an individual and collective right, the DRD and the African Charter are the two major human rights instruments that recognize the right to development as a human right.[145] In contrast to the right-based approach to development, this approach thus goes further to recognize the intrinsic value of development as an entitlement with a corresponding obligation.[146]

Given its holistic, interrelated and indivisible attributes akin to all human rights, the right to development is a comprehensive right with political, social, economic and cultural aspects.[147] In this respect, the DRD re-affirms that "[a] ll human rights and fundamental freedoms are indivisible and interdependent; equal attention and urgent consideration should be given to the implementation, promotion and protection of civil, political, economic, social and cultural rights."[148] By the same token, the African Charter stresses the indivisible and interdependent nature of the right to development and other human rights.[149] A unique feature of the right to development is its conception both as individual and collective entitlements.[150] As an integral element of a collective right to self-determination,[151] the right to development thus envisages people's right to "freely pursue their economic, social and cultural development."[152] Besides its constitutive and instrumental elements, the collective aspect of the right is what befits African context constituted of collective interests, values, and traditions.

Further, it bears noting the distinctive feature of the right-based development approach that stresses the sole duty of the state.[153] In contrast, the collective entitlement inherent in the "right to development" approach underscores the corresponding international dimension of collective duties.[154] In highlighting the significance of an effective international cooperation, the DRD recognizes the extraterritorial obligation of states towards the enjoyment of the right to development.[155] Despite its debatable legal status, the duty of international cooperation is believed to embrace both state and non-state actors such as corporations, international financial institutions and multilateral organizations.[156] This understanding is however not shared among developed nations that dismiss both the right to development and its implication for a corresponding international obligation. As one writer sums it up, the grounds for their opposition relates to "the foundational basis of the right, its legitimacy, justiciability and coherence."[157]

As a result, the right-based approach enjoys prominence among the developed nations in contrast to the "right to development" approach that better suits developing countries such as those in Africa.[158] Yet the rights-based approach is important to complement the "right to development" approach.[159] Eschewing the contentious philosophical and legal issues related to the right at international level,[160] the strategic combination of both approaches will thus offer a broader normative and analytical framework for international human rights in the context of sustainable human development.[161] Given its all-embracing approach, the sustainable development context provides a better framework for addressing development challenges in an interconnected and comprehensive manner.[162]

3.3.4 Sustainable human development context for the right to development

It has been re-affirmed that the right to development as a human right and all human rights are interrelated and interdependent rights.[163] It is thus imperative to (re)frame and realize the right to development in the light of sustainable human development with the human beings at its center. Indeed, the central place accorded to the human person in the right to development and the latter's holistic nature as embodied in the DRD reflect the inclusive notion of sustainable development.[164] In turn, the holistic and interdependent nature of the right to development can be enriched further by the norms of sustainable human development.

Placed within the sustainable human development context, the all-encompassing right proves vital for an integrative realization of the relevant socio-economic rights such as the right to education and author's right to protection of material and moral rights as enshrined in the UDHR and the ICESCR. As the UN resolution on the "Future We Want" reaffirms, "a full access to quality education at all levels is an essential condition for achieving sustainable development."[165] In the same vein, the protection of author's material and moral interests is both important in itself and instrumental for sustainable human development. In effect, the right to education and author's rights are integral to the broader right to development. In this regard, the right to development underlines the role of an integrated approach to address issues of human rights and development.[166]

As highlighted above, there is an increasing emphasis on the linkages between human rights and development in various human rights instruments and related documents. For instance, the Vienna Declaration and Program of Action (1993) is instrumental to highlight the link in its re-affirmation of the right to development as a human right that shares the basic attributes of human rights.[167] Indeed, the Declaration went further to reiterate the right to development as a "universal and inalienable right and an integral part of the fundamental human rights."[168] In the same vein, well-noted in the World Summit on Sustainable Development is the essential role of human rights, including the right to development for achieving sustainable development.[169] From African perspective, the World Summit emphasized the need for actions at all levels to create "an enabling environment" in order to achieve sustainable development and the respect for human rights, including the right to development.[170]

Moreover, the global development initiatives such as the UN Millennium Development Goals (MDGs) and the SDGs constitute an important global development context with an explicit reference to human rights.[171] At the turn of the millennium, the *Human Development Report* (2000) also underlined the existence of a shared motivation and concern between human development and human rights.[172] In particular, advancing human freedom is pointed out as a central and the common purpose of human rights and human development.[173] It is thus stressed that "a broad vision of human rights must be entrenched to achieve sustainable human development."[174] In view of their common objective, "human development is essential for realizing human rights, and human rights are essential for full human development."[175]

From among the global development norms, it is important to mention the arguable international customary status of MDGs[176] and its complementarity with human rights.[177] In this regard, Philip Alston highlights the significance of MDGs context to facilitate the integration of human rights considerations into the development process and the appropriate discussion on the extent of the applicable human rights obligations.[178] Likewise, the *Human Development Report* (2003) stated that MDGs would both "mirror the fundamental motivation for human rights," and "reflect a human rights agenda—rights to food, education, health care and decent living standards."[179]

With a particular emphasis on the right to development, the Working Group on the Right to Development also underlined the contribution of the Millennium Declaration and MDGs for the progressive realization of the right to development.[180] Further, the 2009 UNGA resolution on the Right to Development reaffirms "the objective of making the right to development a reality for everyone, as set out in the United Nations Millennium Declaration."[181] To this end, the resolution calls upon the UN Human Rights Council to ensure the promotion and advancement of sustainable development. In this respect, the Council was reminded of facilitating the achievement of the MDGs towards raising the right to development to the same level with all other human rights and fundamental freedoms.[182] Nonetheless, the integration of human rights into MDGs was found inadequate, *inter alia*, due to the former's lack of effective engagement and its prescriptive norms.[183]

In contrast, the SDGs is considered to have made a better integration of human rights into sustainable development objectives.[184] Drawing on a deeper theoretical basis and calling for a domestic institutional reform,[185] the SDGs represent a comprehensive development agenda with a universalist conception of sustainable development.[186] As such, the realization of the right to development is integral to the SDGs. Indeed, recent developments vindicate the existence of a strong nexus between the right to development and the SDGs, and the instrumental role of the latter for the realization of the right to development. For instance, the Special Rapporteur on the RTD is mandated to contribute towards the realization of the right in the context of an integrated implementation of the SDGs.[187] Thus, the SDGs offers a comprehensive and integrative development context for human rights system that in turn informs the interaction among copyright, higher education, and human development.

It is also vital to note the significance of international cooperation that remains central to the operation of international copyright, human rights and development systems. Although its legal status in each of the systems varies, the principle or duty of international cooperation has been enshrined in the relevant international copyright,[188] human rights[189] and development-related treaties, declarations and global policy instruments, including the WIPO DA, Doha DA, and MDGs/SDGs.[190] From a legal perspective, the duty of international cooperation is a long-standing element of international law,[191] and its due consideration is relevant for the interaction between human rights and copyright in the global context of sustainable human development.

In conclusion, the foregoing discussion sheds light on the notion of sustainable human development as a common and overarching context for copyright and human rights systems. Despite the variance in the scope and approaches adopted by the systems, the need for development was a major *raison d'être* and the ultimate objective for the emergence, development and perpetuating operation of the systems. Indeed, this reality is evident from the various elements or aspects of development. The elements feature in the global policy, legal and institutional frameworks which constitute both copyright and human rights systems. Nonetheless, what remains an issue is the extent to which the systems are responsive to accommodate development concerns. To this end, a sustainable human development context is instrumental to examine the systems and the interaction thereof at global and national levels.

3.4 The interface between copyright and human rights

As can be noted from their respective nexus with sustainable human development, evident is the existence of an interface between IP and human rights. The linkage is also affirmed in the human rights regimes. For instance, both the UDHR and the ICESCR make an explicit mention of the human rights dimensions of IP despite the silence of the existing international IP regimes.[192] In particular, the interface between copyright and human rights is explicit from the relevant provisions of the human rights instruments.[193] Nonetheless, both IP and human rights regimes had remained isolated for quite a long period of time until their recent transformative interactions. There are two major developments that are considered to have triggered a deep interaction between the regimes. The interactive developments are: (a) the increased expansion of IP standards upon its entry into the global trade regime, and (b) the consequent changes in the human rights law, including an increased concern due to the adverse consequences of the expansive IP globalization.[194]

As a central cause of concern, the TRIPs Agreement is at the forefront due to its introduction of a stringent set of IP standards and enforcement mechanisms.[195] In turn, this is further exacerbated through the subsequent proliferation of TRIPs-plus bilateral trade agreements.[196] Indeed, these IP-related trade agreements have increased the tension between IP and human rights regimes with substantive and procedural effects. In so doing, the effects tend to undermine the human rights dimensions while prioritizing a compliance with the stringent requirements of IP.[197] In practice, the effects are manifested in several contexts such as in IP's impact on access to medicines, food, and learning materials. Against this backdrop, the interface between IP and human rights regime has been an ongoing issue of a global debate. Given the burgeoning scholarship on the interface, a concise discussion is made here to highlight the perspectives.

At the global level, the debate on the interaction between human rights and IP is generally framed in three major approaches. The first approach is based on the assumed existence of a fundamental conflict between human rights and IP.[198] In its endorsement of this approach, the UN Sub-Commission on the Promotion and Protection of Human Rights presumes the existence of "actual or potential conflicts [...] between the implementation of the TRIPs Agreement and the realization of economic, social and cultural rights."[199] As a solution, the conflict approach upholds the "primacy of human rights over economic policies and agreements."[200] In contrast, the second approach stresses the possible co-existence between the two regimes.[201] That is, both IP and human rights are regarded to be essentially compatible despite a tension over the point of necessary balance between incentives and access in IP regime.[202] Endorsed by the CESCR in its General Comment No. 17 on creator's right,[203] the co-existence approach emphasizes the possibility to strike a balance between the two legal regimes based on the presumed existence of a common objective.[204] Given the narrow vision of human rights and the reliance of the interface on constrained L&Es,[205] Ruth Okediji finds this approach too inadequate to allow a reform in IP regime that is required to promote human development in the developing countries.[206]

Considered complementary in its perspective, the third approach looks beyond the first two approaches to underscore the shared goals and the complementary objectives of both regimes.[207] Yet, the complementary approach comprises slightly different but related views. Among the views, the first one holds that IP protection can be used *as a means* to promote the realization of human rights.[208] In this respect, copyright protection—as a form of IP—is required to advance human rights ends. For instance, this approach is noted to be adopted in the Marrakesh Treaty that "employs the legal doctrines and policy tools of copyright to achieve human rights objectives."[209]

In a related view, the instrumental role of human rights is emphasized to justify the intended objectives of IP and the legitimacy of the system.[210] Given a strong correlation between copyright and human rights goals,[211] the latter may be used to set an internal limit within the copyright system.[212] To this end, human rights approach to IP is understood in the context of development.[213] The third line of argument notes the possible existence of both conflict and co-existence between the two regimes due to the overlapping human rights and non-human rights attributes.[214] For instance, the authors' right is understood to possess both attributes to entail variance.

Taking a human rights framework towards IP, this variant suggests the adoption of different mechanisms that take into account the attributes to address the issue of interface.[215] From among the proposed solution is the core minimum approach that limits protection of author's material and moral interests to the minimum essential levels of protection.[216] That is, the approach underscores the core minimum obligation that requires the protection of the "basic material interests which are necessary to enable authors to enjoy an adequate standard of living."[217] In drawing from the General Comment No. 3,[218] the core minimum approach is considered to benefit future authors, users and individuals as it sets a maximum limit on IP protection.[219]

Setting such a limit is believed to facilitate a greater access to protected knowledge in order to promote creative innovation and development.[220] In particular, it is argued that a reduction of copyright protection to the core minimum obligations would facilitate an increased access to copyrighted textbooks and software for the realization of the right to education.[221] Nonetheless, the major limitations of the approach lie in: (a) the inability to determine the exact minimum core protection, (b) its lack of guidance on the progressive and maximum limits of protection, and (c) the temptation for a state to transform the floor of the right to a maximum ceiling for the sake of a *mere compliance* with its obligations.[222]

In the context of access to knowledge in general and access to learning materials in particular, the practical implication of the interface is quite pressing at a national level. As will be elaborated in subsequent chapters, it suffices to highlight a more appropriate approach that directs the objectives of the protection of copyright and higher education towards the realization of a sustainable human development. It is noted that copyright, education and development have important human rights dimensions. Furthermore, the issue of interface would arise in respect of access to copyrighted learning materials within the broader context of access to knowledge as the latter involves a human rights dimension. As a noted scholar observes, an access to learning materials are considered to be an essential input for education to implicate human rights.[223]

For addressing the interfaces, the determination of the appropriate approach is subject to "the nature of the conflict, the type of rights involved, the amount of resources available and the urgency of the situation."[224] From among the approaches, a complementary approach to the interfaces fares better to facilitate an adequate access to learning materials. In order to emphasize the complementarities between the various dimensions, this book makes a deliberate choice to exclude the intricacies of normative hierarchies. Noting the limited effect of human rights/IP interface framework,[225] Ruth Okediji rightly underscores the need to re-define the existing framework for IP in order to promote sustainable human development.[226] As suggested in this book, the framework can further be integrated into the more holistic HDCA to rethink or re-direct copyright and higher education towards sustainable human development.[227]

3.5 Conclusion

Despite the differences in the scope and degree of emphasis, the issue of development has been central to both international copyright and human rights systems. In fact, development was the major driving force behind the emergence of both systems. The emergence of international copyright system that dates back to the adoption of the Berne Convention was driven by the economic interests of the right holders and the intermediaries. In the same vein, the issue of development was among the pillar objectives of the UN Charter that include the respect for human rights and fundamental freedoms. In its subsequent articulation, objective was taken further through its incorporation into the UDHR and the ICESCR, among others.

To this end, tracing the breadth and depth of the human development context embedded within the systems requires a closer look at the international copyright and human rights regimes. As noted from the foregoing discussion, both international copyright and human rights systems had evolved in isolation from each other. That is, both emerged at different periods to undertake their own course of evolution. For instance, the emergence of the international copyright system with the Berne Convention in the 1880s has since then led to series of revisions and proliferation of other international copyright treaties. Committed to the expansive trajectory and author-centric approach set in the Berne Convention, the subsequent treaties such as the Rome Convention, the Geneva Phonograms Convention, and the WIPO Internet Treaties altogether constitute the major substantive regimes for the international copyright system. Operating both in the analog and digital environments, all the treaties are dedicated to ensure the protection of the exclusive rights of authors or right holders. To this end, the treaties enshrine a binding set of minimum substantive standards for the rights.

In contrast, the L&Es are left open to member-states to design despite their vital roles to serve the public interest through facilitating access to the protected works. Nonetheless, the reserved policy space is subject to the constraining requirements of the three-step test. An exception to the permissive approach to the L&Es is the Marrakesh Treaty that prescribes for a mandatory set of L&Es for a specific class of users. Marking IP's shift to the global trade regime, the TRIPs Agreement has both globalized and reinforced the existing international copyright system through its incorporation of the major copyright treaties, including the Berne Convention. Further, the international copyright system has been injected with an effective enforcement mechanism under the auspice of the WTO system. In spite of the circumscribed policy and legal spaces, the TRIPs Agreement has left some development-related flexibilities relevant to development needs.

In addition to the substantive legal regimes, the international copyright system has witnessed an institutional transition and consolidation from the BIRPI to the UN-affiliated WIPO. In comparison to its predecessor with a limited administrative scope, the WIPO is rather vested with a broader mandate to promote the global protection of IP, including copyright. Indeed, it has played a key role in facilitating and overseeing the adoption, and implementation of major copyright treaties. In the aftermath of the linkage between copyright and trade regimes, the WTO has also emerged as another strong institutional framework to facilitate the globalization of the international copyright protection and enforcement.

As regards the international human rights system, its emergence is integral to the foundation of the UN system. Enshrined in arts. 55 & 56 of the UN Charter, one of its purposes is to "promote a universal respect for, and observance of, human rights and fundamental freedoms for all" without a discrimination. To this end, all members have pledged themselves to take a joint and separate action in cooperation with the UN. Despite the prior existence of few specific human rights instruments on slavery and labor rights, the adoption of the International Bill of Human Rights marked the emergence of a comprehensive set of human rights.

Founded upon the objectives of the UDHR and its principles, the consequent International Covenants and series of other international human rights instruments are all dedicated to articulate the various human rights and fundamental freedoms. This momentum was taken further to facilitate and shape similar developments at regional levels. A case in point is the adoption of, *inter alia*, the African Charter, the European and the American Conventions on Human Rights. In African context, African Charter is a regime of utmost significance.

As is evident from the human rights regime, most of the major human rights instruments enshrine, *inter alia*, the authors' right to protection of creative works and the right to education. In this regard, the UDHR and the ICESCR articulate both rights while the UNCRC is another important international human rights instrument dealing with the right to education. In particular, the ICESCR and the UNCRC are of a special significance for their detailed articulation of the right to education at all levels. From among the regional human right instruments, the African Charter guarantees both the right to education and the right to development. Indeed, the African Charter is the sole binding regional human rights instrument to recognize the right to development. At the international level, the DRD is dedicated to the right to development. Nonetheless, the transformation of the instrument and the right enshrined therein into a binding status is still contested. In addition to the substantive human rights regimes, there are several international, regional, and national human rights institutions that are mandated to promote the protection of human rights. For instance, important human rights institutions at international and regional levels include the UNHRC, the CESCR, and the African Human Rights Commission.

In both international copyright and human rights regimes, the issue of development has garnered an increasing attention over the recent several decades. Besides the socio-economic rights enshrined in the ICESCR, the prominence of the issue is evident from the subsequent articulation of development as a right in itself. Further, the emerging development norms within the UN system such as the MDGs and SDGs are important initiatives for the enrichment, concretization, and operationalization of the right to development. In the international copyright regime, significant development contexts are the various development-oriented provisions and the WIPO DA that incorporate numerous flexibilities. As is the case with its adoption, the implementation of the WIPO DA is expected to draw a guidance from the UN development goals and priorities. Noting their complementarities, the contributions of copyright and quality higher education must be explored within the broader context of sustainable human development.

In sum, all those elements of development context can be consolidated into a comprehensive framework in the light of the principle of sustainable human development. As a robust and flexible notion under evolution, the principle is noted to reflect a process of change that involves, *inter alia*, the direction of investments and orientation of technological development in order to advance both current and future capabilities to meet human needs and aspirations.[228] Seen through the enriching guidance of the HDCA, the broader and holistic notion of sustainable human development offers a useful context for exploring and guiding the complementarities between copyright and higher education.

Notes

1 Paul Goldstein & P. Bernt Hugenholtz, *International Copyright: Principles, Law and Practice,* 3rd ed (New York: Oxford University Press, 2013) at 6 & 8 [Goldstein & Hugenhotz, *International Copyright*]; see Orit Fischman-Afori, "The Evolution of Copyright Law and Inductive Speculations as to Its Future" (2012) 19 J Intell Prop L 231 at 242–245 & 253–258 [Fischman-Afori, "The Evolution of Copyright Law"].

2 Further, a study shows that higher education levels are strongly correlated with development through "slower population growth, better disease control, more stable and robust political systems" both at national and international levels. Inge Kaul et al., "How to Improve the Provision of Global Public Goods," in Michel Walter & Silke Von Lewinski, ed, *Providing Global Public Goods: Managing Globalization* (New York: Oxford University Press, 2003) at 46.

3 Goldstein & Hugenholtz, *supra* note 1 at 8. It is noted that copyright is useful to "advance the important goals of authorial autonomy and cultural diversity." In so doing, "copyright fosters democracy and free speech..." *Ibid* at 7.

4 See Ruth L. Okediji, "The International Copyright System: Limitations, Exceptions and Public Interest Considerations for Developing Countries" (2006) UNCTAD-ICTSD Issue Paper No. 15 at 12 [Okediji, The International Copyright System].

5 Goldstein & Hugenholtz, *supra* note 1 at 32–33. Given the limited effectiveness of the bilateral treaties, the adoption of the Berne Convention was urged by the expansion of the markets for copyrighted works, the growth of media that facilitated the global dissemination of the works and the consequent desire to ensure their transnational protection against acts of infringement. *Ibid* at 10.

6 *Berne Convention for the Protection of Literary and Artistic Works,* 9 September 1886, as revised at Paris on 24 July 1971, and amended on 29 September 1979, 828 U.N.T.S. 221 [hereinafter Berne Convention].

7 Okediji, "The International Copyright System," *supra* note 4 at 8 & 9.

8 Goldstein & Hugenholtz, *supra* note 1 at 10.

9 Okedjii, "International Copyright System," *supra* note 4 at 5 & 7; see also *Berne Convention, supra* note 6 at art. 20.

10 See Paul Goldstein, *International Copyright: Principles, Law and Practice* (New York: Oxford University Press, 2001) at 72–100 [Goldstein, *International Copyright*].

11 *Ibid.* The new technological developments that led to series of revisions over a period of time include the emergence of technologies such as phonograph, photography, radio, cinematography, television, reprography, and video-technology.

12 Goldstein & Hugenholtz, *supra* note 1 at 10.

13 *Ibid.*

14 *Agreement on Trade-Related Aspects of Intellectual Property Rights,* 15 April 1994, Marrakesh Agreement Establishing the World Trade Organization, arts. 10–13 & 14(5), Annex 1C, 33 ILM1125 (1994) [TRIPS Agreement], The TRIPs Agreement has extended the three-step test to all economic rights, included new subject matters such as computer programs and databases, and additional substantive rights such as rental rights. It has also increased the term of protection from 20 to 50 years for the rights of performers and producers of phonograms. See P. Bernt Hugenholtz & Ruth

L. Okediji, "Conceiving an International Instrument on Limitations and Exceptions to Copyright" (2012) Amsterdam Law School Research Paper No. 2012-2043 at 16–17 & 20 [Hugenholtz & Okediji, "Conceiving an International Instrument"].

15 *World Intellectual Property Organization [WIPO] Copyright Treaty*, 20 December 1996, 36 I.L.M. 65 (entered into force 6 March 2002) [hereinafter WCT]; *WIPO Performances and Phonograms Treaty*, 20 December 1996, 36 I.L.M. 76 (entered into force 20 May 2002) [WPPT].

16 Ruth L. Okediji, "Regulation of Creativity under the WIPO Treaties" (2009) 77 Fordham L Rev 2379 at 2388–2392 [Okediji, "Regulation of Creativity"] (describing the constraining effect of the requirements under art. 20 of the Berne Convention and its impact on the WIPO Internet Treaties). Okediji recounts that "the driving principle of the WCT was to give authors the right to control access to and use of their works on digital networks." *Ibid* at 2399.

17 The United International Bureau for the Protection of Intellectual Property (BIRPI) was the first international organ established to administer both the Berne Convention and the Paris Convention. BIRPI was established in 1893 in order to exercise administrative functions related to both conventions whose initial administration was entrusted to their respective secretariat offices. See Ruth L. Okediji, "The International Relations of Intellectual Property: Narratives of developing Country Participation in the Global Intellectual Property System" (2003) 7 Sing JICL 315 at 330 [Okediji, "The International Relations of IP"]. Adopted in 1883, Paris Convention is the first multilateral agreement that deals with an international protection of industrial property such as patents and trademarks. See *Paris Convention for the Protection of Industrial Property*, as last revised at the Stockholm Revision Conference, 14 July 1967, 828 U.N.T.S. 303 [Paris Convention].

18 *Convention Establishing the World Intellectual Property Organization*, Preamble, paras 2 & 3 *cum* art. 3, 14 July 1967 (as amended on 28 September 1979) (entered into force 26 April 1970) [*WIPO Convention*].

19 See generally Ruth L. Okediji, "WIPO-WTO Relations and the Future of Global Intellectual Property Norms" (2008) 39 Neth Yearb Int Law 69 [Okediji, "WIPO-WTO Relations"]. Although the agreement can serve as a formal commitment to avoid a conflict between the two institutions, it does not clarify the structure of the cooperation with regard to the power to govern IP-norm setting in the future. *Ibid* at 95.

20 Despite its limited role after the establishment of the WIPO and the WTO, the UNSECO was another important organ that forms the broad institutional framework for international copyright system. In particular, its role was instrumental for the adoption and administration of the Universal Copyright Convention for the latter's focus on the interests of less developed countries. Okediji, "WIPO-WTO Relations," *supra* note 19 at 76.

21 *Ibid* at 87. See *Agreement Between the World Intellectual Property Organization and the World Trade Organization*, 22 December 1995, 35 I. L. M. 754 (1996) [*WTO-WIPO Agreement*] (concluded for a cooperation on legal and technical assistance to promote IP protection).

22 See Margaret Chon, "Intellectual Property and the Development Divide" (2006) 27:6 Cardozo L Rev 2813 at 2815 [Chon, "IP and Development Divide"].

23 Peter K. Yu, "Ten Common Questions About Intellectual Property and Human Rights" (2007) 23:4 Ga St U L Rev 709 at 719 [Yu, "Ten Common Question"].

24 Chon, "IP and the Development Divide" *supra* note 22 at 2814. In the context of economic development, innovation and economic growth are the major economic justifications for IP protection. *Ibid* at 2817.

25 *Ibid* at 2815.

26 *U.S Constitution* (1787), Article 1, Section 8, Clause 8. See Goldstein & Hugenholtz, *International Copyright, supra* note 1 at 17.
27 See Goldstein & Hugenholtz, *supra* note 1 at 7; see generally Neil Netanel, "Copyright and a Democratic Civil Society" (1996) 106:2 The Yale L J 283 [Netanel, "Copyright"].
28 It is noted that international copyright system has been driven by the global expansion of markets for knowledge goods and the emergence of multimedia for their dissemination across nations. Goldstein & Hugenholtz, *supra* note 1 at 10.
29 *Ibid.*
30 Goldstein, *International Copyright, supra* note 10 at 8–10
31 See *Berne Convention, supra* note 6, Preamble, para 1 & art. 1.
32 *Ibid.* Goldstein, *International Copyright, supra* note 10 at 26.
33 See *Guide to the Berne Convention for the Protection of Literary and Artistic Works* (Geneva: WIPO, 1978) at 3 [*WIPO Guide to the Berne Convention*].
34 See Sara Bannerman, "Development and International Copyright: A History" (2016) 8:1 The WIPO Journal 11 at 11 & 14–16 (tracing the history of development agenda and development elements as incorporated in the Berne Convention with an increasing emphasis through its revisions).
35 Okediji, "The International Relations of IP," *supra* note 17 at 320–325 (describing the driving commercial interests that led to its inception and continued multilateralism).
36 See Peter K. Yu, "A Tale of Two Development Agendas" (2009) 35 Ohio NUL Rev 465 at 468–511 [Yu, "A Tale of Two"] (describing the first major development agenda that led to the adoption of the Berne Appendix).
37 See *Berne Convention, supra* note 6 at art. 21 cum the Appendix adopted in Paris (1971) that forms an integral part of the Convention. Although the Appendix provides for a scheme of compulsory license to facilitate the reproduction and translation of copyrighted works for educational purposes in the developing countries, the effective utilization of the Appendix has been limited due to lack of transparency and functionality inherent in its "complex and arcane" provisions. See Margaret Chon, "Intellectual Property "from Below": Copyright and Capability for Education" (2007) 3 UC Davis L Rev 805 at 828–829 [Chon, "Intellectual Property from Below"]; Okediji, "International Copyright System," *supra* note 4 at 12–19.
38 Okediji, "International Copyright System," *supra* note 4 at 5 ("The absence of a set of minimum exceptions and/or limitations to copyright in the Berne Convention reflected the practice and understanding that the precise nature of such limitations and exceptions was to be left to the reserved powers of the state to protect the welfare interests of its citizens.").
39 *Ibid.*
40 According to the principle of three-step test under art. 9(2) of the Berne Convention, the limitations and exceptions to reproduction right must: (a) limited to certain special cases, (b) not conflict with the normal exploitation of the work, and (c) not unreasonably prejudice the legitimate interests of the author.
41 It is also important to note the roles of the exceptions for quotation and reporting of current events under arts. 10(1) & 10 *bis* of the Berne Convention to promote social, economic, and cultural development in a democratic society.
42 *Universal Copyright Convention*, 6 September 1952, 216 U.N.T.S. 132 (entered into force 16 September 1955 and revised 24 July 1971) [Universal Copyright Convention].
43 *Universal Copyright Convention*, 1971 Paris Text, Appendix Declaration Relating to Article XVII.
44 Okediji, "The International Relations of IP," *supra* note 17 at 333. The UCC was considered favorable due to its lenient standards that offer a room for flexibility in addressing development concerns. For instance, in addition to the shorter term of

protection, developing states may provide for compulsory licenses as a limitation to reproduction and translation rights in certain circumstances. See *Universal Copyright Convention, supra* note 43, 1971 Paris Text, arts. *Vter* & *Vquater.*

45 *International Convention for the Protection of Performers, Producers of Phonograms and Broadcasting Organizations*, 26 October 1961, 496 U.N.T.S. 43 [Rome Convention].

46 The neighboring rights that have been regulated by the Rome Convention consist of rights of performers, producers of phonograms and that of broadcasting organizations. See *Guide to the Rome Convention and to the Phonograms Convention* (Geneva: WIPO, 1981, reprinted 1994 & 1999) at 7–9 [*WIPO Guide to Rome and Phonograms Conventions*]; Goldstein, *International Copyright, supra* note 10 at 10–11& 36–37.

47 *Rome Convention, supra* note 45 at art. 15. See *WIPO Guide to Rome and Phonograms Convention, supra* note 46 at 57–59. Goldstein, *International Copyright, supra* note 10 at 40.

48 *Convention for the Protection of Producers of Phonograms Against Unauthorized Duplication of Their Phonograms*, 29 October 1971 (entered into force 18 April 1973) [*Geneva Phonograms Convention* (1971)].

49 *Ibid* at art. 6. See *WIPO Guide to the Rome and Phonograms Conventions, supra* note 46 at 105–106. Goldstein, *International Copyright, supra* note 10 at 42.

50 Following the upward trajectory built into the Berne Convention, the primary purpose of the WIPO Internet Treaties is to ensure an extensive copyright protection for the right holders in the digital environment. See WCT, *supra* note 15 at art. 1(1).

51 See WCT, *supra* note 15 at art. 10 & WPPT, *supra* note 15 at art. 16. (See, e.g. WCT under its art. 10 (1): "Contracting Parties may, in their national legislation, provide for limitations of or exceptions to the rights granted to authors of literary and artistic works under this Treaty in certain special cases that do not conflict with a normal exploitation of the work and do not unreasonably prejudice the legitimate interests of the author.") See Chon, "Intellectual Property from Below," *supra* note 37 at 840.

52 WCT & WPPT, *supra* note 15 at Preamble, para 2.

53 WCT&WPPT, *supra* note 15 at Preamble, paras 5 & 4, respectively (emphasis added).

54 Pamela Samuelson, "The U.S. Digital Agenda at WIPO" (1997) 37 Va J Intl L 369 at 409.

55 Okediji, "International Copyright System," *supra* note 4 at 8. In particular, the explicit recognition of education, research and access to information underscores their significance as vital elements of public interest in the course of striking the balance offers a broader and important development context.

56 See Okediji, "The Regulation of Creativity," *supra* note 16 at 2408–2409 ("The impact of TPMs on access to digital content has also been noted by WIPO as being of great concern to DCs and LDCs."). *Ibid* at 2403.

57 *Ibid* at 2409 ("The tendency of global copyright regulation to marginalize the public interest priorities that make copyright law both necessary and relevant is evident in the compromises that yielded the WIPO Internet Treaties.")

58 Chon, "IP and the Development Divide," *supra* note 22 at 2836–2841 (describing the encounter between WIPO and development).

59 *Agreement Between the United Nations and the World Intellectual Property Organization,* art. 1, 17 December 1974, online: WIPO http://www.wipo.int/treaties/en/agreement/index.html [UN-WIPO Agreement], available at; see also *WIPO Convention, supra* note 18 at art. 13 (1).

60 See Rami M. Olwan, *Intellectual Property and Development: Theory and Practice* (Heidelberg: Springer, 2013) at 52. Although the potential promise of 'development' in the context of innovation and technology transfer in developing counties is central to WIPO's strategy in the global administration of IP treaties, its commitment to address the development needs of developing countries is often compromised due to

its budgetary dependence upon and a pressure from developed countries. See *ibid* at 53–54 & 56.

61 WIPO, The 45 Adopted Recommendations Under the WIPO Development Agenda, online: WIPO http://www.wipo.int/ip-development/en/agenda/recommendations.html [WIPO DA]. See also Christopher May, *The World Intellectual Property Organization: Resurgence and the Development Agenda* (London: Routledge, 2007) at 76 (pointing out the need for WIPO's explicit integration of the overall development priorities and goals of the UN and its special agencies into its areas of competence).

62 See Chon, "IP and Development Divide," *supra* note 22 at 2902–2906. See Peter K. Yu, "Five Decades of Intellectual Property and Global Development" (2016) 8:1 The WIPO Journal 1 at 4–5 [Yu, "Five Decades of Intellectual Property"] (stating how the SDGS such as SDG 4, 8, 9 and 17 were indicated to be relevant to the DA); UN Sustainable Development Goals, online: UNDP http://www.un.org/sustainable development/education/ [UNSDGs] (last visited 04 April 2021).

63 See Ruth L. Okediji, "History Lessons for the WIPO Development Agenda," in Neil Netanel, ed, *The Development Agenda: Global Intellectual Property and Developing Countries* (New York: Oxford University Press, 2009) 137 at 140 [Okediji, "History Lessons for the WIPO Development Agenda"] (describing the history of development efforts at WIPO and its DA while reflecting upon its future implications).

64 *Marrakesh Treaty to Facilitate Access to Published Works for Persons Who Are Blind, Visually Impaired, or Otherwise Print Disabled*, 27 June 2013, 52 I.L.M1312 (entered into force 30 June 2016) [Marrakesh Treaty].

65 Margaret Wilkinson, "Copyright Users' Right in International Law" (2014) 60:3 Copyright Column 9 at 11–13 [Wilkinson, "Copyright Users' Right"]; Margaret Wilkinson, "International Copyright: Marrakesh and the Future of Users' Rights Exceptions," in Mark Perry, *Global Governance of Intellectual Property in the 21st Century: Reflecting Policy Through Change* (Switzerland: Springer, 2016) 107 [Wilkinson, "International Copyright"].

66 See *Marrakesh Treaty*, *supra* note 64 at Preamble, para 11. See also Okediji, "History Lessons for the WIPO Development Agenda," *supra* note 63 at 155–160.

67 Laurence R. Helfer, "Intellectual Property and Human Rights: Mapping an Evolving and Contested Relationship," in Rochelle C. Dreyfuss & Justine Pila, eds, *The Oxford Handbook of Intellectual Property Law* (Oxford: Oxford University Press, 2018) 117 at 135; Laurence R. Helfer, et al., *The World Blind Union Guide to the Marrakesh Treaty: Facilitating Access to Books for Print-Disabled Individuals* (New York: Oxford University Press, 2017) at xxiii [Helfer et al., *The World Blind Union Guide*]. The adoption of the Treaty may set an example for future adoption of a comprehensive set mandatory copyright limitations and exceptions that has remained a distant possibility for a decade. See Wilkinson, "Copyright Users' Right," *supra* note 65 at 11.

68 *Marrakesh Treaty*, *supra* note 64, Preamble, para 11 (recalling the importance of the DA recommendations that aim to ensure the integration of development considerations into the WIPO's work).

69 See *Marrakesh Treaty*, *supra* note 64 at Preamble, para 9. It is also important to note that the Marrakesh Treaty goes further to embrace the core principles of non-discrimination, equal opportunity, accessibility, and effective and inclusive participation as embodied in the relevant UN human rights and related regimes. In particular, the Treaty makes an explicit reference to the basic principles embodied in the UDHR and the UN Convention on the Rights of Persons with Disabilities. *Ibid* at para1; see *UN Convention on the Rights of Persons with Disabilities*, 30 March 2007, 2515 UNTS 3 (entered into force 03 May 2008) [CRPD].

70 Helfer, *The World Blind Union Guide*, *supra* note 67 at xxiii.

71 See Chon, "IP and the Development Divide," *supra* note 22 at 2831–2836 (analyzing the relevant development features embedded in the TRIPs Agreement as an instance of the encounter between the WTO and development).

72 See *TRIPs Agreement, supra* note 14, Preamble, paras 5 & 6 and arts. 7 & 8.

73 *TRIPs Agreement, supra* note 14 at art. 8. Carlos Correa notes that the application of art. 8(1) of the TRIPs Agreement is broad enough to accommodate issues arising within and outside IPR regime with implication on IPR. The application of art. 8(1) of may be used as a justification for designing special exceptions that promote public interests in the vital sectors of socio-economic and technological development. See Carlos M. Correa, *Trade Related Aspects of Intellectual Property Rights: A Commentary on the TRIPS Agreement* (Oxford: Oxford University Press, 2007) at 106.

74 Correa, *Trade Related Aspects, supra* note 73 at 104–106 [Correa, *Trade Related Aspects*]; Peter K. Yu, "The Objectives and Principles of the TRIPS Agreement" (2009) 46 Hous L Rev 979 at 1011–1013 [Yu, "The Objectives and Principles"].

75 Correa, *Trade Related Aspects, supra* note 73 at 106.

76 Yu, "Objectives and Principles," *supra* note 74 at 1009–1012. Apparently, art. 8 of the TRIPs Agreement recognizes the special development needs of least-developing countries to maintain maximum flexibility in their domestic implementation of laws and regulations in order to create a sound and viable technological base.

77 *Ibid* at 1013–1015.

78 *WTO Doha Ministerial Declaration,* at para.19, WT/MIN (01) DEC/1/ (20 November 2001), online: WTOhttps://www.wto.org/english/thewto_e/minist_e/min01_e/mindecl_e.htm [Doha Ministerial Declaration].

79 The interpretation and application of the three-step test under art. 13 of the TRIPs Agreement should also be informed by the WIPO DA given the institutional co-operation between WIPO and the WTO, and their respective roles to address development concerns. See *WIPO-WTO Agreement, supra* note 21.

80 *Marrakesh Agreement Establishing the World Trade Organization,* para 1, Annex 1C, 33 ILM1125 (1994) [WTO Agreement].

81 *Ibid.*

82 *Doha Ministerial Declaration, supra* note 78 at para 6.

83 See *WTO Appellate Body Report: United States—Import Prohibition of Certain Shrimp and Shrimp Products,* adopted 12 October 1998, WT/DS58/AB/R, para 129 & 152–155 [*The US Shrimp/Turtle Case*]. The AB opined that considering the specific language of the preamble to the WTO Agreement would give "color, texture and shading to the rights and obligations of members under the WTO Agreement." *Ibid* at para. 155. Robert Howse, "The Appellate Body Rulings in the Shrimp/Turtle Case: A New Legal Baseline for the Trade and Environment Debate" (2002) Colum J Envt'l L 27:2 489 at 500 & 518 (noting how the AB dealt with the issue of "exhaustible natural resources" in the light of the principle of sustainable development as incorporated in the preamble to the WTO Agreement).

84 *The US Shrimp/Turtle Case, supra* note 83 at paras 153 & 155. The AB also noted the general acceptance of the concept of sustainable development "as integrating economic [,] social and environmental protection." *Ibid* at para. 129, footnote 107.

85 Henning Grosse Ruse-Khan, "The Principle of Integration in WTO/TRIPs Jurisprudence" in Marie-Claire Cordonier Segger & C.G Weeramantry, eds, *Sustainable Development Principles in the Decisions of International Courts and Tribunals (1992–2012)* (London &New York; Routledge, 2017) 398 at 406 [Ruse-Khan, "The Principle of Integration"].

86 *Ibid* at 407.

87 *Ibid.*

88 Margaret Chon, "Global Intellectual Property Governance (Under Construction)" (2011) 21:1 Theor Inq L 349 at 360 [Chon, Global IP Governance"]; see Yu, "Objectives and Principles," *supra* note 74 at 1008–1013 & 1018–1044 (explaining at length multiple uses of articles 7 & 8 of the TRIPs Agreement).

89 Okediji, "WIPO-WTO Relations," *supra* note 20 at 110–112; see Chon, "IP and the Development Divide," *supra* note 62 at 2831–2841.
90 See Henning Grosse Ruse-Khan, "Sustainable Development in International Intellectual Property Law–A New Approach From EU Economic Partnership Agreements?" (2010) ICTSD Program on Intellectual Property and Sustainable Development, Issues Paper No. 29 at 8–9 [Ruse-Khan, "Sustainable Development"]. In his detailed scrutiny of the relevant provisions of the EC economic partnership agreements, Ruse-Khan points out the protection and enforcement of IP as a means to foster creativity and innovation that, in turn, serve as means to achieve sustainable development. *Ibid* at 10.
91 *Ibid* at 8–10. See Chon, "IP and the Development Divide," *supra* note 22 at 2828.
92 See Philip Alston, "The UN's Human Rights Record: From San Francisco to Vienna and Beyond" (1994) 16 Hum Rts Q 375 at 375 [Alston, "The UN's Human Rights Record"].
93 *The Charter of the United Nations*, Preamble, para 1 & art. 1 (3), 26 June 1945, Can TS 1945 No.7 (entered into force 24 October 1945) [The UN Charter].
94 *Ibid* at art. 55 & 56.
95 See *Universal Declaration of Human Rights*, GA Res 217A (III), UNGAOR, 3d Sess, 1st plen mtg, UN Doc A/810 (12 December 1948) at art. 26 [UDHR]. See Alston, "The UN's Human Rights Record," *supra* note 92 at 376. Not intended to be a binding legal instrument, the UDHR was a declaration of nations' aspirations and moral commitment towards respect for human rights. Despite its initial adoption as a mere declaration of "common standard of achievement for all peoples and all nations," the legal status of the UDHR has now transformed from a soft-law into a binding hard law through its evolution into rules of international customary law. See generally Bruno Simma and Philip Alston, "The Sources of Human Rights Law: Custom, Jus Cogens, General Principles" (1992) 12 Australian Year Book of International Law 82.
96 See John P Humphrey, "The International Bill of Rights: Scope and Implementation" (1975) 17 Wm & Mary L Rev 527. See *International Covenant on Economic, Social and Cultural Rights,* 16 December 1966, 993 UNTS No 3 (entered into force 3 January 1976) [ICESCR]; *International Covenant on Civil and Political Rights*, 19 December 1966, 999 U.N.T.S 171, 6 I.L.M 368 [ICCPR].
97 See ICCPR, *supra* note 96 at arts. 6, 9, 17, & 19.
98 ICESCR, *supra* note 96 at arts. 11, 13 & 15 [ICESCR].
99 Matthew Craven, *The International Covenant on Economic, Social and Cultural Rights: A Perspective on Its Development* (Oxford: Oxford University Press, 1995) at 129–134 & 136–144.
100 See generally Shedrak C Agbakwa, "Reclaiming Humanity: Economic, Social and Cultural Rights as the Cornerstone of African Human Rights" (2002) 5 Yale Hum Rts & Dev LJ 177. See *African Charter on Human and Peoples' Rights*, 27 June 1981, 21 ILM 58 (entered into force on 21 October 1986) [African *Charter*] (articulating socio-economic rights under arts 14–29).
101 *See World Conference on Human Rights, Vienna Declaration and Program of Action*, para 5, 12 July 1993, GA A/CONF157/23 (Vienna: 14–25 June 1993) [Vienna Declaration].
102 *Ibid*. Indeed, several scholars have underscored the interdependence between and the mutually reinforcing nature of the rights incorporated in the ICCPR and ICESCR. See Craven, *supra* note 99 at 9.
103 *The European Convention for the Protection of Human Rights and Fundamental Freedoms*, adopted 4 November 1950, 213 U.N.T.S. 221 (entered into force 3 September 1953).
104 *The American Convention on Human Rights*, adopted 22 November 1969, 9 I.L.M 673 (entered into force 18 July 1978) [The American Convention].
105 See Richard N. Kiwanuka, "The Meaning of 'People' in the African Charter on Human and Peoples' Rights" (1988) 82 Am J Int'l L 80; see Makau Mutua, "The

Banjul Charter and the African Cultural Fingerprint: An Evaluation of the Language of Duties" (1995) 35 Va J Int'l L 339 [Mutua, "The Banjul Charter"] (describing the cultural, historical and conceptual justifications for the imposition of the duties).

106 See *African Charter on the Rights and Welfare of the Child,* art. 11(3)(c), 01 July 1990, OAU Doc.CAB/LEG/24.9/49 (entered into force 29 November 1999) [ACRWC]; *UN Convention on the Rights of the Child*, 20 November 1989, 1577 UNTS 3 (entered into force on 2 September 1990) at art. 28(1)(c) [UNCRC].

107 ACRWC, *supra* note 106 at art. 11(3) (c).

108 Frans Viljoen, *International Human Rights Law in Africa,* 2nd ed (Oxford: Oxford University Press, 2012) at 6.

109 *Ibid.*

110 *Ibid.*

111 See— "Maastricht Guidelines on Violations of Economic, Social and Cultural Rights" (1998) 20:3 Hum Rts Q 691 at 693–694 [The Maastricht Guidelines]; Committee on Economic, Social and Cultural Rights, *General Comment No.13: The Right to Education,* paras 46–47 & 50, UN Doc E/C 12/1999/10 (8 December 1999) [*CESCR General Comment No.13*]; *CESCR General Comment No. 17: The Right of Everyone to Benefit from the Protection of the Moral and Material Interests Resulting from any scientific, Literary or Artistic Production of Which He or She is the Author (Art. 15 (1) (c) of the Covenant*), paras 28 & 30–34, UN Doc E/C12/GC/17 (Jan.12, 2006) [*CESCR General Comment No. 17*].

112 *CESCR General Comment No.3*: *The Nature of States Parties Obligations (Article 2(1)),* para 9, UN Doc. E/1991/23(14 December 1990); Craven, *supra* note 99 at 128.

113 ICESCR, *supra* note 96 at 2(1). *CESCR General Comment No.3, supra* note 112 at para 9. Craven, *supra* note 99 at 129-34 & 136-44.

114 See Craven, *supra* note 99 at 144-50. "The Limburg Principles on the Implementation of the International Covenant on Economic, Social and Cultural Rights" (1987) 9:2 Hum Rts Q 122 at 126 (paras 29–34) [The Limburg Principles]. Another issue of debate related to the obligations of states in the context of international cooperation is the extraterritorial obligations of states to ensure the realization of human rights outside their jurisdictions. This obligation requires the states to refrain from measures that entail a transnational encroachment on human rights in other nations. In the same vein, states are required to regulate the conduct of third parties such as corporations under their jurisdiction, but that operate in foreign nations. See Klaus D. Beiter "Is the Age of Human Rights Really Over?: The Right to Education in Africa-Domestication, Human Rights-Based Development, and Extraterritorial State Obligations" (2018) 49 Geo J Int'l L 10 at 48–54 [Beiter, "Is the Age of Human Rights Really Over?"].

115 Beiter, "Is the Age of Human Rights Really Over?" *supra* note 114 at 51–54. General Comment No.3 considers international cooperation for development as an obligation incumbent upon states that are capable to offer assistance. *CESCR General Comment No. 3, supra* note 112 at para. 14. In the same vein, *CESCR General Comment No. 13* highlights states' obligation of international assistance and cooperation for the full realization of the right to education. General Comment No.13, *supra* note 111 at para 56.

116 Like its predecessor, the UN Commission for Human Rights (UNCHR) and since 2006, the HRC has been entrusted with the task to serve the core purpose of the UN from among its major pillars. The mandate of HRC includes the responsibility to "address situations of violations of human rights, including gross and systematic violations, and make recommendations thereon." See Human Rights Council, GA Res 60/251, UNGAOR, 60th Sess, UN Doc A/Res/60/251 (2006) at Preamble (para 6) & Main Text, para 3.

117 See David Weissbrodt & Rose Farley, "The UNESCO Human Rights Procedure: An Evaluation" (1994) 16 Hum Rts Q 391 at 394. In this regard, the UNESCO

established a procedure in 1978 to deal with complaints from imprisoned authors, educators, scientists, and other persons facing human rights violations within its purview. In March 1993, it released a report that summarized the results of its procedure. *Ibid* at 391.

118 Makau Mutua, "The Construction of African Human Rights System: Prospects and Pitfalls," in Samantha Power and Graham Allison, eds, *Realizing Human Rights: Moving from Inspiration to Impact* (New York: St. Martin's Press, 2000) 143 at 149 [Mutua, "The Construction of African Human Rights System"]. Substantially drawing on the procedures and experiences of its international counterparts, the African Commission's primary functions are: reception and examination of state reports, consideration of complaints on allegation of violations and elaboration or interpretation of the Charter, when requested. *Ibid.*

119 States' lack of compliance with the decision of the African Commission is one of its basic limitations. Daniel Abebe, "Does International Human Rights Law in African Courts Make a Difference?" (2017) 56 Va J Int'l L 527 at 551–552; see generally Rachel Murray & Debra Long, The Implementation of the Findings of the African Commission on Human and People's Rights 74 (2015); see Mutua, "The Construction of African Human Rights System," *supra* note 118 at 151–152.

120 Abebe, *supra* note 119 at 540.

121 *Ibid* at 576–577. See *Protocol of the Court of Justice of the African Union*, 11 July 2003 (entered into force 11 February 2009), *reprinted* in 113 African Journal of International & Comparative Law 115 (2005).

122 See generally Alona E. Evans, "European Court of Human Rights," (1967) 61 Am J Int'l L 1075.

123 See generally Thomas Buergenthal, "The Inter-American Court of Human Rights," (1982) 76 Am J Int'l L 231.

124 The UN Charter, *supra* note 93 at art. 55. Isabella D. Bunn, "The Right to Development: Implications for International Economic Law" (2000) 15 Am U Int'l L Rev 1425 at 1428–1429 [Bunn, "The Right to Development"].

125 Bunn, "The Right to Development," *supra* note 124 at 1429.

126 See *Balanced and Integrated Economic and Social Progress*, GA Res 1161 (XII), UNGAOR, 3rd Comm., 12th Sess, Agenda Item12, UN Doc. A/3716 (1957) at para 4.

127 *Vienna Declaration and Program of Action*, *supra* note 101 at para 8 ("Democracy, development and respect for human rights and fundamental freedoms are interdependent and mutually reinforcing.").

128 UNDP, *Human Development Reports 2000: Human Rights and Human Development* (New York: UNDP & Oxford University Press, 2000) at 1[UNDP, *Human Development Report 2000*].

129 See Amartya Sen, "Human Rights and Capabilities" (2005) 6:2 Journal of Human Development 151 at 152–155 [Sen, *Human Rights & Human Capabilities*]; Martha C. Nussbaum, "Capabilities and Human Rights" (1997) 66 Fordham L Rev 273 at 293–297 [Nussbaum, "Capabilities and Human Rights"].

130 *Ibid.* Both Sen and Nussbaum underscore the importance of reframing human rights as entitlements to capabilities for human development. Nussbaum notes that "analyzing economic and material rights in terms of capabilities would thus enable us to understand, as we might not otherwise, a rationale we might have for spending unequal amounts of money on the disadvantaged, or creating special programs to assist their transition to full capability." Nussbaum, "Capabilities and Human Rights," *supra* note 129 at 295.

131 See Sen, "Human Rights and Capabilities," *supra* note 129 at 163.

132 Nussbaum "Capabilities and Human Rights," *supra* 129 at 295–296. Nussbaum points out four important roles of the language of rights: (a) justifying claims to capabilities,

(b) emphasizing the significance of the capabilities, (c) offering extra emphasis on people's choice, and (d) settling a disagreement about claims of utility, resources and capabilities. *Ibid.* See also Tristan McCowan, *Education as a Human Right: Principles for a Universal Entitlement to Learning* (London, UK: Bloomsbury, 2013) at 138–140 & 142 (noting the importance of framework of rights for its, *inter alia*, "procedural aspects," universality and "explicit specification of duty-bearer").

133 It should however be borne in mind that a development agenda was at the top of the list of global issues since the early post-WWII period and was thus integral to the new world order embraced by the UN system. See Richard Warren Perry, "Rethinking the Right to Development: After the Critique of Development, After the Critique of Right" (1996) 18: 3/4 Law & Pol'y 225 at 236–240.

134 Bonny Ibhawoh, "The Right to Development: The Politics and Polemics of Power and Resistance" (2011) 33 Hum Rts Q 76 at 81. Arjun Sengupta, "On the Theory and Practice of the Right to Development" (2002) 24:4 Hum Rts Q 837 at 839 [Sengupta, "On the Theory and Practice"].

135 *Ibid.* Also, development was not informed by human rights as the development studies that emerged to be a distinct field of study in 1960s largely focused on policy interventions required to change the existing social orders. See John Harris, "Great Promise, Hubris and Recovery: A Participant's History of Development Studies" in Uma Kothari(ed), *A Radical History of Development Studies: Individuals, Institutions and Ideologies* (London; Zed Books, 2016) 17.

136 *Declaration on the Establishment of a New International Economic Order*, adopted 1 May 1974, U.N. GAOR, 6th Spec. Sess., 229th plen. mtg., U.N. Doc. A/RES/S-6/3201 (1974). The Declaration intended to 'eliminate the widening gap between developed and developing countries and ensure steadily accelerating economic and social development…' As Ibhawoh points out "[b]y redressing the disadvantages of former colonized developing countries in the international economic system, the NIEO agenda aimed to further their economic advances by changing their economic relations with the developed countries." Ibhawoh, *supra* note 134 at 90. For detailed accounts of NIEO, see generally Ruth Gordon, "The Dawn of a New, New International Economic Order?" (2009) 72 Law & Contemp Probs 131.

137 Bunn, "The Right to Development," *supra* note 124 at 1430–1431. For instance, Georges Abi-Saab maintained that the NIEO would be "the only blue-print of the right to development which stands a realistic chance of hardening into law." See Georges Abi-Saab, "The Legal Formulation of a Right to Development," in Rene-Jean Dupuy, ed, The Right to Development at the International Level (1980) Hague Academy of International Law Workshop at 167.

138 *The Charter on Economic Rights and Duties of States*, G.A. Res. 3281 (XXIX), U.N. GAOR, 2d Comm., 29th Sess., Agenda Item 48, art. 7, U.N. Doc. A/RES/3281 (XXIX) (1975)[CERDS]. See also Sushanta K. Chatterjee, "The Charter of Economic Rights and Duties of States: An Evaluation after 15 Years" (1991) 40:3 ICLQ 669.

139 Ibhawoh, *supra* note 134 at 84. In UNICEF's definition of human rights-based approach to programing, "human rights determine the relationship between individuals and groups with valid claims (rights holders) and State and non-state actors with correlative obligations (duty-bearers). It identifies rights-holders and their entitlements, [] corresponding duty-bearers and their obligations, and works towards strengthening the capacities of rights-holders to make their claims, and of duty-bearers to meet their obligations." UNICEF, The State of the World's Children 2004, Annex B, at 91–92 (2004), online: UNICEF www.unicef.org/sowcO4/files/AnnexB.pdf.

140 Obiora Chinedu Okafor, "The Status and Effect of the Right to Development in Contemporary International Law: Towards a North-South 'Entente'" (1995) 7 African Journal of International & Comparative Law 865 at 870. The human rights approach to development assistance offers an international framework for international development

cooperation in the delivery, utilization and evaluation of development assistance. See Stephen P. Marks, "The Human Rights Framework for Development: Seven Approaches," in Arjen Sengupta *et al*, eds, *Reflections on the Right to Development* (New Delhi: Sage Publications, 2005) [Marks, "The Human Rights Framework"]. at 27–33.

141 Philip Alston, "Ships Passing in the Night: The Current State of the Human Rights and Development Debate Seen through the Lens of the Millennium Development Goals" (2005) 27 Hum Rts Q 755 at 799–801 [Alston, "Ships Passing in the Night"]. The integration of human rights standards and principles can provide accountability mechanisms and a system-based response to sustainable development.

142 *Ibid* at 807–813. The approach is useful for asserting rights against the duty-bearer and the consequent accountability. Nevertheless, if not rethought to focus on targeted and selective priorities, the approach is critiqued to offer a little guidance due to its all-embracing, untargeted, and abstract criteria. *Ibid* at 802–807.

143 Stephen Marks, "The Human Right to Development: Between Rhetoric and Reality" (2004) 17 Harv Hum Rts Journal 137 at 138 [Marks, "The Human Right to Development"]. As per one of the categorizations of human rights, and based on their chronological sequence of emergence, civil and political rights are called first generation rights while economic, social and cultural rights are called second generations rights. The third-generation rights include the right to development and environment. *Ibid*. See generally Stephen P. Marks, "Emerging Human Rights: A New Generation for the 1980's?" (1981) 33 Rutgers L. Rev. 435, 435–452 [Marks, "Emerging Human Rights"].

144 Philip Alston, "International Trade as Instrument of Positive Human Rights Policy," (1982) 4:2 Hum Rts Q 155 at 167 [Alston, "International Trade as Instrument"].

145 From the scholars of the time, the Senegalese jurist Keba M'Baye is often regarded as the "father" of the right due to his instrumental role in the conceptualization and the subsequent declaration of the right to development as such. M'Baye's conception of the right drew on African context and his belief of a "necessary nexus between the individual and collective rights." See Perry, *supra* note 133 at 227. See generally *Declaration on the Right to Development*, GA Res 41/128, Annex, UNGAOR, 41st Sess, No. 53, UN Doc A/4/53 (4 December 1986) [DRD]; African Charter, *supra* note 100 at 22.

146 Ibhawoh, *supra* note 134 at 86.

147 DRD, *supra* note 145, Preamble at paras 2 & 10 *cum* art. 1 & 6(2) [hereinafter DRD] ("...that all human rights and fundamental freedoms are indivisible and interdependent..."). See Arjun Sengupta, "Realizing the Right to Development" (2000) 31 Development and Change 553 at 555 & 563 [Sengupta, "Realizing the Right"].

148 DRD, *supra* note 145 at art. 6 (2).

149 *African Charter, supra* note 100, Preamble, para 7 ("[I]t is henceforth essential to pay a particular attention to the right to development and that civil and political rights cannot be dissociated from economic, social and cultural rights in their conception as well as universality and that the satisfaction of economic, social and cultural rights is a guarantee for the enjoyment of civil and political rights.")

150 Ibhawoh, *supra* note 134 at 85. In particular, the conception of the right to development as a collective entitlement encompassing people or community epitomizes a significant departure from the other individual-centered human rights instruments. *Ibid*.

151 Ruth L Gana, "The Myth of Development, The Progress of Rights: Human Rights to Intellectual Property and Development" (1996) 18:3 & 4 Law & Pol'y 315 at 336 [Gana, "The Myth of Development"]; Bunn, "The Right to Development," *supra* note 124 at 1446.

152 *Ibid*. See ICESCR, *supra* note 96 at art. 1 (1); ICCPR, *supra* note 96 at art. 1; UDHR,

supra note 95 at art. 28; *African Charter*, *supra* note 100 at art. 22 (1). Ibhawoh, *supra* note 134 at 91.

153 See Ibhawoh, *supra* note 134 at 98–100. See generally Morten Broberg & Hans-Otto Sano, "Strengths and Weaknesses in a Human Rights-Based Approach to International Development: An Analysis of a Right-Based Approach to Development Assistance Based on Practical Experiences" (2018) 22:5 Int'l JHR 664 (explaining the concept of the approach, its importance and limitations).

154 Ibhawoh, *supra* note 134 at 101. Most developing countries emphasize a collective commitment that undergirds the national and the international obligations for the realization of the right to development.

155 DRD, *supra* note 145 at arts. 3, 4 & 6. This provision should be read in conjunction with ICESCR, art. 2(1). For instance, art. 4 (1) states: "As a complement to the efforts of developing countries, effective international cooperation is essential to providing these countries with appropriate means and facilities to foster their comprehensive development." In this regard, Ibhawoh notes that "[states] have the duty to cooperate in order to achieve this right, and are required to act *collectively* to formulate development policies oriented to the fulfillment of this right." Ibhawoh, *supra* note 134 at 97.

156 UNDP, *Human Development Report 2000*, *supra* note 128 at 1 & 10. Ibhawoh, *supra* note 134 at 101. Sengupta, "Realizing the Right," *supra* note 147 at 559–660 & 564–666.

157 Ibhawoh, *supra* note 134 at 87.

158 In this regard, the African Charter is the sole binding human rights instrument that has espoused the right to development as such. This right has further been interpreted and applied at regional level. The *Endorois* decision is the case in point. In confirming the significance and practical application of the right to development, the African Commission on Human and Peoples' Right has interpreted art. 22 of the African Charter as a constitutive and instrumental right, wherein the violation of either aspect amounts to the violation of the right. See Karin Arts & Atabongawung Tamo, "The Right to Development in the International Law: New Momentum Thirty Years Down the Line?" (2016) 63 Nethl Intl L Rev 222 at 245–246. Given the dedicated role of African jurists such as K' Mabaye in the conceptualization of the right to development both for the DRD and the African Charter and its embodiment in the latter, the right to development is regarded as one of Africa's contribution to the global human rights discourse. See Leslye Obiora, "Beyond the Rhetoric of the Right to Development" (1996) 18:3/4 Law & Pol'y 356 at 358.

159 Ibhawoh, *supra* note 134 at 98.

160 The central debate on the right to development relates to its legal status. That is, its evolution to a binding legal right has faced a persistent and stiff resistance from developed nations. Philip Alston, "Making New Space for Human Rights: The Case of the Right to Development" (1988) 1 Harvard Human Rights Year Book 3 at 20–38. [Alston, "Making New Space for Human Rights"]. For instance, the U.S has been the persistent objector of the human right status of the right to development. Marks, "The Human Right to Development," *supra* note 143 at 141-51. Bunn, "The Right to Development," *supra* note 124 at 1435. See Anthony Carty, "From the Right to Economic Self-Determination to the Right to Development: A Crisis in Legal Theory" (1984) 3 Third World Leg Stud 73 at 75. Perry, *supra* note 566 at 241–242. Obiora, *supra* note 158 at 385–387.

161 Indeed, it has been reiterated time and again in several UN resolutions that sustainable development is a key element of the overarching framework of the UN activities. As such, it is an overarching context and principle for development and human rights that constitute the pillars of the UN objectives. See, e.g. GA Res 64/236, UNGOR, 64th Sess, UN Doc A/Res/64/236 (2010) at paras 8 & 15.

162 Inga T. Winkler & Carmel Williams, "Editorial, The Sustainable Development Goals and Human Rights: A Critical Early Review" (2017) 21:8 Intl JHR 1023 at 1024.
163 See *Vienna Declaration and Program of Action, supra* note 101 at para. 5. (The Declaration states: All human rights are universal, indivisible and interdependent and interrelated. The international community must treat human rights globally in a fair and equal manner, on the same footing, and with the same emphasis.") Sengupta, "Realizing the Right," *supra* note 147 at 556–558.
164 Obiora, *supra* note 158 at 362. This is evident from the very definition of the right to development. See DRD, *supra* note 145 at arts 1(1), 2(1), & 9(1). Nonetheless, given its anthropocentric approach, the ecological aspect of the notion of sustainable development is missing from the definition.
165 See *Resolution on the Future We Want,* GA Res 66/288, UNGOR, A/Res/66/288 (2012) at para 229.
166 Isabella D. Bunn, The *Right to Development and International Economic Law: Legal and Moral Dimensions* (Oxford and Portland: Hart Publishing, 2012) at 5 [Bunn, *The Right to Development and International Economic Law*].
167 *Vienna Declaration and Program of Action, supra* note 101 at para 10. Sengupta, "Realizing the Right," *supra* note 147 at 557.
168 *Vienna Declaration and Program of Action, supra* note 101 at para 10. In the same resolution, the Office of the High Commissioner for Human Rights was entrusted with the responsibility that includes "the promotion and protection of the right to development." See GA Res 48/141, U.N. GAOR, 48th Sess., Supp. No. 49, at 261, U.N. Doc. A/48/141 (1993). In so doing, the Declaration underscores the existence of the interdependent and mutually reinforcing relationship amongst "democracy, development and respect for human rights and fundamental freedoms." *Ibid.*
169 *Report of the World Summit on Sustainable Development*, Res. 2, Annex: Plan of Implementation of the World Summit on Sustainable Development, at 9, para 5, U.N. Doc. A/CONF.199/20 (2002).
170 *Ibid* at 44, para 62(a). The enabling environment is expected to be created at the regional, sub-regional, national and local levels. *Ibid.*
171 See *UN Millennium Development Goals,* G.A. Res. 55/2, U.N. Doc. A/RES/55/2 (2000), online: UN www.un.org/millenniumgoals/index.html.[UNMDGs].
172 UNDP, *Human Development Report 2000, supra* note 128 at 19. (The HDR stated: "Human development and human rights are close enough in motivation and concern to be compatible and congruous, and they are different enough in strategy and design to supplement each other fruitfully. A more integrated approach can thus bring significant rewards, and facilitate in practical ways the shared attempts to advance the dignity, well-being and freedom of individuals in general"). *Ibid.*
173 *Ibid* at 2.
174 *Ibid* at iii.
175 *Ibid* at 2.
176 See Alston, "Ships Passing in the Night," *supra* note 141 at 771–778.
177 *Ibid* at 759–761. In her report submitted to the UN in 2002, the UN High Commissioner for Human Rights also stated that "[t]he strategies to reach the Millennium human rights goals and the Millennium development goals reinforce and complement each other." See *Report of the United Nations High Commissioner for Human Rights to the Economic and Social Council*, U.N. ESCOR, 40th Sess., Agenda Item 14(g), para 10, U.N. Doc. E/2002/68 (2002). Nonetheless, there are criticisms leveled against the MDGs as a top-down, selective and one-size-fits-all framework. Alston, "Ships Passing in the Night," *supra* note 141 at 764–766. See generally Thomas Pogge, "The First United Nations Millennium Development Goal: A Cause for Celebration?" (2004) 5:5 Journal of Human Development 377.

178 Alston, "Ships Passing in the Night," *supra* note 141 at 809–810. From among various instrumental roles of MDGs, Alston observes that "the MDGs can, up to a point, be taken as reflecting the minimum content of certain economic and social rights, so that states that fail to achieve their MDG commitments cannot easily seek to excuse themselves by relying upon a lack of available resources or arguments based on progressive realization." *Ibid* at 823. Hence, he concludes that "there is a sufficiently clear relationship between the explicit MDGs and economic, social and cultural rights norms that the language of rights can be utilized appropriately in many relevant MDG contexts." *Ibid* at 788.

179 See UNDP, *Human Development Report 2003: Millennium Development Goals-A Compact Among Nations to End Human Poverty* (New York: Oxford University Press, 2003) at 27 & 29 [UNDP, *Human Development Report 2003*].

180 See Report of the Working Group on the Right to Development on its fifth session (Geneva, 11–20 February 2004), U.N. ESCOR, Comm'n on Hum. Rts., 60th Sess., 43(g), U.N. Doc. E/CN.4/2004/23 (2004).

181 *UNGA Resolution on the Right to Development,* A/RES/63/178, 26 March 2009, Preamble at para 6. In the Millennium Declaration, the states expressed their commitment 'to making the right to development a reality for everyone and to freeing the entire human race from want.' MDGs, *supra* note 604 at para 11.

182 *Ibid* at para 4.

183 Alston, "Ships Passing in the Night," *supra* note 141 at 755.

184 See Malcolm Langford, "Lost in Transformation? The Politics of the Sustainable Development Goals" (2016) 30:2 Int Aff Ethics 167 at 172–173. See also Beth Simmons, *Mobilizing for Human Rights: International Law in Domestic Politics* (New York: Cambridge University Press, 2009).

185 Langford, *supra* note 184 at 172. Langford notes that "the normative gains within the SDGs provide, therefore, a political resource for selectively defending and promoting targets that require greater attention or legitimation." *Ibid* at 175.

186 *Ibid* at 167. Nonetheless, Langford points out two principal criticisms directed against the SDGs: 'sheer number of commitments' and 'various political compromises' that may undermine the effectiveness of the institutional commitment. *Ibid* at 168. See also Frances Stewart, "The Sustainable Development Goals: A Comment" (2015) 11:3 J Glob Ethics 288 (highlighting problems related to the national implementation, failure to address the existing economic structure and lack of a true integration between suitability and economic goals).

187 Human Rights Council, 'Resolution on the Right to Development', UN Doc. A/HRC/33/L.29, 27 September 2016, para. 14(b). The Special Rapporteur on the RTD is mandated to make contribution to "the promotion, protection and fulfillment of the rights to development in the context of the coherent and integrated implementation of the 2030 Agenda for Sustainable Development and other internationally agreed outcomes of 2015." Furthermore, the special rapporteur is expected to "engage and support efforts to mainstream the right to development among various United Nations bodies, development agencies, international development, financial and trade institutions, and to submit proposals aimed at strengthening the revitalized partnership for sustainable development from the perspective of the right to development." *Ibid* at para. 14(c).

188 See *TRIPs Agreement*, *supra* note 14 at arts. 66(2), 67 & 69; Marrakesh Treaty, *supra* note 64 at art. 9.

189 See ICESCR, *supra* note 96 art. 2(1); UNCRC, *supra* note 106 art. 4, 17(a & b), and 23(4); CRPD, *supra* note 69, Preamble, para (l), arts. 4(2), 32, 37 & 38. See also *CESCR General Comments No. 3*, *supra* note 112 at paras. 13–14.

190 WIPO DA, *supra* note 61; *Doha Ministerial Declaration*, *supra* note 78; MDGs, *supra* note 171, Goal 8(global partnership for development); SDGs, *supra* note 62, Goal: 17

(global partnership for development). At regional level, of similar importance is the African Union (AU) Agenda 2063 that articulates African development aspirations to be achieved over 50 years for the realization of AU's vision of "an integrated, prosperous and peaceful Africa, driven by its own citizens and representing a dynamic force in international arena." Keys among the major aspirations are ensuring "a prosperous Africa based on inclusive and sustainable development" and "...the respect for human rights." See *Agenda 2063: The Africa We Want*, adopted by the 21st Ordinary session of the Assembly of Heads of State and the Government of the African Union, Addis Ababa, 26 May 2013 [AU Agenda 2063].

191 See Arts & Tamo, *supra* note 158 at 239–241.

192 UDHR, *supra* note 95 at art. 22; ICESCR, *supra* note 96 at art. 15(1)(c). Both provisions state that "everyone has the right to the protection of the moral and material interests resulting from any scientific, literary or artistic production of which he is the author." Laurence R. Helfer & Graeme W. Austin, *Human Rights and Intellectual Property: Mapping the Global Interface* (Cambridge & New York: Cambridge University Press, 2011) at 321 [Helfer & Austin, *Human Right and Intellectual Property*].

193 See Philippe Cullet, "Human Rights and Intellectual Property Protection in the TRIPs Era" (2007) 29:2 Human Rights Quarterly 403 at 407–410 (describing the relationship among the right to culture, the right to the benefits of scientific progress and applications, and author's right to protection of material and moral interests under art. 15 of the ICESCR).

194 Helfer & Austin, *Human Rights and Intellectual Property*, *supra* note 192 at 34 & 48–64.

195 *Ibid* at 40.

196 *Ibid*.

197 *Ibid* at 40–41.

198 Laurence R. Helfer, "Human Rights and Intellectual Property: Conflict or Coexistence?" (2003) 5 Minnesota Intellectual Property Review 47 at 48 [Helfer, "Human Rights and Intellectual Property"].

199 *ECOSOC, Sub-Commission on the Promotion and Protection of Human Rights, Intellectual Property Rights and Human Rights*, para.3, Res. 2000/7, U.N. Doc.E/CN.4/Sub.2/RES/2000/7(17 August 2000) [UN Sub-Commission Resolution 2000/7]. In Helfer and Austin's opinion on the endorsed approach, the primacy of human rights urged by the UN human rights bodies overlooks (a) the need for identifying the nature of the conflict, and (b) a legal justification in support of the proposed primacy of human rights. Helfer & Austin, *Human Rights and Intellectual Property*, *supra* note 33 at 65.

200 See *Intellectual Property Rights and Human Rights, Sub-Comm'n on Human Rights* Res 2000/7, 913, UN Doc E/CN 4/Sub 2/RES/2000/7 (2000).

201 Helfer, "Human Rights and Intellectual Property," *supra* note 198 at 48–49.

202 *Ibid*. Helfer & Austin, *Human Rights and Intellectual Property, supra* note 192 at 73.

203 *CESCR General Comment No.17*, *supra* note 111 at para 35.

204 Helfer &Austin "Human Rights and Intellectual Property," *supra* note 192 at 73–79. Audrey R. Chapman, "Approaching Intellectual Property as a Human Right (obligations related to Article 15(1)(c)" (2001) 35 Copyright Bulletin 4 at 14–17 & 28–30.

205 Ruth L. Okediji, "Does Intellectual Property Needs Human Rights?" (2018) 51:1 International Law and Politics 1 at 10, 17, 24 & 25 [Okediji, "Does Intellectual Property Needs Human Rights?"].

206 *Ibid* at 10–37 & 66–67. See generally Ruth L. Okediji, "Intellectual Property in the Image of Human Rights: A Critical Review," in Rochelle Cooper Dreyfuss & Elizabeth Siew-Kuan Ng, ed, *Framing Intellectual Property Law in the 21ST-Century* (Cambridge: Cambridge University Press, 2018) 234 [Okediji, "IP in the Image of Human Rights"]. Underscoring the unintended restrictive effect of the narrow human rights framework and the inadequacy of the existing L&Es, Okediji suggests

policy initiatives for 'a more complete vision' and realization of material conditions envisaged and guaranteed the economic, social and cultural rights. She argues that 'those conditions' are "necessary for the exercise of freedoms that make possible the creation, use and enjoyment of knowledge assets in pursuit of development." *Ibid* at 234–240.

207 See Laurence R. Helfer, "Toward a Human Rights Framework for Intellectual Property" (2007) 40 UC Davis L Rev 971 at 1018–1020 [Helfer, "Toward a Human Rights Framework"].

208 *Ibid.*

209 Helfer et al, The *World Blind Union Guide, supra* note 67 at xxiii. Intersecting both human rights and international copyright law, the implementation and interpretation of the Marrakesh Treaty "must strive to comply with both sets of legal obligations." Ibid. See Molly K. Land, "The Marrakesh Treaty as "Bottom Up" Lawmaking: Supporting Local Human Rights Action on IP Policies "(2018) 8 UC Irvine L Rev 513 at 549–551.

210 Ruth L. Okediji, "Securing Intellectual Property Objectives: New Approaches to Human Rights Considerations," in Margot E. Salomon et al, eds, *Casting the Net Wide: Human Rights, Development and New Duty-Bearer* (Intersentia, 2007) 211 at 213–214 & 234 [Okediji, "Securing Intellectual Property Objectives"].

211 *Ibid* at 227–229.

212 *Ibid* at 234.

213 See generally Ruth L. Gana, "The Myth of Development, the Progress of Rights: Human Rights to Intellectual Property and Development" (1996) 18 Law & Pol'y 315. In particular, Gana argues that 'any human rights to IP must be understood in the context of the right to development' in order to allow developing countries to design IP regimes consistent with their development objectives. *Ibid* at 323–328.

214 Peter K. Yu, "Re-conceptualizing Intellectual Property Interests in a Human Rights Framework" (2007) 40 UC Davis L Rev 1039 at 1077–1078 [Yu, "Re-Conceptualizing Intellectual Property"]. It is argued that only some attributes of intellectual property rights are regarded as human rights while the remaining attributes have no human rights basis. Further, as pointed out in the *General Comment No. 17*, IP regimes "that primarily protect business and corporate interests and investments" lack human rights basis as corporate entities' "entitlements...are not protected at the level of human rights." *CESCR General Comment No. 17, supra* note 111 at paras 2 & 7.

215 *Ibid.* The three mechanisms suggested as possible solutions are (a) the just remunerative approach, (b) the core minimum approach, and (c) the progressive realization approach. While the first approach focuses on the protection of the core minimum level of human rights, the progressive realization approach aims at state's increasing utilization of available resources for the full realization of economic, social and cultural rights as incorporated in the relevant human rights instruments. In contrast, the just remunerative approach highlights author's right to receive a fair remuneration for a limitation imposed on the enjoyment of his human rights over creative works. *Ibid* at 1095–1130.

216 *Ibid* at 1105–1109.

217 *CESCR General Comment No.17, supra* note 111 at para 2.

218 *CESCR General Comment No.3, supra* note 112 at para 10.

219 Yu, "Re-conceptualizing Intellectual Property," *supra* note 214 at 1108.

220 *Ibid* at 1109.

221 *Ibid* at 1118.

222 *Ibid* at 1109–1113.

223 Peter K. Yu, "Ten Common Questions About Intellectual Property and Human Rights" (2007) 23:4 Ga St U L Rev 709 at 719–720.

224 Yu, "Re-Conceptualizing Intellectual Property," *supra* note 214 at 1123.

225 Okediji, "Does Intellectual Property Needs Human Rights?" *supra* note 205 at 10–37.
226 *Ibid* at 57–67. Okediji, "IP in the Image of Human Rights," *supra* note 206 at 363–389.
227 *Ibid* at 62–67. In this regard, Okediji concludes that "[p]rogress toward attaining the highest levels of human flourishing will require novel approaches in the IP and in the human rights legal space." *Ibid* at 67.
228 See UNWCED, *Our Common Future, supra* note 400 at 48. Yu, "Re-conceptualizing Intellectual Property," *supra* note 647 at 1117.

4 Higher education and creative innovation: exploring copyright flexibilities

4.1 Introduction

From the CA-driven human development perspective, the objectives of both authors' right and higher education should be understood to complement each other in order to advance sustainable human development. As noted from the development context of the relevant international legal instruments and the underpinning theoretical justifications, both regimes share a common human rights framework. In addition to their intrinsic values, both higher education and copyright—a means for protection of author's right—are instrumental for sustainable human development. For the advancement of their respective purpose—creative innovation and development of human personalities, both copyright and higher education depend upon each other in the production, access to, and dissemination of knowledge. In this regard, critical is the role of copyright-related flexibilities under the international legal regimes for quality higher education and a sustainable creative innovation.

At this juncture, it is important to describe the usage of the notion of "creative innovation" in this book. In one of its landmark precedents that articulated the *raison d'être* of copyright protection, the Supreme Court of Canada once used the term to underscore a balance in the public interests underpinning copyright.[1] Sharing a similar view, the term "creative innovation" is adopted in this book for three major reasons. First, the term is suggestive of the overlapping aspects of creativity and innovation associated with copyright. In the same vein, both elements are the products of knowledge generated through education.[2] Second, the usage of the term is opted for a convenience and to avoid the joint or interchangeable usage of the terms "creativity" and "innovation." Third, there is no clear-cut line of distinction between creativity and innovation. Hence, this book does not attempt to draw one. Nor does it categorize IP along the lines as all forms of IP often involve both aspects, irrespective of the variance in the degree.

It is however conceded that the preferred term remains a loose combination of the two terms with their own conceptual reach. Further, it is not in a perfect fit with the firm-oriented conventional notion of innovation embodied in the Oslo Manual.[3] Noted in a broader sense and without a universal

DOI: 10.4324/9781003214298-4

definition, the term "innovation" has been a buzzword among scholars, businesspersons and policy makers.[4] Leaving aside the definitional deficit, the notion of creative innovation has been central to IP and development.

In both realms of copyright and higher education, the notion of creative innovation is undergoing a significant transformation. With the converging roles of authors and users in the process of creative innovation, there emerges the notion of innovation as an open, collaborative and dynamic process. For instance, Bengt-Ake Lundval—a well-established expert in the field—has long observed innovation "not primarily as a single event, but rather *as a process*."[5] In this dynamic process, the sustainable production and diffusion of knowledge are integral to the cumulative and interactive learning process of creative innovation.[6] In particular, subsequent to its inception in Henry Chesbrough's seminal work that emphasizes the inflow and outflow of knowledge or ideas between firms to drive innovation,[7] the notion of open innovation has garnered a significant traction. Further, consistent with an open innovation is Eric von Hippel's notion of "users-driven innovation" that underscores individual users' role and their collaborative efforts to drive a collective creative innovation.[8]

In the context of copyright, illuminative of users' creative and collaborative roles is Benkler's articulation of commons-based peer production of creative works relevant for education.[9] With the advent of internet as its enabler, an open and collaborative innovation marks the democratic, cumulative and dynamic nature of creative innovation.[10] In effect, this conceptual shift demands a similar reorientation in copyright, higher education and the relevant copyright-related flexibilities that underpin their linkages. Further, the role of an open approach to a creative innovation and its resonance with open access models[11] underline the need for a suitable normative and policy framework to align with the relevant copyright flexibilities.

Seen as their common objective, creative innovation is integral to the linkage between higher education and copyright, and their contributions for sustainable human development. As noted in this book, a higher education is critical to generate relevant knowledge, produce human capital and foster human capabilities that altogether constitute essential inputs for creative innovation. Indeed, quality higher education and scientific research are instrumental to cultivate and nurture the capabilities required for translating the knowledge generated into a creative innovation.[12] As an instrument of human development, an advanced education is a key to unlock and unleash the creative potential of the learners. The intellectual development of a nation through an advanced education expands the human capabilities of the people to engage in a sustainable creative innovation.

In the same vein, a balanced copyright protection is crucial to incentivize the production, dissemination and efficient utilization of knowledge for creative innovation, advanced education and scientific research. For a creative innovation to flourish through a robust copyright system, quite crucial is a continuous investment in human beings through a quality education.[13] Both learning and creative freedoms are thus vital to enrich people's creative capabilities required for human development through creative innovations.

In a nutshell, the promotion of creative innovation and quality higher education are interdependent for, and contingent upon, access to knowledge and human capital.[14] As argued in this book, the linkage extends to human capabilities. In turn, this multidimensional linkage is interwoven through and dependent upon the role of copyright flexibilities permitted under the existing international copyright regime. In particular, copyright flexibilities are instrumental for promoting higher education and a robust creative innovation through enhanced access to knowledge or learning materials.

4.2 Higher education and creative innovation for human development

Noted within the broader framework of the HDCA, human development is measured in terms of enhanced freedoms or expansion of human capabilities. As emphasized in this book, essential for a human development to flourish are educational and creative innovation capabilities. Further, both higher education and creative innovation are noted as interdependent and constitutive elements of human development. From among various instances of interdependence, what remain vital are the linkages between the regimes in the context of (a) access to knowledge, (b) human capital, and (c) human capabilities. The first two contexts tend to highlight the instrumental aspects of the linkage as vital resources. In contrast, the third context reflects the substantive linkages between both higher education and creative innovation as important human capabilities with both instrumental and intrinsic values. For example, education of all levels is integral to the indicators of HDI that measures human development as an enlargement of real opportunities or expansion of capabilities.

In the same vein, cultivated through an advanced education and understood as a form of capabilities or freedom, creative innovation is instrumental to enlarge a set of other real opportunities.[15] In the CA, the freedom "to produce one's own expressive work" is among Martha Nussbaum's central human capabilities.[16] In this context, the linkage between higher education and creative innovation is further based upon access to knowledge and human capital. In fact, both access to knowledge and human capital are essential elements of, *and* inputs for, expansion of human capabilities.

Noted in terms of human capabilities, knowledge is "central to human freedom and human development."[17] Within this broad framework of access to knowledge, the *Human Development Report* (2016) underscores the crucial role of access to relevant learning materials for quality higher education to advance quality human development.[18] As "the stock of knowledge in all its multiple forms that contribute to productive work,"[19] human capital is thus another important element of human capabilities that links higher education and creative innovation. Acknowledging the instrumental significance of human capital, Sen rather goes further to underscore the need for its integration into the broader framework of human capabilities.[20]

Therefore, the expansion of human capabilities remains a common denominator for higher education, creative innovation, and their linkages towards a sustainable human development. Against this backdrop as a normative context, this chapter thus explores the international copyright flexibilities. It also highlights the instrumental role of the flexibilities to facilitate or bridge a linkage between higher education and copyright towards human development.

4.3 International copyright flexibilities

As noted in the preceding chapter, the international copyright regime is constituted of series of multilateral copyright and trade agreements. Being the first international copyright instrument, the Berne Convention is known for setting the minimum standards for author's right with a built-in expansive trajectory.[21] Built upon that baseline, the international copyright regime has since then evolved both in its breadth and depth to ensure an ever-increasing protection of author's/right holder's right. An epitome of these developments is the international copyright regime's aggressive venture into the global trade and digital environments that now form a complex web of interlinkage and enforcement mechanisms.

Leaving aside the proliferating free trade agreements (FTAs) with a TRIPs-plus effect,[22] the TRIPs Agreement and the WIPO Internet Treaties have paved the way for copyright's entry into the respective trade and digital environments. In particular, the TRIPs Agreement's integration of the trade-sanctioned enforcement mechanism and the WIPO Internet Treaties' introduction of technological protection measures (TPMs) into the copyright regime are worth noting. In all these right-holders' interest-driven expansive efforts, the issue of the flexibilities has been largely left to an individual state to handle, *albeit* subject to the circumscribing effect of the three-step test.

As elaborated in this chapter, the three-step test has been cast wider to encompass all exclusive rights and entrench the minimum standards enshrined in the treaties. To this effect, the TRIPs Agreement has set itself in a firm foundation with an enforcement mechanism as its unwavering safeguard. The three-step test is thus both a determinative and preemptive test intended to curb the "discretionary" power of the states. Although the interpretative guidance of the objectives and the preamble is noted to offer some policy space, the breadth and depth of flexibilities are required to be determined on the basis of the requirements of the test within the overall consistency requirement of the TRIPs Agreement. In this chapter, the various flexibilities relevant to education will be explored from the perspective of human development while the importance of the flexibilities for creative innovation will also be highlighted.

4.3.1 General flexibilities for education and creative innovation

In the absence of a harmonized set of international copyright flexibilities, various flexibilities are permitted or embodied in the international copyright system. The flexibilities are of various categories. In addition to the flexibilities inherent in the relevant preamble, objectives, and principles, the categories are based on the protected subject matter, conditions of protection, duration, the type of use, and beneficiaries. In particular, the most common form of flexibilities is composed of compensated and uncompensated L&Es to the exclusive rights.[23] Below are the various and relevant flexibilities enshrined in the major treaties.

A General flexibilities under the Berne and Rome conventions

As the major international copyright treaties, both Berne and Rome conventions are foundational for the international protection of copyright and related or neighboring rights. In setting minimum standards for a legal protection, both conventions have reserved to member states the freedom to formulate their respective flexibilities. In addition to its specific L&Es, *inter alia*, for private use and uses for teaching or scientific research,[24] the Rome Convention leaves member states with a discretion to emulate the Berne Convention's approach in devising appropriate and corresponding flexibilities.[25] As such, the discussion on the Berne Convention is *mutatis mutandis* applicable to the flexibilities envisaged under the Rome Convention. Given its authors'-centric approach that underpins the primacy of exclusive rights, Ruth Okediji notes the Berne Convention's approach to flexibilities as "an explicit expression of retained sovereignty as well as its deference to such sovereignty."[26] Further, she also observes the Convention's implicit recognition of the inherent limiting effect of the public interest on authors' rights.[27] Although the permissive approach in itself appears to be an aspect of flexibilities, the Berne Convention marks the baseline for a set of mandatory minimum standards for the authors' right.[28]

In effect, the exercise of the discretion deferred to member states is circumscribed within the initial built-in copyright protection trajectory and the mandatory nature of the minimum standards.[29] Further, the Convention's introduction of the three-step test in its latest revision is another significant restraint on the L&Es to reproduction right.[30] Fenced within this structural confine, the flexibilities under the Berne Convention relate to the subject matter of copyright, its duration, conditions of protection, and specific flexibilities for copyrighted works. The Convention stipulates or allows for various specific flexibilities in the form of compensated and uncompensated limitations.[31] Depending upon the type of the L&Es, the exercise of the flexibilities can thus be permitted with or without remuneration. Save for quotation exception,[32] most of the L&Es incorporated in the Berne convention are permissive in nature.

From the general flexibilities related to the copyrightable subject matter, the Berne Convention provides for mandatory and permissive exclusions. An instance of the former is art. 2 (8) of the Berne Convention that excludes "news of the day or miscellaneous facts having the character of a mere press of information."[33] In Okediji's observation, this provision refers to a factual content of the news that cannot fit into the notion of works of authorship.[34] From within the eligible subject matters of protection, the Convention also leaves member-states with a discretion to determine the protection of official texts of legislative, administrative and legal nature as well as the official translations thereof.[35] Likewise, member-states are at liberty to exclude, in whole or in part, from a legal protection both "political speeches and speeches delivered in the course of a legal proceedings."[36] In both cases, the permissive exclusion relates to subject matters that are eligible for protection, but which are available for exclusion *ab initio* when the public interest so demands.[37]

Another mode of exclusion is based upon the principle of idea/expression that limits protection to the *expression* of ideas and excludes the protection of *mere* ideas, facts, procedures, methods of operation, and mathematical concepts as such.[38] Developed in the United States and recognized in several jurisdictions, this doctrine of idea/expression distinction is used to distinguish between eligible and ineligible subject matter.[39] Prior to its explicit incorporation in the TRIPs Agreement,[40] the principle was implicit in the notion of authorship, creative or original works and in the exclusion of factual works under the Berne Convention.[41] Subject to a judicial determination, the application of this principle relates to the substantive condition of protection that excludes a work for want of originality. As a rule, copyright is limited to an *original expression* of ideas.

For all copyrightable works, originality is an essential requirement for the legal protection of the works.[42] In contrast, despite its wide acceptance among states, fixation constitutes an optional requirement for copyright protection.[43] In effect, the requirements of originality and fixation constitute the two conditions of copyright protection. As it leaves out some works, strict application of the criteria has the potential to offer a room for flexibilities. In this regard, apart from formalities or administrative requirements that are excluded, the Berne Convention allows members states to impose the conditions of protection.[44]

For instance, the requirement of originality, though not mentioned, is already implicit in the notion of works of authorship under the Berne Convention.[45] In fact, the requirement of originality remains integral to the protectable subject matter and its qualification for protection. It is undisputed that originality constitutes the *essence* of copyright protection as *a work of independent intellectual creation*.[46] Nonetheless, its actual application offers member states a considerable freedom to determine the appropriate threshold with inevitable variance across nations.[47] Related to the principle of idea/expression dichotomy that leaves out ideas and mere facts for free use,[48] a stringent application of originality could exclude unoriginal works from a legal protection. This is true of a merger doctrine as well.

In contrast to its implicit embodiment of originality, the Berne Convention makes an explicit mention of the *optional* requirement of fixation.[49] In the opinion of a distinguished commentator, the Convention's optional approach to the requirement is indicative of its deference to the natural-law based justifications that entitle an author to authorship right upon a mere creation of the work.[50] Yet, fixation in a material form, as required in common law jurisdictions, is of a manifold practical importance. For instance, it is significant for its evidentiary benefit in "the objective determination of the existence of a work."[51] It is also instrumental for its facilitative role for creative innovation, preservation and dissemination of copyrighted works.[52] Given its significance, most states require fixation of a creative work in a tangible medium.[53] As a result, creative works that do not meet the statutory requirements will fall into the public domain for all to use. Thus, the conditions of copyright protection can offer a state a policy space to exploit in devising flexibilities.

The other general limitation is based on the duration of the copyright protection. Despite its longer term, the protection of copyright is not as perpetual as it appears. In fact, the longest required term of protection under the Berne Convention is a minimum duration of author's lifetime plus 50 years for most works.[54] The shortest duration the Convention sets is a minimum of 25 years for photographic works and works of applied art.[55] Given the EU and US extension of the *post-mortem* duration to 70 years and their persistent effort for its integration into other jurisdictions through FTAs, the flexibility related to the duration is already under threat. For a member-state that avoids the Berne-plus obligation, the duration under the Berne Convention remains the governing rule for legal protection. Once the term of protection elapses, the works will be available for free access and utilization. A shorter duration is thus vital to ensure a quick return of the works to the public domain for the latter to flourish. Vital as it is, the enrichment of a public domain in turn promotes a sustainable creative innovation and other public interests such as education.

In addition to the flexibilities highlighted above, the three-step test that will be explored in depth after a while is often considered as an aspect of general flexibilities. Introduced in 1967, the three-step test was enshrined under art. 9(2) of the Berne Convention as a parameter for a limitation on author's reproduction right. As indicated below, the test has now morphed into an all-encompassing parameter under the TRIPs Agreement. Under the Convention, the test leaves member states with an *option* to permit the reproduction of protected works in certain cases. Incorporated into several copyright treaties, the three-step test operates "in certain cases, provided that the reproduction does not conflict with a normal exploitation of the works nor does it unreasonably prejudice the legitimate interests of the author."[56] Indeed, as Okediji notes, the cumulative three-step test was rather intended to serve both as *a limit* on the discretion of member states and *a parameter* for their formulation of L&Es to the exclusive right.[57]

Adopted in a response to the demand of developing countries,[58] the disputed and less-utilized Berne Appendix is another aspect of flexibilities that operates subject to remuneration.[59] In its intended application for reproduction and translation right, the purpose of the Appendix was to facilitate a bulk access to and utilization of copyrighted works for development purposes, including education.[60] Given its complex procedure and administrative costs, the Appendix has failed to serve as an effective element of the permitted flexibilities.[61]

In addition to other specific L&Es that will be examined below, the various general flexibilities enshrined under the Berne Convention are instrumental both for higher education and creative innovation that necessitate access to existing works. Nevertheless, most of the flexibilities are both *permissive* and *subordinate* to the overriding author-oriented approach of the Berne Convention. In effect, the general flexibilities embodied in the Convention are not sufficiently oriented towards human development. Noting this gap, Margaret Chon recommends the application of the principle of substantive equality for "the fullest exploitation of the Berne-endorsed exception."[62] In so doing, Chon calls for deference to a flexible interpretation and application of the relevant flexibilities in order to promote access to educational materials for the purposes of human development.[63]

B Flexibilities under the TRIPs Agreement

Marking a significant shift in the international copyright regime into the global trade system, the TRIPs Agreement has made an explicit integration of the Berne Convention into the trade-sanctioned system.[64] As such, the TRIPs Agreement has introduced several changes to the existing copyright flexibilities. First, it has expanded both the subject matter and the scope of exclusive economic rights with a profound impact upon the existing flexibilities.[65] Second, the TRIPs Agreement has transformed the *author's right* into the expansive notion of right-holder's right that entitles corporate entities to acquire exclusive economic rights.[66] Third, the Agreement has expanded the scope of the three-step test to encompass *all existing and new* exclusive economic rights.[67] The ramification of the expansive test has been an issue of heated debates in the existing legal scholarship with multiple suggestions for its interpretation and application at national levels.[68] Fourth, it has introduced an effective enforcement mechanism including criminal measure against violation of the exclusive rights.[69]

Nevertheless, the TRIPs Agreement has made explicit the hitherto implicit principle of idea/expression distinction that helps delineate between copyrightable and non-copyrightable works.[70] One cannot but admit the role of the explicit reiteration of the principle and the flexibilities in its preamble, objectives and principles. In its overall effect, the TRIPs Agreement is however a Berne-plus special agreement with expansive rights that constrain the space for flexibilities.[71] In particular, the restrictive aspects have the tendency to generate a perceived or actual restraint on the freedom of states to devise flexibilities for fear of trade sanctions or due to their integration into the TRIPs-plus FTAs. A brief exploration of some of the relevant general flexibilities is thus in order.

To start with its objectives and principles, the TRIPs Agreement provides for a set of general flexibilities. As elaborated elsewhere in this book, a development-oriented reading of the preamble, art. 7 & 8 of the TRIPs Agreement and their interpretative guidance for the substantive provisions would offer member states some rooms for flexibilities that serve their development needs.[72] In this respect, a critical policy and legislative space relevant to advance a quality higher education and creative innovation is the open-ended notion of the public interest "in sectors of vital importance for socio-economic and technological development."[73] Further, similar flexibilities can be carved out from the core objectives enshrined in art. 7 of the TRIPs Agreement. To this end, the provision highlights the purpose of IP to promote innovation and dissemination of knowledge, a respect for the mutual advantage of producers and users, an account for social and economic welfare, and the notion of a balance between rights and obligations.[74]

Despite the TRIPs Agreement's disputed "one-size-fit-all approach,"[75] the interpretation and application of these open-ended words or principles with due regard to a nation's specific context have the potential to provide a "wiggle room" or general flexibilities for human development.[76] Indeed, several commentators agree that a strategic application of the aforementioned provisions within the framework of the overarching principle of sustainable development is useful to generate considerable flexibilities that serve nation's development goals.[77] Nonetheless, the general flexibilities are subject to the constraining effect of the *necessity and consistency requirements* embedded in the TRIPs Agreement.[78]

In relation to the protected subject matter or set of exclusive rights, the flexibilities under the TRIPs Agreement are rather more constrained than its predecessor due to the Agreement's extension to new subject matters. In terms of protectable subject matters, the TRIPs Agreement has introduced or clarified computer programs as literary works and original compilations of data or other material that constitutes intellectual creation.[79] In the same vein, the recognition of rental right as an exclusive right for computer programs and cinematographic works is an instance of the expansion in the economic rights.[80] Nonetheless, a Berne-minus approach is taken to exclude the corresponding moral rights.[81] With regard to the conditions and duration of protection, the TRIPs Agreement maintains similar minimum standards set under the Berne Convention. In the course of integration, a constraining ceiling has been placed upon the corresponding flexibilities. From among permitted and compensated limitations, the Berne Appendix has been made integral to the TRIPs Agreement without the long-sought reform.[82] One notable exclusion is however the principle of exhaustion. Left to the sovereign discretion of member states to regulate, states are thus free to tailor the application of the principle to their domestic needs.[83]

Another copyright-related aspect of general flexibilities worth noting is art. 40 of the TRIPs Agreement that prohibits anti-competitive practices. In its flexible application, the prohibition is treated as a disciplinary measure setting an external limit to copyright.[84] It is thus important to prevent an abusive exploitation of the exclusive right to the detriment of the users.[85] In its enforcement measures, the TRIPs Agreement offers some flexibilities in the modes, standards of enforcement and remedies as well as in the notions of "infringement" and "commercial scale."[86]

C Flexibilities under the WTO Internet Treaties

Adopted within their respective framework of the Berne and Rome Conventions,[87] the WCT and the WPPT have extended the substantive minimum standards of copyright protection into the digital environment. Given their developments in the post–TRIPs Agreement regime, their adoption was subject to the overbearing effect of the Agreement.[88] Necessitated due to the emerging socio-economic and technological development, the treaties were adopted to offer a much more extensive and stronger protection.[89] For instance, pursuant to art. 20 of the Berne Convention, the WCT has further entrenched the expansive scope of minimum standards for digital copyrighted works through the addition of making available right.[90] As noted from the consistency requirement indicated in the Agreed statements, the WCT epitomizes a continuing momentum created under the TRIPs Agreement to consolidate and strengthen the protection of copyright in the digital environment.[91]

Indeed, both WCT and WPPT have added another layer of protection--often called "para-copyright"--through their introduction of the rights against circumvention of TPMs and alteration or removal of rights management information (RMI).[92] While these technological measures have a far-reaching effect to frustrate or undermine the legitimate use of the existing flexibilities, states are left with the discretion to determine the legal means for their protection.[93] In protecting the TPMs, the criteria of *adequacy* and *effectiveness* of the digital locks and their limited use for *legitimate rights* might offer some flexibilities. With regard to the flexibilities, the WIPO Internet Treaties emulate their respective predecessors in permitting or providing for set of general flexibilities. To this effect, both WCT and WPPT allow states to provide for L&Es, subject to the all-encompassing three-step test inherited from the TRIPs Agreement.[94]

As elaborated earlier, all the general flexibilities pertaining to the subject matter and conditions of protection, term limits, and the three-step test would thus be applicable, *mutatis mutandis,* for the protection under the WIPO Internet Treaties. In contrast to their predecessors, the WIPO Internet Treaties make an explicit reference to and recognition of the need to *maintain balance* between the rights and *the public interest*, such as education, research and access to information in their preambles.[95] In this sense, some flexibilities can be derived from a pro-development interpretation of the *notion of balancing* and *the public interest* along with a particular mention of education and research. To this end, a right-based human development perspective is useful to offer a flexible and inclusive normative tool for the balance sought to advance public interest. Further, as the relevant established rule of interpretation dictates,[96] the aforementioned paragraphs in the preamble would be used to inform the interpretation and application of the substantive provisions. The policy space envisaged in the preambles is however undercut by the combined effect of the restrictive legal and pervasive technological mechanisms embedded in the substantive provisions.[97]

D Flexibilities under the Marrakesh and the Beijing Treaties

As the first international copyright treaty on L&Es, the Marrakesh Treaty primarily deals with the various flexibilities that promote special class of users' access to copyrighted works. In fact, the Treaty remains distinct and historic due to: (a) its provision of mandatory L&Es to the exclusive rights of copyright owners, and (b) its designation of print-disabled individuals as the beneficiaries.[98] Further, the Marrakesh Treaty is the sole copyright treaty that makes an explicit reference to international human rights instruments such as the UDHR and CRPD.[99] From among a long list of rights, both human rights instruments make a specific mention of the right to education,[100] and the right to participate in cultural life.[101] Adopted within the domain of international copyright system, the Treaty is useful for the realization of these fundamental rights, among others.[102] In this context, the Marrakesh Treaty is regarded as "an international agreement that employs the legal doctrines and policy tools of copyright to advance human rights ends."[103]

While noting the importance of the prevailing economic justification,[104] its embrace of the human rights approach to the copyright flexibilities marks a significant step towards human development. The Treaty is thus pivotal for its: (a) incorporation of basic principles of access and effective participation, and (b) reference to the WIPO's Development Agenda recommendations that reflect relevant flexibilities.[105] Further, the Treaty's acknowledgment of the need for a balance between the rights of authors and public interests, such as education, research and access to information, is another important aspect of general flexibilities.[106] Quite relevant, the Treaty's preamble refers to education both in the context of right and the larger public interest.[107] Such an emphasis mirrors the weight attached to the importance of education and access to copyrighted works for its realization.

In its substantive part, the Marrakesh Treaty requires the contracting parties to provide for L&Es to the exclusive economic rights in order to facilitate the availability of works in accessible formats. In general, the Treaty's requirement for mandatory L&Es, its provisions on cross-border exchange of accessible formats, and the restriction on the use of TPMs are relevant flexibilities that can be used to facilitate access to copyrighted learning materials.[108] Nonetheless, the utilization of these flexibilities requires a state's compliance with its existing obligations under the international copyright regime. In particular, the implementation of the flexibilities is subject to the requirements of the three-step test drawn from the Berne Convention, TRIPs Agreement and the WCT.[109] Given the human rights-oriented objectives of the Treaty, the broader interpretation of its three-step test may however offer states a better room to devise L&Es consistent with the Treaty's objectives.[110] In terms of its normative significance, it is useful to note the Treaty's embrace of users' rights approach and its lesson for a future comprehensive approach to flexibilities. Nonetheless, its implementation still remains within the expansive international copyright framework.

From among recent treaties, the Beijing Treaty is a right-holders-oriented treaty intended to ensure the effective protection of rights of performers in the audiovisual works.[111] In a departure from its predecessors, the Treaty's preamble makes an explicit recognition of the importance of the WIPO DA's recommendations and the need for maintaining a balance.[112] As regards the balance, the Treaty mimics the WPPT to underscore the need for a balance between the exclusive rights of performers and the larger public interest.[113] In its substantive content, the Beijing Treaty allows contracting parties to provide for a set of L&Es corresponding to those provided for literary and artistic works subject to the requirement of the three-step test.[114]

Therefore, the development-oriented interpretation and implementation of general flexibilities embodied in both treaties can be exploited to facilitate access to learning materials for higher education towards human development. In its integrative approach, the Marrakesh Treaty combines both the economic "incentive and reward" justification for right-holders and the "enhancement of "opportunities" for everyone.[115] More resonant with the latter prong and quite instrumental for the effective use of the flexibilities, the CA-driven human development perspective offers a better normative and evaluative guidance than the utilitarianism underpinning narrow economic considerations. In fact, the HDCA is apt to embrace both aspects and reframe the underpinning objectives in terms of capabilities for human development.

4.3.2 *Specific flexibilities relevant for higher education*

Within the ambit of the general flexibilities explored earlier, there are relevant flexibilities with a specific reference to education. In the same vein, there are other specific flexibilities that are quite relevant for education without an explicit mention of the term as a ground. Hence, this sub-section explores the relevant specific flexibilities under international copyright regime.

A Utilization for teaching purposes

Given the compelling need for access to most copyrighted works for educational purposes, a teaching exception was long recognized in the Berne Convention. Despite its subsequent marginalization, the promotion of learning was in fact central to the very purpose of copyright upon its inception.[116] Incorporated under art. 10(2) of the Berne Convention, the exception for the purpose of teaching is one of the most important specific flexibilities permitted for education. As such, the relevant part of the afore-cited article reads as follows:

> It shall be a matter for legislation in countries of the Union...to permit the utilization, *to the extent justified by the purpose*, of a literary or artistic works *by way of illustration* in publications, broadcasts or sound or visual recordings for teaching, provided such utilization is *compatible with fair practice* [emphasis added].

As is evident from the reading of this provision, it is up to a member-state to formulate an exception that facilitates the utilization of copyrighted works for educational purpose in its jurisdiction within the permitted limit.[117] In doing so, the member-state can thus design appropriate L&Es in a manner that promotes access to copyrighted learning materials for education at all levels.

Embedded in the teaching exception are several elements of flexibilities worth noting. First, the permitted utilization is applicable for all relevant works in publications, broadcasts and sound or visual recordings. In this respect, Ricketson and Ginsburg consider the utilization to be technology-neutral to encompass a digital fixation of works.[118] In the same vein, the authors opine that the ambit of the embraced broadcast can extend to its public performance, *albeit* to the exclusion of distribution of a work and digital or on-demand transmissions.[119] In terms of the categories of works, the exception is applicable to all works protected under the Berne Convention.[120]

Second, the references made to "the extent justified by the purpose" and "compatible with fair practice" render the provision an open-ended and a flexible exception. There is no quantitative limitation, except for the restriction related to the words "by way of illustration."[121] It is argued that the flexible interpretation of the words "purpose" and "fair practice" is dictated by the relevant national context. Although the exception appears to be somehow restrictive in its scope, the above-mentioned commentators note that the restriction "would not exclude the use of the whole work in appropriate circumstances." [122] As a result, multiple copies of a copyrighted work can be made for teaching purposes, subject to the qualification of "fair practice."[123]

It still remains unclear whether or not the scope of the phrase "by way of illustration" is broad enough to allow the use of compilations (anthologies) or a course-pack consisting of book chapters.[124] In this respect, the practice varies across jurisdictions. For instance, some jurisdictions such the United States and the United Kingdom adopt a licensing scheme to cover course-packs for higher education.[125] In contrast, the recent jurisprudence in Canada and India allow the use of course-packs for the purpose of education under the liberal reading of a fair dealing exception.[126] A much more liberal interpretation of the exception is imperative for education in the developing countries. As such, a development-oriented and context-based approach is important for the assessment of fairness to balance the interests of both authors and users. Third, the word "teaching" is interpreted to encompass teaching at all levels and in all modes—classroom instruction, distance, and online education as "there is no reason to exclude" the latter from its ambit.[127] In a restrictive interpretation of the term, "teaching" is noted to include a formal education in all educational institutions and universities, excluding general teaching that takes place outside the institutions.[128]

Furthermore, as a specific exception provided in the Berne Convention, debatable is whether or not the teaching exception is subject to the requirements of the three-step test. Noting the requirement of "fair practice" as a question left for the national tribunals to address, the first line of interpretation supports the possible evaluation of the exception in light of the test.[129] The other line of interpretation regards the exception as a self-contained and particular exception that is not subject to the curtailing effect of the three-step test.[130] Bearing in mind the guiding significance of the jurisprudence on the test *as found appropriate*, this author subscribes to the latter view. It is rightly argued that the superimposition of the three-step test upon a specific exception would rather entail a double restriction of the exception on top of the latter's an in-built limitation.[131] For a teaching exception with its own specific conditions, its further subjection to the three-step test would unduly narrow its scope and undermine the intended purpose of its contemplated flexibilities.[132]

According to Correa, the imposition of an additional scrutiny through the test upon the specific L&Es provided under the Berne Convention does not concur with the intention of the drafters and the literal meaning of art. 13 of the TRIPS Agreement.[133] In case an issue of compliance arises, Margaret Chon underscores the need to determine the alignment between art. 10 (2) and the three-step test in the light of arts. 7 & 8 of the TRIPs Agreement that refer to development.[134] In this context, as Chon argues, it is important for a decision maker to consider the public policy behind the exception and defer to the country's stated purpose of promoting education for human development.[135]

B Quotation exception

From among the specific flexibilities, relevant for educational purpose is the exception that allows quotation of copyrighted works for scholarship, review and criticism. As enshrined in the Berne Convention, the relevant part of art. 10 (1) provides that "it shall be permissible to make quotations from a work which has already been lawfully made available to the public." As a basic and *mandatory exception* to exclusive rights, quotation is integral to several intellectual activities, including for "scientific, critical, informatory and educational purposes."[136] In addition to the *lawful availability of a work to the public* by "any means," including a compulsory licensing,[137] the operation of the exception is further required to be "compatible with fair practice" and limited to the extent "justified by the purpose."[138] In the absence of a quantitative limit, commentators observe that "an objective appreciation" of the purpose is determinant for a compliance with "fair practice" although the length of the quotation is still relevant for the assessment.[139] In fact, the word "fair practice" itself is a flexible concept that remains subject to a judicial determination.[140]

In principle, quotation is deemed a self-contained exception.[141] Nevertheless, the determination of the fairness criterion may draw on a jurisprudence related to the three-step test's requirements of non-conflict with normal exploitation and absence of unreasonable prejudice with author's legitimate interests.[142] The requirement of "the extent justified by purpose" is also flexible as its determination depends upon the purpose that necessitates the quotation. For instance, a lengthy quotation could remain compatible both with "fair practice" and the "purpose" if its use is sought for a critical review or work of scholarship.[143] In sum, three points are worth noting in relation to its interpretation. First, the quotation exception is applicable for all kinds of use, work and exclusive rights in the absence of a restriction to suggest otherwise.[144] Second, there is no quantitative limitation on the length of quotation. Subject to the requirements, a quotation of the whole work may thus be justifiable in some circumstances.[145] Third, the exception is mandatory in its character and is an exception "that comes closest to embodying a 'user right' to make quotations."[146]

C Compulsory licensing including the Berne Appendix

For the exploitation of exclusive economic rights, voluntary licensing is a rule integral to the freedom of the rights holder. In most cases, this freedom or mode of exploitation is exercised through the active role of collective management organizations (CMOs).[147] Nonetheless, the exploitation of the economic rights through the licensing scheme is subject to the existence of a relevant market as well as an efficient and effective CMOs. Due to a market failure, lack of efficient CMOs, or the abusive use of the copyright, a compulsory licensing may be granted without the consent of the right holder in order to serve the public interests.[148] Justified on the grounds of public interest, compulsory licensing is thus an important form of copyright flexibilities relevant for higher education. In addition to the uncompensated statutory L&Es for the purposes of teaching, quotation, press usage, and news reporting,[149] the international copyright regime incorporates few instances of a statutory compulsory licensing with an equitable remuneration.

For instance, the Berne Convention permits a compulsory licensing with an equitable remuneration for the broadcast of literary and artistic works, recording of musical works and making of a cinematographic works.[150] For the operation of the compulsory licenses often regarded as statutory licenses, the required equitable remuneration may be fixed in the relevant legislation or its determination might be entrusted to a competent authority.[151] As commentators note, a compulsory license related to broadcasts is underpinned by public interest considerations.[152] Despite its limited practical utility and subject to the overdue reform, the Berne Appendix is a special compulsory licensing scheme designed for educational purposes in developing countries.

Intended to facilitate a bulk access to copyrighted materials, the Berne Appendix—now integral to the TRIPs Agreement and WCT—imposes a limitation on the reproduction and translation rights of authors under certain conditions for teaching, scholarship and scientific research purposes. Nonetheless, the utilization of the compulsory licensing is subject to both an equitable remuneration and a compliance with set of complex procedures, including notification requirement.[153]

From among the cumbersome conditions, the major conditions under the Appendix are:[154] (a) a long waiting period of three to seven years, with a further grace period, (b) the need for a competent authority to issue the license, and (c) the restriction on parallel imports and the translation license, and (d) the limitation of the license to use in connection with systematic instructional activities. Further, the use of Berne Appendix is limited due to the high transaction costs arising from its complex requirements and the unaffordable equitable remuneration required. Hence, the Berne Appendix is critiqued for its failure to achieve its intended purpose of facilitating a bulk access to learning materials and for its arguable exclusion of "private study, research and distance education."[155] Subject to the practical limitations, the Berne Appendix and other instances of compulsory licensing schemes constitute part of the relevant flexibilities.[156]

D The principle of exhaustion and parallel importation

Developed in the first decade of the twentieth century, the principle of exhaustion is known as the "first-sale" doctrine in the United States or the doctrine of exhaustion in other jurisdictions.[157] In facilitating the distinct economic exploitation of tangible and intangible property, the principle of exhaustion serves as "a public policy tool that limits an economic exploitation of intellectual property rights following the first lawful transfer of a physical object in which the intellectual property is embodied, unless otherwise prescribed in the law."[158] As its regulation lies within the ambit of a state's discretion, the application of the principle remains an important aspect of the relevant flexibilities.[159] Noted as the exhaustion of an author's exclusive economic rights to the copies of a copyrighted work after their lawful sale (with the author's consent), the principle allows the resale or transfer of the copies without further authorization.[160]

Although the application of the principle may encompass any potential "use" of the material object or copies transferred,[161] most common is the exhaustion of the distribution right of an author in respect of the lawful copies sold.[162] In terms of its geographical scope of application, the principle of exhaustion can operate as a domestic/national, regional, and international exhaustion. The national principle of exhaustion is applicable for copyrighted works first sold on the national market to allow their further unimpeded distribution or use within that jurisdiction.[163] As a result, the application of national exhaustion precludes parallel imports of copyrighted works without authors' consent to the detriment of the users or consumers. In jurisdictions that prohibit parallel importation, rights holders derive an additional economic benefit from the practice of price discrimination through market segregation across nations based on the variance in the demand and purchasing power.[164]

In contrast, the application of the principle at regional level exhausts authors' distribution right over the resale or alienation of the copies throughout the jurisdictions of all the states that constitute the regional union or regional market.[165] For instance, the principle of regional exhaustion has been central to the EU's internal market founded upon the free movement of goods, among its other pillars.[166] In the United States, the Supreme Court has clarified the country's approach in its recent jurisprudence related to a copyright over textbooks.[167] In its precedent, the Court has affirmed the adoption of the principle of international exhaustion In effect, this will facilitate the global distribution of the protected copies once the works are put on a market by or with the consent of the rights holder.[168] Central to the regional and international exhaustion, it is thus crucial for developing nations to utilize unimpeded parallel imports and benefit from the consequent price reduction through competition.[169] In general, the principle of exhaustion is important to "create secondary markets for used knowledge goods."[170] In so doing, the principle promotes a market competition that in turn enables consumers or users to purchase protected knowledge goods such as learning materials at a lesser price.[171]

From the international copyright legal regimes, the incorporation of principle of national exhaustion is argued to be implicit in the Berne Convention due to the underpinning principle of territoriality. Further, the relevant provisions on the seizure of infringing copies and sound recordings prohibit parallel imports without a permission. Likewise, the Convention does not permit exportation of copies made under the Berne Appendix. The foregoing instances are often cited to corroborate the argument against parallel imports while several countries dispute this assertion in the absence of an explicit obligation.[172] In contrast, art. 6 (2) of the WCT, art. 12 (2) and art. 6 of the TRIPs Agreement make an explicit mention of the principle without imposing an obligation to regulate it. In particular, the TRIPs Agreement leaves member-states with the discretion to adopt the principle of exhaustion with a geographical reach of their choice. Except in the context of the principles of non-discrimination, the issue of the exhaustion is not subject to the dispute settlement under the Agreement.[173]

In terms of its economic benefit, the reserved policy space is thus very critical for developing countries to adopt an international exhaustion that facilitates importation of relevant learning materials for education.[174] In adopting international exhaustion, developing countries can provide for specific legal provisions permitting parallel imports. This allows users to enjoy the benefit of consumer choice and lower prices from the application of the principle.[175] Nonetheless, its extension to creative works in the digital environment is still not settled and needs a careful policy consideration.[176]

E Regulation of anti-competitive practices for bulk or affordable access

Intended to foster a fair competition, a reasonable restraint on the exclusive rights is relevant both for a follow-on creative innovation and higher education. Premised upon the existence of a market for the works, a regulatory measure related to anti-competitive practices can be used as an instrument to facilitate an affordable access to learning materials for educational purposes. In this regard, member-states were left with the freedom to regulate anticompetitive practices or abuses of monopoly under the Berne Convention.[177] An explicit introduction of the measure was later made through the TRIPs Agreement within the framework of a global trade regime.[178] It is noted that regulation of anti-competitive practices is not part of the L&Es *internal* to the international copyright system.[179] In effect, the regulatory action is not subject to the three-step test that is intended to serve as a general rule for the L&Es internal to the copyright system.[180]

As a public policy measure that lies within the ambit of competition law and that marks the latter's interface with copyright system, the regulation of the anti-competitive practice is called for and intended to prevent the abusive action of the exclusive rights.[181] The adoption of the anti-competitive measures is permitted within the framework of the basic principle under art. 8(2) of the TRIPs Agreement. Intended to prevent abuses of IPRs, developing countries with strong domestic competition law and policy may exploit the flexibilities in regulating the anti-competitive practices of copyright owners.[182] In the digital environment, the regulatory measure on this ground can include the prevention or restricted use of technological controls that impede a legitimate access to learning materials.[183]

Further, adhesive and restrictive contractual terms such as click-wrap agreements that are intended to limit a lawful use of copyrighted works may constitute anti-competitive practice in the digital environment.[184] In particular, a concern relates to licensing agreements for software products that prevent reverse-engineering or use of non-copyrightable aspects of the software.[185] In general, art. 40 of the TRIPs Agreement is an enumerative list. Thus, similar anti-competitive practices can be invoked to avoid an excessive impediment against access.[186] As the relevant jurisprudence evolving elsewhere indicates, the refusal to license on reasonable terms, excessive pricing, and price fixing might constitute anti-competitive practices to justify the grant of a compulsory license, subject to an equitable remuneration.[187] It is argued that the effective use of art. 40 of the TRIPs Agreement may serve the purpose of facilitating a bulk access to copyrighted materials for educational purposes.[188]

Nonetheless, the potential benefits of the flexibilities related to anti-competitive practices are quite limited in the context of developing countries. First, there is lack of a robust competition policy and strong judicial systems in developing countries.[189] Second, it is difficult to satisfy the product market criterion that requires the availability of substitute goods for the copyrighted works with a monopoly price relative to the market.[190] In fact, the main problem in most developing countries is the unavailability or lack of affordable access to copyrighted works on the market. From among other factors, the major ones are low purchasing power and infrastructural constraints that are further exacerbated by stringent copyright protection.[191]

As for creative works in the digital environment, a legtimate access to the works is further precluded due to technological controls.[192] Further, lack of internet and computers is among the infrastructural barriers against access to the relevant learning materials available online in digital formats for users and educators. From reasons related to copyright, an actual access to, and the acquisition of, the digital learning materials are thus restricted due to digital locks and exorbitant price or subscription fees. In sum, the cumulative effect of these factors generates anti-competitive practices that stifle a robust competition to the detriment of the users or potential consumers.

F Limitations and exceptions for library and archival uses

In addition to their mission of collecting, preserving, and disseminating knowledge, the role of libraries and archives is critical for educational purposes.[193] In particular, in developing countries with a limited access, libraries are instrumental for their facilitative or enabling access to learning materials.[194] In this context, although there is no explicit exception for library and archival uses under the Berne Convention, the exception can be justified both within the broader context of educational purposes and the three-step test under art. 9(2) of the Convention and art. 13 of the TRIPs Agreement.[195] Indeed, the increasing roles of libraries and the lack of explicit L&Es in the international copyright regime are among the major reasons for the ongoing WIPO's consideration of the L&Es for libraries, archives, and museums.[196] It is indisputable that an explicit exception that facilitates the roles of library and archives is crucial to complement the relevant flexibilities for higher education. In the meantime, the application of the three-step test in light of arts. 7 & 8 of the TRIPs can be used to provide for appropriate flexibilities. Permitted for users of libraries and archives, this set of general flexibilities are useful to facilitate access to copyrighted learning materials for promoting, *inter alia*, higher education towards development.

In conclusion, the effective operation of the aforementioned flexibilities in the form of L&Es such as those for educational and quotation purposes depend upon the availability of access to the protected works. For digital learning materials, the implementation of anti-circumvention of TPMs is a challenge that undermines the flexibilities due to its indiscriminate impediment of access to the works even for the legitimate uses. As Okediji observes, this challenge can be overcome through a permitted circumvention of the TPMs in order to allow an access to relevant digital copyrighted materials.[197] This observation is in line with the *Agreed Statement* to the WCT/WPPT that emphasizes member states' freedom to "devise new L&Es that are appropriate in the digital network environment."[198]

For works in the digital environment, "developing countries should carefully consider what new limitations and exceptions are needed to encourage access to digital works in a manner consistent with identified development goals and the general public interest."[199] For example, Okediji suggests the formulation of an exception that allows the circumvention of technological controls to facilitate access to and use of works for educational or personal purposes.[200] Under the TRIPs Agreement, member states are free to prevent the application of anti-circumvention measures as its protection is not required under the Agreement.[201]

4.3.3 The double-edged three-step test: element and parameter of flexibilities

As noted previously, the emergence of the three-step test dates back to the revision of the Berne Convention at Stockholm in 1967. With the advent of the TRIPs Agreement, its initial application for a reproduction right under the Convention was further expanded in its reach to encompass all exclusive economic rights both within the international copyright and the IP regimes as a whole. In the international copyright regime, the test has been seen as an overarching principle for the L&Es under all subsequent copyright treaties and the TRIPs Agreement. In the aftermath of its entrenchment in the TRIPs Agreement for all exclusive economic rights, the three-step test has made its way into the WIPO Internet Treaties, the Marrakesh Treaty, and the Beijing Treaty.

Given its vague construction, the three-step test tends to entail a double-edged effect of *enabling* and *limiting* the utilization of relevant flexibilities. In particular, the application of the test has a significant implication both for higher education and creative innovation in the context of access to copyrighted materials. In order is thus the exploration of the test and its dual functions for the domestic utilization of the relevant flexibilities.

A The content of the three-step test

In its extensive embodiment of the test, art. 13 of the TRIPs Agreement that enshrines the three steps reads as follows:

> Members shall confine limitations and exceptions to exclusive rights to *certain special cases* which do *not conflict with a normal exploitation of the work* and do *not unreasonably prejudice the legitimate interest* of the right holder [emphasis added].

I CERTAIN SPECIAL CASES

As the first condition of the test, the wording of "certain special cases" has been interpreted to require a clear delineation of limitation or exception under the national legislation.[202] In its interpretation of the step, the WTO Panel emphasized the term "certain" to include an exception whose scope is "known and particularized" in order to "guarantee a sufficient degree of legal certainty."[203] The WTO Panel has also interpreted the term "special" as an additional requirement imposed upon the defined exception to be "limited in its field of application or exceptional in its scope."[204] That is, the exception "should be narrow in a quantitative as well as qualitative sense."[205] In contrast to the Panel's dictionary meaning approach, Ricketson has noted Panel's dictionary meaning approach "special" to mean an exception with a purpose and public policy justification.[206] In the recent edition of their joint commentary, Ricketson and Ginsburg interpret the condition to endorse exceptions that are "finite and limited in scope."[207] Despite the disputed open-ended U.S. fair use exception's compliance with the condition,[208] most purpose-specific exceptions such as private uses, and uses for research and scholarship are often considered to meet the condition as certain special cases.[209]

II NO CONFLICT WITH A NORMAL EXPLOITATION

As noted in the WTO Panel's interpretation of this condition, the condition of the test derives its meaning from the words "exploitation" and "normal." As obvious as it appears, the term "exploitation" is understood to mean copyright owners' use of the exclusive rights "to extract economic value from their rights to those works."[210] That is, the exploitation of the work covers any use intended to maximize the value of the rights.[211] The term "normal" which, *inter alia,* means "regular" or "conventional" is noted to reflect two possible connotations—empirical nature and normative standard.[212] The phrase "normal exploitation" is thus interpreted to include both current forms of exploitation with tangible revenue and "those forms of exploitation which have acquired, or could acquire considerable economic or practical importance."[213] According to this line of interpretation, an exception or limitation interferes with the normal exploitation of the exclusive economic rights when it entails *an economic competition* with the owners and deprives them of *significant* market or commercial gains.[214]

Thus, as the WTO Panel has made it clear, not all uses of the creative works covered by the scope of exclusive rights and that involve commercial gains would necessarily lead to a conflict with the normal exploitation requirement.[215] In addition to the covered uses that still fall below the threshold, uses such as private use or uses for non-commercial research seem to pass muster under the condition.[216] An economic competition with an owner and the consequent loss of significant commercial gains are determinative of the condition.[217] Once found, a violation of the condition warrants the proscription of an exception.[218]

Nonetheless, the overriding economic considerations of the step tend to make it an issue of less importance in countries without a significant commercial exploitation or in those with a market failure due to users inability to pay.[219] In some cases, this market situation might be used to justify a liberal application of the flexibilities to facilitate the non-commercial use of copyrighted materials for education and scientific research.[220]

Given the WTO Panel's emphasis on the economic aspect in its interpretation of the test, Ricketson and Ginsburg point out the unaddressed issue of non-economic normative considerations. Noting the existing exceptions with strong non-economic normative aspects, the commentators suggest taking a contextual treaty interpretation to embrace both economic and non-economic normative considerations.[221] In this respect, Ricketson and Ginsburg draw attention to the overriding non-economic normative aspect of the public policy-driven exceptions such as free speech, education and scholarship.[222] Indeed, their interpretation seems to be premised upon the application of the three-step test to all other exceptions to the reproduction right. That is, the non-economic normative considerations of the L&Es subject to the three-step test should be given a due weight in the evaluation of the second condition that animates an economic justification.[223]

It is argued that the inclusion of the non-economic normative considerations is useful to offer a more flexible policy space to accommodate public interests within the stated objective of the Berne Convention.[224] Inherent in the notion of public interest and development objectives contemplated in the TRIPs Agreement, the non-economic normative considerations should take into account relevant human rights.[225] Further, in view of the variance in nation's conception of public interest and different levels of development,[226] the determination of the normative considerations should be made in the light of sustainable human development.

III NO UNREASONABLE PREJUDICE TO THE LEGITIMATE INTEREST

In the event of a non-interference with the normal exploitation of the work, there will arise a need for the assessment of unreasonable prejudice to right holder's legitimate interests. As a logical extension of the second step, the third step is deemed to be the most difficult condition to interpret.[227] Further, it is considered the most important prong of the three-step test as its examination involves public policy considerations.[228] To this end, both unreasonable prejudice and legitimate interests are important elements. In the WTO Panel's interpretation of "legitimate interests" of the right holder, it is noted to "encompass a legal right" wherein the connotation of "interests" is "not necessarily limited to actual or potential economic advantage or detriment."[229] Not confined to a legal positivist perspective, the protection of the "legitimate interests" requires a normative justification "in the light of the objectives that underlie the protection of exclusive rights."[230] As Gervais observes, taking a broader view "could reflect a systemic option to balance the rights of copyright holders and users."[231]

Once the legitimate interest is determined, important is assessing the occurrence of "unreasonable prejudice" to the legitimate interests of the right holder. As is evident from the condition, not all levels of prejudice are relevant to determine a compliance between an exception or a limitation and the condition. Rather, a critical factor is the existence of "unreasonable" level of prejudice that entails a "substantial" harm or damage. In its reference to the term as an economic loss, the WTO Panel held the view that a "prejudice to the legitimate interests of right holders reaches an unreasonable level if an exception or limitation causes or has the potential to cause an unreasonable loss of income to the copyright owner."[232] In this respect, as prejudice *per se* is not prohibited, leading commentators argue that the "unreasonable prejudice" can be avoided through an equitable remuneration system.[233] In particular, Correa contends that the Panel seemed to agree with this view as long as "a system of compulsory licensing or equitable remuneration is available."[234]

As Foster observes, the absence of a relevant market for normal exploitation in the LDCs or a market failure makes the "unreasonable level of prejudice" a matter of limited occurrence due to insignificant loss of income and a strong public interest considerations such as the human right to education.[235] It is contended that the criterion of reasonableness or justifiable prejudice offers a room for public interest justification that allows legislators to strike a balance between the rights of the right holders and the needs or interests of users.[236] In this context, Gervais points out the importance of human rights principles to inform the interpretation of the public interest considerations.[237] In concurring with this view, Goldstein and Hugenholtz argue that "the word legitimate and reasonable inject normative meaning into the test and admit a variety of public interest into the equation."[238]

Some writers also observe that the step permits the WTO members to resolve a conflict between fundamental rights through the application of a proportionality test that offers states a margin of appreciation.[239] In the same vein, the Munich's Declaration on the balanced interpretation of the three-step test calls for the consideration of *the legitimate interest of third parties* akin to the test provided for patent under art. 30 of the TRIPs Agreement.[240] The significance of the Declaration lies in its holistic approach that treats the steps as "individual elements informing one overall assessment."[241] Yet, the proposed interpretation is critiqued for its "overemphasis" on the users' aspect of public interest without a "due" regard for that of right holders.[242] Favoring a sequential approach to the application of the test,[243] this critique tends to mask the long entrenched private rights in the copyright system. Given copyright's twin public interest aspects, a holistic or an integrated approach to the test is rather both flexible and reasonable to maintain the balance that remains central to the purpose of copyright itself.[244]

In sum, the application of the conditions of the three-step test would determine whether or not an exception or a limitation to an exclusive right is justifiable. In contrast to the first condition which most purpose-specific exceptions would readily meet,[245] the two remaining conditions demand a rigorous act of balancing competing interests. As the criteria are both open-ended and abstract, their actual application at the national level could entail a variance within the overarching requirements of necessity and consistency with the TRIPs Agreement. It should be noted that the application of the test under other copyright treaties such as the WIPO Internet Treaties would essentially remain similar to the three-step test under the TRIPs Agreement.[246]

B The dual function of the test: flexibility and parameter for flexibilities

As is evident from the burgeoning scholarship and the jurisprudence it has generated, there seems to be a consensus about the dual aspects of the test. From users' perspective, the significance of the three-step test has drawn both skepticism and support. For instance, mindful of its emergence as a compromise and its limited flexibilities,[247] Okediji views the three-step test as a constraint on member states' freedom to design the permitted national flexibilities.[248] This observation stems from the adoption of the test within an overarching parameter of the right-oriented framework and its subsequent expansive integration into the TRIPs Agreement.[249] Taking the TRIPs Agreement as a "given,"[250] other scholars consider the three-step test an open-ended norm or balancing instrument that offers a "considerable room" for flexibilities.

For example, in their recent joint work titled "The Three-Step Test Revisited," Geiger, Gervais and Senftleben argue that the three-step test "was intended to serve as a flexible balancing tool offering national policy makers *sufficient* breathing space to satisfy economic, social, and cultural needs."[251] In their observation, the three-step test can be used to devise L&Es such as those for libraries, archives and museums as well as exemptions of reproduction required for judicial, administrative or parliamentary proceedings.[252] To this effect, Gervais suggests a reverse application of the test with an emphasis upon the importance of the third step.[253] In his argument for a model fair use doctrine based on the three-step test for the EU, Senftleben regards the test as a "flexible framework" with the "function of creating room for the introduction of copyright limitations at the national level."[254] In his opinion, the three-step test is a "flexible balancing tool" with a "fundamental role in enabling limitations and enhancing the flexibility of the copyright system."[255] Subject to the overall consistency requirement, it is true that the three-step test allows members some rooms to devise domestic flexibilities in order to balance private and public interests.[256]

Nonetheless, as its evolution and intended effect suggest, the purpose of the test was not to "create" or "enable" the creation of "sufficient" flexibilities. Instead, it was *primarily* designed and then was extended further to place a ceiling upon the hitherto sovereign discretion reserved to states.[257] In fact, the issue of flexibilities somehow inherent in the test seems to be subordinate to its primary function. In this sense, the test deviates from the objective of a copyright system that requires equivalent considerations. As a parameter, the test stands to serve its primary function. After all, this is the overriding reason that makes a compliance with the test a matter of serious concern to developed nations.

In this respect, the purpose of the test is explicit in the international copyright regime. That is, the prime function of the three-step test is to confine the scope of the national copyright flexibilities such as L&Es.[258] Operating as such, the test is an international rule with the most direct constraint on the discretion of policy makers in designing new L&Es.[259] Adopted within the global copyright system underpinned by the primacy of the interest of authors/right holders,[260] the test is *primarily* intended to set a limit on the freedom of the states to regulate the permitted flexibilities.[261] Construed to reflect the desire to maintain the status quo and intended to govern the flexibilities appropriate in the digital environment,[262] the three-step test's guiding function was emphasized in the *Agreed Statement* to art. 10 of the WCT. Adopted against a backdrop of an intended, but disputed restrictive approach,[263] the *Statement* makes clear that art. 10(2) "neither reduces nor extends" the scope of the L&Es permitted under the Berne Convention.[264]

Although this reading seems to maintain the existing scope, it reaffirms the objective of the test to circumscribe the scope of the L&Es. Intended to preserve or extend the scope of protection, the *Statement* rules out a room for the expansion of flexibilities. Further, despite the Treaty's central aim to advance the human rights of the beneficiaries,[265] the integration of the three-step test into the Marrakesh Treaty reinforces the test's restrictive function as a parameter for flexibilities. Designed to be more of a constraining parameter than an "enabling" one, the test stands firm to preempt legislative or judicial inroads into the expansive exclusive domains once secured.

For its operation within the broad parameter of the global copyright system, below are the salient points related to the application of the three-step test as a specific parameter for flexibilities. First, including for unpublished works,[266] the application of the test is vital for L&Es that are not specified under the international copyright treaties.[267] Except for those specified under the existing international copyright regime, the formulation of L&Es is required to meet the conditions of the three-step test to qualify as permitted flexibilities. For instance, the L&Es that are subject to the guidance of the test for their formulation and application include private use, exceptions for scientific research and scholarship as well as those for libraries, archives, and museums.[268]

Despite its dubious compliance with the test,[269] the application or adoption of the four-factor US fair use doctrine[270]—called a bundle of L&Es—is subject to the guidance of the three-step test.[271] Second, the application of the three-step test as a parameter should be understood within the broad development objectives and principles of the TRIPs Agreement.[272] This understanding comports with the established rule of treaty interpretation and is useful to take into account the national development context.[273] Given the public interest considerations inherent in the test, its interpretation should draw a guidance from the relevant human rights principles as recognized in the Marrakesh Treaty.[274]

Third, member states are free to adopt a user-right or human development-oriented approach as an appropriate "legal means" for compliance with the test. Fourth, it is contended that the domestic application of the three-step test would not govern the self-contained specific L&Es such as the teaching exception under the Berne Convention.[275] In this regard, Ricketson and Ginsburg note the overlap between art. 13 of the TRIPs Agreement and the exception for all practical purposes as the reference to "fairness" corresponds to the requirements of the three-step test.[276] As long as it is not required as such, its application to those specific L&Es should be resisted. Five, outside the ambit of the test is perhaps the regulation of exhaustion of exclusive rights as such a regulation was excluded from the dispute settlement mechanism.[277]

It could be contended that the principle could entail a competition with the normal exploitation of the right and a loss of income. But, central to the justification of exhaustion and important to reject such an argument is the right holder's recoupment through the income once derived from a prior exploitation. Thus, its exclusion from the WTO dispute settlement would foreclose a legal challenge on this ground at international level. By the same token, as Okediji observes, outside the reach of the test is the regulation of anti-competitive practices that falls within the ambit of a national competition law.[278]

From the foregoing discussion on its dual functions the test is *primarily* designed to set a limitation on nation's sovereign discretion to devise the permitted flexibilities. While this restrictive parameter is intended to advance the interests of the right holders, the test is noted to leave "some 'flexibilities." Given its built-in dual features, the test can still be considered both a parameter for, and a form of, flexibilities.[279] As there is no "one-size-fits-all" approach for a mechanical implementation of the abstract criteria, developing countries could benefit from an appropriate implementation of the test in a manner that ensures the fullest utilization of its inherent and related flexibilities. To this effect, as noted above, scholars have suggested a number of approaches ranging from reversing the steps with an emphasis on the third one,[280] reading into the third step the interests of third parties[281] to the adoption of the three-step-test infused with fair use doctrine.[282] In this regard, the emerging user-right based approach as informed by human development perspective and human rights norms can help countries leverage the flexibilities for the realization of quality higher education and user-driven creative innovation.

In sum, a balanced approach to creative innovation and higher education requires a due consideration of the twin—protection and access—aspects of the public interests to be integral to the *intended* objective of a copyright protection. Due to their conceptual overlap, the infusion between human rights norms and the HDCA-driven sustainable human development is useful to offer a normative guidance that informs the utilization of the flexibilities.[283]

4.4 Conclusion

The utilization of international copyright flexibilities is instrumental both for a sustainable creative innovation and quality higher education in the context of access to knowledge and human capital. Further, much more important is the role of the flexibilities for the expansion of human capabilities that constitute an enriching and overarching conceptual framework for a sustainable human development. From this perspective, the set of relevant flexibilities under the existing international copyright system is neither directed towards nor informed by the core objective of sustainable human development. Given the primacy of exclusive rights under the existing international copyright legal regime, there lacks a harmonization for the corresponding flexibilities that should be treated as an integral part of the regime. For instance, the Berne Convention which sets the international baseline for the international copyright system leaves the matter to member states, subject to its built-in upward trajectory of authors' right. Nonetheless, it provides for a specific teaching exception, exception for quotation and the contested Berne Appendix for the purposes of education.

Further, various general flexibilities related to the subject matter, conditions of protection, and duration are embodied in the Convention. In accordance with the compliance requirements, the various general flexibilities enshrined in or permitted under other treaties such as TRIPs Agreement and the WIPO treaties could also be utilized for further creative innovation and higher education in order to promote human development. From among the existing international copyright treaties, the Marrakesh Treaty is the sole legal regime that provides for mandatory set of international L&Es. Integral to all copyright treaties, the application of the all-encompassing three-step test operates to serve its dual functions. Serving as a parameter, the test is designed *primarily* to limit the scope of the L&Es. In its limited role, the test somehow allows the utilization of copyright flexibilities contemplated under the international copyright system.

In view of their central role for human development, various approaches have been highlighted in the legal scholarship and emerging jurisprudence. In addition to the traditional approach that subordinates flexibilities to the exclusive rights, the emerging approaches to copyright flexibilities regard the flexibilities as development policy tools and/or users' rights.[284] Going further and with the potential to embrace them, the HDCA is important to enhance the instrumental role of the international copyright flexibilities for higher education and creative innovation. Given its normative reach to encompass the emerging approaches to the copyright flexibilities, the HDCA reinforces the significance of the flexibilities to facilitate access to knowledge or learning materials for higher education.

Accommodative and multifaceted in its nature, the HDCA is thus suited to serve as a policy and normative tool to balance authors' and users' interests. Indeed, the approach is crucial to inform flexibilities whether framed as public policy goals or rights grounded in human rights norms. Further, human development perspective is more useful for the interpretation and application of the notion of "development" in the TRIPs Agreement and other international copyright treaties. In particular, the HDCA is pivotal for an explicit articulation of human development as the core objective of international copyright and reframing its flexibilities as an instrumental aspect of human capabilities.

As noted in the preamble to the WTO Agreement, the interpretation and application of the development objectives and relevant flexibilities embodied in the TRIPs Agreement is required to be guided by the principle of sustainable development. Indeed, this principle is well-suited to embrace human development out of which emerges a notion of sustainable human development. For the international copyright regime, the principle can serve as an entry point for rethinking and reintegrating the flexibilities in the light of the broader framework of sustainable human development.

Notes

1 In its reasoning on the need for balanced public policy objectives underpinning copyright, the Court pointed out how excessive copyright protection would unduly limit the ability of the public domain to foster and embellish '*creative innovation*' in the long-term of society as a whole, or create practical obstacles to proper utilization." *Theberge v Galerie d'Art du Petit Chaplain* Inc, et al., 2S.C. R 336, 2002 SCC 34, para 32.

2 See David Gurteen, "Knowledge, Creativity and innovation" (1998) 2:1 J Knowl Manag 5–13. As Gurteen notes, "creativity and innovation concern the process of creating and applying new knowledge." *Ibid* at 5.

3 *Oslo Manual: Guidelines for Collecting and Interpreting Innovation Data,* 3rd ed (OECD Publishing, 2005) at 46.

4 Jeremy de Beer, Chidi Oguamanam, & Tobais Schonwetter, "Innovation, Intellectual Property and Development Narratives in Africa," in De Beer et al, eds, *Innovation and Intellectual Property Collaborative Dynamics in Africa* (Cape Town: UCT Press, 2014) at 9 [de Beer, Oguamanam & Schonwetter, "Innovation, IP and Development"].

5 Bengt-Ake Lundval, *The Learning Economy and the Economics of Hope* (London: Anthem Press, 2016) at 93 (emphasis in the original).

6 *Ibid* at 93–94.

7 See generally Henry Chesbrough, "The Era of Open Innovation" (2003) 44:3 MIT Sloan Manag Rev 35; Henry Chesbrough, *Open Innovation: The New Imperative for Creating and Profiting from Technology* (Massachusetts: Harvard Business School Press, 2006). An open innovation is defined "a paradigm that assumes that firms can and should use external ideas, as well as internal ideas and internal and external paths to market, as the firms look to advance their technology." Ibid at xxiv.

8 See Eric Von Hippel, *The Sources of Innovation* (Oxford: Oxford University press, 1988) at 11–26; Hippel, "Innovation by User communities: Learning from Open-Source Software" (2001) MIT Sloan Manag Rev 82; Hippel, *Free Innovation* (Massachusetts: MIT Press, 2017).

9 Yochai Benkler & Helen Nissenbaum, "Commons-Based Peer Production and Virtue" (2006) 14:4 J Polit Philos 394–419 [Benkler, "Common-Based"]; see generally Yochai Benkler, *The Wealth of Networks: How Social Production Transforms Markets and Freedom* (New Haven, CT: Yale University Press, 2006) [Benkler, *The Wealth of Networks*].

10 See generally Eric von Hippel, *Democratizing Innovation* (Cambridge, MA: MIT Press, 2006)[Hippel, *Democratizing Innovation*]. Benkler, *The Wealth of Networks, supra* note 9 at 2–10.

11 See Henry Chesbrough & Melissa Appleyard, "Open Innovation and Strategy" (2007) 50:1 Calif Manag Rev 57 at 61–73.

12 Rohinton P. Medhora, *New Thinking on Innovation: Introduction,* Center for International Innovation Governance, Special Report 2017, at 5 & 8.

13 Michael Spence, *Innovation and Prosperity in an Age of Transition: Foreword,* in CIGI Special Report 2017, *supra* note 12 at xiii ("[P]eople as [the] most important investable resource … are the source of innovation, creativity and dynamism.").

14 See Stuart Cunningham and Luke Jaaniste, "The Policy Journey Toward Education for Creative Economy," in Daniel Araya and Michael A. Peters, eds, *Education in the Creative Economy: Knowledge and Learning in the Age of Innovation* (New York: Peter Lang, 2010) 29 at 36–41.

15 See Amartya Sen, *Development as Freedom* (New York: Anchor Books, 1999) at 75–76 [Sen, *Development as Freedom*].

16 Martha Nussbaum, *Creating Capabilities: The Human Development Approach* (Cambridge: Harvard University Press, 2011) at 33 [Nussbaum, *Creating Capabilities*].

17 Benkler, *The Wealth of Networks, supra* note 9 at 1.

18 UNDP, *Human Development Report 2016: Human Development for Everyone* (New York: UNDP, 2016) at 67–69 [UNDP, *Human Development Report 2016*]; ("Inequality in access to advanced, high quality education, health care and other services restricts the ability of some people to expand their capabilities. Access to information is crucial to high-quality education and thus for expanding opportunities and capabilities among children and youth."). *Ibid* at 68 & 69.

19 Orly Lobel, "The New Cognitive Property: Human Capital Law and the Reach of Intellectual Property" (2015) 93 Tex L Rev 789 at 834.

20 Sen, *Development as Freedom, supra* note 15 at 292–297. As Sen points out, "we must go beyond the notion of human capital, after acknowledging its relevance and reach." *Ibid* at 296. Given the inclusive potential of the capability perspective, "there is a strong need to go well beyond that rather limited and circumscribed role of human capital in understanding development as freedom." *Ibid* at 297.

21 See Ruth L. Okediji, "The International Copyright System: Limitations, Exceptions and Public Interest Considerations for Developing Countries" (2006) UNCTAD-ICTSD Issue Paper No. 15 at 7–8 [Okediji, The International Copyright System].

22 *Ibid* at 4 & 23–24. Peter K. Yu, "The International Enclosure Movement," (2007) 82 Indiana LJ 827 at 867–870 [Yu, "The International Enclosure"]; Peter K. Yu, "TRIPS and Its Discontents," (2006) 10 Marq Intell Prop L Rev 369 at 383–386 [Yu, TRIPS and Its Discontents"]; Peter Drahos, "BITs and BIPs: Bilateralism in Intellectual Property" (2001) 4 J World Intellect Prop 791.

23 Okediji, "International Copyright System," *supra* note 21 at 12–14.

24 *International Convention for the Protection of Performers, Producers of Phonograms and Broadcasting Organizations,* art. 15(1), 26 October 1961, 496 U.N.T.S. 43 [Rome Convention].

25 *Ibid* at art. 15(2).

26 Okediji, "International Copyright System," *supra* note 21 at 7.

27 *Ibid.* In particular, Okediji argues that "the narrow set of limitations recognized in the Berne Convention reflected enduring principles of access to copyrighted works in the interest of the public at large." *Ibid* at 7 & 8. For example, the limitation for educational purposes and dissemination of scientific works places education and scientific advancement among "the still enduring aspects of the public interest in access to protected works." *Ibid* at 8; Sam Ricketson, "U.S Accession to the Berne Convention:

An Outsider's Appreciation" (1993) 8 Intellectual Property Journal 87 [Ricketson, "U.S Accession"].

28 See *Guide to the Berne Convention for the Protection of Literary and Artistic Works* (Geneva: WIPO, 1978) at 5–11 [*WIPO Guide to the Berne Convention*]; Bernt Hugenhotz & Ruth Okediji, "Contours of an International Instrument on Limitations and Exceptions" in Neil Weinstock Netanel, ed, *The Development Agenda: Global Intellectual Property and Developing Countries* (Oxford: Oxford University Press, 2008) 474 at 475 [Okediji & Hugenholtz, "Contours of an International Instrument"]; see Alan Story, "Burn Berne: Why the Leading International Copyright Convention Must Be Repealed" (2003) 40 Hous L Rev 763 at 788–790.

29 The in-built expansive trajectory was explicitly set in the Berne Convention in order to prohibit an agreement with a regressive effect on the minimum standards set in the Convention. Berne Convention, art. 20. In the absence of a corresponding mandatory set of flexibilities, the mandatory minimum standards underpinned by the principle of national treatment is another structural restraint on the sovereign discretion of member states. See Okediji, "International Copyright System," *supra* note 21 at 12.

30 *Berne Convention for the Protection of Literary and Artistic Works,* art. 9(2), 9 September 1886, as revised at Paris on 24 July 1971, and amended on 29 September 1979, 828 U.N.T.S. 221 [hereinafter Berne Convention]. Okediji, "International Copyright System," *supra* note 21 at 13.

31 Paul Goldstein and P. Bernt Hugenholtz, *International Copyright: Principles, Law and Practice,* 3rd ed (New York: Oxford University Press, 2013) at 372 [Goldstein & Hugenhotz, *International Copyright*]. Okediji, "International Copyright system" *supra* note 21 at 12. For example, use of Berne Appendix is an instance of compensated limitations while uncompensated limitations include quotations (art. 10(1)), uses for teaching purposes (10 (2)), press usage (art. 10 *bis* (1)), reporting of current events (art. 10 bis (2)), etc. Okediji &Hugenholtz, "Contours of an International Instrument", *supra* note 28 at 480.

32 Okediji & Hugenholtz, "Contours of an International Instrument" *supra* note 28 at 481 (noting the mandatory nature of the exception for quotation and its rationale to lie in the freedom of expression).

33 Hugenhotz & Okediji, "Contours of International Instrument" *supra* note 28 at 478.

34 Okediji, International Copyright System, *supra* note 21 at 10. Both Hugenholtz and Okediji point out lack of a clear evidence in the historical record. Hugenholtz & Okediji, "Contours of an International Instrument" *supra* note 28 at 478.

35 *Berne Convention, supra* note 30 at art. 2(4).

36 *Ibid* at art. 2*bis* (1).

37 See Sam Ricketson, *The Berne Convention for the Protection of Literary and Artistic Works: 1886–1986* (London: Kluwer, 1987) at para 6.67 [Ricketson, *The Berne Convention*].

38 See *Agreement on Trade-Related Aspects of Intellectual Property Rights, art. 9(2), 15 April 1994, Marrakesh Agreement Establishing the World Trade Organization*, Annex 1C, 33 ILM1125 (1994) [TRIPS Agreement].

39 See J.A.L. Sterling, *World Copyright Law*, 3rd ed (London: Sweet and Maxwell, 2008) at 221.

40 See *TRIPs Agreement, supra* note 38 at 9(2) & 10(2).

41 *Berne Convention, supra* note 30 at art. 2(1) & (8); As Goldstein and Hugenholtz observes, this principle was embedded in the in the Berne Convention's requirements of authorship and originality. Goldstein & Hugenholtz, *supra* note 31 at 220; Okediji, "International Copyright System" *supra* note 21 at 11; Ruth L. Okediji, "Regulation of Creativity under the WIPO Treaties" (2009) 77 Fordham L Rev 2379 at 2394 & fn. 82 [Okediji, "Regulation of Creativity"].

42 Daniel Gervais, *(Re)structuring Copyright: A Comprehensive Path to International Copyright Reform* (Cheltenham: Edward Elgar, 2017) at 94–118 [Gervais, *Restructuring Copyright*].

43 *Berne Convention, supra* note 30 at art. 2(2).
44 Okedi, "International Copyright System" *supra* note 21 at 11. The condition of originality is implicit in the notion of authorship. Hugenholtz & Okediji, "Contours of an International Instrument" *supra* note 28 at 478.
45 See *Berne Convention, supra* note 30 at art. 2(1). In particular, one can infer the implicit requirement from the reading of art. 2(3) that reads "...a literary or artistic work shall be protected as *original works* without prejudice to the copyright in *the original work (emphasis added).*" Okediji, "International Copyright System" *supra* note 21 at 11.
46 See *Berne Convention, supra* note 30 at art. 2(3). See also *TRIPs Agreement,* art. 10(2) in reference to the protection of compilations of data or other material as long as they constitute "intellectual creations." As a manifestation of 'creative choices' made by the author of his own free will, originality is the only adequate and determinative test for the protection of a work. Gervais, *Restructuring Copyright, supra* note 42 at 114–119.
47 For the requirement of originality and its evolution in the U.S legal system, see Robert Brauneis, "The Transformation of Originality in the Progressive-Era Debate over Copyright in News" (2009) 27 Cardozo Arts & Ent LJ 321. For instance, in the U.S an independent creation with a modicum of creativity is required. In the EU, expression 'intellectual creation' is used as a test. In the UK, 'the skill, judgement and/or labor' of the author is the standard. As a middle ground, in Canada, an original work must 'originate from an author and must be the product of an author's exercise of skill and judgement.' Ruth L. Okediji, "Creative Markets and Copyright in the Fourth Industrial Era: Reconfiguring the Public Benefit for a Digital Economy," ICTSD, Issue Paper No. 43 at 15–16 [Okediji, "Creative Markets and Copyright"].
48 See Goldstein & Hugenholtz, *supra* note 31 at 5.
49 *Berne Convention, supra* note 30 at art. 2(2). Okediji, "International Copyright System" *supra* note 21 at 11.
50 Jane Ginsburg, "A Tale of Two Copyrights: Literary Property in Revolutionary France and America" (1990) 64 Tul L Rev 991 at 994. As Ginsburg notes, for an author's right justified by the natural rights or personality theory, "the sole relevant act is the work's creation." *Ibid*; Gervais, *(Re)structuring Copyright, supra* note 42 at 259–260.
51 Gervais, *Restructuring Copyright, supra* note 42 at 120.
52 *Ibid* at 120. Fixation 'serves as an expression of author's intent to create a more or less permanent work' and as a means for its consequent commercial exploitation. *Ibid.* Okediji, "International Copyright system" *supra* note 21 at 11.
53 For instance, fixation is a constitutional requirement for copyright protection in the United States. *Ibid.* Sam Ricketson and Jane Ginsburg, *International Copyright and Neighboring Rights: The Berne Convention and Beyond*, Volume I, 2nd ed (Oxford: Oxford University Press, 2006) at 417–419 [Ricketson & Ginsburg (Vol. I)].
54 *Berne Convention, supra* note 30 at art. 7(1).
55 *Ibid* at art. 7(4).
56 *Ibid* at art. 9(2).
57 Okediji, "International Copyright System" *supra* note 21 at 13–14; Margaret Chon, "Intellectual Property "from Below": Copyright and Capability for Education" (2007) 3 UC Davis L Rev 805 at 842–843 [Chon, "Intellectual Property from Below"].
58 See Sara Bannerman, *International Copyright and Access to Knowledge* (Cambridge: Cambridge University Press, 2016) at 24–25 [Bannerman, *International Copyright*].
59 Okediji, "International Copyright System" *supra* note 21 at 15; Chon, "Intellectual Property 'from Below,'" *supra* note 57 at 835.
60 *Ibid.*
61 Okediji, "International Copyright System" *supra* note 21 at 15; Chon, "Intellectual Property 'from Below'" *supra* note 57 at 829 & 835; Ruth Okediji, "Sustainable Access to Copyrighted to Digital Information Works in Developing Countries, in Keith Maskus & Jerome Reichman, eds, *International Public Goods and Transfer of*

Technology Under a Globalized Intellectual Property Regime (Cambridge: Cambridge University Press, 2005) 142 at 162–166 [Okediji, "Sustainable Access"].

62 Chon, "Intellectual Property 'from Below'" *supra* note 57 at 815 & 838. Informed by the CA, the substantive equality or an "approach from below" not only emphasizes distributive justice outcomes, but also underscores the inclusion of the perspectives and actions of the least empowered people to go beyond a formal equality in shaping a normative legal agenda. *Ibid* at 815.

63 *Ibid* at 833–834 & 843–844. Chon argues that "a decision maker should explicitly consider and defer to a developing country's stated policy of promoting education for development." *Ibid* at 844.

64 *TRIPs Agreement, supra* note 38 at art. 2(1). Daniel Gervais, *The TRIPs Agreement: Drafting History and Analysis* (London: Thomson Reuters/Sweet & Maxwell, 2008) at 175–176 & 213 [Gervais, *The TRIPs Agreement*].

65 See Ricketson & Ginsburg (Vol. I), *supra* note 53 at 850–856. For instance, both computer program (subject matter) and rental right (exclusive right) are introduced.

66 See *TRIPs Agreement, supra* note 38 at art. 1(3) and its fn 1 that indicate the term 'nationals' to include 'legal persons.' In particular, this is evident from a specific reference to the term'right holder' in arts. 8(2), 13 & 14(4). Okediji, "International Copyright System," *supra* note 21 at 1.

67 *TRIPs Agreement, supra* note 38 at art. 13. Ricketson & Ginsburg, *supra* note 53 at 852.

68 For a discussion on the various approaches suggested, see Christophe Geiger, Daniel Gervais & Martin Senftleben, "The Three-Step Test Revisited: How to Use the Test's Flexibility in National Copyright Law" (2014) 29:3 Am U Int'l L Rev 581 at 605–609 [Geiger, Gervais & Senftleben, "The Three-Step Test Revisited"]; Kamiel Koelman, "Fixing the Three Step Test" (2006) 28 Eur IP Rev 407 at 410; Christophe Geiger et al., "Towards a Balanced Interpretation of the 'Three-Step Test' for Copyright Exceptions" (2008) Eur IP Rev 489 [Geiger et al, "Towards a Balanced Interpretation"].

69 See *TRIPs Agreement, supra* note 38 at arts. 41–61 & 63–64.

70 *Ibid* at art. 9(2) & 10(2).

71 Gervais, *The TRIPs Agreement, supra* note 64 at 175. Adopted within the framework of art. 20 of the Berne Convention, the TRIPs Agreement can cannot derogate from existing obligations while it "can curtail flexibilities contained in the pre-exiting conventions." The main reason is that most flexibilities were not part of the existing obligations. *Ibid.*

72 See Peter K. Yu, "The Objectives and Principles of the TRIPS Agreement" (2009) 46 Hous L Rev 979 at 1018–1046; As Correa notes, arts. 7 & 8 constitute "a central piece for the implementation and interpretation of the TRIPs Agreement." Carlos M. Correa, *Trade Related Aspects of Intellectual Property Rights: A Commentary on the TRIPS Agreement* (Oxford: Oxford University Press, 2007) at 108 [Correa, *Trade Related Aspects*].

73 See TRIPs Agreement, *supra* note 38 at art. 8. Gervais, *The TRIPs Agreement, supra* note 64 at 209–210; Correa, *Trade Related Aspects, supra* note 72 at 105–107; Yu, "The Objectives and Principles", *supra* note 72 at 1008–1012.

74 Gervais, *The TRIPs Agreement, supra* note 64 at 203–224 & 207; Yu, "The Objectives and Principles," *supra* note 72 at 1000–1008; Correa, *Trade Related Aspects, supra* note 72 at 105–106.

75 Yu, "The Objectives and Principles," *supra* note 72 at 981; James Boyle, "A Manifesto on WIPO and the Future of Intellectual Property" (2004) 9 Duke L & Tech Rev at 3–4.

76 Correa, *Trade Related Aspects, supra* note 72 at 105–106; Hugenholtz & Okediji, "The Contours of an International Instrument" *supra* note 28 at 477–489; Yu, "TRIPs and Its Discontents", *supra* note 22 at 387; Jerome H Reichman, "From Free Riders to Fair Followers: Global Competition under the TRIPs Agreement" (1997) 29 NYUJ Int'l 7

Pol 11 at 28 (claiming the existence of sufficient 'wiggle room' in the TRIPs Agreement for public interest in free competition).

77 Yu, "TRIPs and Its Discontents," *supra* note 22 at 387–395; Yu, "The Objectives and Principles," *supra* note 72 at 1018–1046; Grosse Ruse-Khan, "The (Non)Use of Treaty Object and Purpose in Intellectual property Disputes in the WTO" (2012) Max Planck Institute for Intellectual Property and Competition Law Research Paper No. 11–15 at 1–35; Gervais, *The TRIPs Agreement, supra* note 64 at 202-11; Correa, *Trade Related Aspects, supra* note 72 at 105–109; Carlos Correa, *Intellectual Property Rights, the WTO and Developing Countries: The TRIPs Agreement and Policy Options* (London & New York: Zed Books, 2000) 6–8 & 21; Jerome Reichman, "Intellectual Property in the Twenty-First Century: Will the Developing Countries Lead or Follow?" 46:4 Hous L Rev 1115 at 1125–1176 & 1182 (also emphasizing the need for developing countries' optimal utilization of the flexibilities).

78 *TRIPs Agreement, supra* note 38 at art. 8. The measures to be adopted by members under art. 8 are required to be "consistent with the provision of the Agreement." Gervais, *The TRIPs Agreement, supra* note 64 at 204 & 209; Yu, "Objectives and Principles," *supra* note 72 at 1013–1018.

79 *TRIPs Agreement, supra* note 38 at art. 10. Ricketson & Ginsburg (Vol. I), *supra* note 53 at 514–522.

80 *TRIPs Agreement, supra* note 38 at art. 11. Ricketson & Ginsburg (Vol. I), *supra* note 53 at 690–692.

81 *TRIPs Agreement, supra* note 38 at 9(1). Ricketson & Ginsburg (Vol. I), *supra* note 53 at 615–619.

82 *TRIPs Agreement, supra* note 38 at art. 9(1). Gervais, *The TRIPs Agreement, supra* note 64 at 213; Okediji, "International Copyright system," *supra* note 21 at 15–16 & 19; Gervais, *Restructuring Copyright, supra* note 42 at 41–43.

83 Gervais, *The TRIPs Agreement, supra* note 64 at 198–201; Correa, *Trade Related Aspects, supra* note 72 at 78–89.

84 Okediji, "International Copyright System," *supra* note 21 at 16–17.

85 *Ibid* at 17–19. Subject to the existence of a robust competition law regime and a competitive market, Okediji points out the potential of art. 40 to serve as a policy tool in order to facilitate access to affordable copyrighted works. *Ibid.*

86 See generally Peter Yu, "The TRIPs Enforcement Dispute" (2011) 89 Neb L Rev 1046–1131[Yu, "The TRIPs Enforcement"]; Jerome Reichman, "Enforcing the Enforcement Procedures of the TRIPs Agreement: Comments" (1997) 37 Va J Int'l L 335–356. See Correa, *Trade Related Aspects, supra* note 72 at 410–450.

87 Okediji, "The Regulation of Creativity," *supra* note 41 at 2388–2389; Mihaly Ficsor, *The Law of Copyright and the Internet: The 1996 WIPO Treaties, Their Interpretation and Implementation* (Oxford: Oxford University Press, 2002) at 409–410 & 591 [Ficsor, *The Law of Copyright*]. See *World Intellectual Property Organization [WIPO] Copyright Treaty*, art. 1, 20 December 1996, 36 I.L.M. 65 (entered into force 6 March 2002) [hereinafter WCT] & Berne Convention, *supra* note 30 at art. 20; WIPO Performances and Phonograms Treaty, art. 1, 20 December 1996, 36 I.L.M. 76 (entered into force 20 May 2002) [WPPT] & Rome Convention, *supra* note 24 at art. 22.

88 Not only have the WIPO Treaties carried forward the new rights that emerged under the TRIPs Agreement, the contracting parties which are members to the TRIPs Agreement have also issued a set of agreed statements to ensure consistency with the Agreement. For WCT, this is evident from the agreed statements concerning art. 4 (computer programs), art. 5 (databases), and art. 7 (rental rights).

89 Okediji, "The Regulation of Creativity," *supra* note 41 at 2388–2391(noting the in-built maximalist approach for an ever-increasing protection of authors' right). See Ricketson, *The Berne Convention, supra* note 37 at 683–685; Berne Convention, *supra*

note 30 at art. 20; Rome Convention, *supra* note 24 at art. 22 (stating states' right to enter into special agreements 'so far as such agreements *grant more extensive rights*....').
90 WCT, *supra* note 87 at art. 8; see also WPPT, *supra* note 87 at arts. 10 & 14.
91 See the Agreed Statements concerning the arts. 4, 5 & 7 of the WCT; Okediji, "The Regulation of Creativity," *supra* note 41 at 2393–2395. While they can serve as source of interpretation for TRIPs Agreement, as Okediji notes, the provisions of the WCT are however not formally subject to the WTO dispute settlement mechanism. *Ibid* at 2394.
92 WCT, *supra* note 87 at arts. 11 & 12; WPPT, *supra* note 87 at arts. 18 & 19.
93 Okediji, "The Regulation of Creativity," *supra* note 41 at 2400–2401; Jane Ginsburg, "Legal Protection of Technological Measures Protecting Works of Authorship: International Obligations and the US Experience" (2005) 29 Columbia Journal of Law & Arts 11 at 20 [Ginsburg, "Legal Protection of Technological Measures"]. For example, outside copyright law, *sui generis* law or unfair competition law can be used to comply with the obligation.
94 WCT, *supra* note 87 at art 10; WPPT, *supra* note 87 at art. 16.
95 WCT, *supra* note 87 at Preamble, para 5; WPPT, *supra* note 87 at Preamble, para 4.
96 See *Vienna Convention on the Law of Treaties*, 23 May 1969, 1155 UNTS 331, 8 ILM 679 (entered into force 27 January 1980) at arts. 31(1) & (2) [Vienna Convention]; See Sir Ian Sinclair, *The Vienna Convention on the Law of Treaties*, 2nd ed (Oxford: Manchester University Press, 1984) at 119–135.
97 Okediji, "The Regulation of Creativity," *supra* note 41 at 2400–2410. As Okediji remarks, "the WIPO Internet Treaties have considerably fell short [in their mission] to provide a relevant and credible source of norms to facilitate knowledge creation in the global digital context." *Ibid* at 2380; Gervais, *Restructuring Copyright*, *supra* note 42 at 55–56 (pointing out the reference to maintaining 'balance' as a 'rhetorical nod').
98 Laurence R. Helfer, et al., *The World Blind Union Guide to the Marrakesh Treaty: Facilitating Access to Books for Print-Disabled Individuals* (New York: Oxford University Press, 2017) at xix [Helfer et al, *The World Blind Union Guide*].
99 *Ibid* at 1, 15 & 21; Molly K. Land, "The Marrakesh Treaty as "Bottom Up" Lawmaking: Supporting Local Human Rights Action on IP Policies "(2018) 8 UC Irvine L Rev 513 at 548–550; *Marrakesh Treaty to Facilitate Access to Published Works for Persons Who Are Blind, Visually Impaired, or Otherwise Print Disabled*, Preamble, para 1, 27 June 2013, 52 I.L.M1312 (entered into force 30 June 2016) [Marrakesh Treaty].
100 *Universal Declaration of Human Rights*, GA Res 217A (III), UNGAOR, 3d Sess, 1st plen mtg, UN Doc A/810 (12 December 1948) at art. 26 [UDHR]; *UN Convention on the Rights of Persons with Disabilities*, art. 24, 30 March 2007, 2515 UNTS 3 (entered into force 03 May 2008) [CRPD].
101 UDHR, *supra* note 100 at art. 27; CRPD, *supra* note 100 at art. 30.
102 Helfer et al, *The World Blind Union, supra* note 98 at 8–19. As observed by Helfer and others, the "overarching object and purpose" of the Marrakesh Treaty is "to promote the human rights of individuals with print disabilities by expanding access to copyrighted works." *Ibid* at 13.
103 *Ibid* at xviii, 1 & 8–15. *See generally* Land, *supra* note 99.
104 *Marrakesh Treaty*, *supra* note 99 at Preamble, para 3.
105 *Ibid* at para 1 & 11.
106 *Ibid* at para 9.
107 *Ibid* at para 2 & 9. The enjoyment of "the right to education and the opportunity to conduct research" are noted along with other rights for "the complete development of persons with visual impairments or with other print disabilities." *Ibid* at para 2.
108 *Ibid* at arts. 4, 5, 6, 7 & 9; Land, *supra* note 99 at 547; see Helfer et al, *The World Blind Union Guide*, *supra* note 98 at 38–66.

109 Helfer et al., *The World Blind Union Guide, supra* note 98 at 67–70. *Marrakesh Treaty, supra* note 99 at Preamble, para 10.
110 Helfer et al., *The World Blind Union Guide, supra* note 98 at 71–74. It is argued that a flexible application of the three-step test can further be informed by international human rights law, including art. 30(3) of the CRPD that obligates states 'to take all appropriate steps" to prohibit unreasonable or discriminatory barrier on access to cultural materials. *Ibid* at 73.
111 See *Beijing Treaty on Audiovisual Performances,* Preamble, paras 1 & 3, 24 June 2012, 51 ILM 1211(2012)[*Beijing Treaty*] (not in effect at the moment).
112 *Ibid* at para 2. Silke von Lewinski, "The Beijing Treaty on Audiovisual Performances" (--) Max Plank Research Institute for Intellectual Property and Competition Law Research Paper No. 13–08 at 8–9 (noting the limited impact but 'symbolic value' of the reference to the WIPO DA for developing countries).
113 *Beijing Treaty, supra* note 111 at para 5.
114 *Ibid* at art. 13.
115 *Marrakesh Treaty, supra* note 99 at Preamble, para 3.
116 See Myra Tawfik, "History in the Balance: Copyright and Access to Knowledge," in Michael Geist, ed, *From Radical Extremism to Balanced Copyright: Canadian Copyright and the Digital Agenda* (Toronto: Irwin Law, 2010) 69 at 70–74 [Tawfik, "History in the Balance"]; Ronan Deazley, *On the Origin of the Right to Copy: Charting the Movement of Copyright Law in the Eighteenth Century* (1695–1775) (Oxford: Hart publishing, 2004) at xxiv. Deazley notes "the encouragement and spread of education with the continued production of useful books" as an aspect of public interest that underpinned the Statute of Anne. *Ibid.*
117 Sam Ricketson, "WIPO Study on Limitations and Exceptions of Copyright and Related Rights in the Digital Environment, Standing Committee on Copyright and Related Rights," at 14–15, Ninth session, Geneva, June 23–27, 2003, online: <www.wipo.int/edocs/mdocs/copyright/en/sccr_9/sccr_9_7.pdf> (last visited on 10 April 2021) [Ricketson, "WIPO Study on L&Es"].
118 Ricketson & Ginsburg (Vol. I), *supra* note 53 at 793.
119 *Ibid* at 794.
120 *Ibid* at 795.
121 *Ibid* at 793–795; Ricketson, "WIPO Study on L & Es," *supra* note 117 at 14.
122 *Ibid* at 792 & 794. The contemplated circumstances may justify the use of an artistic work or a short literary work in its entirety. *Ibid* at 794.
123 Ricketson, "WIPO Study on L & Es," *supra* note 117 at 15.
124 Ricketson & Ginsburg (Vol. I), *supra* note 53 at 794.
125 Gervais, *Restructuring Copyright, supra* note 42 at 90–91.
126 *Alberta (Education) v Canadian Copyright Licensing Agency (Access Copyright),* 2012 SCC 37; *University of Oxford v. Rameshwari Photocopy Services (2016)* 2016 SCC OnLine Del 5128 (India); Okediji, "Creative Market and Copyright" *supra* note 47 at 35 & 39.
127 Ricketson & Ginsburg, *supra* note 53 at 792–793; Okediji, "International Copyright System" *supra* note 21 at 21.
128 Ricketson & Ginsburg (Vol. I), *supra* note 53 at 792–793.
129 *Ibid* at 793 & 858. Ricketson and Ginsburg argue that the reference to 'compatible with fair practice' may correspond to the second and third steps of the three-step test while its limited scope is regarded to be within the first step. *Ibid* at 858. Gervais, *(Re) structuring Copyright, supra* note 42 at 90–93 & 227–229. In order to determine the issue of 'fair practice,' Gervais opines that 'a WTO panel is likely to apply a rule of reason compatible with the three-step test.' *Ibid* at 93.
130 Okediji, "International Copyright System," *supra* note 21 at 14; Chon, "Intellectual Property from Below," *supra* note 57 at 843; Ricketson, "WIPO Study on L & Es," *supra* note 117 at 21.

131 Geiger, Gervais, & Senftleben, "The Three-Step Test Revisited," *supra* note 68 at 617–618 (noting the restrictive effect of the test upon specific exceptions and limitations).
132 Correa, *The Trade Related Aspect, supra* note 72 at 145; Pamela Samuelson, "The US Digital Agenda at WIPO" (1997) 37 Va J Int'l L 369 at 370 & 402–403.
133 Correa, *Trade Related Aspects, supra* note 72 at 139.
134 Chon, "Intellectual Property 'from Below,'" *supra* note 57 at 843; Andres Moncayo von Hase, "The Application and Interpretation of the Agreement on Trade-Related Aspects of Intellectual Property Rights," in Carlos M. Correa & Abdulqawi A. Yusuf eds., *Intellectual Property and International Trade: The TRIPS Agreement* (The Netherlands: Kluwer, 1998) 93 at 134.
135 Chon, "Intellectual Property 'from Below,'" *supra* note 57 at 844.
136 Ricketson & Ginsburg (Vol. I), *supra* note 53 at 785–786.
137 *Ibid* at 785 & 786. That is, its scope is not limited only to copies of the works made available, but also extends to the public performance or broadcast of dramatic or musical works. *Ibid* at 785.
138 *Berne Convention, supra* note 30 at art. 10(1).
139 Ricketson & Ginsburg (Vol. I), *supra* note 53 at 786 & 788.
140 *Ibid.*
141 Okedji, "International Copyright System," *supra* note 21 at 14.
142 Ricketson & Ginsburg (Vol. I), *supra* note 53 at 786–788.
143 *Ibid.*
144 *Ibid* at 786 & 788; Okediji, "International Copyright System," *supra* note 21 at 13. In concert to other limitations under the Berne convention, Okediji observes that "Article 10(1) is not limited by prescribed uses—quotations may be made for any purpose so long as they are done within the stipulated context (citation omitted)." *Ibid.*
145 Ricketson & Ginsburg (Vol. I), *supra* note 53 at 788. From among the various uses, the quotation exception can be used liberally for 'books reviews, criticism and news commentary. Okediji, "International Copyright System" *supra* note 21 at 13.
146 Ricketson & Ginsburg (Vol. I), *supra* note 53 at 788–789; Goldstein & Hugenholtz, *supra* note 31 at 392.
147 See Gervais, *Restructuring Copyright, supra* note 42 at 237–256.
148 Ricketson & Ginsburg (Vol. I), *supra* note 53 at 844–847.
149 Hugenholtz & Okediji, "Contours", *supra* note 28 at 480. In most jurisdictions, national exception for private use is also regarded as an instance of a statutory compulsory license without remuneration. Ruth Okediji, "Sustainable Access to Copyrighted to Digital Information Works in Developing Countries, in Keith Maskus & Jerome Reichman, eds, *International Public Goods and Transfer of Technology Under a Globalized Intellectual Property Regime* (Cambridge: Cambridge University Press, 2005)142 at 147-52 [Okediji, "Sustainable Access"].
150 Berne Convention, *supra* note 30 at art. 11 *bis,* 13 & 14 *bis* 2(b). *WIPO Guide to the Berne Convention, supra* note 28 at 70 & 79–80; Michael Freegrad, "The Berne Convention, Compulsory Licensing and Collecting Societies" (1986) 11 Columbia-VLA Journal of Law and the arts. 137 at 140–142; Okedji, "International Copyright System" *supra* note 21 at 14–15 & 20. For detailed discussions, see Ricketson & Ginsburg, *supra* note 53 at 808–824.
151 See Carlos Correa, "Intellectual Property Rights and the Use of Compulsory Licenses: Options for Developing Countries" (1999) South Centre Working Paper No. 5 at 4–5; *WIPO Guide to the Berne Convention, supra* note 28 at 70 & 80.
152 Ricketson & Ginsburg (Vol. I), *supra* note 53 at 819 (pointing out the emphasis placed upon the educational and informatory role of broadcasting).
153 Okediji, "International Copyright System" *supra* note 21 at 15–16; Okediji, "Sustainable Access" *supra* note 149 at 162–169 & 177–178; Chon, "Intellectual

Property from Below" *supra* note 57 at 829–835; Gervais, *Restructuring Copyright, supra* note 42 at 43–46.

154 Berne Appendix to Paris Act of Berne Convention (1971), at arts. I–IV; Gervais, *Restructuring Copyright, supra* note 42 at 341-44; Okediji, "Sustainable Access, "*supra* note 149 at 163–169.

155 Okediji, "International Copyright System" *supra* note 21 at 15–16 & 29; Okediji, "Sustainable Access" *supra* note 149 at 162–169; Chon, Intellectual Property 'from Below', *supra* note 57 at 829 & 835; Susan Isikoˇ Strba, *International Copyright Law and Access to Education in Developing Countries: Exploring Multilateral Legal and Quasi-Legal Solutions* (Leiden: Martinus Nijhoff, 2012) at 203–240.

156 Okediji, "International Copyright System," *supra* note 21 at 19; Okediji, "Sustainable Access" *supra* note 149 at 166–168.

157 Jeremy de Beer & Robert Tomkowicz, "Exhaustion of Intellectual Property Rights in Canada" (2009) 25 CIPR 3 at 6.

158 *Ibid* at 7 (citation omitted).

159 Okediji, "Creative Markets and Copyright," *supra* note 47 at 24; see Peter Mezei, *Copyright Exhaustion: Law and Policy in the United States and the European Union* (Cambridge: Cambridge University Press, 2018) at 6–58.

160 Goldstein & Hugenholtz, *supra* note 31 at 311. For its application in the digital environment, as the emerging jurisprudence in the EU indicates, the principle of exhaustion covers *both tangible and tangible copies* of works, such as computer programs. Mezei, *supra* note 159 at 94–98; Ricketson & Ginsburg (Vol. I), *supra* note 53 at 658.

161 de Beer & Tomkowicz, *supra* note 157 at 7–8. Nonetheless, the scope of the principle may be limited for copyrighted works by a statute that can exclude uses such as rental, lease and lending of certain works including computer programs or in the case of a patent, an act of making the invention that corresponds to a reproduction right in a copyright. *Ibid* at 8–9.

162 *Ibid.* In contrast to art. 6 of the WCT, it should be noted that there is no general recognition of the distribution right in the Berne Convention. Ricketson & Ginsburg (Vol. I), *supra* note 53 at 659, 666 & 694.

163 *Ibid.* Frederick Abbot, Thomas Cottier & Francis Gurry, *International Intellectual Property in an Integrated World Economy* (New York: Aspen Publishers, 2007) at 513.

164 *Ibid.*

165 *Ibid.*

166 See Domenico Sindico, "On Parallel Importation, TRIPs and European Court of Justice Decisions" (2002) 5:4 The Journal of World Intellectual Property 505–516; Correa, *Trade Related Aspects, supra* note 72 at 79. de Beer & Tomkowicz, *supra* note 157 at 10–11.

167 *Kistaeng v. John Wiley & Sons, Inc.,* 568 U.S. 133 S.Ct. 1351(2013); Shubha Gosh, "The Implementation of Exhaustion Policies: Lessons from National Experiences" (2013) International Centre for Trade and Sustainable Development Issue Paper No.40 at 21–23.

168 Gervais, *TRIPs Agreement, supra* note 64 at 199.

169 Mezei, *supra* note 159 at 21. See Gervais, *TRIPs Agreement, supra* note 64 at 198–201.

170 See Okediji, "International Copyright System" *supra* note 21 at 2; Okediji, "Creative Markets and Copyright' *supra* note 47 at 24.

171 Ruth Anthony Reese, "The First Sale Doctrine in the Era of Digital Networks" (2003) 44 Boston College L Rev 577 at 585–589. For consumers, affordable retail price competition, secondary markets, rental markets and public lending are the benefits that drive from the application of the principle of exhaustion. *Ibid.*

172 Gervais, *TRIPs Agreement, supra* note 64 at 200. The relevant provisions cited in this regard are art. 16 on seizure of infringing copies despite its lawful nature in the country of importation, art. 13(3) on the seizure of sounding recordings imported without

permission and art. IV(4)(a) of the Berne Appendix. In contrast, there is no explicit provisions of this sort nor is there a specific provision on the principle under other copyright treaties. *Ibid* at 201.

173 TRIPs Agreement, *supra* note 38 art. 6; Correa, *Trade Related Aspects, supra* note 72 at 69. Nonetheless, the application of the preferred principle of exhaustion is subject to the non-discriminatory principles (arts. 3 & 4) under the Agreement. In the Doha declaration on Public Health, the principle of international exhaustion has been confirmed to enable member states to benefit from the flexibilities with regard to patents. *Ibid* at 80 & 86.

174 Okediji, "Creative Markets and Copyright, *supra* note 47 at 31. As Okediji notes, the principle 'plays a critical role in the overall architecture of copyright law by ensuring that secondary markets of lower-cost copyrighted goods remain available to the consuming public." *Ibid*. Chon, "Intellectual Property from Below" *supra* note 57 at 839.

175 Correa, *Trade Related Aspects, supra* note 72 at 86–89. Gervais, *TRIPs Agreement, supra* note 64 at 200.

176 Okediji, "Creative Markets and Copyright" *supra* note 47 at 28–31. In the absence of an action to adapt the principle to the digital environment, Okediji observes that "the gradual shift to digital content distribution threatens the vitality of exhaustion and its concomitant benefits." *Ibid* at 31.

177 Ricketson & Ginsburg (Vol. I), *supra* note 53 at 844–847.

178 TRIPs Agreement, *supra* note 38 at art. 40.

179 Goldstein & Hugenholtz, *supra* note at 31 at 403–405.

180 Okediji, "International Copyright System, *supra* note 21 at 14.

181 *Ibid*.

182 Okediji, "International Copyright System," *supra* note 21 at 33.

183 *Ibid*.

184 See generally Nathan Davis, "Presumed Assent: The Judicial Acceptance of Click-wrap" (2007) 22 BTLJ 577; Dale Clapperton & Stephen Corones, "Unfair Terms in 'Click-wrap' and Other Electronic Contracts" (2007) 35 Aust'l Bus L Rev 156.

185 Okediji, "International Copyright System" supra note 21 at 17.

186 *Ibid*. Correa, *Trade Related Aspects, supra* note 72 at 398–404.

187 Correa, *Trade Related Aspects, supra* note 72 at 399. Ricketson & Ginsburg, *supra* note 53 at 846-47; For a jurisprudence on refusal to license as a form of anti-competitive practices, see *Joined Cases C-241/91 P radio Telefis Eirean and Independent Television Publications Ltd v. EC Commission* [1995] ECR I-743, [1995] All ER (EC) 4161;

188 Okediji, "International Copyright System" *supra* note 21 at 16–19. Its potential to facilitate a bulk access is however subject to the existence of a robust competition policy and law with competent enforcement authorities both of which are often missing in the developing countries. *Ibid* at 17–18.

189 *Ibid* at 16–18.

190 *Ibid* at 33.

191 *Ibid* at 17–18 & 33; Chon, "Intellectual Property from Below" *supra* note 57 at 821–828.

192 Okediji, "International Copyright System" *supra* note 21 at 17–18.

193 *Ibid* at 22.

194 Bannerman, *supra* note 58 at 75–76. Chris Armstrong *et al*., eds, *Access to Knowledge in Africa: The Role of Copyright* (Cape Town: University of Cape Town Press, 2010) at 324 & 335–336.

195 *Ibid*. Ricketson & Ginsburg (Vol. I), *supra* note 53 at 783; Geiger, Gervais & Senftelben, "The Three-Step Test Revisited," *supra* note 68 at 617.

196 Bannerman, *supra* note 58 at 75–77.

197 Okedjij, "International Copyright System" *supra* note 21 at 33. Gervais, *Restructuring Copyright, supra* note 42 at 222–223.
198 Okediji, "International Copyright System" *supra* note 21 at 33.
199 *Ibid.*
200 *Ibid* at 27 & 33.
201 Correa, *Trade Related Aspects, supra* note 72 at 35.
202 *Ibid* at 151. See also WTO Report of the Panel WT/DS160/R of 15 June 2000 on *United States-Section 110(5) of the US Copyright Act*, para 6. 108–109.
203 WTO Panel, *supra* note 202 at para 6. 109.
204 *Ibid* at para 6.109. The WTO Panel indicated the interpretation to suggest 'a narrow scope as well as an exceptional or distinctive objective.' *Ibid.*
205 Correa, *Trade Related Aspects, supra* note 72 at 151.
206 Ricketson, *The Berne Convention, supra* note 37 at 482.
207 Ricketson & Ginsburg (Vol. I), *supra* note 53 at 767.
208 Gervais, *Restructuring Copyright, supra* note 42 at 64–66. For instance, Okediji points out the apparent inconsistency between fair use and the test. Ruth Okediji, Towards International Fair Use Doctrine (2000) 39 Columbia Journal of Transnational Law 75 [Okediji, "Towards International Fair Use Doctrine"]. In contrast, Correa points out its possible compliance with the test. Correa, *Trade Related Aspects, supra* note 72 at 146–148; In a recent work, Geiger, Gervais and Senftleben, suggest the fair use to bee 'seen as three steps forming a whole' to justify a legislative approach of using open-ended exceptions and limitations. Geiger, Gervais & Senflteben, "The Three-Step Test Revisited," *supra* note 68 at 581–626.
209 Gervais, *Restructuring Copyright, supra* note 42 at 64; Goldstein & Hugenholtz, *supra* note 31 at 380–383; Ricketson & Ginsburg (Vol. I), *supra* note 53 at 766; Jane Ginsburg, "Towards Supranational Copyright Law? The WTO Panel: Decision and the 'Three-Step Test' for Copyright Exceptions" (2001) 187 RIDA 3.
210 WTO Panel, *supra* note 202 at 44.
211 Ficsor, *The Law of Copyright, supra* note 87 at section 5.56.
212 Gervais, *Restructuring Copyright, supra* note 42 at 66; Ricketson & Ginsburg (Vol. I), *supra* note 53 at 768-69; WTO Panel, *supra* note 202 at para 6.178–80; Ficsor, *The Law of Copyright, supra* note 87 at 285.
213 WTO Panel, *supra* note 202 at para 6.180. Ricketson & Ginsburg (Vol. I), *supra* note 53 at 769.
214 WTO Panel, *supra* note 202 at para 6.183; The consideration of both actual and potential impacts of an exception or limitation was emphasized in the ruling. *Ibid* at para 6.183–84; Gervais, *Restructuring Copyright, supra* note 42 at 67; Ficsor, *The Law of Copyright, supra* note 87 at 516.
215 WTO Panel, *supra* note 202 at para 6.182.
216 Gervais, *Restructuring Copyright, supra* note 42 at 88–89 & 213; Ricketson & Ginsburg (Vol. I), *supra* note 53 at 779–782.
217 See Gervais, *Restructuring Copyright, supra* note 42 at 67; Goldstein & Hugenholtz, *supra* note 31 at 378; Ficsor, *The Law of Copyright, supra* note 87 at 516;
218 Ricketson & Ginsburg (Vol. I), *supra* note 53 at 773 (pointing out the interference with the normal exploitation, both economic and non-economic, as the end of the matter and a sufficient ground for prohibiting an exception).
219 Sharon E. Foster, "The Conflict between the Human Right to Education and Copyright" in Paul Torremans, ed, *Intellectual Property and Human Rights: Enhanced Edition of Copyright and Human Rights* (The Netherlands: Kluwer Law International, 2008) 287 at 30–3-06; see Wendy Gordon, "Fair Use as a Market Failure: A structural and Economic Analysis of the Betamax and Its Predecessors" (1982) 82 Colum L Rev 1600 at 1614–1621[Gordon, "Fair Use"]; Gervais, *Restructuring Copyright, supra* note 42 at 71.
220 See Gervais, *Restructuring Copyright, supra* note 42 at 88–93.

221 Ricketson & Ginsburg (Vol. I), *supra* note 53 at 771–772.
222 *Ibid* at 772–773.
223 *Ibid* at 772.
224 *Ibid* at 772–773. It is also noted that 'normal exploitation' is of no guidance to assess the non-economic normative justifications the determination of which will be matter for national legislation, subject to a public interest justification. *Ibid* at 773.
225 For the WTO's possible considerations of human rights in its jurisprudence, see Gabrielle Marceau, "WTO Dispute Settlement and Human Rights" (2002) 13:4 Eur J Int'l L 753–814.
226 Correa, *Trade Related Aspects*, *supra* note 72 at 105–108 (articulating the possible variance in the notion of 'the public interest' contemplated in art. 8(1). As he notes, "the definition of what constitutes the 'public interest' rests with the concerned member." *Ibid* at 105.
227 Gervais, *Restructuring Copyright*, *supra* note 42 at 67.
228 Geiger, Gervais & Senftleben, "The Three-Step Test Revisited," *supra* note 68 at 604. For Ricketson and Ginsburg, the second step seems to be more important. Ricketson & Ginsburg (Vol. I), *supra* note 53 at 767.
229 WTO Panel, *supra* note 202 at para 6.223. As articulated in the ruling, "'interest' may encompass a legal right or title to a property or to use or benefit of a property (including intellectual property)." *Ibid.*
230 *Ibid* at para 6.224. As the WTO Panel noted, "'legitimate'…. has also the connotation of legitimacy from a more normative perspective, in the context of calling for the protection of interests that are justifiable in the light of the objectives that underlie the protection of exclusive rights." *Ibid.* Ricketson & Ginsburg (Vol. I), *supra* note 53 at 774.
231 Gervais, *Restructuring Copyright*, *supra* note 42 at 67; Martin Senftleben, *Copyright, Limitations and the Three Step Test: An Analysis of the Three Step Test in International and EC Copyright Law* (The Netherlands: Kluwer, 2004) at 226–227.
232 WTO Panel, *supra* note 202 at para 6.229.
233 Ricketson & Ginsburg (Vol. I), *supra* note 53 at 775–777; Gervais, *Restructuring Copyright*, *supra* note 42 at 69; Goldstein & Hugenholtz, *supra* note 31 at 379.
234 Correa, *Trade Related Aspects*, *supra* note 72 at 155; WTO Panel, *supra* note 202 at para 6.229, fn 205.
235 Foster, *supra* note 219 at 306. Given the issue of a market failure in the developing countries, Fosters regards the relationship between copyright and the right to education as an instance of 'false conflict' to point out the lack of actual conflict. *Ibid* at 305–306; see Gordon, *supra* note 219 at 1618–1619.
236 Gervais, *Restructuring Copyright*, *supra* note 42 at 69–70 (noting a public interest imperative for a government to impose justifiable exception to copyright despite a loss of revenue for copyright holders); Daniel Gervais, "Towards a New Core International Copyright Norm: The Reverse Three-Step Test," (2005) 9 Marq Intell Prop L Rev 1 at 18–19 (2005) [Gervais, "The Reverse Three-Step Test"]; Ricketson & Ginsburg (Vol. I), *supra* note 53 at 775; Ficsor, *The Law of Copyright*, *supra* note 87 at 516.
237 Daniel Gervais, "Intellectual Property and Human Rights: Learning to Live Together," in Paul Torremans, ed, *Intellectual Property and Human Rights*, *supra* note 219, at 18 [Gervais, "Intellectual Property and Human Rights"].
238 Goldstein & Hugenholtz, *supra* note 31 at 378. See —Declaration: Balanced Interpretation of the "Three Step Test" in Copyright Law 39 IIC 107 (2008).
239 Martin Senftleben," Towards a Horizontal Standard for Limiting Intellectual Property Rights? WTO Panel Reports Shed Light on the Three-Step Test in Copyright Law and Related Tests in Patent and Trademark Law" (2006) 37 International Review of Intellectual Property & Competition Law 407 at 438 [Senftleben, "Towards a Horizontal Standard"]; Christophe Geiger, "Fundamental Rights: A Safeguard for the Coherence of Intellectual Property Law?" (2004) International Review of Intellectual Property & Competition Law

268 at 277. For a discussion on the principle of proportionality, see Henning Ruse-Khan, "Proportionality and Balancing within the Objectives for Intellectual Property," in Torremans, ed, *Intellectual Property and Human Rights, supra* note 219 at 161–193.

240 Christophe Geiger et al., "Declaration: A Balanced Interpretation of the Three-Step Test in Copyright Law" (2010) 1 Journal of Intellectual Property, Information Technology and E-Commerce 119 at 121 [hereinafter Geiger et al., Declaration].

241 *Ibid* at 119–120.

242 Geiger, Gervais and Senftleben, "The Three-Step Test Revisited," *supra* note 68 at 609–610.

243 For the critique on this line, see Mihály Ficsor, "Munich Declaration on the Three-Step Test–Respectable Objective, Wrong Way to Try to Achieve It" (2012), cited in Geiger, Gervais and Senftleben, "The Three-Step Test Revisited," *supra* note 68 at 609.

244 Geiger, "Declaration" *supra* note 240 at 120; Geiger, Gervais and Senftleben, "The Three-Step Test Revisited" *supra* note 68 at 610–611; Andre Lucas, "For a Reasonable Interpretation of the Three-Step Test" (2010) 32 Eur IP Rev 277 at 277–278.

245 Gervais, *Restructuring Copyright, supra* note 42 at 64.

246 Ficsor, *The Law of Copyright, supra* note 87 at 517–520.

247 See Okediji, "International Copyright System," *supra* note 21 at 5 & 7.

248 *Ibid* at 9.

249 *Ibid.*

250 Daniel Gervais, "TRIPs and Development," in *Intellectual Property, Trade and Development: Strategies to Optimize Economic Development in a TRIPs-Plus Era* (Oxford: Oxford University Press, 2007) 3 at 4; Gervais, *Restructuring Copyright, supra* note 42 at 284.

251 Geiger, Gervais & Senftleben, "The Three-Step Test Revisited," supra note 68 at 582.

252 *Ibid* at 617.

253 See Gervais, "The Reverse Three-Step Test", *supra* note 236 at 27–35.

254 Martin Senftleben, "The International Three-Step Test: A model Provision for EC Fair Use Legislation" (2010) 1 Journal of Intellectual Property and Information Technology 67 at 75 [Senftleben, "The International Three-Step Test"].

255 *Ibid* at 75 & 77.

256 Correa, *Trade Related Aspects, supra* note 72 at 139.

257 See Okediji, "International Copyright System," *supra* note 21 at 7–9.

258 See Correa, *Trade Related Aspects, supra* note 137 at 134–145; TRIPs Agreement, art. 13 (stating '[m]embers *shall confine*...) [emphasis added]; Guido Westkamp, "The Three-Step Test and Copyright Limitations in Europe: European Copyright Law between Approximation and National Decision Making" (2008) 56 Journal of Copyright Society of USA 1 at 3–12.

259 Gervais, *Restructuring Copyright, supra* note 42 at 59.

260 Okediji, "International Copyright System," *supra* note 21 at 1–2 & 7.

261 *Ibid* at 7–9.

262 Ricketson & Ginsburg (Vol. I), *supra* note 53 at 868 & 871–872.

263 *Ibid* at 868–869. As Ricketson & Ginsburg recount, what was suggested in the initial proposal may imply greater restrictions on the scope of permissible exceptions. *Ibid. Comp.* Correa, *Trade Related Aspects, supra* note 72 at 143–145 (arguing that the test under art. 10 of WCT and art. 13 of the TRIPs Agreement does not impose additional requirements on those specific exceptions under the Berne Convention).

264 *Agreed Statement* to art. 10 of the WCT, *supra* note 87.

265 Helfer et al, *The World Blind Union Guide, supra* note 98 at 8–15.

266 Ricketson & Ginsburg (Vol. I), *supra* note 53 at 777–778 (in the absence of a specific

reference to published work or otherwise, the three-step test is deemed to cover both published and unpublished works).

267 *Ibid* at 779–783; Correa, *Trade Related Aspects*, *supra* note 72 at 134–145; Ricketson & Ginsburg (Vol. I), *supra* note 53 at 852–857.

268 Ricketson & Ginsburg (Vol. I), *supra* note 53 at 779–783.

269 Okediji, "Toward an International Fair Use Doctrine" *supra* note 208 at 78–79 & 85–87.

270 The four factors integral to the US fair use doctrine are: the purpose or character of the use, the nature of the copyrighted work, the amount of the work used, and the effect of the use on the potential market. See US Copyright Act, §107; see generally Pierre Laval, "Toward a Fair Use Standard" (1990) 103:5 Harv L Rev 1105–1136.

271 Okediji, "Toward an International Fair Use Doctrine," *supra* note 208 at 114–136.

272 *Ibid* at 141; Ricketson & Ginsburg (Vol. I), *supra* note 53 at 852–853; see Yu, "Objectives and Principles" *supra* note 72 at 1000–1046.

273 Okediji, "Toward an International Fair Use Doctrine," *supra* note 208 at 139–141; See generally Susy Frankel, "The WTO's Application of 'the Customary Rules of Interpretation of Public International Law' to Intellectual Property" (2005) 46 Va J Int'l L 563–431.

274 Gervais, "Intellectual Property and Human Rights" *supra* note 237 at 18. Helfer et al, *The World Blind Union Gide, supra* note 98 at 8–18.

275 Correa, *Trade Related Aspects*, *supra* note 72 at 140 & 145.

276 Ricketson & Ginsburg (Vol. I), *supra* note 53 at 858.

277 See Correa, *Trade Related Aspects, supra* note 72 at 79–83; Gervais, *TRIPs Agreement, supra* note 64 at 198–202.

278 Okediji, "International Copyright System," *supra* note 21 at 14. In this regard, Okediji argues that measures taken pursuant to art. 40 of the TRIPs Agreement will not be subject to the scrutiny of the three-step test as such measures are not deemed proper limitations or exceptions within the international copyright system. *Ibid.*

279 See Christophe Geiger, "From Berne to National Law, via the Copyright Directive: The Dangerous Mutations of the Three-Step Test" (2007) 29 Eur IP Rev 486 at 489 (stating both the enabling and restricting functions of the test).

280 Gervais, "The Reverse Three-Step Test," *supra* note 236 at 27–35; Geiger, Gervais & Senftleben, "The Three-Step Test Revisited," *supra* note 254 at 625–626.

281 See generally Geiger et al., "Declaration," *supra* note 240; Annette Kur, "Of Oceans, Islands, and Inland Water – How Much Room for Exceptions and Limitations Under the Three-Step Test? (2009) 8 Richmond Journal of Global Law & Business 287 at 340–350.

282 *See generally* Senftleben, "The International Three-Step Test" *supra* note 254; Okediji, "Toward an International Fair use Doctrine" *supra* note 208 at 151–175.

283 Laurence R. Helfer & Graeme W. Austin, *Human Rights and Intellectual Property: Mapping the Global Interface* (Cambridge & New York: Cambridge University Press, 2011) at 211; Gervais, "Intellectual Property and Human Rights," *supra* note 237 at 18–23; see Margaret Chon, "Intellectual Property and the Development Divide" (2006) 27:6 Cardozo L Rev 2813 at 2874–2911; Martha Nussbaum, Capabilities and Social Justice (2002) 4 International Studies Review 123 at 132 (stating that 'human capabilities extend a moral claim that they should be developed').

284 Ruth Okediji, "Reframing International Copyright Limitations and Exceptions as Development Policy," in *Copyright Law in an Age of Limitations and Exceptions* (Cambridge: Cambridge University, 2017) 429 at 475 & 482–489. *See* TRIPs Agreement, *supra* note 38 at Preamble at paras 6 & 7 and art. 8; Correa, *Trade Related Aspects, supra* note 72 at 104–107; David Vaver, "Copyright Defenses as User Rights" (2013) 60:4 J Copyright Soc'y USA 661 at 661–672; Carys Craig, "Globalizing User

5 Copyright and higher education for human development: HDCA for rethinking flexibilities

5.1 Introduction

In the preceding chapters, has been argued that both copyright and higher education are instrumental for sustainable human development through the enlargement of creative and learning capabilities. In particular, the production and dissemination of knowledge are central to the roles of copyright and higher education. In furtherance of their roles, both regimes are interdependent for access to the knowledge in order to facilitate sustainable creative innovation, formation of human capital and expansion of human capabilities. Nonetheless, the effectiveness of their roles and complementarities to advance human development depend upon the existence of development-oriented, coherent and well-aligned policy, legal and institutional frameworks. As is evident from the interface between human rights and copyright regimes, there exist significant gaps and incoherencies between the existing policy, legal, and institutional regimes of copyright and higher education. In the same vein, there is lack of a proper orientation towards sustainable human development. Against this backdrop, the central finding of this book laments the insufficient and narrow conception of relevant copyright-related flexibilities. In the existing international copyright system, the various L&Es are often designed as mere grounds of defenses against owners' claims of infringements. In such a constrained and unbalanced system, access to knowledge is unduly restricted for want of appropriate flexibilities.

Implicating far-reaching ramifications, all these gaps operate to undermine the positive roles of copyright and higher education to promote the sustainable human development. Noting this core problem, this chapter underscores the significance of rethinking flexibilities as users' rights and vital instruments of expanding human capabilities. Further, combining both features as useful aspects of the various flexibilities is crucial to facilitate a coherent alignment between copyright and higher education. In turn, this will strengthen their complementarities for promoting human development. While underscoring the need to rethink the existing regimes of copyright flexibilities, this chapter explores the major approaches for the (re)integration of relevant flexibilities essential for human development. To this end, the HDCA is regarded as a

DOI: 10.4324/9781003214298-5

more appropriate framework to reframe and undergird the flexibilities as a set of development-oriented users' rights directed towards human development.

5.2 Approaches towards (re)integration of flexibilities

As explored in this book, the existing international copyright regime provides or permits various copyright and related flexibilities for educational and creative innovation purposes. Furthermore, the treaties that constitute the international copyright regime require the application of the three-step test to guide the domestic utilization of the flexibilities. In this respect, three major approaches can be gleaned from the relevant scholarship and jurisprudence on copyright flexibilities. In terms of their orientation or emphasis, the approaches can be referred to as defensive, development policy tool and users' rights approach.

5.2.1 The traditional defensive approach

Given its explicit right-holders-oriented feature, the existing international copyright system underscores the primacy of the exclusive rights of an author/ rights holder.[1] As a result, the interests of the author/rights holder are both framed and articulated as exclusive rights. In contrast, the interests of users or the public at large are construed as L&Es with strings of conditions attached thereto. That is, despite their central roles, the flexibilities are not regarded as indispensable and integral elements of the existing global copyright system.[2] Instead, the flexibilities are often considered as mere grounds of defense to be raised against the infringement claims of authors/rights holders.

For instance, a fair use or a fair dealing doctrine is traditionally viewed as one of the grounds of affirmative defense against a copyright infringement.[3] Designed to safeguard the primacy of authors'/rights holders' exclusive rights, the defensive approach deprives the permitted L&Es of a positive legal status to be asserted as users' rights on an equal footing with the exclusive rights. As Elkin-Koren opines, "this narrow view overlooks the users' critical role in serving the goals of copyright law and may therefore ultimately lead to inefficient outcomes."[4]

Further, this restrictive/narrow approach contradicts the very notion of the balance integral to a copyright system.[5] In the words of Vaver, "balancing a right against an exception is either nonsensical or starts off with a linguistic bias against the exception."[6] In fact, these conceptual and functional incongruities are often overlooked to emphasize the expansive exclusive rights. The L&Es are thus relegated and subject to the traditional defensive approach embedded in the international copyright system. This imbalanced and restrictive approach has long been critiqued and found inapt for advancing human development.[7] Inclined towards excessive protection, the approach is not suitable to facilitate a reasonable access to creative works for the promotion of a sustainable creative innovation and higher education.

5.2.2 The development policy tools approach

Seen from the perspective of development, a broader development-oriented approach is proposed to underscore the role of various copyright flexibilities as a development policy tool for development objectives. In its breadth, this approach draws on the broader notion of flexibilities that encompass rights, measures and options as embodied in the existing international legal regimes.[8] Noting their potential for human development, Okediji highlights the need to reframe the international copyright policy and its flexibilities as a development policy tool.[9] It is believed that this approach would allow developing countries a better policy space to design or reframe a set of copyright flexibilities suited to their domestic development needs.[10]

In a broader context, Correa underlines the importance of the policy space reserved under the TRIPs Agreement for members to exploit it for their development needs.[11] For example, members are permitted to "adopt measures necessary (…) to promote the public interest in sectors of vital importance to their socio-economic and technological development" as relevant flexibilities for development objectives at a national level.[12] In other words, the recognition of members' discretion to adopt the necessary measures or flexibilities underlines the role of the 'wiggle room' for sustainable human development.

Exploring the interpretative significance of art. 7 & 8 of the TRIPs Agreement, Peter Yu states that the Agreement "includes a number of flexibilities to facilitate development and to protect the public interest."[13] From the substantive rules, the three-step test is considered a guiding rule of specific flexibilities that "allows national law makers to satisfy domestic social, cultural, and economic needs."[14] For some commentators, the three-step test is "intended to serve as a flexible balancing tool for nations to address their socio-economic development objectives."[15] In the application of the test, the approach is considered useful to take into account relevant human rights obligations.[16]

Setting aside the debate on the test, central to the development policy approach is the underpinning malleable notion of public interests that guides the utilization of flexibilities to meet development needs.[17] Given the international recognition of the public interest goals of copyright, Okediji asserts that "[a]n international fair use doctrine would promote and preserve the public interest as an integral component of the post-TRIPS copyright regime"[18] Nonetheless, most developing and LDCs have not made an effective use of the relevant flexibilities.[19] From among several factors, the major reasons for the non-utilization can be attributed to an overbearing pressure of developed nations, the threat of trade sanctions, weak institutions, the WIPO's right-holders-centric technical assistance, and the proliferating FTAs.[20] Hence, the LDCs are often less equipped to benefit from the limited development-oriented flexibilities embedded in the international copyright regime.

5.2.3 The emerging users' rights approach

Still undergoing conceptual transformation, the emerging users' rights approach reframes copyright flexibilities as users' rights. In Elkin-Koren's observation, "[a] user-rights approach holds that permissible uses under copyright law should be articulated and treated as rights."[21] In spite of its recent prominence, the conception of the approach traces back to Layman Patterson and Stanley Lindberg's seminal contribution that claims the copyright system itself as a regime of users' rights.[22] In the context of L&Es, David Vaver's articulation of the notion of users' right was instrumental to shape the recent copyright jurisprudence of Canada.[23]

In his critique of the traditional defensive approach to L&Es as mere 'loopholes,' Vaver underlined the need for a 'fair and balanced reading' of owners and users' rights.[24] The subsequent judicial embrace of this view led to the articulation and reification of users' right in the *CHH v. Law Society of Upper Canada.*[25] In its ruling that has become a watershed in the jurisprudence of users' rights, the Supreme Court of Canada (SCC) stated: "the fair dealing exception, like other exceptions in the Copyright Act, is a user's right."[26]

In reiterating a fair dealing as *an integral element* of copyright system, the Court has laid down a principle that underscores the L&Es as users' rights on an equal footing with the exclusive rights.[27] Indeed, it is a significant departure from the predominant right-holder-centered perspective.[28] The approach is considered vital to underline the active creative role of users to promote the objectives of copyright.[29] In so doing, the users' rights approach calls for a due and balanced consideration of "the rights and duties of both users and authors."[30] For both interests, this approach marks a shift in the baseline for the required balance from the hitherto author's right to the creative process itself.[31]

In a case related to access to learning materials for the purpose of education, the SCC has re-emphasized the approach in the *Alberta v. Canadian Copyright Licensing Agency.*[32] In essence, the case involved teachers' reproduction of educational material for classroom use. In its ruling, the Court underscored the users-right based nature of the claim and referred to a fair dealing as a "user's right" that can be used for allowable purpose.[33] A similar trend is gathering a momentum in other jurisdictions.[34] From among the recent copyright treaties, the Marrakesh Treaty is the first international legal instrument to embrace this approach.[35] Above all, the approach has drawn a significant attention in the recent legal scholarship.[36]

Further, the approach is considered useful to reframe users' right in the context of human rights.[37] From a human rights perspective, the approach can be used to maintain a balance between the interest of the public and authors' rights to protection of his/her material and moral interests. In the balancing exercise, the human rights justifications might be invoked to underpin users' rights in the context of the right to culture, the right to benefits of scientific progress and its applications, and the freedom indispensable for scientific research and creative activities.[38] In fact, art. 15 of the ICESCR provides for authors' rights on a par with the aforementioned rights. Besides, the intended general balance among the human rights within the Covenant also brings into the equation the right to education in the context of affordable access to learning materials.[39] Hence, the approach is important to inject into the balancing equilibrium pertinent human rights considerations.

Although the users' rights approach has garnered a significant traction, it is not immune to limitations. For instance, scholars caution against the 'double-edged effect' of the approach and its indeterminate nature.[40] The usual critiques of rights aside,[41] two major reasons are worth mentioning here. First, users' rights approach tends to create two competing individual rights that might reinforce the owner-centric rights-based copyright regime.[42] In Craig's observation, this approach might result in its legitimation of the entrenched authors' rights as a baseline for balancing.[43] In effect, "the concern is that the judicial embrace of user rights will actually backfire to slow our progress towards a fairer copyright regime."[44] From a human rights perspective, a matter of critical concern is the increasing corporations' abusive assertion of human rights.[45] For example, corporation's claim of this sort seems to emerge in the recent jurisprudence in the EU.[46]

Second, the approach's apparent reduction of the public interest goals into individual claims not only overlooks the overlapping role of creators and users, but also encroaches upon policy room for a flexible public interest.[47] In view of these drawbacks, Craig notes that "[t]he reliance on rights rhetoric therefore threatens to impoverish our discussion around the public interest and the social values at stake in the copyright context."[48] From its inception, the judicial articulation of users' right has however been made within the broader public interest objectives.[49] In particular, users' rights are regarded as *a means* or an 'essential part' in the furtherance of the public interest objectives of copyright.[50]

Noting its possible limitations, a strategic use of users-rights approach along with the development policy approach can serve as a powerful tool to counter the effect of the ratchet up in the copyright regime.[51] For the concern related to a human rights-based corporate claim, worth reminding is the CESCR's categorical rejection of such a claim. In its General Comment No.17, the Committee underscored IPRs as *a means* of providing incentives for creative innovation.[52]

Even within the human rights regime, there is an implicit room in the General Comment No.17 that can augment the flexibilities. In this regard, the CESCR is notable for its articulation of the purpose of material interests of an individual author to safeguard an *adequate standard of living*—a notion that in itself is flexible to determine.[53] This line of interpretation is significant for two reasons. First, it rejects the overemphasis on the dominant exclusive economic rights driven by the neoliberal economic theories. Second, the notion of *adequate standard of living* can be used to restore the necessary balance between author's and users' rights. As noted by Gervais, taking this "human rights approach brings values back into the [copyright] system."[54] In effect, this human rights approach to the flexibilities would accommodate the underpinning utilitarian and natural rights justifications for both copyright and human rights to complement each other.[55]

To this end, the emerging users'-rights-approach is instrumental for its rhetorical and normative significance.[56] Encapsulated in the language of users' right, the approach allows users to invoke the rights against others, including a copyright holder.[57] That is, a due recognition of users' right bestows upon users the privilege to vindicate copyright flexibilities as enforceable claims against the right holders. As a result, the latter will be obligated to refrain from encroaching upon the flexibilities.[58] For instance, "[c]onceptualized as a right, fair dealing establishes a corresponding duty on behalf of the owner to honor the user's right."[59] From a human rights perspective, Vaver opines that "[e]quating user rights with human rights would certainly help transform users' rights beyond mere defenses and give them substantive content."[60]

In highlighting its significance at a global level, Craig also notes that "[t]he international recognition of 'users rights,' it seems reasonable to assert, might provide a more reliable shield for users against the incursion of copyright."[61] In spite of its limitations, the users right approach has thus the potential to facilitate a better access to copyrighted learning materials. As Craig cautiously notes, "[u]ser rights may still be the most effective tool at our disposal to advance the interests of users of protected works and the public in general in the face of the powerful rights-based claims of authors and corporate owners."[62] Nevertheless, in Craig's insightful observation, it is better to emphasize "not whether but how the language of the rights will be used."[63] Hence, a more appropriate approach is needed to place it in a broader framework to harness its rhetorical potential for human development.

5.2.4 HDCA as a more inclusive framework

It is noted that both development policy and users-rights approaches have their own merits and demerits. Yet, advancing public interest constitutes the common goal of the approaches.[64] In Craig's opinion, "the stated objectives of our copyright system require a teleological lens."[65] In contrast, "claims to right focus on origins and present-day entitlements"[66] In spite of its limited focus, the approach has a 'protective function of [safe]guarding individuals [and] their entitlements' to rights.[67] That said, the balancing mechanism grounded in the users-rights approach is not flexible enough to accommodate a development-oriented objective of copyright to advance a broader public interest.[68] In harnessing its strategic rhetorical force, one would thus suggest placing the users' rights approach within the more flexible development policy approach. In its framing, the latter is firmly anchored in a broader public interest for sustainable creative innovation.[69] Further, the strategic combination of the approaches should be oriented towards the rich goals of human development.

Building upon the underpinning public interests, the HDCA offers a better framework to accommodate both development policy tools and users' rights perspectives. Indeed, as its recent articulation affirms,[70] the development policy approach dovetails with the CA-driven human development.[71] In the same vein, the users' rights approach can serve as "a particular institutional and rhetorical means"[72] for the advancement of basic human or social values such as creative innovation and education.[73] In rethinking the objective of copyright for the promotion of sustainable human development, the HDCA provides a sufficient flexible normative room to mediate and direct the perspectives towards their common ends—promoting public interest. For the desired policy and legal reform, a human development perspective offers a robust normative foundation to reframe copyright and related flexibilities in terms of human capabilities.

In order to advance human development, it is thus vital to reframe the users-rights and related general flexibilities as users' freedoms or human capabilities. As Elkin-Koren notes, "[u]nderstanding users rights as a matter of freedom (…) may strengthen the theoretical basis for user rights."[74] In this respect, the human capabilities are understood as individual's creative freedoms to access and use the relevant knowledge for individual and collective human development.[75] Due to its multifaceted nature to serve as a policy and normative tool to balance author's and users' interests, the HDCA is useful to inform flexibilities whether framed as public policy goals or rights grounded in human rights norms.[76]

In this regard, worth noting is the existence of a conceptual overlap between CA and human rights as well as their potential to complement each other.[77] Indeed, the Human Development Reports (2000) has long underscored the conceptual and functional complementarities between human rights and human development.[78] As Martha Nussbaum points out, "[c]apabilities can supplement the language of rights in clarifying the basic concept of human rights, by emphasizing the material and social aspect of all rights and the need for government action to protect and secure all rights."[79] In the same vein, "[h]uman rights makes clear that the idea of capabilities is not an optional entitlement, but an urgent demand that should not be ignored nor compromised in pursuit of other objectives such as expansion of aggregate wealth."[80]

Hence, "[c]apabilities are complementary to and augment, rather than competing with, human rights."[81] It is noted that 'a more integrated approach can thus bring significant rewards' for the advancement of human development.[82] In our case, a human development perspective will allow the integration of the users' rights and the development policy tool into a coherent whole to enlarge users' opportunities for access to, creation, and dissemination, of knowledge. As Benkler notes, "the freedom to use basic resources [such as knowledge] and capabilities allows an improved participation in the production of information and information-dependent components of human development."[83]

Grounded in the public interests,[84] the integration of international copyright and related flexibilities should thus be directed towards enhancing individual's creative freedoms to access and use the creative works for education and creative innovation. In sum, the inclusive framework of HDCA offers a broader perspective to evaluate or analyze the instrumental role of copyright and its flexibilities to promote sustainable human development. Further, this human-centric development framework is useful to guide appropriate policy and legal reforms to redirect the objectives of copyright and higher education towards sustainable human development. Likewise, the HDCA brings together the relevant human rights and constitutional dimensions to inform the (re)incorporation and application of copyright flexibilities for enhanced access to learning materials.

5.3 Re-orienting policy, legal and institutional regimes towards human development

As highlighted in the preceding chapters, international copyright and human rights systems lack a proper alignment with each other. Yet, development objectives remain their common denominator. In view of their respective contributions and common objectives, both copyright and education are vital for the advancement of human development. In particular, it is essential to emphasize their potential complementarities and instrumental roles for enhancement of human capabilities.

In practice, copyright and higher education are neither well aligned nor oriented towards human development. In this regard, gaps and incoherencies are often evident from the relevant policies, legal and institutional frameworks of international copyright and higher education systems. In the same vein, the development policy objectives underpinning copyright and educational systems are not sufficiently oriented towards a sustainable human development. The lack of sufficient orientation is in part attributed to the overriding emphasis on the market-driven economic growth.

Hence, an effective re-orientation and re-integration of appropriate flexibilities require similar re-orientations in the broader policy, legal and institutional regimes of copyright and education in a manner that promotes sustainable human development. In particular, a strategic shift in the development orientation and creation of coherence between the respective regimes are essential to strengthen their complementarities and reorient them towards sustainable human development. For its rich normative and evaluative significance, the framework of the HDCA should be used for appropriate policy, legal and institutional reforms to advance sustainable human development.

5.3.1 Revisiting and forging coherence among policy objectives

As explained in this book, an appropriate coherence among relevant policies and the latter's proper orientation are essential for human development. Nonetheless, there often lacks a coherence between copyright and higher education policies in LDCs. In some LDCS, there exists no comprehensive copyright policy. For instance, in the LDCs such as Ethiopia, the pertinent policy regimes are neither consistent nor aligned with the appropriate national policy objectives. Further, there is a similar misfit or incoherence even between copyright's intended objectives and its relevant substantive content. In this regard, the perusal of Ethiopian copyright law unveils the gap between its substantive provisions and the intended role of creative works for, *inter alia*, scientific, technological and cultural development.[85] That is, the substantive provisions are not directed towards the stated aspects of development.

In most LDCs with policy gaps, the prevailing problems of policy incoherencies and fragmentations necessitate an integrative reformulation of a comprehensive and coherent policy framework to promote creative innovation and an equitable access thereto. As emphasized in this book, both objectives are integral to a balanced copyright system. For the achievement of the objectives, vital are the facilitative role and the legislative incorporation of appropriate copyright flexibilities. In developing their respective national copyright and educational policies, the LDCs known for low ranking development index should take the inclusive HDCA that guides both the design, formulation and implementation of the policies in line with their human development policy objectives. For a robust human development-oriented copyright policy, the guiding parameter and central policy objective should be promoting the creation and dissemination of creative works as essential constitutive and instrument elements of human capabilities.[86] To this end, the overarching policy objective of copyright should envision to 'maximize the development of human [creative innovation]'[87] through enhanced freedoms.

In this regard, the HDCA is a useful normative framework to both promote and balance author's opportunities or freedoms to create and users' opportunities to access and learn from the creative works. In taking such a board and multidimensional approach, the policy framework can be grounded in the constitutional policy development objectives to promote technological, socio-economic and cultural development. Setting human development—'human flourishing in its fullest sense'[88]—as its ultimate objective, the policy framework should build upon insights from creators and users as well as other stakeholders through a democratic, participatory, and transparent process of policy formulation.

Placed within the inclusive framework of human development, the process of policy-making and its implementation at international, continental, and national levels should integrate the relevant human rights dimensions to support appropriate human capabilities. In particular, the integration of human rights dimensions is useful to inject into the policy frameworks the *triple human rights obligations* of states' and non-state actors to *respect, protect and fulfill* the human rights of creators and users. For the expansion of creative human capabilities, this right-based human development framework offers the policy a legal scaffolding to make the stakeholders more committed, accountable and responsible for its appropriate implementation.[89]

Like the market-driven copyright policy oriented towards economic growth, the overriding policy objectives of the higher education system are often producing human capital and scientific research to promote an economic growth. Such an overemphasis upon human capital renders the learners a mere instrument of economic growth. In consequence, this narrow focus on economic growth in effect neglects or undermines the broad human development objectives education needs to advance.

As is for a copyright policy, it is thus essential to reconsider the existing higher education systems to develop coherent policies and re-conceptualize higher education itself in terms of human capabilities. In contrast to the market-driven educational policies, a proper re-orientation of higher education towards human development is both inclusive of its role for human capital and crucial to foreground the expansion of human capabilities as its core objective.[90] To this end, Melanie Walker notes that "[h]uman development and human capabilities [approach] offers a rich resource to policy-makers and to universities for addressing the formation of socially good graduates, while also taking up access, equity and quality, and educational processes and outcomes."[91]

For a higher education's policy orientation towards sustainable human development, human development values such as well-being, equity, democratic justice and social inclusion, sustainability, active participation, and empowerment are all important to inform the policy objectives.[92] In embracing these values, the framework would enhance the freedom of learners and educators to be active agents of changes in the process of sustainable human development.[93] In this context, Walker underscores universities' potential role to "form graduate citizens who are self-knowing agents capable of purposeful action for individual and collective change."[94] In short, promoting a sustainable human development should be considered an overarching policy objective of higher education through the formation of human capabilities.[95]

For a cross-sectoral policy coherence and integrative re-orientation, the respective policy orientation and coherence made for copyright and higher education should further be aligned with a shared set of human development objectives. The alignment and integration should in turn be consolidated into a coherent whole to reinforce their complementarities for the advancement of sustainable human development. As studies on policy regimes in the LDCs reveal, there is often a significant gap and cross-sectoral policy incoherence between copyright and higher education. In principle, an inter-sectoral policy incoherence or the problem of coordination stems from "a structural misalignment between government policies and the regulatory frameworks in place to achieve intended policy objectives."[96] In turn, the misalignment undermines the complementarities between the sectors and their appropriate orientation towards their ultimate objective—sustainable human development.

Therefore, it is imperative to take an integrated or holistic approach in rethinking and reforming the relevant policies in order to facilitate a cross-sectoral policy collaboration and coherence for the expansion of creative innovation and learning capabilities. In formulating a coherent and consistent copyright policy framework, the norm-setting process should be evidence-based, inclusive, deliberative, and participatory to reflect nations' priorities and levels of development.[97] In this respect, the integrative policy collaboration should also take into account the linkages between copyright and other pertinent policies such as innovation, cultural and competition policies.[98] As recommended in the WIPO DA, such a development-oriented norm-setting approach is vital for the promotion of creative innovation and knowledge diffusion "to the mutual advantage of producers and users of technological knowledge and in a manner conducive to social and economic welfare, and to a balance of rights and obligations."[99]

Within this broader context of societal interests, an appropriate bridge must be built between copyright and higher education policies through relevant policy flexibilities. Once the linkage is created, the flexibilities can be used to promote the policy objectives for the expansion of human capabilities. Both the human capital and the narrow metric of economic growth that animate the national development policies of most LDCs should be revisited and subsumed within the robust and broad framework of sustainable human development. In so doing, the HDCA can inform a proper alignment among the policy regimes and direct them towards sustainable human development.

Complementing the framework of human development, relevant human rights instruments should be integrated into the human development objectives to guide the overall policy alignment and re-orientation. In her version of the CA, Nussbaum contends that her list of central human capabilities—inclusive of creative and learning capabilities—can serve as basic constitutional principles to underpin human rights dimensions.[100]

5.3.2 Revisiting legal frameworks for better coherence

As is often apparent from the relevant national legal frameworks, the existence or lack of a coherence between copyright and higher education can be considered at several levels. For a legal coherence between authors' rights and education with human rights dimensions, a legal coherence of prime significance is the integration and implementation of the human rights instruments. In countries that recognize the human rights dimension in their national constitutions, the constitutional dimension of authors' rights and higher education is another important layer of legal coherence.

To this effect, a constitutional coherence might be built upon an explicit reference to author's rights and higher education or a set of relevant constitutional flexibilities grounded in public interests. When embodied in a national constitution, the constitutional flexibilities and the underpinning public interests need to be cascaded down and incorporated into the respective copyright and higher education legal regimes. In this respect, a relevant jurisprudence might prove useful and flexible to bridge an appropriate linkage between the legal and/or constitutional/human rights provisions.

Hence, the role of the courts is crucial where there lacks an explicit and clear articulation of the constitutional dimensions of copyright and higher education. The same holds true for incoherencies and gaps between copyright regime and higher education. For instance, the teaching exception in copyright law might be quite narrow without a due regard for development-oriented educational objectives.

Within the broader sustainable human development objectives, a nation needs to build a bridge between its policy objectives and the appropriate legal frameworks. The problem of coordination or incoherence among relevant laws might occur due to a defect in the design of the legislation themselves that fail to forge an appropriate linkage to achieve the common objectives.[101] In the context of access to copyrighted learning materials, it is important to rethink the often-narrow-scoped copyright flexibilities and align them with the educational objectives of the higher education legal regimes.

For instance, in its recent copyright bill, South Africa enshrines a myriad of L&Es that mirror its development-oriented IP policy objectives.[102] In addition to a long list of the L&Es, the bill incorporates a catch-all cause of a fair-use doctrine that draws on the major attributes of the doctrine under the US law. For a better integration of the flexibilities, a context-sensitive and users' rights–oriented human development approach should be considered for appropriate legislative reforms. Given their roles for enhanced access to knowledge required for human capabilities, the human rights dimensions of both author's right and higher education themselves should be well-oriented towards the right to sustainable human development.

To this effect, a proper, inclusive, and coherent integration is thus essential for the progressive realization of the right to sustainable human development. Further, the existing international, regional, and national legal frameworks should be placed within the framework of sustainable human development. For the LDCs with low levels of human development, it is important to articulate the constitutional and human rights aspects, forge reinforcing legal coherences, and re-orient the linkages towards sustainable human development. In this regard, the constitutional and human rights dimensions of sustainable development can serve as a springboard to establish the legal basis for the framework of sustainable human development.

For this purpose, legislative and judicial measures should be taken to rethink the existing legal frameworks and integrate appropriate legal flexibilities that are geared towards sustainable human development. In line with the suggested inclusive framework of the HDCA for national policy reforms, both international lawmaking process and national legislative measures should be (re) oriented towards human development. In particular, rethinking and integrating relevant international copyright-related flexibilities should be scrutinized to reflect nations' respective levels of human development.[103]

5.3.3 Building institutional coherence and collaboration

An institutional coherence builds upon policy and legal coherence to promote the institutional coordination and collaboration. One of the reasons for the problem of poor coordination is the existence of weak institutions and lack of collaboration on policy formulation and implementation.[104] Further, an institutional practice reflects the misalignment in the underpinning policy and legal regimes. As noted above, the incoherencies in the policy and legal frameworks of copyright and higher education have implications for the institutional coherence. For instance, the lack of coordination and collaboration in the relevant institutional frameworks often led to inconsistent institutional practices. Absent appropriate linkages, the gaps in the policy, legal, and institutional frameworks would further constrain the collaborative operation of the relevant regimes to promote human capabilities.

Therefore, it is crucial to build an appropriate bridge between the institutional frameworks of copyright and higher education in a manner that facilitates their mutual and cooperative operations for the realization of sustainable human development objectives. For instance, "universities should embrace their obligations to promote well-being and quality of life in society through their research, [societal engagement], and educative functions."[105] In the same vein, copyright administrative institutions and creative industries' core functions should be oriented towards advancing human development.[106] Moreover, this broad and integrative development approach should be taken to galvanize the institutional reforms and forge an interdepartmental collaboration among the sectoral institutions.

In so doing, the institutional recalibration and coherence ought to be geared towards the expansion of learning and creative human capabilities. In particular, the institutional cooperation and collaboration should facilitate access to knowledge or learning materials in order to enhance quality higher education and creative innovation. To this effect, the HDCA is vital to inform the institutional policy and legal frameworks, regulations, and practices through the incorporation of appropriate flexibilities. Including the role of courts, the existence of strong and conducive institutional environment is essential to translate the international flexibilities into national development-inducing flexibilities.[107]

5.4 Revisiting and re-orienting copyright-related flexibilities

As explained in this book, international copyright flexibilities are both inadequate and constrained with significant implications for access to knowledge. Worse still, developed nations continue championing a more restrictive and owners-oriented international copyright system through TRIPs-plus bilateral and regional trade agreements. For the LDCs that are net importers of knowledge goods critical for their development imperatives, such an access-restrictive approach is quite detrimental to a development-oriented access to the creative works for a sustainable creative innovation and educational purposes. In effect, this would encroach upon the human/constitutional aspects of users' rights and hinder the realization of the right to sustainable human development.

In order to remove the impediment, the existing legal regimes should be rethought to re-integrate a minimum set of relevant and access-enhancing copyright flexibilities that counter the misguided ratchet in the copyright system. In addition to the reform, a strategic integration of the flexibilities is crucial for the advancement of human development through enhanced access to creative works. To this effect, the inclusive framework of the HDCA should be taken to rethink or (re)integrate copyright flexibilities as users' rights and indispensable components of the copyright regimes at all levels.

5.4.1 Rethinking and reintegrating general copyright-related flexibilities

A Human rights and constitutional dimensions

In the preceding chapter, various general flexibilities with possible constitutional and human rights aspects have been elaborated. Given their normative significance, the pertinent human rights and constitutional dimensions should inform the integration of the relevant general copyright-related flexibilities explored in the chapter. To achieve this purpose, the HDCA should be adopted due to its integrative approach to accommodate both development policy and the emerging-rights-based approaches to copyright flexibilities. As emphasized in this book, this integrative and inclusive normative framework offers a broader room with maximum flexibilities in order to address the national development priorities and realities.

From the general flexibilities, the public interest considerations that are often embodied in constitutional and the human rights regimes are pivotal to strike an appropriate balance between creators and users' interests/rights.[108] In particular, relevant constitutional and human rights aspects should be articulated or recognized in national copyright and related legislation.[109] Further, the constitutional and human rights norms should be regarded as a set of overarching guide in the incorporation, interpretation, and application of the copyright flexibilities for the advancement of human development.[110] Taking into account human rights dimensions offers a teleological lens for L&Es and guide courts in their interpretation.[111] Further, human rights have a normative role in re-scoping the exclusive rights.[112]

B International norms of development-oriented flexibilities

From the international norms of development flexibilities, both the policy and legislative reforms should draw on the flexibilities inherent in arts. 7&8 of the TRIPs Agreement to entrench a balance between the twin aspects of the public interest that underlie a robust copyright system. In line with the provisions, an explicit recognition of education at all levels and in all modes should be made to underscore its role as a 'sector of vital importance' and an instrument of sustainable human development. It is worth noting that the principle of sustainable development enshrined in the WTO Agreement can serve as an overarching guidance for the integration of the TRIPs-development flexibilities.

In the same vein, the norm-setting process of flexibilities envisaged in the WIPO DA is pertinent to emphasize the roles of copyright flexibilities for the advancement of human development. In the national integration of the flexibilities, the above-mentioned general development objectives and principles are relevant to inform the policy formulation and legislative reform in a manner that reflects nations' levels of development and national contexts.[113]

C Public interest–driven flexibilities and remunerative approach

From within the copyright system, a human development–oriented approach should inform the interpretation of the principle of idea/expression distinction, conditions of protection, and the exclusions of optional works such as legislative and administrative documents. Such a holistic approach is useful to advance the intended public interest via a robust public domain. In order to curb its 'enclosure' and advance the public interest,[114] the enrichment of a public domain should be at the centerpiece of the policy and legal reforms intended for the promotion of creative innovation. Further, a structural reform in the copyright regime is worth considering in order to accommodate a non-market approach more suited to creative works in the educational sector.

In most LDCs, despite its growing expansion in the private sector, higher education still remains integral to the core public-funded sectors. Hence, a blend of incentive mechanisms should be explored to reflect the countries' respective socio-economic contexts. For instance, an equitable remunerative mechanism is more suitable for creative works in the educational sector. Considered as an alternative or in combination with the existing approach, the remunerative mechanism can be tailored to address development needs. In developed nations themselves, not all creative sectors depend upon the exclusive rights regime for incentives.[115] It is thus vital to consider appropriate incentive mechanisms for better reforms in the sectors.

For the structural reform, a useful insight can be drawn from Gervais' recent proposed four-quadrants reform approach that distinguishes between the kind of copyrighted works, industries, and categories of creators/users.[116] In particular, his suggested structural reform under quadrant I (for public dedication) and II (for non-commercialization) resonates with educational sector as a sector of vital importance.[117] In fact, the creators in both quadrants are often active in creative process and share the values in the education sector.[118] For the creators, both public funding and non-economic considerations are the prime incentive mechanisms to drive knowledge creation and diffusion.[119] For instance, authors such as academics and scientists depend upon a distinct incentive mechanism (a mix of salary, grants, and reputation) and are often supportive of the emerging open access models.[120] As a distinct sector, the educational sector can be illustrative of the inappropriateness of the 'one-size-fits-all' and exclusive proprietary regime.[121] As scholars suggest, "liability rules may be preferable to property rights in certain sectors such as education or scientific publishing."[122] The proponents contend that liability rules regime is useful to prevent misappropriation while it facilitates access to creative works and spur a follow-on creative innovation.[123]

As an alternative to the exclusive rights approach, the equitable (just) remunerative mechanism is thus instrumental for enhanced access to learning materials.[124] From a human rights perspective, the remunerative mechanism is consistent with the required protection of authors' material interests for the purpose of an adequate living standard.[125] As stated in the *General Comment No. 17*, under certain circumstances, limitations may be imposed subject to "compensatory measures, such as payment of adequate compensation for the use of scientific, literary or artistic productions in the public interest."[126] The remunerative scheme can thus be used to avoid authors' unreasonable loss of income and facilitate access to their creative works.[127]

At this juncture, worth inquiring is the approach's compliance with the international three-step test. As hinted at in the WTO jurisprudence but left undefined,[128] the existence of stronger normative considerations may justify an equitable remunerative scheme within the reach of the three-step test as long as there is no conflict with a right-holder's normal exploitation.[129] In this respect, the Max Planck Institute's proposed interpretation of the test is relevant for its articulation of normative considerations in the context of public interest.[130] While taking into account the public interest of users' access, the remunerative scheme would avoid 'unreasonable prejudice to the legitimate interest' of the right-holders.[131] As noted in the proposed interpretation, this approach will offer a room for the legitimate interest of third parties. Further, a nation's economic realities might evidence the lack of opportunities for a commercial exploitation and the practical insignificance of the anticipated conflict with the normal exploitation.[132] That is, there is a scenario of market failure as most consumers (learners and educators) are unable to afford the price of learning materials such as books.[133]

In Foster's observation of the interface between copyright and right to education, this scenario of market failure entails a 'false conflict' for want of material interest or trade impact.[134] In the absence of market opportunities for normal exploitation, the remunerative mechanism would preempt a concern related to the three-step test. In dealing with the test, the public interest that underpins education as a sector of vital importance with a constitutional and human rights dimensions should suffice to constitute stronger normative considerations.[135] In the same vein, a remunerative mechanism may be justified for related works to serve similar ends.[136] In sum, facilitating adequate access to relevant learning materials requires a structural reform that takes into account a combination of compensation schemes for the creators, appropriate set of L&Es and public investment in the cultural institutions such as libraries and archives.[137]

D Retracting the TRIPs-plus approach

Given the overbearing impact of a diplomatic pressure, misguided technical assistance, and restrictive FTAs, the LDCs often adopt a TRIPs-plus approach that undercuts their potentials for an optimal utilization of relevant copyright flexibilities. It is thus imperative to revisit the ill-advised TRIPs-plus approach applied to the scope, terms of protection and enforcement measures. Its continued existence entails serious ramifications for a vibrant creative innovation and quality education through a severe restraint on access to knowledge in general and learning materials in particular. For instance, the default term of protection adopted for works of applied art should be kept to the international minimum standard (i.e. 25 years).

Setting appropriate term limits is critical to promote a vibrant public domain that allows a free use and sustainable access to creative works. Likewise, unnecessary restrictions on rental and public lending rights must be retracted or at least exempted for educational and library purposes. Consistent with the TRIPs Agreement, the legislative action is vital to facilitate unrestricted rental of relevant works and interlibrary lending of learning materials. Reframed as rights of remuneration in lieu of exclusive rights, the rights can be safeguarded against unreasonable acts of commercialization through an equitable remuneration.

In revisiting the scope of exclusive rights in general, Gervais underscores the significance of setting proper limits to the rights in accordance with their intended purpose.[138] Situated within copyright's 'inherent teleological limit' as their 'normative anchor',[139] a new perspective is essential for re-scoping exclusive rights. For instance, the author proposes an 'effect-based' analysis of use or a demonstrable 'interference with actual or predictable commercial exploitation' as a determining factor to redefine the scope of economic rights.[140] As an actual or predictable commercial impact is the crux of the exploitation, this perspective is useful to inform both legislative reform and judicial interpretations to exempt non-commercial uses.

In addition to re-scoping the rights, there is a need to rethink the strict enforcement measures that undermine the very purpose of copyright itself and frustrate users' rights. In particular, unintentional and non-commercial acts of infringement should be exonerated from an indiscriminate criminalization and its severe penalties. In principle, the use of creative works for educational purposes falls within acts of non-commercial uses. It is thus plausible to consider a total exoneration of the acts from criminalization. Instead, the combination of provisional measures and civil remedies should suffice to safeguard authors' rights or maintain the *necessary* incentive.

Indeed, the criminalization required under international copyright regime is limited to commercial acts of infringement and leaves out from its scope non-commercial acts for educational purposes. In a broader context, the flexible requirements of 'piracy on a commercial scale' might be inserted into national copyright laws. In the same vein, the TRIPs-plus border measures, including seizure of goods in transit, should be aligned with corresponding measures under the relevant customs law. It must be noted that a harsh enforcement mechanism is often counterproductive and tends to undermine a respect for the laws.[141]

E Crafting a blend of three-step test and open-ended fair use

As a general rule of copyright flexibilities, an appropriate (re)integration of the three-step test is important to exploit the international copyright flexibilities. Given the restrictive effect of the TRIPs Agreement and relevant copyright treaties, countries such as the LDCs should take a strategic proactive measure to (re)integrate the test in light of their human rights obligations and sustainable human development objectives. In their critique of the test for its vagueness and double-edged effect,[142] scholars have suggested a number of approaches for its adoption and application at national levels. From the range of proposed approaches,[143] the Max Planck Institute's public-interest-oriented holistic approach to the test can be used for its national adoption.[144] Yet it remains to be seen whether or not the WTO DSB will endorse this interpretative approach. For the sake of a compliance, worth keeping in view is thus the evolving WTO jurisprudence on the test although the existing one has drawn mixed comments.[145]

Further, the proposed infusion of the test with the open-ended US fair-use doctrine is useful to consider for the domestic application of the various flexibilities.[146] It is important to note that the three-step test is an international *guiding rule* for states to design domestic flexibilities.[147] In contrast, the fair-use doctrine serves as a *legal standard* for national courts to apply the flexibilities.[148] Within the international limit, states can opt for the doctrine or an enumerative list of flexibilities or a combination of both models. For countries that are net importers of knowledge, a strategic blend of both models may prove useful to reframe specific flexibilities as users' rights. In this respect, a rich and useful lesson on users' rights perspective can be drawn from the Canadian fair dealing jurisprudence.[149]

For its open-ended nature and subject to customization, the flexible US fair-use doctrine[150] is worth adopting. In effect, a blend of the perspectives is believed to offer courts with a concrete and flexible balancing tool for the interpretation and application of the test to advance public interests. As Elkin-Koren points out, interpreting a fair use as a right is "necessary in order to achieve the goals that copyright law is designed to promote."[151] It should be kept in mind that embracing a fair use doctrine itself involves legal uncertainties[152] and its application requires a rich judicial experience.

However, the adoption of fair use doctrine as a catch-all clause along with an illustrative list of L&Es would mitigate the uncertainties and rigidities associated with the respective models of flexibilities.[153] In this regard, South Africa's copyright bill that adopts a new version of fair-use doctrine can offer a good lesson.[154] Elsewhere, Peter Yu has explored the various modalities nations have taken to adopt the doctrine.[155] In so doing, he underscores the need for a proper customization of the US fair-use doctrine as an instance of legal transplants.[156] Crafting a blend of an open-ended fair use and the three-step test as a guiding rule of users rights needs to take into account the local legal and institutional context.

5.4.2 Rethinking specific copyright-related flexibilities

As emphasized in this book, it should be recalled that a CA-driven human perspective is suggested for its potential to subsume both the development policy strategy and the emerging users' rights approaches. Hence, the integrative HDCA should be used for rethinking and an optimal (re)integration of copyright and related flexibilities. Including the copyright system itself, the development policy prong of the approach is useful to accommodate the general flexibilities. Within this broader framework and in line with the relevant constitutional and human rights dimensions, the users' rights component of the approach is vital to underscore the normative significance of the specific copyright flexibilities as users' rights.[157] Recast as users' rights, the flexibilities should thus be articulated, interpreted, and applied on a par with author's exclusive rights.[158] As Elkin-Koren notes, "[t]he framing of permissible uses as rights offers a legal framework for analyzing the potential threats to desirable uses which serve copyright purposes."[159] In effect, restoring the long-sought balance will advance its objectives.

The restoration of the balance can be achieved through the imposition of a corresponding obligation upon the right-holders to respect the rights of users.[160] To leverage its rhetorical significance, the users' right approach should be kept in view to integrate the appropriate specific flexibilities as an integral component of a balanced copyright system. As reitrated in the *CCH v Law Society*, "[b]oth owner rights and user rights should therefore be given the fair and balanced reading that befits remedial legislation."[161] Nonetheless, it must be noted that not all flexibilities readily fit into the users-rights framework. For instance, a non-statutory compulsory licensing may better be understood as a regulatory mechanism than an *ex ante* designated users' right. Perhaps, once granted, the permissible use might be claimed as users' rights. As for the specific flexibilities, it is crucial to (re)incorporate the flexibilities into the international and national legal regimes as mandatory L&Es and integral elements of the copyright system.

A Private use exception

In this digital era that holds a great promise for creative users across the globe, private users' access to knowledge is essential for individual human development through creative participation in cultural life and learning process.[162] Nonetheless, the existing exception is too restrictive to allow users a sufficient freedom to access and use creative works for personal purposes. It is thus important to redesign or rethink the existing exception as a *mandatory* user's right available for both natural and juridical persons. Further, save the specific exclusions such as original works of fine art, the private use should be extended to all creative works and all categories of exclusive rights as long as the use is for private or personal purposes. To claim it as such, the exception should be reframed as a user's right.

It should also be made clear that the exception is applicable for both digital and non-digital works. To this end, the exception should be construed broadly to encompass all creative works that are *lawfully made available to the public.* In the digital environment, this user's right must be safeguarded against an abusive digital and contractual restriction. In the same vein, the exception should be exempted from a wholesale criminalization presumed to curb a piracy on a commercial scale. For the sake of a compliance with the international three-step test, the suggested fair-use-infused test will serve to set the exception within a proper limit.

B Quotation exception

It should be recalled that quotation exception is the sole mandatory exception under the Berne Convention. Framed as 'a mandatory user freedom,'[163] the exception's special status is said to reflect a 'freedom of expression' and authors' 'essential privilege' to quote.[164] Given its role for creative freedom, education and scientific research, an exception for quotation should be reframed as a mandatory user's right in a national copyright law.

As a self-contained exception, the requirements of fair practice, the extent justified by the purpose and the proper attribution are intended to maintain a balance between authors and users' interests. It is thus useful to both reframe the exception and shield its legitimate exercise against digital locks and criminalization. In the academic sector where the prohibition of plagiarism discourages a substantial quotation without due attribution, the social norm itself is more effective than criminalization.

C Teaching and scientific research exceptions

As noted in this book, the teaching exception is the most direct and crucial exception for educational purposes. Nonetheless, the scope of the existing exception under national laws varies across nations. Likewise, their incorporation into national laws also takes different approaches. For instance, most continental countries adopting a closed list of L&Es prefer specific exceptions for scientific research and scholarship. In contrast, the common law countries such as the United States and Canada that are known for their open-ended fair-use or fair-dealing doctrine provide for the exceptions within the framework of the doctrine. From Africa, South Africa's recent bill opts for a blend approach of specific L&Es and a catch-all clause of fair-use doctrine.

Despite the variance in the approaches and the consequent difference in scope, the overarching purpose remains the same. In view of their purpose, it is thus vital to reframe the exceptions for teaching, scholarship, and scientific research as essential users' rights.[165] Further, the exceptions should cover all exclusive rights over works lawfully made to the public in both analog and digital environments. In particular, it is important to extend the exceptions to encompass acts of translation, adaptation, distribution, communication, importation, rental/lending, display, and so on for *non-commercial uses*. For instance, an access to a work for a distance or online education implicates several exclusive rights.[166]

Placed within the proposed fair-use-driven three-steep test,[167] the introduction of a suitable exception for scientific research and a scholarship will promote quality higher education and scientific research for human development.[168] Due to its instrumental role, Reichman and Okediji recommend the adoption of a tailor-made mandatory exemption for scientific research without the restrictions of commercial/non-commercial distinction, digital locks and contractual overrides.[169] Indeed, carving out development-oriented L&Es for education and research are contemplated in the WIPO Internet and Marrakesh Treaties. In their respective preambles, the Treaties recognize 'the need to maintain a balance between the rights of authors and the larger public interest, particularly *education, research and access to information*.'[170]

As mentioned earlier, the exceptions for teaching, scholarship and scientific research should be exempted from the digital locks.[171] In this respect, worth a lesson is Morocco's exemption of L&Es for educational institutions from TPMs.[172] This carve-out is crucial to facilitate a legitimate access to and use of the creative works. Further, subject to the requirement of fair practice, the teaching exception should make clear the possible use of course packs for educational purposes in order to legitimize the existing practice.[173] An explicit provision is also needed to exempt the L&Es from a threat of criminalization. Given the growing significance of distance or online education, the teaching exception must be applicable for education of all levels and modes.[174] After all, promoting education both as an essential element of human rights and basic capabilities is vital for the realization of human development.

Set within the broad framework of flexibilities critical for human development, providing for mandatory teaching, and scientific research exceptions is thus vital to facilitate access to digital and non-digital learning materials.[175] For their optimal utilization, the *mandatory status* of the L&Es will be important to shield users against technological and contractual overrides.[176] A set of mandatory L&Es is also useful to promote affordable access to disadvantaged learners.[177] To this end, governments can use the L&Es as a strategic baseline to negotiate with publishers over the price of learning materials.[178]

D Limitations and exceptions for libraries and archives

Given their roles to facilitate access to learning materials for higher education and scientific research,[179] the L&Es for libraries and archives are other vital flexibilities that need to be reframed as users' rights and adapted to the digital environment. It is undisputed that the growing digital information technologies have transformed the roles of libraries. As Okediji observes, libraries and archives are "the most accessible and dependable source of information, scientific materials and knowledge."[180] Nonetheless, the lack of appropriate L&Es constitutes an impediment to their role of facilitating access to knowledge, supporting education and providing opportunities for knowledge accumulation.[181]

In several LDCs, the L&Es for libraries and archives are often restricted to the narrow scope of reproduction limited to published journal articles and short extracts of books. For instance, the L&Es permitted for libraries and archives in Ethiopia exclude acts of distribution, making available digital copies, adaptation, and public lending. In both developed nations and the LDCs, unreasonable prohibition of access is detrimental to the public interest roles of libraries in the digital environment.[182] Further, the reproduction of the whole works such as books and unpublished works is often not allowed. To avoid such a severe restriction of the roles of libraries, a broader set of L&Es should encompass all the relevant exclusive rights. In terms of the works, it should be applicable for all works lawfully made available to the public. In the LDCs, the strict conditions that are often attached to the L&Es need to be relaxed. In this regard, lessons can be drawn from countries with boarder L&Es for libraries.

In setting or taking a legislative inspiration, the LDCs should also devise a corpus of appropriate mandatory L&Es in compliance with the broadest possible interpretation of the three-step test. It is important to reframe the L&Es as users rights in order to enable users to assert the rights against restrictive practices. In recognition of their roles to advance public interest, the L&Es must further be insulated against an indiscriminate criminalization and the restrictive effects of TPMs.[183] Indeed, reframing and safeguarding appropriate L&Es for libraries and archives are crucial to advance human development through access to creative works.[184]

E Exhaustion doctrine and parallel imports

As noted earlier, the TRIPs Agreement has left the issue of exhaustion or parallel imports quite open for member states to determine. In view of its role to facilitate affordable access to learning materials,[185] copyright law, competition and the pertinent customs laws need a proper alignment to facilitate parallel imports of the relevant learning materials after their lawful first sale. Given their reliance upon imported learning materials as net importers of knowledge goods, the LDCs stand to benefit from adopting international doctrine of exhaustion that facilitates unimpeded parallel importation. In this regard, useful lessons can be drawn from developed and developing nations. For example, the United States that champions a stronger protection has adopted the rule of international exhaustion in order to advance its public interests. In Africa, both Egypt and South Africa (in its new bill) are among countries that provide for the doctrine of international exhaustion.[186]

Noting the functional equivalence between the first sale and commercial licensing in the online markets, scholars also argue for the doctrine's reasonable extension to the digital environment so as to facilitate access to digital copies.[187] In short, the TRIPs-plus approach must be avoided in order to integrate the doctrine as an important form of flexibilities.

F Compulsory licensing

Intended to advance public interests, the role of compulsory license is crucial to facilitate access to creative works needed for higher education and creative innovation. Not all creators and users are able to reach successful negotiations for an authorized access to protected knowledge. In most LDCs, absent local CMOs or due to their inefficient operation, the compensated scheme becomes the sole avenue for access to protected knowledge goods. Even when there is one, as a remedial measure to address the concerns of anticompetitive or unfair licensing practices, a compulsory licensing regime remains instrumental to facilitate access to learning materials. For an optimal utilization of this compensated scheme, the procedures and conditions of compulsory licensing should be simplified to avoid undue complexities that undermine its operation and the intended benefits.

Encompassing all works *lawfully made available to the public,* compulsory licensing should be applicable for all acts of exclusive rights, including distribution and making available rights. From among others, the latter rights are critical for educational institutions and libraries. Further, a resort to compulsory license should be indicated in the appropriate laws as an authorized measure to regulate anticompetitive or unfair practices. To this end, a coherent linkage must be created between copyright and competition (antitrust) laws. As a public policy tool, a compulsory license should primarily be designed to serve the public interest.

G Limitations and exceptions for persons with disabilities

Embodied in the Marrakesh Treaty, the L&Es for persons with disabilities are vital for advancing the human capabilities of the persons. As of this writing, several countries have ratified or acceded to the Marrakesh Treaty that requires domestic implementation of the international instrument. Preceding the Treaty, the ratification of the UNCRPD marked a significant milestone to address the needs of persons with disabilities within the human rights system. From among several other rights, access to education is central to the Convention. In addition to its reference, *inter alia*, to the UNCRPD, the preamble to the Marrakesh Treaty is cognizant of the challenges persons with disabilities face in their enjoyment of the right to education and the opportunity to conduct scientific research. For the advancement of their human capabilities, users with disabilities should be allowed an adequate access to knowledge for creative innovation and access to education. In this regard, both international instruments thus underscore the need to provide relevant L&Es to allow disabled users an access to copyrighted materials in appropriate formats.

In order to conform to its international obligations, contracting parties are required to integrate into their respective copyright systems the relevant flexibilities enshrined in the Marrakesh Treaty. Predating the Treaty, art. 30(3) of the UNCRPD itself obligates states to take 'all appropriate steps' to remove IP-related 'discriminatory barrier to access by persons with disabilities to cultural materials.' In adopting the appropriate flexibilities to facilitate the beneficiaries' access to learning materials, commentators suggest taking into account the overarching human rights objectives of the treaties and a broader definition of beneficiaries.[188] In so doing, a member-state is required to enable persons with disabilities to "[e]njoy access to cultural materials in accessible formats" for their sustainable human development.[189] To this end, relevant entities should be authorized to promote access to copyrighted materials in accessible formats.

In sum, the reintegration of the specific copyright-related flexibilities should be made in order to facilitate access to copyrighted learning materials. Seen through the prism of human development, the broader public interest objectives should be used for the reintegration and utilization of the flexibilities as users' rights. Provided as development-inducing mandatory L&Es,[190] the flexibilities should be immune to both wholesale criminalization and abusive TPMs. In this regard, the WIPO's technical assistance to LDCs that often promotes, *inter alia,* an indiscriminate use of TPMs should be resisted or considered with a great caution. It must be underlined that the protection of TPMs is not required to be made "in a manner inconsistent with copyright's fundamental goals."[191]

5.5 Conclusion

As discussed in this book, there is a plethora of copyright and related flexibilities that are scattered and embedded in various legal regimes. Despite this fact, a significant number of relevant international copyright flexibilities are left underutilized in several LDCs. In addition to copyright law that remains the principal legal regime, the national constitutions, ratified human rights instruments, competition law, and higher education legislation often provide for pertinent flexibilities to promote access to learning materials. In most LDCs, there however lacks an appropriate coherence among the relevant policy, legal, and institutional frameworks. As a result, the disparate flexibilities are often not tied together into a coherent whole to facilitate the collaborative realization of the underlying development objectives. For their coherent integration, it is imperative to rethink the development orientation and create a proper alignment among the policy, legal and institutional regimes in order to promote a sustainable human development.

Seen through the HDCA lens, making appropriate policy and legal reforms are essential to rethink and ensure a coherent integration of the flexibilities, including the open access licensing models. In the integration of the pertinent flexibilities, a set of broad and mandatory L&Es should be designed, *inter alia,* for private use, quotation, teaching, scientific research, libraries, and archives as well as for persons with disabilities. Framed as users' rights, this set of flexibilities will prove crucial for higher education and creative innovation. In the same vein, an appropriate compulsory licensing schemes aligned with the doctrine of international exhaustion should be adopted to facilitate affordable or bulk access to copyrighted materials. Informed by the human rights and constitutional dimensions, it is crucial to reframe the flexibilities as positive users' rights. Further, these flexibilities should be insulated from criminalization, digital locks and abusive contractual overrides. For concerns related to digital locks, scholars point out the roles of a competition authority and positive users' right to allow a legitimate circumvention of TPMs for lawful purposes.[192]

In a nutshell, the integrative and rights-based HDCA should be adopted to rethink, reincorporate and align relevant development-oriented flexibilities. In particular, the formulation of robust and comprehensive copyright and educational policies should embrace both the existing international copyright-related flexibilities and the emerging open access models. With a proper alignment and coherence, a strategic combination of the flexibilities is useful to facilitate enhanced access to knowledge in general and learning materials in particular. Considering their respective contexts and levels of human development, countries should reframe or reintegrate the relevant legal flexibilities as users' rights in order to empower their users and promote the expansion of human capabilities. To this end, the proper integration and effective utilization of flexibilities require strong, robust and collaborative institutions. Thus, promoting institutional collaboration and capacity building is also vital for sustainable human development.

Notes

1 Ruth Okediji, "Reframing International Copyright Limitations and Exceptions as Development Policy," in *Copyright Law in an Age of Limitations and Exceptions* (Cambridge: Cambridge University, 2017) 429 at 443–445 [Okediji, "Reframing International Copyright"]; Ruth L. Okediji, "The International Copyright System: Limitations, Exceptions and Public Interest Considerations for Developing Countries" (2006) UNCTAD-ICTSD Issue Paper No.15 at 7–8 &12 [Okediji, The International Copyright System].

2 See Okediji, "International Copyright System," *supra* note 1 at ix, xii & 6–9.

3 David Vaver, "Copyright Defenses as User Rights" (2013) 60:4 J Copyr Soc USA 661 at 667 [Vaver, "Copyright Defenses"].

4 Niva Elkin-Koren, "Copyright in a Digital Ecosystem: A User Right Approach," in Okediji, ed, *Copyright Law in an Age of Limitations and Exceptions, supra note* 154 at 134 [Elkin-Koren, "Copyright in a Digital Ecosystem"].

5 David Vaver, *Copyright Law* (Toronto: Irwin Law, 2000) at 171 [Vaver, *Copyright Law*]. As Vaver puts it, "the policy of copyright policy has always been to balance competing owner and user interests according to both contemporary exigencies and transcendental imperatives such as free speech and free trade."

6 Vaver, "Copyright Defenses," *supra* note 3 at 669.

7 See Okediji, "Reframing International Copyright" *supra* note 1 at 447–460.

8 See Carolyn Deere, *The Implementation Game: The TRIPs Agreement and the Global Politics of Intellectual Property reform in Developing Countries* (Oxford: Oxford University Press, 2009) at 68 [Deere, *The Implementation Guide*].

9 See generally Okediji, "Reframing International Copyright" *supra* note 1.

10 *Ibid* at 475 & 482–489.

11 *See* Carlos M. Correa, *Trade Related Aspects of Intellectual Property Rights: A Commentary on the TRIPS Agreement* (Oxford: Oxford University Press, 2007) at 104–107[Correa, *Trade Related Aspects*].

12 *Ibid. Agreement on Trade-Related Aspects of Intellectual Property Rights*, 15 April 1994, Marrakesh Agreement Establishing the World Trade Organization, Preamble, paras 6 & 7 *cum* art. 8, Annex 1C, 33 ILM1125 (1994) [*TRIPS Agreement*].

13 Peter K. Yu, "The Objectives and Principles of the TRIPS Agreement" (2009) 46 Hous L Rev 979 at 981 [Yu, "The Objectives and Principles"]; Peter K. Yu, "The International Enclosure Movement," (2007) 82 Indiana LJ 827 at 863–866 [Yu, "The International Enclosure"]; Peter K. Yu, "TRIPS and Its Discontents," (2006) 10 Marq Intell Prop L Rev 369 at 387–401 [Yu, TRIPS and Its Discontents"].

14 Martin Senftleben, "The International Three-Step Test: A Model Provision for EC Fair Use Legislation" (2010) 1 JIPIT 67 at 67 [Senftleben, "The International Three-Step Test"].

15 Christophe Geiger, Daniel Gervais & Martin Senftleben, "The Three-Step Test Revisited: How to Use the Test's Flexibility in National Copyright Law" (2014) 29:3 Am U Int'l L Rev 581 at 582 [Giger, Gervais & Senftleben, "The Three-Step Test Revisited"].

16 *Ibid* at 601–605.

17 Okediji, "Reframing International Copyright," *supra* note 1 at 440–447 & 494–495; Ruth Okediji, Towards International Fair Use Doctrine (2000) 39 Colum J Transnat'l L 75 at 87–90 [Okediji, "Towards International Fair Use Doctrine"].

18 Okediji, "Toward an International Fair Use Doctrine" *supra* note 17 at 90.

19 Okediji, "Reframing International Copyright" *supra* note 1 at 436, 439, 475 & 481–482. The reasons relate to (a) a misalignment between copyright law and domestic institutional environment, and (b) the failure to adopt a strategic and development-oriented policy measures that facilitate access to knowledge goods. *Ibid.*

20 See Okediji, Reframing International Copyright" *supra* note 1 at 436–440; Okediji, International Copyright system," *supra* note 1 at 20 & 30–31; see Deer, *Implementation Game, supra* note 8 at 196–232 & 303–320.

21 Elkin-Koren, "Copyright in a Digital Ecosystem" *supra* note 4 at 132. For courts and commentators, "user rights" are often referred to "as an all-encompassing category, loosely describing the public domain, exceptions and limitations and other permissible uses." *Ibid* at 158.

22 See Layman Patterson & Stanley Lindberg, *The Nature of Copyright: The Law of Users' Rights* (Athens & London: The University of Georgia Press, 1991). Elkin-Koren, "Copyright in a Digital Ecosystem" *supra* note 4 at 155–156.

23 Vaver, *Copyright Law, supra* note 5 at 171; See *Alberta v. Canadian Copyright Licensing Agency*, [2012] 2 S.C.R. 345 (Can.); *Society of Composers, Authors and Music Publishers of Can. v. Bell Can.*, [2012] 2 S.C.R. 326 (Can.). *See generally* Michael Geist, ed, *The Copyright Pentalogy: How the Supreme Court of Canada Shook the Foundations of Canadian Copyright Law* (Toronto: Irwin Law, 2013).

24 Vaver, *Copyright Law, supra* note 5 at 171.

25 See *CCH Canadian Ltd vs Law Society of Upper Canada, [2004] 1 S.C.R. 339* at paras 147–150 [*CCH vs Law Society*]. See also Teresa Scassa, "Recalibrating Copyright Law?: A Comment on the Supreme Court of Canada's Decision in CC Canadian Limited et al v. Law Society of Upper Canada" (2004) 3:2 CJLT 89 at 93–98 [Scassa, "Recalibrating Copyright Law?"].

26 *CCH vs Law Society, supra* note 25 at para 48.
27 *Ibid.* See generally Teresa Scassa, "Users' Rights in the Balance: Recent Developments in Copyright Law at the Supreme Court of Canada", (2005) 22 CIPR 133.
28 While appraising the 'salutary effect' of the Canadian approach and the SCC's positive step in support of user's rights, Scassa opines that "the new Canadian orientation may be too little, too late in copyright larger scheme of where copyright law is heading." Scassa, *Recalibrating Copyright Law, supra* note 25 at 89 & 97. In this regard, the major reasons she points out are Canada's international obligation under copyright treaties and the consequent constraining impact of legislative measures. *Ibid* at 89 & 97–98.
29 Elkin-Koren, "Copyright in a Digital Ecosystem," *supra* note 4 at 132 & 134–135.
30 *Ibid* at 132.
31 *Ibid* at 132 & 143–148.
32 *Alberta v. Canadian Copyright Licensing Agency, supra* note 23.
33 *Ibid* at para 360; Carys Craig, "Globalizing User Rights-Talk: On Copyright Limits and Rhetorical Risks" (2017) 33:1 Am U Int'l L Rev 2 at 24–25 [Craig, "Globalizing User Rights-Talk"].
34 Craig, "Globalizing User Rights-Talk" *supra* note 33 at 27–37; Elkin-Koren, "Copyright in a Digital Ecosystem," *supra* note 4 at 132.
35 Margaret Wilkinson, "International Copyright: Marrakesh and the Future of Users' Rights Exceptions," in Mark Perry, ed., *Global Governance of Intellectual Property in the 21st Century: Reflecting Policy Through Change* (Switzerland: Springer, 2016)107 at 107–127 [Wilkinson, "International Copyright"]. In the words of Wilkinson, "there is no question that Marrakesh [Treaty] is historic, because it is the first international treaty focused on user's rights." *Ibid* at 118.
36 *Ibid.* See generally, e.g. Patterson & Lindberg, *The Nature of Copyright, supra* note 22; Vaver, "Copyright Defenses," *supra* note 3; David Vaver, "*User Rights*" (2013) 25 Intell Prop J 105; Craig, "Globalizing User Rights-Talk" *supra* note 33; Elkin-Koren, "Copyright in the Digital Ecosystem," *supra* note 4; Pascale Chapdelaine, *Copyright Users Rights: Contracts and the Erosion of Property* (Oxford: Oxford University Press, 2017); Abraham Drassinower, "Taking User Rights Seriously," in Michael Geist, ed, *In the Public Interest: The Future of Canadian Copyright Law* (Toronto: Irwin Law Journal, 2005) 462.
37 Vaver, "Copyright Defenses" *supra* note 3 at 672.
38 *International Covenant on Economic, Social and Cultural Rights,* art. 15(1)(a & b), 16 December 1966, 993 UNTS No 3 (entered into force 3 January 1976) [ICESCR]; *Universal Declaration of Human Rights*, GA Res 217A (III), UNGAOR, 3d Sess, 1st plen mtg, UN Doc A/810 (12 December 1948) at art. 27(1) [UDHR]; *CESCR General Comment No.17: The Right of Everyone to Benefit from the Protection of the Moral and Material Interests Resulting from any scientific, Literary or Artistic Production of Which He or She is the Author (Art. 15 (1) (c) of the Covenant)*, para 4, UN Doc E/C12/GC/17 (Jan.12, 2006) [*CESCR General Comment No.17*].
39 *CESCR General Comment No.17, supra* note 38 at para 35; see Peter K. Yu, "Re-conceptualizing Intellectual Property Interests in a Human Rights Framework" (2007) 40 UC Davis L Rev 1039 at 1071–1074 [Yu, "Re-Conceptualizing Intellectual Property"]; Yu, "Challenges to the Development of a Human-Rights Framework for Intellectual Property," in Paul Torremans, ed., *Intellectual Property and Human Rights: Enhanced Edition of Copyright and Human Rights* (The Netherlands: Kluwer Law International, 2008) [Yu, "Challenges"]; Laurence R. Helfer, "Toward a Human Rights Framework for Intellectual Property" (2007) 40 UC Davis L Rev 971 at 996 [Helfer, "Toward a Human Rights Framework"] (pointing out the need for balancing with other rights recognized in the ICESCR as required.)
40 Craig, "Globalizing User Rights-Talk" *supra* note 33 at 42–73.
41 *Ibid* at 53–64 (explaining the various critiques based critical legal studies). See Mark Tushnet, "The Critique of Rights," (1994) 47:1 SMU L Rev 23–34; Mark Tushnet,

"An Essay on Rights," (1984) 62:8 Tex L Rev 1363–1403; Duncan Kennedy, "The Critique of Rights in Critical Legal Studies," in Wendy Brown & Janet Halley, eds., *Left Legalism/ Left Critique* (Durham: Duke University Press, 2002) 178–228.
42 Craig, "Globalizing User Rights-Talk" *supra* note 33 at 53.
43 *Ibid* at 62. As Craig notes, "the claim that users' rights are duly recognized within the copyright system will produce "a narrative of legitimation," a language for concluding that the system is fair, objective and unbiased." [footnote omitted]. *Ibid.*
44 *Ibid.*
45 See Yu, "Challenges" *supra* note 39 at 84–91.
46 *Anheuser-Busch, Inc. v. Portugal*, [2007] ECHR 73049/01; Laurence Helfer, "The New Frontier? Intellectual Property and European Court of Human Rights 2008 49: Harv Int'l LJ 1–52 [Helfer, The New Frontier].
47 Craig, "Globalizing User Rights-Talk" *supra* note 33 at 50–51 &71–73; Helfer, "Toward a Human Rights Framework" *supra* note 39 at 994–997. In his observation of the multiple test for a restriction on author's human rights, Helfer states that the test is "more constraining than the now ubiquitous 'three-step test' used to assess the treaty-compatibility of exceptions and limitations in national copyright and patent laws." *Ibid* at 994.
48 Craig, "Globalizing User Rights-Talk" *supra* note 33 at 62.
49 *Ibid* at 52.
50 *Ibid.* In emphasizing the role of copyright for promoting public interest, the Supreme Court of Canada has reiterated its stance on users' rights as "an essential part of furthering the public interest objectives of the Copyright Act." *Society of Composers, Authors and Music Publishers of Canada v. Bell Canada*, [2012] 2 S.C.R. 326, paras. 9–11 (Can.)
51 See Craig, "Globalizing User Rights-Talk" *supra* note 33 at 64–70 & 72–73.
52 *CESR General Comment No.17*, *supra* note 38 at paras 1 & 2. As the Committee has observed, "intellectual property rights are first and foremost a *means* by which States seek to provide incentives for inventiveness and creativity ... for the benefit of society as a whole (emphasis added)." *Ibid* at para 1. Yu, "Challenges" *supra* note 39 at 85.
53 *CESCR General Comment No.17*, *supra* note 38 at para 2. Yu, "Reconceptualizing Intellectual Property," *supra* note 39 at 1081–1090.
54 Daniel Gervais, "Intellectual Property and Human Rights: Learning to Live Together," in Paul Torremans, ed, *Intellectual Property and Human Rights, supra* note 39, at 15 [Gervais, "Intellectual Property and Human Rights"].
55 *Ibid* at 13–23.
56 Craig, "Globalizing User Rights-Talk" *supra* note 33 at 56–58 & 71–72.
57 Carys Craig, "Digital Locks and the Fate of Fair Dealing in Canada: In Pursuit of 'Prescriptive Parallelism'" (2010) 13: 4 J World Intellect Prop 503 at 511 [Craig, "Digital Locks"].
58 *Ibid.*
59 *Ibid.*
60 Vaver, "Copyright Defenses" *supra* note 3 at 672.
61 Craig, "Globalizing User Rights-Talk" *supra* note 33 at 41.
62 *Ibid* at 72.
63 *Ibid.*
64 See Okediji, "Reframing International Copyright" *supra* note 1 at 440–447 & 472–479; Craig, "Globalizing User Rights-Talk" *supra* note 33 at 52.
65 Craig, "Globalizing User Rights-Talk" supra note 33 at 63.
66 *Ibid* at 63.
67 Carys Craig, "Technological Neutrality: Recalibrating Copyright in the Information Age" (2016) 17 Theor Inq L 601 at 626[Craig, "Technological Neutrality"].
68 *Ibid* at 627; Craig, "Globalizing User Rights-Talk" *supra* note 33 at 50.

69 See Craig, "Technological Neutrality" *supra* note 67 at 626; Okediji, "Reframing International Copyright" *supra* note 1 at 440–447 & 482–489.

70 See generally Okediji, "Reframing International Copyright" *supra* note 1; Ruth L. Okediji, "The Limits of International Copyright Exceptions for Developing Countries" (2019) 21:3 Vand J Ent & Tech L 689 [Okediji, "The Limits of International Copyright"].

71 See Okediji, "Reframing International Copyright" *supra* note 1 at 441 & 494–495.

72 For instance, Jennifer Nedelsky notes rights as "a particular institutional and rhetorical means of expressing, contesting, and implementing… values." Jennifer Nedelsky, *Law's Relations: A Relational Theory of Self, Autonomy, and Law* (Oxford: Oxford University Press, 2011) at 238 & 241.

73 Craig, "Technological Neutrality" *supra* note 67 at 627–629. For Nedelsky, value means "any of the big abstractions used to articulate what a given society sees as essential to humanity or to the good life for its members." Nedelsky, *supra* note 72 at 241 & 246.

74 Elkin-Koren, "Copyright in the Digital Ecosystem" *supra* note 4 at 168.

75 Okediji, "Reframing International Copyright" *supra* note 1 at 440.

76 *Ibid* at 440–447.

77 Laurence R. Helfer & Graeme W. Austin, *Human Rights and Intellectual Property: Mapping the Global Interface* (Cambridge & New York: Cambridge University Press, 2011) at 211 [Helfer & Austin, *Human Right and Intellectual Property*].

78 UNDP, *Human Development Reports 2000: Human Rights and Human Development* (New York: UNDP & Oxford University Press, 2000) at 19–26 [UNDP, *Human Development Report 2000*]; see generally Sakiko Fakuda-Parr, "The Metrics of Human Rights: Complementarities of the Human Development and Capabilities Approach" (2011) 12:1 J Hum Dev Capab 73–89.

79 Martha Nussbaum, "Capabilities, Entitlements, Rights: Supplementation and Critique" (2011) 12:1 J Hum Dev Capab 23 at 26 [Nussbaum, "Capabilities"].

80 *Ibid.*

81 *Ibid.*

82 UNDP, *Human Development Reports* (2000), *supra* note 78 at 19.

83 Yochai Benkler, *The Wealth of Networks: How Social Production Transforms Markets and Freedom* (New Haven, CT: Yale University Press, 2006) at 14 [Benkler, *The Wealth of Networks*].

84 Okediji, "Reframing International Copyright" *supra* note 1 at 440–447. Okediji, however, observes the expansion of the international copyright's protection without 'any overarching theory of an international public interest.' *Ibid* at 444–445.

85 See *Copyright Proclamation No.410/2004*, *Federal Negarit Gazette*, 10th Year No.55, Addis Ababa, 19th July, 2004, Preamble at para1 [*Copyright Proc. No.410/2004*]. This gap is evident from the readings of its preamble & the substantive provisions with restrictive exceptions.

86 It is important to recast copyright as the freedoms (capabilities) *to create* that needs to be balanced against, *inter alia*, the freedom to access knowledge and participate in cultural life. See Gervais, "Intellectual Property and Human Rights" *supra* note 54 at 22–33.

87 Daniel Gervais, *(Re)structuring Copyright: A Comprehensive Path to International Copyright Reform* (Cheltenham: Edward Elgar, 2017) at 216 & 279 [Gervais, *Restructuring Copyright*].

88 Sabina Alkire, "Dimensions of Human Development" (2002) 30:2 World Dev 181 at 182.

89 Nussbaum, "Capabilities, Entitlements and Rights," *supra* note 79 at 31–36; Marth C. Nussbaum, "Capabilities and Human Rights" (1997) 66 Fordham L Rev 273 at 295–297 [Nussbaum, "Capabilities and Human Rights"].

90 Melanie Walker, "A Human Development and Capabilities 'Prospective Analysis' of Global Higher Education Policy" (2010) 25:4 J Educ Policy 485 at 488–489 [Walker,

"A Human Development and Capabilities"]. Walker argues that "human capital goals ought to be subsumed into the more expansive policy of human development." *Ibid* at 489.

91 *Ibid* at 497.

92 *Ibid* at 492. Melanie Walker, "Universities and a Human Development Ethics: A Capabilities Approach to Curriculum" (2012) 47:3 Eur J Educ 448 at 454 & 456–457 [Walker, "Universities and Human Development"].

93 Walker, "Universities and Human Development" *supra* note 92 at 456. Walker, "A Human Development and Capabilities," *supra* note 90 at 487–488 & 493–494. As Walker notes, "graduates equipped with knowledge, practical skills and public service values can make a positive difference in the everyday lives of the people with whom they come into contact." *Ibid* at 487.

94 Walker, "A Human Development and Capabilities" *supra* note 90 at 494.

95 *Ibid* at 488–490 & 493–496.

96 Okediji, "Reframing International Copyright" *supra* note 1 at 466. In Okediji's observation, the major reasons for the policy incoherence or problem of coordination in developing and least developing countries are: defect in the design of the law, weak institutions, under enforcement of laws and underinvestment in research and development. *Ibid* at 466–467.

97 See WIPO DA, Cluster B: Norm-Setting, Flexibilities, Public Policy and Public Domain, Recommendations No.15.

98 See WIPO DA, Cluster B: Norm-Setting, Flexibilities, Public Policy and Public Domain, Recommendations No.22 & 23; Cluster C: Technology Transfer, Information Communication Technology (ICT) and Access to Knowledge, Recommendations 25, 28 & 32. See Gervais, *Restructuring Copyright, supra* note 87 at 217 & 280 (noting the emerging global perspective on copyright in particular and IP in general 'as part of a broader landscape of innovation policies').

99 See WIPO DA, Cluster F: Other Issues, Recommendations No. 45; TRIPs Agreement, *supra* note 12 at art. 7.

100 Nussbaum, "Capabilities and Human Rights" *supra* note 89 at 277. Martha Nussbaum, "Introduction: Aspirations and the Capabilities List" (2016) 17:3 J Hum Dev Capab 301 at 301. Nussbaum, regards her list of capabilities as a 'blueprint' for nations' to take them into account as 'fundamental constitutional entitlements.' *Ibid.*

101 Okediji, "Reframing International Copyright" *supra* note 1 at 467.

102 See *South African Copyright Amendment Bill* [B13-B-2017], § 12 (A-D) & 19(B-D), Republic of South Africa, online https://www.gov.za/sites/default/files/gcis_document/201705/b13-2017copyright170516.pdf; see also Intellectual Property Policy of the Republic of South Africa, Phase I, International Trade and Development, November 2018, online: dti www.dti.gov.za/gazzettes/IP_Policy.pdf

103 See WIPO DA, Cluster A: Technical Assistance and Capacity Building, Recommendations No. 1 & 13. It is worth mentioning that WIPO's technical assistance given to various LDCs has the potential to shape the domestic copyright systems. As indicated in the DA, "WIPO's legislative assistance shall be, *inter alia*, development-oriented and demand-driven, taking into account the priorities and the special needs of developing countries, especially LDCs, as well as the different levels of development of member states." *Ibid* at Recommendation No. 13.

104 Okedij, "Reframing International Copyright" *supra* note 1 at 467.

105 Walker, "A Human Development and Capabilities" *supra* note 90 at 493.

106 See Gervais, *Restructuring Copyright, supra* note 87 at 279–294. In general, Gervais notes the goal of copyright—'maximiz[ing] the development of human creativity and innovation'—to be 'justified as a matter of human development' and 'welfare enhancing.' *Ibid* at 279.

107 One of the reasons that affect the optimal implementation of flexibilities is "the misalignment between the design of copyright law and the domestic institutional environment." Okediji, "Reframing International Copyright" *supra* note 1 at 475. Okediji, "International Copyright System," *supra* note 1 at 20 & 30–31.

108 See Christophe Geiger, "The Constitutional Dimension of Intellectual Property" in Paul Torremans, ed, *Intellectual Property and Human Rights, supra* note 39 at 114–131 [Geiger, "Constitutional Dimension"].

109 *Ibid* at 115–122.

110 See Gervais, "Intellectual Property and Human Rights" *supra* note 54 at 13–23.

111 *Ibid* at 18. As Gervais notes, "a human rights framework can provide specific normative guidance in the elaboration and interpretation of copyright rules." *Ibid* at 23. For him, 'human rights provide purpose' to L & Es. Daniel Gervais, "Human Rights and the Philosophical Foundations of Intellectual Property," in Christophe Geiger, *Research Handbook on Human Rights and Intellectual Property* (Cheltenham: Edward Elgar Publishing, 2015) at 90 & 97 [Gervais, "HRs & Philosophical Foundations"].

112 Gervais, "Intellectual Property and Human Rights" *supra* note 54 at 21.

113 The WIPO DA acknowledges taking due account of the level of development in norm-setting process for flexibilities. WIPO DA, Recommendation No. 13.

114 See generally James Boyle, "The Second Enclosure Movement and the Construction of the Public Domain" (2003) 66 Law & Contemp Probs 34–74.

115 Gervais, *Restructuring Copyright, supra* note 87 at 193 & 286–291. As Gervais observes, "[n]ot all IP rights are the same, nor do all industries respond the same to changes in IP protection." *Ibid* at 289.

116 *Ibid* at 192–206 & 289–290. For Gervais, authors in quadrant I are those who 'dedicate their work to the public domain' while authors in quadrant II are creators who are 'otherwise compensated for their work' and care about attribution. In contrast, those in quadrant III care about both income and attribution, but lack a real control over the dissemination. This category is considered 'a very significant part of the core of copyright policy.' Called 'commercial custodian,' those in quadrant IV represent copyright industries engaged in active commercial exploitation of the works. *Ibid* at 193–198.

117 *Ibid* at 289–291.

118 *Ibid* at 204–205. Given their primary concern with attribution in lieu of commercialization, several academics and scientists fall in this quadrant II while those waive protection altogether and dedicate their works to the public domain belong to quadrant I. *Ibid.*

119 *Ibid* at 195 & 290–291.

120 *Ibid* at 195, 198 & 204–205.

121 Instead, as Okediji points out, "[a]ddressing access to education and knowledge in developing countries will require a combination of policy instruments ranging from compensation schemes for producers of educational materials, educational L&Es, and public investments in cultural institutions such as libraries, archives, and museums." Okediji, "Reframing International Copyright" supra note 1 at 487. For the problems related to the 'one-size-fits-all' paradigms, see Michael Carroll, "One Size Does Not Fit All: A Framework for Tailoring Intellectual Property Rights" (2009) 70 Ohio State Law J 1361; Jerome Reichman & David Lange, "Bargaining Around the TRIPs Agreement: The Case for Ongoing Public-Private Initiatives to Facilitate Worldwide Intellectual Property Transactions" (1998) 9 Duke J Comp & Int'l L 11 at 50.

122 Okediji, "Reframing International Copyright" *supra* note 1 at 476.

123 Jerome Reichman & Tracy Lewis, "Using Liability Rules to Stimulate Local Innovations in Developing Countries" in Keith Maskus & Jerome Reichman, eds, *International Public Goods and Transfer of Technology Under a Globalized Intellectual Property Regime* (Cambridge: Cambridge University Press, 2005) 337 at 349–351; But see

Robert Merges, "Contracting into Liability Rules: Intellectual Property Rights and Collective Rights Organizations" (1996) 84 Cal L Rev 1293 (disputing the appropriateness of liability rules and in particular compulsory licenses for digital content).

124 Several jurisdictions have adopted an equitable remuneration scheme for works that are relevant for educational purposes. See Jane Ginsburg, "Fair Use for Free, Permitted-but-Paid?" (2014) 29 BTLJ 1383 at 417–432.

125 *General Comment No.17, supra* note 38 at paras 16 & 24; Yu, "Reconceptualizing Intellectual Property," *supra* note 39 at 1089–1092.

126 *General Comment No.17, supra* note 38 at para 24.

127 Gervais, *Restructuring Copyright, supra* note 87 at 195, 198, 204–205 & 289.

128 Jerome Reichman & Ruth Okediji, "When Copyright Law and Science Collide: Empowering Digitally Integrated Research Methods on a Global Scale" (2012) 96 Minn L Rev 1362 at 1390–1393, 1402–1403 & 1436 [Reichman & Okediji, "When Copyright Law and Science Collide"].

129 *Ibid* at 1403 & 1409–1410; see Sam Ricketson and Jane Ginsburg, *International Copyright and Neighboring Rights: The Berne Convention and Beyond*, Volume I, 2nd ed (Oxford: Oxford University Press, 2006) at 769–776, 853 & 859 [Ricketson & Ginsburg (Vol. I)]. Gervais, "Intellectual Property and Human Rights" *supra* note 54 at 8–10 & 18–23; Correa, *Trade Related Aspects, supra* note 11 at 154–155.

130 See generally Christophe Geiger et al., "Towards a Balanced Interpretation of the 'Three-Step Test' for Copyright Exceptions" (2008) Eur IP Rev 489 [Geiger et al, "Towards a Balanced Interpretation"]; Patrick Goold, "The Interpretive Argument for a Balanced Three-Step Test?" (2017) 33:1 Am U Int'l L Rev 187–230.

131 Ricketson & Ginsburg (Vol. I), *supra* note 129 at 773–777; Okediji, "Towards International Fair Use Doctrine," *supra* note 17 at 111–113.

132 In the absence of actual or potential market for the learning materials, there exists no actual conflict with the author's or publishers' normal(commercial) exploitation. It is important to bear in mind that the average per capita income in Ethiopia (≈$800) is less than or almost equal to the price of most important textbooks published abroad and sold online the costs of which includes shipping and related expenses.

133 Sharon E. Foster, "The Conflict between the Human Right to Education and Copyright" in Paul Torremans, ed, *Intellectual Property and Human Rights, supra note 39* at 305–306; see Wendy Gordon, "Fair Use as a Market Failure: A structural and Economic Analysis of the Betamax and Its Predecessors" (1982) 82 Colum L Rev 1600 at 1605–1627 [Gordon, "Fair Use"].

134 Foster, *supra* note 133 at 305–306. As Foster notes, "[i]n the case of market failure due to a state's inability to afford to pay there would be a false conflict as there is no reasonable expectation of material gain but moral interests would have to be protected." *Ibid* at 306.

135 *Ibid* at 305–306; Ricketson & Ginsburg (Vol. I), *supra* note 129 at 771–173; See Reichman & Okediji, *supra* note 128 at 1402–1403. Gervais, "Intellectual Property and Human Rights" *supra* note 54 at 8–10 & 18–23.

136 From the proposed Gervais' quadrant, this can be accommodated under quadrant III for authors (poets, artists, singers, etc) who demand a fair remuneration and attribution. Gervais, *Restructuring Copyright, supra* note 87 at 195–196, 198 & 203.

137 See Okediji, "Reframing International Copyright" *supra* note 1 at 487.

138 Gervais, *Restructuring Copyright, supra* note 87 at 213.

139 *Ibid.*

140 *Ibid* at 213–214. Drawing on the three-step test and subject to the appropriate limitations, Gervais, in proposing this approach, argues that "the objective is to *build intrinsic limits in the scope of the right itself* and make it *independent of the technical nature of the use* made." [emphasis in the original]. *Ibid* at 214. For the effects-based perspective, what matters is not the use but the effect/impact of the use on the commercial

exploitation of the work. In Gervais' opinion, this approach is flexible to exempt private use or use for research. *Ibid* at 211–214.

141 *Ibid* at 229–230; Chris Armstrong *et al.*, eds, *Access to Knowledge in Africa: The Role of Copyright* (Cape Town: University of Cape Town Press, 2010) at 333.

142 *Ibid* at 84. See Okediji, "International Copyright System," *supra* note 1 at 13–14.

143 See generally Daniel Gervais, "Towards a New Core International Copyright Norm: The Reverse Three-Step Test," (2005) 9 Marq Intell Prop L Rev 1 (2005) [Gervais, "The Reverse Three-Step Test"]. In contrast, Okediji has proposed the adoption of international standard of fair use. See generally Okediji, "Toward International Fair Use" *supra* note 17. Nonetheless, Okediji acknowledges the possible challenges against the adoption of the international fair use on the grounds of its indeterminacy and breadth. *Ibid* at 124–136.

144 See generally Geiger, et al, "Towards a Balanced Interpretation," *supra* note 130.

145 See Justin Hughes, "Fair Use and Its Politics-at Home and Abroad," in Okediji, *Copyright in an Age of Digital Limitations and Exceptions, supra* note 1 at 241–246 [Hughes, "Fair Use and Its Politics"].

146 Senfteleben, "The International Three-Step Test," *supra* note 14. Comp. Okediji, "Toward an International Fair Use Doctrine" *supra* note 17 at 141.

147 Gervais, *Restructuring Copyright, supra* note 87 at 65.

148 *Ibid.*

149 *See CCH Canadian, Ltd. v. Law Society of Upper Canada, supra* note 25; *SOCAN v. Bell Canada SOCAN, supra* note 23; *Alberta (Educ.) v. Canadian Copyright Licensing Agency, supra* note 23. Vaver, "Copyright Defenses" *supra* note 3 at 667–670.

150 See generally Piere Leval, "Toward a Fair Use Standard," *supra* note 930; Martin Senftleben, "The Perfect Match: Civil Law Judges and Open-Ended Fair Use Provisions" (2017) 33 Am U Intl L Rev 231–286. Okediji, "Toward International Fair Use," *supra* note 131. But see, Hughes, "Fair Use and Its Politics" *supra* note 145 at 234 at 234–274 (arguing that US should not lobby for its adoption).

151 Elkin-Koren, "Copyright in the Digital Ecosystem" *supra* note 4 at 156. Yet this reframing a fair use as a user right is critiqued, inter alia, due to its indeterminacy and for want of correlative duties. *Ibid* at 161–162.

152 Hughes, "Fair Use and Its Politics" *supra* note 145 at 255–256.

153 Tobias Schonwetter & Caroline Ncube, "New Hope for Africa? Copyright and Access to Knowledge in the Digital Age" (2011) 13:3 Info 64 at 67–68.

154 As a catch-all clause intended to complement the specific L&Es, South Africa's new fair use doctrine is farmed as an open-ended doctrine with an illustrative list of purposes. See *South African Copyright Amendment Bill[B13B-2017], supra* note 102, § 12A.

155 Peter Yu, "Customizing the Fair Use Transplants" (2018) 7:9 Laws 1–15 [Yu, "Customizing the Fair Use"].

156 *Ibid.*

157 Elkin-Koren, "Copyright in the Digital Ecosystem," *supra* note 4 at 164-66; Craig, "Using Global Rights-Talk" *supra* note 33 at 58–59.

158 Vaver, "Copyright Defenses" *supra* note 2 at 669. Users' rights approach is thus useful to restore the real balance between author's right and user's rights. *Ibid*. Elkin-Koren "Copyright in the Digital Ecosystem," *supra* note 4 at 134.

159 Elkin-Koren, "Copyright in the Digital Ecosystem," *supra* note 4 at 135.

160 *Ibid* at 134–135; Craig, "Globalizing User Rights-Talk" *supra* note 33 at 58.

161 *CCH Canadian Ltd v. Law Society of Upper Canada, supra* note 25 at para 48. Vaver, *Copyright Law, supra* note 5 at 171.

162 See Elkin-Koren, "Copyright in the Digital Ecosystem," *supra* note 4 at 153–155.

163 Bernt Hugenhotz & Ruth Okediji, "Contours of an International Instrument on Limitations and Exceptions" in Neil Weinstock Netanel, ed, *The Development Agenda: Global Intellectual Property and Developing Countries* (Oxford: Oxford University Press, 2008) 474 at 481.

164 *Ibid.*
165 See Elkin-Koren, "Copyright in the Digital Ecosystem," *supra* note 4 at 151–153.
166 Kenneth Crews, "Distance Education and Copyright Law: The Limits and Meaning of Copyright Policy" (2000) 27:1 JC & UL 15 at 21–24.
167 See generally Senftleben, "The International Three-Step Test" *supra* note 14.
168 See Ricketson & Ginsburg (Vol. I), *supra* note 129 at 783. Gervais, *Restructuring Copyright, supra* note 87 at 88–89. Reichman & Okediji, *supra* note 128 at 1439–1449.
169 Reichman & Okediji, *supra* note 128 at 1439–1449. In their view, "any mandatory exception for scientific research must [] be cloaked in some substantive content that promotes flexibility within an inherently pro-science framework and deflects narrowing legalistic interpretation in advance." *Ibid* at 1433.
170 *World Intellectual Property Organization [WIPO] Copyright Treaty*, Preamble, para 5, 20 December 1996, 36 ILM 65 (entered into force 6 March 2002) [WCT]; WIPO Performances and Phonograms Treaty, Preamble, para 4, 20 December 1996, 36 ILM 76 (entered into force 20 May 2002) [WPPT]; *Marrakesh Treaty to Facilitate Access to Published Works for Persons Who Are Blind, Visually Impaired, or Otherwise Print Disabled*, Preamble, para 9, 27 June 2013, 52 ILM 1312 (entered into force 30 June 2016) [*Marrakesh Treaty*].
171 See Okediji, "International Copyright System," *supra* note 1 at 27.
172 *Copyright and Related Rights Law No.2-00* (as amended by Law. 34–05 on 14 February 2006), art. 65.1 (TPMs are not applicable to non-profit entities: libraries, archive services, educational institutions and public broadcasting organizations); Schonwetter & Ncube, "New Hope for Africa," *supra* note 153 at 70–72.
173 For instance, a clear provision that allows use of course-packs has been included in South Africa's copyright amendment bill. Copyright Amendment Bill [B13B-2017], *supra* note 102, § 12D (2).
174 Ricketson & Ginsburg (Vol. I), *supra* note 129 at 792–793. Okediji, *International Copyright System, supra* note 1 at 21; Susan Strba, "A Model for Access to Educational Resources and Innovation in the Developing World" in Daniel Gervais, *Intellectual Property, Trade and Development: Strategies to Optimize Economic Development in a TRIPS-Plus Era*, 2nd ed (Oxford: Oxford University Press, 2014) 287 at 297–298 [Strba, "A Model for Access"].
175 See Okediji, "Reframing International Copyright" *supra* note 1 at 487 & 493.
176 Elkin-Koren, "Copyright in the Digital Ecosystem" *supra* note 4 at 166. Reichman & Okediji, *supra* note 128 at 1371, 1414–1418, & 1441–1449.
177 Okediji, "Reframing International Copyright," *supra* note 1 at 469.
178 *Ibid.*
179 See Okediji, "The Limits of International Copyright," *supra* note 70 at 732–733.
180 Okediji, "Reframing International Copyright" *supra* note 1 at 490.
181 *Ibid* at 491.
182 Okediji, "Reframing International Copyright," *supra* note 1 at 489–492; Elkin-Koren, "Copyright in a Digital Ecosystem," *supra* note 4 at 137–139.
183 Okediji, "International Copyright System," *supra* note 1 at 28; Schonwetter & Ncube, "New Hope for Africa," *supra* note 153 at 71 & 72 (recommending either permitted circumvention for or exemption of L&Es from TPMs). As mentioned above, it is important to adopt the approach followed by Morocco that exempts, inter alia, libraries and archives from TPMs. See *Moroccan Copyright and Related Rights Law No.2-00* (as amended by Law 34-05), art. 65.1.
184 See Okediji, "Reframing International Copyright," *supra* note 1 at 491–492. Elkin-Koren, "Copyright in the Digital Ecosystem," *supra* note 4 at 138–140 & 166. As mentioned above, it is important to adopt the approach followed by Morocco that exempts, *inter alia*, libraries and archives from TPMs. Scohnwetter & Ncube, "New Hope for Africa," *supra* note 153 at 70–72.

185 Daniel Gervais, *The TRIPs Agreement: Drafting History and Analysis* (London: Thomson Reuters/Sweet & Maxwell, 2008) at 200 [Gervais, *The TRIPs Agreement*]. In terms of its economic significance, parallel importation is 'one way of reducing the cost of learning materials.' Strba, "A Model for Access" *supra* note 174 at 294.

186 See *Egypt Law on the Protection of Intellectual Property Rights, Law No.82 of 2002,* art. 147; South African Copyright Amendment Bill [B13B-2017], *supra* note 102, § 12 B (6).

187 See generally Caterina Sganga, "A Plea for Digital Exhaustion in EU Copyright Law" (2018) 9 JIPITEC 211 at 237–239; Aaron Perzanowski & Jason Schultz, "Digital Exhaustion" (2011) 58 UCLA L Rev 890 at 890–946; Ruth L. Okediji, "Creative Markets and Copyright in the Fourth Industrial Era: Reconfiguring the Public Benefit for a Digital Economy," ICTSD, Issue Paper No.43 at 24–31 [Okediji, "Creative Markets and Copyright"]. For instance, the doctrine's extension is considered appropriate for e-books. *Ibid* at 31.

188 Laurence R. Helfer, et al., *The World Blind Union Guide to the Marrakesh Treaty: Facilitating Access to Books for Print-Disabled Individuals* (New York: Oxford University Press, 2017) at 38.

189 UN Convention on the Rights of Persons with Disabilities, Preamble, para g & art. 30(1), 30 March 2007, 2515 UNTS 3 (entered into force 03 May 2008) [CRPD].

190 Okediji, "The Limits of International Copyright" *supra* note 70 at 733 (stating that "[m]andatory L&Es for libraries, archives, and other educational and cultural institutions are essential to facilitate both liberty-enhancing and development-inducing goals.").

191 See, e.g Okediji, "International Copyright System," *supra* note 1 at 27.

192 See, e.g Michel Geist, "Anti-Circumvention Legislation and Competition Policy: Defining a Canadian Way?" in Geist, ed., *In The Public Interest, supra* note 36 at 248–250.

6 Re-integrating licensing regimes into the framework of flexibilities

6.1 Introduction

In principle, licensing models applicable to IP are often emphasized as modes of exploitation and dissemination of protected knowledge goods.[1] Central to the licensing regimes for copyrighted works are market conditions, competition rules and laws of contracts. Yet, copyright law remains the underpinning legal regime. Designed to strike a balance between the protection and access dimensions of copyright system, the underpinning legal regime offers a room for flexibilities. In a contractual licensing, the market and licensing terms are negotiated between creators and users. In contrast, the access prong of copyright and rules of market competition step in to facilitate the operation of a compulsory licensing against abusive impediments. In an open access, the creators exercise their unfettered discretion to determine the rules of the private ordering. In all these licensing models, there exist various degrees of flexibilities that serve to facilitate access to knowledge. Nonetheless, it should be noted that lack of harmonization in copyright licensing regimes might pose a serious challenge to an effective operation of cross-border licensing practices.[2] This factor will in effect impede access to knowledge across borders through remunerative licensing schemes.

Hence, licensing models are used both as modes of knowledge appropriation and channels of diffusion that should be rethought and integrated into the broader framework of flexibilities. The proper integration and effective utilization of the various licensing models as elements of flexibilities have the potential to: facilitate access to knowledge, foster creative innovation and promote advanced learning. Embraced within the framework of the HDCA, the appropriate design, integration, and effective utilization of the licensing regimes as flexibilities are instrumental to facilitate the expansion of creative and learning capabilities required for sustainable human development.

DOI: 10.4324/9781003214298-6

6.2 Licensing models as an element of flexibilities: an avenue for access to knowledge

6.2.1 Blanket and extended collective licensing models

For the exploitation and dissemination of creative works, there exist a number of licensing models. Each one of the models has its own merits and limitations. No single licensing model does suit all categories of works and markets. For instance, blanket (repertoire) licensing is considered useful to offer "an attractive alternative in the online environment."[3] Thus, an appropriate combination of licensing schemes offers better benefits. In addition to the traditional individual/transactional licensing, both blanket licensing and extended collective licensing (ECL) models are important models CMOs often depend on to operate. Considered "the mainstay of most CMOs," blanket licensing facilitates "the unlimited use of all works within the organization's repertoire for a specific period of time."[4]

In facilitating an "immediate access to a broad array of creative content," blanket licensing is both time and cost efficient to reduce transaction costs associated with negotiation for specific works.[5] Nonetheless, given its "all or nothing" bargaining nature, it is less flexible and quite expensive for selective or particularized use of the repertoire.[6] For universities and colleges in the LDCs that have severe financial constraints, this inflexible and expensive licensing scheme would foreclose the options available for affordable and selective access to relevant learning materials. Further, it will remain a challenge for the nascent CMOs to reach a reciprocal agreement with their foreign counterparts for the repertoire. For the model to prove more useful, the mitigation of the drawbacks of blanket licensing requires an appropriate regulation.[7]

Built upon the same principles and known in the Nordic countries, the ECL is rather deemed more useful for a range of creative works including learning materials for educational purposes and libraries.[8] Subject to the opt-out clause for the non-members, the ECL offers an efficient access to significant portion of foreign copyrighted works through local CMOs.[9] Indeed, the ECL is considered a more comprehensive option for being inclusive of both national and foreign right holders.[10] As used in Norway, the ECL is also important to facilitate a mass digitization of out-of-print books and access to the digital databases of in-copyright works.[11] The ECL can thus be quite useful to promote access to orphan works.[12] Given the importance of vast amount of orphan works for both educational and creative innovation purposes, the instrumental role of the ECL should beroles of commercial licensing harnessed to facilitate access to relevant knowledge.

Despite its considerable merits and the need for appropriate legislative measures,[13] there are however some limitations related to the operation of the ECL. First, while foreclosing other options,[14] the ECL requires effective CMOs, and works best where right-holders are well informed and organized.[15] Second, given its unsettled consonance with the international copyright regime,[16] the use of ECL in a mass digitization of works might be constrained due to the three-step test.[17] Third, foreign rights holders might not get a due remuneration as the ECL tends to favor local authors.[18] In both models of collective licensing, the blanket licensing is useful to allow an efficient access to the entire repertoire of learning materials for education and research.[19] In addition to its inaptness for some works,[20] the licensing has its own limitations.

From users' perspectives, its potential might be undermined due to the practice of "big deals" commercial publishers or CMOs often use in a compulsive "all or nothing" bargain for an authorized access to the repertoire.[21] Absent appropriate L&Es and regulation through antitrust law at a national level, the exploitative subscription fees attached to blanket licensing would constitute an impediment for academic libraries. For the local CMOs, an administrative approval of the licensing tariffs might mitigate the concern related to anti-competitive practices, such as excessive fees. In a nutshell, the benefits of the foregoing licensing models presuppose an effective operation of the CMOs. For example, their actual benefits might be limited due to the CMOs' underdevelopment and inexperience.[22] Further, a market failure is another challenge undermining the roles of commercial licensing schemes.

6.2.2 Open access licensing models as emerging flexibilities

Suited to unencumbered access to and dissemination of knowledge, an open access (OA) licensing model is another emerging licensing regime with an increasing significance in the academic environment.[23] As mentioned elsewhere, OA licensing mechanisms are founded upon the proprietary copyright regime *albeit* with added flexibilities.[24] In fact, OA is anchored in the access prong of the public interest with a prime focus on collaborative creation and dissemination in lieu of a commercial exploitation. In contrast to the exclusive all-rights-reserved practice, the OA licensing model operates on the basis of "some rights-reserved" approach.[25] To this extent, a national copyright law remains the basis to regulate the reserved rights—attribution, integrity, and related aspects.[26] In the same vein, users-driven contractual regime plays a key role for the operation of OA.[27]

In contrast to the proprietary licensing schemes, the OA licensing scheme has attracted a greater interest due to its potential to facilitate access to knowledge. An OA is often understood as "a free online access to scholarly literature and scientific publications."[28] As adopted in the *Budapest Open Access Initiative* (2002),[29] the notion of OA is not limited to peer-reviewed articles. Instead, it goes further to encompass a "barrier-free" access to *any* digital content that can be used for higher education such as journals, monographs, textbooks, periodicals, and research reports.[30] In the words of Peter Suber, OA content is "digital, online, free of charge, and free of most copyright and licensing restrictions."[31]

Subject to the consent of right-holders, an OA allows users to overcome the significant copyright-related access-barriers to most learning materials.[32]

Nonetheless, given an access to the Internet, the actual benefits of OA depend upon the effective functioning of the appropriate licensing schemes such as creative commons (CC) and General Public Licensing (GPL). Inspired by the GPL that was developed for software products,[33] the CC licensing scheme created for digital contents is the most dominant form of an open content licensing scheme. In particular, the CC scheme "offers users series of an easy to use, standardized and automated licenses" attached to the work.[34] In view of its significance, Eric Priest regards such a nonexclusive licensing scheme as "the lifeblood of open access."[35]

Due to its resonance with the freedoms of users and creators to unencumbered access, collaborative creation and diffusion of knowledge in the educational sector,[36] OA licensing mechanism has become quite popular among educators and scholars. Further, policy, legislative and institutional initiatives have been taken across countries and continents such as the United States, Europe, Asia, Latin America, and South Africa to promote OA for public-funded research reports and publications.[37]

In particular, several higher educational institutions such as MIT, Harvard University, University of Cambridge, University of Oxford, and University of Toronto are among those universities in the Global North that have embraced OA. In Africa, an inspiring initiative is the Egyptian Knowledge Bank—an online knowledge bank of digital repositories—that allows all Egyptians free access to databases of knowledge housed in several regional and international publishing industries. Following the universities in the South Africa, several higher educational institutions across the continent are also starting to explore OA to mitigate the negative impact of knowledge resource constraints.

In order to address a nation's human development imperatives, these access-oriented attributes of OA licensing models have the potential to *complement* appropriate copyright-related flexibilities and facilitate enhanced access to learning materials for education. It is thus important to examine the prospects and challenges of adopting the licensing mechanism for enhanced access to knowledge.

6.3 Re-integrating OA into the framework of flexibilities: HDCA for (re)integration

6.3.1 Introduction

In addition to the various flexibilities embedded in the treaties and national laws, a set of contract-based flexibilities are also useful to facilitate access to knowledge or learning materials. While the law remains the baseline, an access to copyrighted learning materials is obtained through various licensing schemes. Compared to other licensing models, OA licensing schemes offer more rooms to facilitate a legitimate access to copyrighted content in general and learning materials in particular. From among the licensing schemes, OA thus constitutes an emerging aspect of access-oriented flexibilities based on a private ordering.

Including OA, the set of voluntary licensing models is distinct from a compulsory or statutory license issued against the consent of the authors or right-holders. Central to their points of distinction, a blend of copyright and contract laws is used to regulate the contractual licensing models to facilitate access to knowledge. In terms of the licensing fees, except OA licensing model that allows a free access to digital content, the remaining licensing models operate subject to royalties for all protected creative works. From within the proprietary licensing schemes, a transactional/individual licensing model functions on the basis of a direct contractual negotiation between right-holders such as publishers, and users in respect of a copyrighted work.[38]

In contrast, a collective licensing scheme is known among CMOs that use the model to grant users an access to a catalogue of copyrighted works in their repertoire.[39] In particular, a collective blanket licensing is used in this regard to authorize users an access to ranges of works in the repertoire in a single transaction.[40] Similar to the conventional collective licensing, albeit with enhanced benefits, the ECL allows CMOs to license works of non-members with the discretion of the latter to opt out.[41] Despite the varying benefits attached to individual, collective blanket licensing and ECL schemes in terms of the associated costs and the degree of flexibilities, the latter two schemes are more cost-efficient to facilitate access to learning materials required for higher education.

In sum, the strategic combination and utilization of the various licensing models is important to supplement other flexibilities to allow more access to educational or learning materials required for higher education.[42] In these regards, this book explores the appropriate policy and legal options which developing countries might consider useful to harness the potential of the various licensing models as an integral set of flexibilities. In particular, an in-depth exploration of the prospects and challenges of the OA model is made from a human development perspective.

6.3.2 Prospects of OA licensing models

In view of its increasing acceptance among educators, researchers, libraries and academic publishers, OA holds a great promise for a free access to relevant digital learning materials such as scientific journals, software and research reports. Indeed, several public and private initiatives have been taken both in developed and developing nations to adopt OA mechanisms in order to promote collaborative creation, sharing, and dissemination of digital contents. In this regard, it is important to note the widespread use of the OA licensing models such as GNU/GPL for open source software and the CC for digital contents. Often used for scientific publications, the CC "offers a number of licenses with different degrees of permission barriers."[43]

Constituted of four general elements, the CC offers a combination of six core licenses operating on three levels.[44] For instance, "attribution" being the basic element of all the combinations, the CC Attribution License (CC BY) offers users the utmost freedom to reproduce, distribute, adapt and use creative works for all purposes subject to an attribution to the original creator.[45] With a lesser freedom, the CC BY-SA version encourages sharing of digital contents, including derivate ones under the same rules. Indeed, the CC licensing model becomes popular for its users-oriented flexibilities.[46] Somehow, there still remains a concern on the issue of moral right in relation to allowing derivative works across jurisdictions.[47] In spite of its limited creative freedom, the CC BY-NC-ND is often used to resolve the concern and ensure the non-commercialization of the digital contents.[48] This version however limits users' freedom to create derivate works and commercialize them to cover their expenses for sustainable creative activities.[49]

For a number of reasons, OA mechanism has the potential to complement the existing flexibilities and mitigate the impediments against access to knowledge in developing and least developed countries. First, OA is more suited to the reputation-induced ethos of scholars and academic researchers that produce a large amount of scientific publications and research reports.[50] In a reputation-driven academic environment, OA enlarges the authors' audience, makes the works visible and increases their impact through a wider dissemination.[51] In addition to academic reputation, peer recognition and readership as the driving non-pecuniary incentive mechanism, the academic authors depend upon a blend of salaries, grants/prizes, and public funding for compensation.[52]

Second, the advent of digital technologies, the commercial publishers' sky-rocketing prices or subscription fees, and the consequent shift in demands have all led to a growing OA publishing market.[53] Serving as an access-driven viable business model, the OA academic publishing operates on the basis of the gold (open access journals) and green roads (self-archiving or repositories) for scientific journals.[54] In fact, the commercial publishers have started to adopt a hybrid model to offer an OA to articles published through articles processing fees (ACP).[55] In effect, this has led to the so-called "author pays" rule to determine OA to the articles.[56]

Third, the OA models facilitate both North-South as well as South-South transnational collaborative creation and efficient dissemination of digital works at a lesser cost. In so doing, OA is instrumental to bridge the digital divide, overcome geographical barriers and reduce the transaction costs related to the traditional licensing negotiation and distribution.[57] This constitutes a significant technical and economic advantage over the limited access to print materials fenced within the exclusive copyright regime. In harnessing online educational opportunities, critical is the importance of access to digital contents and open educational resources (OERs), including the massive online open courses (MOOCS).[58] The combination of OA and OERs facilitates both national and transnational access to higher education.[59]

In facilitating access to education, OA enlarges the educational opportunities of population for sustainable human development. Given the infrastructural and resource constraints for education in the global South, creating learning opportunities is vital to fill in the gaps and expand the human capabilities of people. To advance interactive learning and creative innovation, OA is thus instrumental to promote a collaborative creation and sharing of global educational resources from across the globe.[60] In particular, the South-South collaboration across nations and universities within a nation promotes access to relevant knowledge that is more suited to the local context of the nation.[61] Given its role in fostering knowledge sharing and collaboration, several studies exploring the potential roles of OA for advanced learning and scientific research support the adoption of OA.

From a creative innovation perspective, OA comports with the users'-driven open, commons-based peer production and collaborative innovation process.[62] In this regard, digital technologies such as Internet or ICT can be harnessed to facilitate a cross-border access to knowledge for the purposes of creative innovation and higher education. To this effect, an increased investment in the ICT as a tool for development is important to pave the roads towards embracing OA models. From human development perspective, ICT and networked digital platforms are considered to "hold great promise for human flourishing even in the most desperate communities around the world."[63] It is noted that "inexpensive and reliable access to the Internet is becoming essential to the development of capabilities in other areas, such as education."[64] Facilitated through Internet, "[a]ccess to information is crucial for high-quality education and thus for expanding opportunities."[65]

In harnessing the potential of OA, the technological platforms are instrumental to facilitate a wider range of access to and dissemination of knowledge, creative interactions, and collaborative opportunities for the enlargement of human capabilities. Fourth, the adoption of OA licensing models would offer options that augment the existing copyright system.[66] As the economics of OA reveals, "a well-designed system of OA journals will not destroy the authors' or the publishers' incentives to provide and disseminate academic articles."[67] In support of OA, this finding attenuates publishers' concern of an incentive mechanism that drives publishing industries. Indeed, a study concludes that OA "should be the future of academic publishing."[68] As Margaret Chon observes, "[o]pen course content initiatives in the tertiary textbook arena indicate that market-based mechanisms for distribution are only one possible means for providing access to textbooks."[69]

6.3.3 Policy and legal rooms for (re)integration of OA at national levels

In view of their potential to facilitate free or affordable access to relevant learning materials, OA licensing models require appropriate policy and legal environments. For the necessary policy and legal actions, it is important to curve out policy and legal rooms available under the relevant national and international regimes. From a policy perspective, OA models need to be emphasized as a strategy or a form of flexibilities intended to promote, *inter alia*, the policy objectives of creative innovation and education for sustainable human development. Critical in this regard is the linkage between OA and the ICT for their collaborative roles in promoting sustainable human development.[70] To this effect, the explicit adoption of OA models is useful to complement the exiting flexibilities. The (re)integration of the models into the relevant policies are thus vital to facilitate collaborative production and enhanced diffusion of knowledge for creative innovation and education.

While making relevant policy reforms, it is important to consider all possible options to respect authors' freedom to publish their research outputs in outlets of their choice. In the event a closed publication outlet is chosen, the authors' would then be required to self-archive the publications. As discussed in this book, facilitating this additional option requires a coherent policy and legislative approach. To this end, this book underscores the need for a *development-oriented* national policy and legal frameworks that consolidate the existing initiatives into a coherent policy to guide the development of consistent institutional policies.

In particular, the formulation of the national policy is expected to be aligned with the copyright and other pertinent regimes. Such an integrative policy initiative will encourage academic and research institutions to embrace OA and develop a consistent set of institutional policies. For the policy formulation or implementation, relevant insights can be drawn from soft norms such as the draft treaty on access to knowledge, the various OA declarations and the national practices of other nations. It is vital to have an all-inclusive and integrated OA policy across relevant sectors.

In addition to the initiatives for a policy regime, there are rooms in the existing legal regimes for the legislative measures needed to ensure the adoption of OA. From the international perspective, both the TRIPs Agreement and the WCT do recognize a possible variance in the *legal means* for the implementation of the treaties as long as the national law remains consistent. For instance, art. 1.1 of the TRIPs Agreement states that "members shall be free to determine the appropriate method of implementing the provisions of this agreement within their own legal systems and practice."[71] Save for the minimum standards,[72] no *specific form* of implementation is required from states.[73] Further, a legal room can be carved out from the recognition accorded to the public interest in the sectors of vital importance and the need to maintain a balance between rights and obligations.[74] In this context, education should thus be considered a critical element of a public interest that falls within the reserved policy space.

In this respect, the WCT is more explicit in its reference to education, research and access to information as essential aspects of the public interest.[75] For its implementation, art. 14(1) of the WCT allows member states "to adopt, in accordance with their legal systems the necessary measures" to ensure the application of the treaty. As Reichman and Okediji observe, the afore-cited provisions allow a flexible room for appropriate legislative measures.[76] Taking advantage of the policy space under the treaties, a nation can adopt policy and legislative measures that accommodate OA to advance its public interest. In particular, the LDCs with low-ranking human development should take appropriate policy steps to exploit the policy space in order to promote its public interest through enhanced access to knowledge for education and research.

Yet, carving out L&Es to integrate OA will be constrained due to the three-step test unless otherwise the test is relaxed to offer a sufficient room.[77] For instance, Marc Sheufen argues that the Max Planck's interpretation of the test and its proposed insertion of "the legitimate interest of third parties" into the test can serve as an entry point to embrace OA.[78] Indeed, worth considering are the relevant insights from the proposed interpretation. In particular, the "legitimate interest of third parties" can be considered an integral element of the broad public interest. In turn, this will open up a policy space to facilitate the integration of OA into the national innovation system without contradicting the existing copyright regime. In the same vein, relevant dimensions are the human rights to development and the right of everyone to share in scientific advancement and its benefits.

In a knowledge era, it is obvious that the realization of these human rights and the advancement of public interests require unfettered access to knowledge through broader access mechanisms. Further, relevant higher education laws that require universities' public dedication of the knowledge produced for academic purposes are useful to support OA for research publications. For instance, the laws might mandate higher educational institutions adoption of the model for all public-funded research in order for the research outputs to be available for public use through OA. In taking a legislative measure, it is essential to ensure a proper alignment between the copyright law and other relevant laws.

6.3.4 The challenges of (re)integrating open access

In spite of the prospects of the OA model to enhance access to learning materials, there remain a number of challenges. Seeking a political will for resolution, the first set of challenges relates to policy and legal constraints. In principle, OA requires no legislative action to operate as it is a regime of private ordering. In a national context, there however needs to be a coherent approach towards creating development-oriented enabling policy and legislative environments that support the (re)integration of OA for enhanced access to knowledge. In addition to the general reforms, revisiting the work-for-hire doctrine and introducing a "teacher exception" are vital for the operation of OA in the educational sector.[79]

As there is no "one-size-fits-all" incentive mechanism,[80] it is argued that an equitable remunerative mechanism is more suited to educational sector.[81] Indeed, it is not in the best interest of both academics and scientists to lock up their works for the sake of permission and commercialization. Rather, their major interest lies in the widest dissemination of the works and the consequent reputation. To this end, the non-exclusive mechanism is more appropriate to serve their interest through OA with a proper attribution of authorship.[82]

Further, the equitable remuneration will remain consistent with author's human right. In considering this approach, countries should make a strategic use of the available policy space for their integration of relevant flexibilities.

Absent treaties that allow more flexibilities, countries bear international duties to take the existing global copyright system as a "given."[83] Yet, possible amendments to the national laws are still critical to (re)integrate OA into the existing framework of flexibilities. For instance, introducing a statutory "teacher/researcher" exception to the doctrine of work-for-hire will entitle academic authors/researchers to ownership of rights over their creative works.[84] As a national doctrine, nations are free to design the doctrine as it is deemed fit for the purpose. Vested with the right, authors will be able to retain their right of authorship while granting the recruiting research and academic institutions a non-exclusive license over the creative works.[85] Otherwise, divesting academic authors of rights over their works tends to conflict with their academic freedom and limits the operation of OA.[86]

In practice, academic authors often seem to bypass the doctrine of work-for-hire and transfer copyright ownership to reputable academic publishers. To avoid inconsistent practices, appropriate policy and legal reforms are thus important to empower academic authors to both publish and self-archive their works without undue restriction. In the same vein, the non-exclusive license vested in educational institutions will enable the institutions to self-archive or dedicate the academic works for public use as might be required in the relevant higher education legislation.[87] For authors, contractual mandates from their educational institutions or funders can be used to induce or encourage self-archiving.[88] In the exclusive and proprietary copyright regime, it is useful to consider the introduction of an inalienable non-exclusive right that remains operative after a copyright transfer to publishers. In the digital era, scholars even question publishers' automatic entitlement to exclusive rights over authors' research publications.[89] It is rather suggested that publishers should be remunerated for their publishing services.[90]

In addition to allowing the academic authors the freedom to use and adapt their works after a copyright transfer, the retention of a non-exclusive right would facilitate authors' second publication or self-archiving.[91] It also minimizes the bargaining imbalance and protects academic authors against exploitative commercial publishers that force a copyright assignment from the authors on a routine basis.[92] In this respect, a lesson can be drawn from the German copyright law that provides for an inalienable right of a secondary publication.[93] From Africa, South Africa is poised to be one of the countries allowing a similar right for state-funded research publications.[94]

In short, both policy implementation and legislative measures should be taken at a national level to create an enabling environment that promotes OA in consonance with the existing international copyright, human rights and development obligations. Nonetheless, a national legislative reform will still be constrained for want of a global harmonization of L&Es that create uncertainties for a cross-border OA.[95] Like that of remunerative licensing schemes, the lack of harmonization might give rise to the issue of conflict of laws that undermines the potential of OA.[96] It should be noted that harnessing the potential of OA to the fullest depends upon a networked and global collaboration. Building a global partnership for development requires taking context-sensitive and development-tailored policy and legislative measures. In this regard, drawing lessons from relevant countries, and forging institutional collaborations or consortia with relevant global partners are important steps to mitigate the implications of the challenges.

As for several developing countries, the challenges most LDCs face stem from their economic and technical constraints. The implementation of OA requires both financial and technical capacities to invest in the relevant infrastructure and harness its potential. Despite the recent developments, a better internet access at higher educational institutions, and the ubiquitous cell phones in the LDCs, there still remain severe economic and technical factors. These factors are implicated in building and maintaining ICT infrastructure, ensuring sustainable and high-speed Internet bandwidth, electric power, and acquisition of relevant hardware and software equipment.[97]

In particular, the financial and technical resources are critical for academic and research institutions to run sustainable and functioning institutional repositories for the green OA models. It is noted that public universities and colleges' increasing investment in the ICT infrastructure offers some leverages to reduce the challenges. A lasting solution to overcome the hurdles however demands a concerted effort from the government, funding organizations, universities and relevant stakeholders.[98] For academic scholars to embrace OA journals, the financial implication for "author pays" model requires a sustainable funding scheme and subsidies.[99] Further, there needs to be an improvement in the existing incentive mechanisms in place for academic authors with insufficient income. In most African countries, several underpaid academics that earn their basic living from the sales of their books might lack an incentive to forego the commercial exploitation of their works. In effect, the economic situations of the authors would discourage them from choosing OA for the unimpeded and free distribution of their works.

The third challenge arises from social factors. For instance, the lack of awareness among the stakeholders, resistance from market-driven publishers, authors' preference of closed access journals for their reputational advantage, are among the social factors.[100] Some of the factors are related to the issues of quality, publication (APC) costs and mandates.[101] In order to mitigate the challenges, it is crucial to set up a sustainable incentive and effective quality assurance mechanisms that encourage authors to embrace OA journals.[102] For the OA mandate to be effective, academic and funding institutions should also use contractual requirements to facilitate archiving of digital contents.[103]

From the global perspective, there still remains a challenge due to the existing Global North–oriented metrics for the assessment of the quality and impact factor of journals.[104] As a result, few journals from the Global South fit into the established metrics of reputable journals to earn a significant impact factor and attract experienced authors. Lamenting the status quo, scholars hope that a wider embrace of OA has the potential to counter the biased and hegemonic global publishing system.[105]

6.4 Conclusion

In sum, it is argued that the OA has enormous benefits to promote creative innovation and higher education across borders through enhanced access to knowledge. Yet, legal, financial, technical, and social factors constitute critical challenges against the potentials of the OA licensing models. Hence, appropriate steps should be taken to address the challenges in order to harness its benefits. In addition to the need for investments in the necessary infrastructure, inclusive policy and legal reforms are vital to integrate OA into the broad framework of copyright-related flexibilities to promote access to creative works. As suggested for other flexibilities, the HDCA is useful to facilitate the (re)integration of the licensing regimes and their roles for promoting users' rights.

From among various models of OA, the licensing models such as GNU/GPL for open source/free software and CC licenses for OA journals are instrumental to promote access to digital contents.[106] For the policy and prospective legal reforms to take root, an institutional mandate or funders' contractual requirement is vital to facilitate scholars' embrace of OA for the public-funded research publications.[107] In a nutshell, it is important to underscore the potential of OA towards enhanced freedoms of access, interactive learning and collaborative innovation to facilitate the expansion of human capabilities.

Notes

1 See generally Alain Strowel & Bernard Vanbrabant, "Copyright Licensing: A European View," in Jacques de Werra, ed, *Research Handbook on Intellectual Property Licensing* (Cheltenham, UK: Edward Elgar, 2013) 29 at 29–53.

2 *Ibid* at 48–53.

3 Daniel Gervais, *(Re)structuring Copyright: A Comprehensive Path to International Copyright Reform* (Cheltenham: Edward Elgar, 2017) at 250 [Gervais, *Restructuring Copyright*].

4 Laurence R. Helfer, "Collective Management of Copyright and Human Rights: An Easy Alliance Revisited," in Daniel Gervais, ed., *Collective Management of Copyright and Related Rights*, 3rd ed. (The Netherlands: Kluwer Law International, 2015) 81 at 95. Jeremy de Beer, "Legal Strategies To Profit From Peer-Production" (2008) 46 Can Bus LJ 269 at 284 [de Beer, "Legal Strategies"] (stating that "[c]ollective blanket licensing could also work well to enable the creation of a wide range of derivative works.")

5 Helfer, "Collective management of Copyright," *supra* note 4 at 95.

6 *Ibid*.

7 Ibid at 96–108.

8 Alain Strowel, "The European 'Extended Collective Licensing' Model" (2011) 34:4 Colum JL & Arts 665 at 666 [Strowel, "Extended Collective Licensing"]; Pamela Samuelson, "Legislative Alternatives to the Google Book Settlement" (2011) 34:4 Colum JL & Arts 697 at 706 [Samuelson, "Legislative Alternatives"].

9 Gervais, *Restructuring Copyright, supra* note 3 at 251; Daniel Gervais, "Collective Management of Copyright and Neighboring Rights in Canada: An International Perspective" (2002) 1:2 CJLT 21 at 30 [Gervais, "Collective Management"].

10 Helfer, "Collective Management of Copyright," *supra* note 4 at 98.

11 Samuelson, "Legislative Alternatives," *supra* note 8 at 709–710. Strowel, "Extended Collective Licensing," *supra* note 8 at 666–667.

12 Strowel, Strowel, "Extended Collective Licensing," *supra* note 8 at 667 & 69; Samuelson, "Legislative Alternatives," *supra* note 8 at 719–721; Gervais, *Restructuring Copyright, supra* note 3 at 251.

13 Samuelson, "Legislative Alternatives," *supra* note 8 at 714–729 (describing the various benefits of ECL to facilitate access to copyrighted works).

14 De Beer, "Legal Strategies," *supra* note 4 at 287 (pointing out the difficulty for "licensees to choose to use only pre-cleared or Creative common contents").

15 Gervais, "Collective Management," *supra* note 9 at 30.

16 Samuelson, "Legislative Alternatives," *supra* note 8 at 714–715. In this regard, Gervais dismisses the argument of alleged inconsistency with art. 5(2) of Berne Convention as long as there is efficient, transparent and uncostly opt-out system; Gervais, *Restructuring Copyright, supra* note 3 at 252. Mahly Ficsor, "Collective Rights Management from the Viewpoint of International Treaties, with Special Attention to the EU'Acquis", in Gervais ed., *Collective Management of Copyright, supra* note 1716, 31 at 66–68 (pointing out four conditions for ECL's compliance with international copyright regime).

17 Strowel, "Extended Collective Licensing," *supra* note 8 at 668–669.

18 *Ibid* at 669; Samuelson, "Legislative Alternatives," *supra* note 8 at 714.

19 Gervais, "Collective Management," *supra* note 9 at 30.

20 De Beer, "Legal strategies" *supra* note 4 at 286 (noting the complex clearance process for audiovisual works and the inefficiencies related to negotiation for fragmented rights).

21 Helfer, "Collective Management of Copyright," *supra* note 4 at 90. For a discussion on the practice of 'big deals,' see generally Aaron S. Eldin & Daniel L. Rubinfeld, "Exclusion or Efficient Pricing?: The Big Deal Bundling of Academic Journals" (2004) 72:1 Antitrust LJ 119.

22 As Helfer has noted, "many developing countries have *only limited experience* in encouraging creativity within their borders and *in promoting the licensing of copyrighted works*." Emphasis added. Helfer, Collective Management of Copyright, *supra* note 4 at 94.

23 Paulo Guarda, "Creation of Software within the Academic Context: Knowledge Transfer, Intellectual Property Rights and Licences" (2013) 44 IIC 494 at 514.

24 See Peter Suber, *Open Access* (Massachusetts: MIT Press, 2013) at 1–27 [Suber, *Open Access*](explaining open access).

25 Marc Sheufen, *Copyright Versus Open Access: On the Organization and Political Economy of Access to Scientific Knowledge* (Geneva: Springer, 2015) at 110 [Sheufen, *Copyright Versus Open Access*]. In particular, this is true for the OA model based on creative commons. Niva Elkin-Koren, "What contracts Cannot Do: The Limits of Private Ordering in Facilitating Creative Commons" (2005) 74 Fordham L Rev 375 at 389 [Elkin-Koren, "What Contracts Cannot Do"].

26 Jeremy de Beer & Chidi Oguamanam, "Open Minds: Lessons from Nigeria on Intellectual Property, Innovation and Development," in Mattew L. Smith and Katherine M.A. Reilly, eds., *Open Development: Networked Innovations in International Development* (Cambridge, MA: The MIT Press, 2013) 249 at 264 [de Beer & Oguamanan, "Open Minds"]. For instance, CC licenses essentially depend on rights management information practices and end user license agreements for managing digital rights. *Ibid.* Elkin-Koren, "What Contracts Cannot Do" *supra* note 25 at 392–394.

27 Elkin-Koren, "What Contracts Cannot Do" *supra* note 25 at 406–420 (exploring the merits and demerits of the contractual regime that underpins the Creative Commons).

28 Mikael Laakso et al., "The Development of Open Access Journal Publishing from 1993 to 2009" (2011) 6 PLOS ONE at 6.

29 See *Budapest Open Access Initiative*, February 14, 2002, Budapest, Hungary, online: http://www.budapestopenaccessinitiative.org/read (last visited 15 April 2021).

30 Suber, *Open Access, supra* note 24 at 9 & 17.

31 *Ibid* at 4. An open access can be taken to mean any digital access to scholarly works that are free from financial, technical and legal barriers. See Leslie Chan and Eve Gray, "Centering the Knowledge Peripheries through Open Access: Implications for Future Research and Discourse on Knowledge for Development," in Smith & Reilly, eds., *Open Development, supra* note 26, 197 at 203.

32 In this respect, both Bethesda and Berlin Open Access initiatives underscore the significance of authors' advance consent to enable users to "copy, use, distribute, transmit and display the work publicly and to make and distribute derivative works, in any digital medium for any responsible purpose, subject to proper attribution of authorship." See Bethesda Statement on Open Access Publishing, June 20, 2003, online: http://legacy.earlham.edu/~peters/fos/bethesda.htm (last visited 10 April 2021); Berlin Declaration on Open Access to Knowledge in the Sciences and Humanities, 23 October 2003, online: https://openaccess.mpg.de/Berlin-Declaration (last visited 10 April 2021).

33 See Volker Grassmuk, "Towards a New Social Contract: Free-Licensing into the Knowledge Commons," in Lucie Guibault & Christina Angelopoulos, eds, *Open Content Licensing: From Theory to Practice* (Amsterdam: Amsterdam University Press, 2011) 21 at 52–58.

34 Lucie Guibault, "Owning the Right to Open Up Access to Scientific Publications," in Guibault & Angelopoulos, ed., *Open Content Licensing, supra* note 33 at 158 [Guibault, "Owning the Right to Open Up Access"].

35 See Eric Priest, "Copyright and the Harvard Open Access Mandate," (2012) 10:7 Nw J Tech & Intell Prop 377 at 418 [Priest, "Copyright"]; Nicolas Robinson-Garcia, Rodrigo Costas & Thed N. van Leeuwen, "Open Access Uptake By Universities Worldwide," (2020) *Peer J.* DOI 10.7717/peerj.9410.

36 See Helfer, "Collective Management of Copyright," *supra* note 4 at 97. In allowing uses without remuneration, open content licenses "facilitate sharing of ideas, information and protected content between authors and users and directly promote 'the public interest in enjoying broad access to new knowledge' –two goals endorsed by Article 15 of the Covenant and by the ICESCR Committee." *Ibid.*

37 Sheufen, *Copyright versus Open Access, supra* note 25 at 69–75; Thomas Eger & Marc Sheufen, *The Economics of Open Access: On the Future of Academic Publishing* (Cheltenham: Edward Elgar, 2018) at 81 & 87.

38 See Ivan L. Pitt, *Direct Licensing and the Music Industry: How Technology, Innovation and Competition Reshaped Direct Licensing* (New York: Springer, 2015) at 135–155 [Pitt, *Direct Licensing*] (making a detailed treatment of a direct licensing as an emerging alternative to the blanket licensing for musical works).

39 See Johan Axhamn, "Exceptions, Limitations and Collective Management of Rights as Vehicles for Access to Information," in Dana Beldiman, ed., *Access to Information and Knowledge: 21st Century Challenges in Intellectual Property and Knowledge Governance* (Cheltenham, UK: Edward Elgar, 2013) at 177.

40 See Glen A. Clark, "Blanket Licensing: The Clash Between Copyright Protection and the Sherman Act" (1980) 55 Notre Dame L Rev 729 at 732–733 & 747.

41 See Axhamn, *supra* note 39 at 185–186. For a further discussion of an extended collective licensing scheme, see Daniel Gervais, "Collective Management of Copyright: Theory and Practice in the Digital Age," in Daniel Gervais, ed., *Collective Management*

of Copyright and Related Rights, 2nd ed. (The Netherlands: Kluwer Law International, 2010) 1 at 21–26 [Gervais, "Collective Management of Copyright"].

42 *See* Axhamn, *supra* note 39 at 185–186.

43 Eger & Sheufen, *supra* note 37 at 14. Nonetheless, the creative commons' strategy is critiqued for lack of standardization in licenses, reliance on proprietary and contractual regimes, and the consequent limitation of access. See generally Elkin-Koren, "What Contracts Cannot Do," *supra* note 25. Guibault, "Owning the Right to Open Up Access," *supra* note 34 at 158–159.

44 Sheufen, *Copyright Versus Open Access, supra* note 25 at 110. See Creative Commons, About the Licenses, online:https://creativecommons.org/licenses/.

45 *Ibid.* Marshall Smith, "Open Educational Resources: Opportunities and Challenges for the Developing World," in Smith & Reilly, ed., *Open Development, supra* note 26 at 133 [Smith, "Open Educational Resources"].

46 See Catharina Maracke, "Creative Commons International: The International License Porting Project – Origins, Experiences, and Challenges" (2010) 1 JIPITEC 4–18.

47 *Ibid* at 7–9.

48 Elkin-Koren, "What Contracts Cannot Do" *supra* note 25 at 401.

49 Smith, "Open Educational Resources" *supra* note 45 at 1745. Elkin-Koren, "What Contracts Cannot Do" *supra* note 25 at 401.

50 Jerome Reichman & Ruth Okediji, "When Copyright Law and Science Collide: Empowering Digitally Integrated Research Methods on a Global Scale" (2012) 96 Minn L Rev 1362 at 1427 [Reichman & Okediji, "When Copyright and Science Collide"]. De Beer, "Legal Strategies,' supra note 4 at 284 & 86. As de Beer observes, "Creative Commons licences are especially well suited to non-commercial contexts where peers produce content for reasons other than financial reward." *Ibid* at 286.

51 Sheufen, *Copyright versus Open Access, supra* note 25 at 121; Peter Suber, *Science Dissemination Using Open Access: A Compendium of Selected Literature on Open Access* (The Abdu Selam International Centre for Theoretical Physics, 2008) at 12.

52 Eger & Sheufen, *supra* note 37 at 11 & 47–55. Guibault, "Owning the Right to Open Up Access," *supra* note 34 at 160.

53 *Ibid* at 29–32; Priest, "Copyright," *supra* note 35 at 390. Guibault, "Owning the Right to Open Up Access," *supra* note 34 at 137–138.

54 Eger & Sheufen, *supra* note 37 at 29–32; see Guibault, "Owning the Right to Open Up Access," *supra* note 34 at 139 & 153–157 (for a discussion on the gold and green roads).

55 *Ibid* at 33.

56 *Ibid.* For instance, for OA journals published by the big commercial academic publishers, authors are charged ACP or submission fee of up to USD 3000. *Ibid.*

57 Sheufen, *Copyright versus Open Access, supra* note 25 at 120.

58 It is important to note that several prestigious universities in the developed nations such as Harvard University, UC Berkley, MIT and so on have embraced OA to run MOOCs that are accessible to students all over the world. Smith, "Open Educational Resources" *supra* note 45 at 138–139.

59 *Ibid* at 145–148 & 150–157.

60 Chan & Gray, "Centering the Knowledge Peripheries through Open Access," *supra* note 31 at 197.

61 *Ibid.* Chan & Gray note that the South-South flow of knowledge is "far more essential for local [research] and development since the Global Southern countries have more in common than those of the Global North." *Ibid.* Guibault, "Owning the Right to Open Up Access," *supra* note 34 at 137.

62 See generally Yochai Benkler, *The Wealth of Networks: How Social Production Transforms Markets and Freedom* (New Haven, CT: Yale University Press, 2006) [Benkler, *The Wealth of Networks*]; Eric Von Hippel, *Democratizing Innovation* (Cambridge: The MIT

Press, 2005); Reichman & Okediji, "When Copyright Law and Science Collide," *supra* note 50 at 1478–1479.

63 Ruth Okediji, "Reframing International Copyright Limitations and Exceptions as Development Policy," in *Copyright Law in an Age of Limitations and Exceptions* (Cambridge: Cambridge University, 2017) 429 at 457 [Okediji, "Reframing International Copyright"] [original citations omitted].

64 UNDP, *Human Development Report 2016: Human Development for Everyone* (New York: UNDP, 2016) at 69 [UNDP, *Human Development Report 2016*].

65 *Ibid.*

66 It should be borne in mind that OA licensing models are based upon a combination of copyright and contractual regimes. Nevertheless, lack of international standardization in the CC licensing model and the principle of choice of law grounded in territoriality would pose a challenge. Sheufen, *Copyright versus Open Access, supra* note 25 at 112.

67 *Ibid* at 122.

68 *Ibid* at 141.

69 Margaret Chon, "Intellectual Property "from Below": Copyright and Capability for Education" (2007) 3 UC Davis L Rev 805 at 842 [Chon, "Intellectual Property from Below"].

70 See Dalindyebo Shabalala, "Knowledge and Education: Pro-access Implications of New Technologies" in Tzen Wong & Graham Dutfield, eds., *Intellectual Property and Human Development: Current Trends and Future Scenarios* (Cambridge: Cambridge University Press, 2011) 250 at 251–257.

71 See also *World Intellectual Property Organization [WIPO] Copyright Treaty*, art. 14(1), 20 December 1996, 36 ILM 65 (entered into force 6 March 2002) [hereinafter WCT]. The afore-cited provision authorizes members to "undertake to adopt, in accordance with their legal systems, the measures necessary to ensure the application of this treaty."

72 Okediji, "Reframing International Copyright," *supra* note 63 at 437–438. The international minimum standards include "what counts as protectable expression, and the terms and conditions of access and use of protected works." *Ibid* at 437.

73 As Myra Tawfik has rightly noted, "the international copyright law system does not mandate or compel specific outcomes for domestic legislation nor does it require the international harmonization of laws. National legislatures retain a great measure of discretion in the way in which they interpret and implement their international copyright obligations." Myra Tawfik, "International Copyright Law: Wi[h]ether User Rights?" in Michael Geist, ed., *In the Public Interest: The Future of Canadian Copyright Law* (Toronto: Irwin Law Journal, 2005) at 72.

74 *Ibid* at 76–77. *Agreement on Trade-Related Aspects of Intellectual Property Rights*,arts. 7 & 8, 15 April 1994, Marrakesh Agreement Establishing the World Trade Organization, Annex 1C, 33 ILM1125 (1994) [*TRIPS Agreement*].

75 WCT, *supra* note 71 at Preamble, para 5.

76 Reichman & Okediji, "When Copyright Law and Science Collide," *supra* note 50 at 1452–1453.

77 *Ibid* at 1453.

78 Sheufen, *Copyright versus Open Access, supra* note 25 at 106–108; Reichman & Okediji, "When Copyright Law and Science Collide," *supra* note 50 at 1454–1455 (noting the importance of incorporating the proposal in reinterpreting the test).

79 See Priest, "Copyright," *supra* note 35 at 400–408 (discussing the application of the doctrine in the United States, the unclarity on teacher's exception and suggesting the need for a clear teacher exception for works that are academic in nature to facilitate OA).

80 See Gervais, *Restructuring Copyright, supra* note 3 at 191–206 & 287 (explaining the various categories of creators/industries and the respective motivation or incentive mechanisms). Priest, "Copyright," *supra* note 35 at 398–400.

81 This scheme is more apt to embrace OA as authors will have a non-exclusive right to equitable remuneration. Once equitable compensation is made, the works will then be available for public use without restriction, save for moral rights.
82 Jerome Reichman, "The Limits of 'Limitations and Exceptions' in the Copyright Law," in Okediji, *Copyright Law in an Age of Limitations and Exceptions*, *supra* note 63 at 308–314 [Reichman, "The Limits of L&Es"].
83 See Daniel Gervais, "IP, Trade and Development: The State of Play" (2005) 74 Fordham L Rev 505 at 535 [Gervais, "IP, Trade and Development"] (stating that "TRIPs should be seen, and accepted, as a given").
84 Priest, "Copyright," *supra* note 35 at 403–408. It should be noted that art. 21(4) of the *Copyright Proc. 410/2004* does not provide for a statutory exception to the doctrine. Rather, it provides for a general doctrine of work-for-hire unless agreed otherwise.
85 Priest, "Copyright," *supra* note 35 at 403–408. To quote Priest, "[n]on-exclusive licenses, therefore, are the lifeblood of open access." *Ibid* at 418; Guibault, "Owning the Right to Open Up Access," supra note 34 at 163.
86 *Ibid* at 411–417. Eger & Sheufen, *supra* note 37 at 106 & 114–115 (noting that an absolute mandate be a challenge for OA journals due to lack of reputation and a conflict with academic freedom).
87 For example, the higher education legislation in Ethiopia requires such a public dedication of academic works. See *Higher Education Proclamation, Proc. No. 1152/2019*, art. 25(5), Federal Negarit Gazetta of the Federal Democratic Republic of Ethiopia, 25th Year No. 78, Addis Ababa, 12 September 2019. See Priest, "Copyright," *supra* note 35 at 423–424.
88 Reichman & Okediji, *supra* note 50 at 1469–1470; Sheufen, *Copyright versus Open Access, supra* note 25 at 115. Priest, "Copyright," *supra* note 35 at 396–397.
89 Reichman & Okediji, "When Copyright Law and Science Collide," *supra* note 50 at 1465–1469. The authors argue that "[r]ecognizing that publishers must charge for their technical *services* need not extend to endowing them with exclusive rights to downstream uses or reuses of the scientific *product* they make available." *Ibid* at 1466. Reichman, "The Limits of L & Es" *supra* note 82 at 308.
90 *Ibid.* Guilibat, "Owning the Right to Open Up Access," supra note 34 at 148–150 (articulating how publishers acquire broader rights from authors).
91 Sheufen, *Copyright versus Open Access*, *supra* note 25 at 155. Suber, *Open Access, supra* note 75 at 125–132. Guibault, "Owning the Right to Open Up Access," *supra* note 34 at 161–162.
92 See Reichman & Okediji, "When Copyright Law and Science Collide," *supra* note 50 at 1460 & 1476.
93 For instance, German copyright law provides for the retention of right of secondary publication 12 months after the original publication. *German Copyright Act*, art. 38(4). See Copyright Act of 9 September 1965, § 38(4), (as last amended by Article 1 of the Act of 1 September 2017) [Federal Law Gazette I p. 3346]. Sheufen, *Copyright versus Open Access*, *supra* note 25 at 118.
94 See *Copyright Amendment Bill [B13-B-2017]*, §12D (7), Republic of South Africa, online: https://www.gov.za/sites/default/files/gcis_document/201705/b13–2017copyright170516.pdf,
95 See Maracke, *supra* note 46 at 7; Okediji, "Reframing International Copyright" *supra* note 63 at 89–94; see generally Andrew Rens, "Implementing WIPO's Development Agenda: Treaty Provisions on Minimum Exceptions and Limitations for Education," in Jeremey de Beer, ed, *Implementing WIPO's Development Agenda* (Ottawa: Wilfred University Press, 2009) 158 at 158–169.
96 Maracke, *supra* note 46 at 11–13. Rens, *supra* note 95 at 165–166.
97 Sheufen, *Copyright versus Open Access*, *supra* note 25 at 100.

98 Reichman & Okediji, "When Copyright Law and Science Collide," *supra* note 50 at 1474–1475.

99 *Ibid* at 1464.

100 *Ibid* at 1463–1464 & 1471–1472.

101 Eger & Sheufen, *supra* note 37 at 102–106 & 108–115. Eger & Sheufen note that mandate is not helpful for green OA journals due to lack of reputation and a conflict with academic freedom. *Ibid* at 106 & 114–115. Sheufen, *Copyright versus Open Access*, *supra* note 25 at 154–155 (suggesting, inter alia, monitoring mandates, reconsideration of incentive structure, awareness creation).

102 *Ibid* at 108–115. Chan & Gray, *supra* note 31 at 208–209.

103 Reichman & Okediji, "When Copyright Law and Science Collide," *supra* note 50 at 1469–1472.

104 Chan & Gray, *supra* note 31 at 200–203 & 211.

105 *Ibid* at 198 & 206–208. If not countered, such systemic marginalization of relevant knowledge from the global south would both deepen the existing knowledge divide and perpetuate the epistemological bias.

106 Reichman & Okediji, "When Copyright Law and Science Collide," *supra* note 50 at 1470.

107 *Ibid* at 1466–1467 & 1469–1470. Priest, "Copyright," *supra* note 35 at 394–395. Guilibat, "Owning the Right to Open Up Access," *supra* note 34 at 158–159.

7 Concluding remarks

7.1 Introduction

Despite the challenges associated with rapid population growth, populous countries are blessed with rich and untapped human wealth for development opportunities. As a crucial form of investment in and transformation of the human wealth, educating the youths and tapping into their potentials will create enormous opportunities for human development. Long affirmed in the *Human Development Report (1990)*, it remains indisputable that 'people are the real wealth of a nation.'[1] As a matter of fact, the assertion made before decades now underpins the dominance of knowledge-driven development. In this context, access to quality higher education remains an essential prerequisite for a nation to harness its human potentials for sustainable human development.

Given its established instrumental role, education in general has long been considered a key tool for economic growth through the formation of human capital. Yet, it needs to be redefined and emphasized as an element of human capabilities. Rethinking education as an essential element of human capabilities helps embrace and enrich the narrow and economic conception of human capital. It is in the latter context that education serves as a vital tool for the advancement of sustainable human development. After decades of investment in the basic and secondary levels of education, several LDCs have thus undertaken an intensified campaign for mass expansion of higher educational institutions in order to promote access to higher education. In consequence, there is an increasing demand for a bulk access to copyrighted learning materials both for advanced education and scientific research. In most countries, students bear the larger chunk of the spiraling costs of access to knowledge relevant for higher education.

In particular, several LDCs face a more serious challenge due to the dire economic conditions of learners and educators. Further, lack of robust local publishers and the rising global licensing fees are some of the major infrastructural and financial hurdles most LDCs find difficult to overcome. Access to knowledge is a prerequisite for quality higher education and scientific research. In disregard for this prerequisite, the failure to meet the increasing demand for access to relevant learning materials has an implication for the

DOI: 10.4324/9781003214298-7

expansion of advanced human capabilities. It is in this context that a copyright system interfaces with higher education to impact sustainable human development. From among several factors, a restrictive copyright regime constitutes a significant impediment against access to relevant copyrighted learning materials. As the findings reveal, a restrictive copyright regime exacerbates the conditions and impedes access to knowledge. In turn, a limited access to relevant knowledge has far-reaching repercussions for creative innovation, higher education, and development.

In principle, copyright protection is premised on the desire to promote the production and dissemination of creative works for the purpose of public interest. In particular, the Anglo-American utilitarian objective of promoting "the progress of useful arts" emphasizes the primacy of the interest of the public at large.[2] In contrast, the continental conception of copyright is grounded in the individualistic natural-right based creative freedom of an author.[3] In spite of the variance in their respective emphasis, both perspectives are instrumental for the advancement of sustainable human development.[4]

In its instrumental role for human development, copyright is further interlinked with education. Indeed, promoting learning as one of the vital public interests has been integral to copyright system from its inception. Within the broader framework of access to knowledge, the most direct interaction occurs in the context of access to learning materials. As essential inputs required for higher education, most learning materials are subject to copyright protection.[5] This scenario brings to the fore the relationship between copyright and higher education as well as their respective roles for human development. Given its fundamental significance for human development, education has been recognized in legal regimes at various levels.

In fact, both international and regional human rights instruments underscore the need to take all appropriate measures to make higher education accessible to all. At international level, the human right status of higher education with an immediate application is contested and its provision is rather contingent upon capacities and/or merits. Nevertheless, the legal context of African countries should be seen in tandem with art. 14 of the African Charter that suggests the existence of a less debatable human rights status of higher education. In line with the Charter's distinctive approach, its generic right to education of all levels, and its affirmation in the relevant jurisprudence, higher education—an integral element of the recognized right—should be embraced as such at national levels.

The normative conundrum aside, the progressive realization of higher education is both essential in itself and instrumental for the realization of other human rights. In view of its prime objective and instrumental link, higher education is thus pivotal for sustainable human development. In the LDCs such as Ethiopia, the issue of sustainable human development is so vital that it is accorded both constitutional and human right status. Indeed, Ethiopia's low level of human development itself constitutes a compelling reason for its treatment as the core and overarching national policy objective.

As adopted in this book, the notion of human development is understood as the enlargement of freedoms or human capabilities for valuable achievements. Education of all levels is instrumental for the expansion of freedoms. As a matter of fact, the realization of higher education and its instrumental role for human development depend, *inter alia,* upon the availability of or access to relevant learning materials. In turn, access to relevant copyrighted learning materials is contingent upon the existence of appropriate copyright flexibilities.

Given this interdependence, the central issues examined in this book are explorations of: (a) relevant international copyright flexibilities and (b) approaches for rethinking and comprehensive integration of all relevant copyright-related flexibilities in order to promote human development. The central argument that underpins the research questions assumes (a) lack of a comprehensive and human development-oriented copyright flexibilities, (b) the consequent restricted access to protected knowledge, and (c) the negative implications for the progressive realization of sustainable human development. In this book, the findings affirm the assumptions and answer the research questions in affirmative.

7.2 Copyright and higher education for human development

7.2.1 Mapping the conceptual linkage

As indicated above, both copyright and education share common objectives of promoting sustainable human development. Designed for the protection of original creative works, copyright contributes to human development by promoting creative innovation and scientific progress. In the same vein, education fosters human development through the cultivation of human personalities and advanced skills. Thus, development is the ultimate end of both regimes. Indeed, human development is a critical issue at global, regional and local levels. Despite its disputed status at international level, the right to development has been embodied in the African Charter as a binding human right in Africa.[6] Hence, both copyright protection and higher education are instrumental for the progressive realization of this right to development in the continent.

In their immediate linkage, the instrumental roles of copyright and higher education for human development center upon access to learning materials. In other words, the need for an access to copyrighted learning materials constitutes a ground for the interaction between copyright and education. This point of nexus requires a careful examination in the light of their intended common goals towards sustainable human development. In principle, a balanced copyright protection is crucial to incentivize the production and efficient utilization of knowledge for creative innovation, advanced education, and scientific research. That is, copyright serves as a means for the generation, appropriation and dissemination of knowledge. In turn, the generated knowledge is an essential input for both creative innovation and higher education that contribute for sustainable human development. It is important to note that a robust creative innovation itself depends upon balanced copyright system and quality education.[7]

In addition to knowledge generation, higher education is crucial for the formation of human capital and expansion of human capabilities. These are all essential inputs for vibrant creative innovation. Hence, quality higher education and scientific research are instrumental to cultivate range of capabilities used for sustainable creative innovation.[8] Indeed, an advanced education is a key to unleash the creative potential of the learners and expand their human capabilities. In this context, both copyright and higher education complement each other for the expansion of creative and learning capabilities. The enlargement of people's creative and educational capabilities will foster sustainable human development.

7.2.2 Theoretical justifications of copyright, education, and development

The emergence and development of copyright, education, and human development are grounded in their respective philosophical foundations. The theoretical foundations are useful to offer insights into the purpose, significance, and attributes of each of the subject matters under consideration. Despite some overlapping attributes, each theoretical justification has evolved to advance various values and interests. Yet, subject to a variance, the theoretical justifications share one basic objective—development.

For instance, anchored in the economic incentive, the utilitarian justification predominates copyright protection. Intended to advance an aggregate welfare of the society, the legal protection is granted to recompense and safeguard a necessary incentive for the development of creative works.[9] The justification is however critiqued for its overemphasis on welfare maximization without a due regard for distributional concerns. In contrast, the labor theory is used to justify copyright protection as a product of an author's labor mixed with commons.[10] Subject to Locke's provisos of non-waste and leaving 'enough and as good' commons for others, creators are entitled to rights due to the labor invested in the creative works. It bears noting that the provisos are meant to recognize public interests. Entrenched in a similar natural rights tradition, the personality theory justifies the protection of authors' rights for the purpose of self-actualization or personal development.[11] As an embodiment of individual freedom, the protection of a creative work is essential for the personhood of the creator and its manifestation.

Evident in the short-term and disclosure-bound patent regime, the contractarian theory is another justification with some relevance for copyright regime.[12] From copyright's perspective, the justification is anchored in an implicit social contract between creators and the public at large for their mutual interests.[13] Related to this justification is the social planning theory under construction. Considered an eclectic blend of the above-mentioned justifications, the social planning paradigm underscores the role of copyright to foster a just and democratic culture.[14] As such, it emphasizes the need to strike a balance and accommodate social goals. In short, combinations of various theoretical justifications underpin the existing legal protection of copyright.

As timeless and unconditional entitlements, the protection of human rights shares similar natural rights justification that foregrounds human rights in a human dignity. From among the natural, social justice/deliberative, protest, and discursive schools of thought, the first two have been explored in this book. According to the dominant natural rights theory, a human person is entitled to human rights upon birth by virtue of humanity.[15] That is, human rights are inherent in the human person.

Emerging as an alternative view, the social justice theory conceives human rights as a subset of social justice and products of social cooperation.[16] In contrast to others, the major focus of this theory are the socio-economic rights. In essence, the *inherency* and the *acquisition* of human rights and the respective sources remain the basic distinction between the theories. It is worth noting that both theories have their own critiques directed against their respective philosophical basis. In fact, the same holds true for the protest and discourse schools of thought.

As for education, its significance is justified both on intrinsic and instrumental grounds. For instance, the liberal (general) theory of education underscores the value of education for the development of a democratic individual freedom and social interaction.[17] Distinct from the liberal model, the human capital theory underpins the instrumental role of education for an economic growth.[18] It is, however, critiqued for its treatment of human beings as a *mere means* of economic development. In the quest for a more inclusive justification, the capability approach is adapted to underline both intrinsic and instrumental values of education.[19] As a robust normative tool, the approach treats education as an essential form of human capabilities. Education is thus valued both for its enhancement of individual freedoms and its instrumental roles in advancing a socio-economic development. Further, the proponents tend to construe the right to education as an entitlement to human capabilities.[20]

For both copyright and education at all levels, it is undisputed that a sustainable human development should remain central to their objectives and respective human rights/constitutional dimensions. Like its constituents, the notion of development itself has different philosophical justifications. Despite the recent shift in the notion and theoretical foundations of development, almost all the theories that evolved in the last several decades focus on an economic development. This is true of the neoliberal and the contemporary theories of economic development. From among others, capital accumulation, technological progress, labor, investment, and markets are all common to most of the theories. The extent of the roles of the market and government intervention are the central points of distinction among the theories and within their major variants. Associated with the knowledge-based economies, the endogenous growth model has become prominent for its treatment of knowledge as the driver of economic development.[21]

In its departure from the rest, the HDCA has emerged to be comprehensive enough to accommodate the hitherto neglected social aspects of development. Indeed, the approach has made a major shift both in the notion and the conventional metrics of development. Placing human beings at its center, the HDCA reframes development as the expansion or enlargement of individuals' freedom to lead worthwhile lives. As used in the *Human Development Reports* for decades, the measure of human development is thus the expansion of the human capabilities that are essential for valuable functionings.[22] In line with this robust notion, the HDCA is adopted in this book both as a normative and analytical framework to explore the complementarities between copyright and higher education, and their roles for a sustainable human development. Gaining a traction among IP scholars for being a better framework to explore IP's role for development, the HDCA is quite suitable to embrace the above justifications for human flourishing.

7.2.3 International development context

Despite the difference in the scope and degree of emphasis, the issue of development has been central to both international copyright and human rights systems. In fact, development was one of the major driving forces behind the emergence of both systems. From its inception, the expansion of international copyright system has been attributed to the economic interests of the rights holders and the intermediaries. In the same vein, the issue of development has been among the pillar objectives of the UN Charter. In furtherance of the Charter's objectives, the UDHR and ICESCR, among others, have all articulated and enshrined various aspects of development. As hinted above, there remains a variance in the depth and breadth of development notion embodied in the international copyright and human rights regimes. In terms of historical junctures, both regimes emerged at different times and have thence evolved with their own prime orientation.

In the evolution of the international copyright system, the Berne Convention is the cornerstone with in-built principles for the subsequent proliferation of other international copyright treaties. In particular, the expansive trajectory and author-centric approach set in the Berne Convention have remained the governing rules. Building upon the core rules, the Rome Convention, the Geneva Phonograms Convention, and the WIPO Internet Treaties altogether constitute the major substantive regimes for the international copyright system. All the treaties are dedicated to ensure the protection of the rights of authors or right holders.

Marking IP's shift to the trade regime, the TRIPs Agreement has both globalized and reinforced the existing international copyright system through its incorporation of the major copyright treaties, including the Berne Convention. Further, the copyright system has been injected with effective enforcement measures under the auspice of the WTO system. For its firm entrenchment, a binding set of minimum substantive standards is developed to ensure the legal protection of the rights both in the analog and digital environments.

Given its lopsided evolution, the international copyright regime lacks a holistic approach to development. A critical gap in this regard the regime's overemphasis on economic growth and the consequent marginalization of L&Es from among relevant copyright flexibilities. As a manifestation of an imbalanced system, this author-centeric approach undermines the integral role of the indispensable flexibilities to serve the public interest through access to the protected works. It is true that states are permitted to design their own L&Es and incorporate the available flexibilities. In this context, arts. 7 & 8 of the TRIPs Agreement and pertinent copyright treaties allow considerable development related-flexibilities. The incorporation of the permissible flexibilities is however subject to the in-built structural restriction and the constraining requirements of the three-step test. Adopted within the restrictive system, the Marrakesh Treaty is the sole international instrument with a mandatory set of L&Es for a specific class of users. In short, the marginalization of the L&Es in the copyright regime is counterproductive for sustainable human development.

Besides the substantive legal regimes, both the UN-affiliated WIPO and the WTO are central components of the global copyright system. Vested with a broad mandate to promote the global protection of IP, the WIPO has played a key role in facilitating and overseeing the adoption and implementation of major copyright treaties. For an obvious reason, the WIPO also advocates for a stronger IP protection through its technical assistance. In the aftermath of IP's integration into the global trade regime, the WTO has emerged as a strong institutional framework intended, *inter alia,* to promote the globalization and enforcement of copyright protection.

In contrast to the copyright regime, the evolution of international human rights system is a recent phenomenon. In fact, its emergence has been integral to the foundation of the UN system in the post-WWII period. As indicated in arts. 55 & 56 of the UN Charter, one of its pillars is promoting "a universal respect for, and observance of, human rights and fundamental freedoms for all" without a discrimination. This commitment led to the emergence of a comprehensive set of human rights. Originating from the UDHR that served as their blueprint, the International Covenants and other human rights instruments were all adopted to articulate the various human rights and fundamental freedoms.

In addition, the adoption of, *inter alia*, the African Charter, the European and the American Conventions on Human Rights were foundational for the development of the regional human rights system within the international framework. In addition to the substantive human rights regimes, there are several international, regional and national human rights institutions that are mandated to promote the protection of human rights. For instance, the UNHRC, the CESCR, and the African Human Rights Commission are among the most important institutions at international and regional levels.

From among a range of human rights, authors' rights, the right to education and other constituent elements of the right to development are enshrined in most of the major human rights instruments. In this regard, the UDHR and the ICESCR articulate both rights. In contrast, the UNCRC is another relevant human rights instrument dealing with the right to education. In particular, the ICESCR and the UNCRC are more significant for their detailed articulation of the right to education at all levels. From among the regional human rights instruments, the African Charter is notable for its recognition of the right to property, the right to education and the right to development.

Indeed, the African Charter is the sole binding regional human rights instrument to recognize the right to development. At international level, the DRD is dedicated to the right to development. Nonetheless, its evolution into a binding status is still a subject of debate. Following its articulation as a human right in the DRD and the African Charter, its status as such has been reaffirmed in several declarations and resolutions. In terms of their legal status, the declarations and resolutions however remain unenforceable soft norms.

Further, the emerging development norms within the UN system such as the MDGs and SDGs are important initiatives for the enrichment, concretization, and operationalization of the right to development. In the international copyright regime, similar important development context is constituted of the various development-oriented provisions and the WIPO DA that incorporate numerous flexibilities. Dedicated to the issue of development, the implementation of the WIPO DA is expected to align with the UN development goals and priorities. Thus, the roles of copyright and higher education for human development should be explored within the broader development context. Indeed, situating both regimes in the broader development context is essential for a nation to underscore their complementarities and promote its human development.

In sum, all the relevant elements of development context should further be consolidated in the light of the principle of sustainable human development. The notion of sustainable development is noted as a process of sustainable change with socio-economic and environmental dimensions. This intergenerational and inclusive process of change involves, *inter alia*, the direction of investments and orientation of technological development in order to advance both current and future capabilities to meet human needs and aspirations.[23] From the perspective of the CA-driven human development that enriches and guides the development objective of copyright and higher education, the broader and holistic notion of sustainable human development offers a useful context.

7.3 Exploring copyright-related flexibilities for human development

7.3.1 International copyright-related flexibilities

The appropriate incorporation of international copyright flexibilities is instrumental both for a sustainable creative innovation and quality higher education in the context of access to knowledge and formation of human capital. Further, more important is the role of the flexibilities for the expansion of human capabilities. Indeed, the enlargement of human capabilities constitutes an enriching and overarching conceptual framework for a sustainable human development. From this perspective, the set of relevant flexibilities under the existing international copyright system is neither directed towards nor informed by the core objective of human development. In the existing international copyright legal regime, an issue of central focus has been the harmonization and primacy of exclusive rights. In contrast, the corresponding flexibilities are neither harmonized nor treated as an integral part of the regime.

Instead, their domestic integration is left to members *albeit* with a significant circumscription. Setting a baseline for the exclusive rights, the Berne Convention leaves to member states the discretion to design most domestic L&Es. This discretion is nonetheless subject to the Convention's built-in upward trajectory of author's right and the three-step test. From the few L&Es provided in the Convention, pertinent are the teaching exception, exception for quotation and the contested Berne Appendix for the purposes of education. Except for the self-contained ones, the L&Es to reproduction right are thus cabined within the three-step test.

Further, the general flexibilities related to the subject matter, conditions of protection, and term limits are embodied in the Convention. The various general flexibilities enshrined in or permitted under the TRIPs Agreement and the WIPO treaties could also be utilized for further creative innovation and higher education in order to promote human development. From among the existing international copyright treaties, the Marrakesh Treaty is the sole legal regime that provides for mandatory L&Es. In a Berne-plus approach, common to all copyright treaties is the all-encompassing application of the three-step test as introduced in the TRIPs Agreement. Serving as a parameter, the test is intended to safeguard the exclusive rights. In the same vein, it is a guiding rule for the national incorporation or creation of copyright flexibilities contemplated under the international copyright system.

In view of their central role for human development, various approaches have been highlighted in the legal scholarship and emerging jurisprudence. In addition to the traditional approach that subordinates flexibilities to the exclusive rights, the emerging approaches to copyright flexibilities regard the flexibilities as development policy tools and/or users' rights.[24] Going further and with the potential to embrace both, the CA-based human development perspective is important to enhance the instrumental role of the international copyright flexibilities for higher education and creative innovation. Given its normative reach, the HDCA is both equitable and inclusive to encompass the emerging approaches to the copyright flexibilities. In so doing, the framework reinforces the significance of the flexibilities to facilitate access to knowledge or learning materials for higher education.

Due to its multifaceted nature to serve as a policy and normative tool to balance authors' and users' interests, the HDCA is crucial to inform flexibilities whether framed as public policy goals or rights grounded in human rights norms. Further, this human-centered framework is more useful for rethinking, interpretation and application of the notion of "development" in the TRIPs Agreement and other international copyright treaties. In particular, the HDCA is pivotal for an explicit articulation of human development as the core objective of copyright.[25] In the same vein, it is useful to reframe flexibilities as an instrumental aspect of human capabilities.[26]

As noted in the preamble to the WTO Agreement, the principle of sustainable development can be a useful guide for the interpretation and application of the development objectives and relevant flexibilities embodied in the TRIPs Agreement.[27] Indeed, this integrative principle is well-suited to embrace human development to underscore a notion of sustainable human development. For the international copyright regime, the principle provides an entry point for a coherent reintegration of the flexibilities in the light of a broad framework of sustainable human development.

7.3.2 Exploring national copyright-related flexibilities

As emphasized in this book, both copyright and higher education are crucial for the realization of sustainable human development, *inter alia*, through the expansion of human capabilities. As opposed to developed nations that dispute its human right status, African countries that subscribe to the African Charter endorse the right to sustainable development with its human rights, and in some jurisdictions, constitutional dimensions as well. Nevertheless, the intrinsic and instrumental roles of copyright and higher education for sustainable human development depend upon the existence of appropriate flexibilities that facilitate access to knowledge. In this regard, countries might take their respective approaches to incorporate in their national copyright systems the various copyright and related flexibilities. In order to facilitate a better access to knowledge, countries should take into account their respective human development imperatives.

First, the notion of sustainable development itself should be construed as a broad framework of flexibilities to accommodate various interests.[28] Framed as an important right, sustainable development has both human rights and constitutional dimensions to guide the interpretation of specific flexibilities. Second, there is a relevant set of general flexibilities with similar dimensions. For instance, the constitutional public interest is a significant and core aspect of general flexibilities. Often embedded in a national constitution, the public interest underscores a constitutional justification to limit and guide copyright as *a means* of private property protection that should *serve a social function*.[29]

In the same vein, the public interest undergirds the role of copyright to advance the freedom of expression. Indeed, the latter constitutes an external constitutional constraint upon the former to serve as a ground for flexibilities. Likewise, striking a balance between higher education and authors' rights itself requires appropriate flexibilities to ensure their interdependence and complementarities for their progressive realization. Further, the subjective *adequate standard of living* suggested for author's right to material interests and the variance in its scope from the expansive scope of copyright might offer another general aspect of legal flexibilities.

As explained in this book, most general and specific copyright flexibilities are embodied in the global copyright system. Curved out for member-states to utilize, the general flexibilities integral to the international copyright treaties include the principle of idea/expression distinction, subject matters-related exclusion, conditions and terms of protection. For the integration of a balanced set of relevant flexibilities, the pressure for adoption of a TRIPs-plus approach should be resisted to avoid the erosion or waiver of the available flexibilities. Enclosing the flexibilities, the erosion of a flexible policy space also occurs through the untamed expansion and introduction of exclusive rights.

For instance, *unconditional exclusive* rental right for all works, provision of resale right and introduction of an *exclusive* public lending right are all instances of the TRIPs-plus approach that need a careful consideration. In the same vein, the copyright law should avoid an excessive and stringent set of enforcement measures, including an *indiscriminate* criminalization of *all acts of infringement*. An expansive legislative action is counterproductive as it often impoverishes the public domain that ought to flourish in order to foster a sustainable creative innovation. Indeed, the erosion of the available flexibilities has far-reaching implications for the constitutional and human rights aspects of the right to sustainable human development.

From among the specific copyright flexibilities, the L&Es that are instrumental for access to copyrighted learning materials include exceptions for private use, quotation, teaching, and libraries. Further, an effective compulsory license, when aligned with a doctrine of international exhaustion, can be used to facilitate access to domestic and imported learning materials at affordable prices. From the vantage point of categories of disadvantaged users, a copyright law should incorporate appropriate L&Es for persons with disabilities. From a human rights perspective, member-states are required to take appropriate steps in order to observe their international obligations under the UNCRPD. Dedicated to the disabled users, the Marrakesh Treaty is an international copyright instrument that *requires* the contracting parties to incorporate into their domestic laws appropriate L&Es. From both perspectives, the HDCA is thus vital to incorporate mandatory L&Es for users with disabilities.

In sum, member-states should embrace the human-centered approach for a better integration of a number of legal flexibilities relevant to facilitate a sustainable creative innovation and access to learning materials for higher education. To this effect, human development-oriented reform measures should be taken to rethink the existing restrictive approach and reintegrate appropriate flexibilities suited to reinforce the complementing roles of copyright and higher education for enhanced human development.

7.4 Rethinking policy and legal flexibilities for human development

7.4.1 Rethinking policy, legal, and institutional regimes

Sharing a common overarching objective, both copyright and higher education are interlinked in their contributions to sustainable human development. In practice, the policy and legal linkages between copyright and higher education often lack the relevant attributes of human development. For instance, despite their inevitable linkage in the context of access to learning materials or knowledge, the gaps or incoherences arise from lack of appropriate set of general policy and legal flexibilities. In consequence, the lack of coherence undermines their potential to complement each other in their roles for sustainable human development. Thus, it is imperative to forge a coherence between the policy and legal frameworks. In doing so, crucial is an incorporation of the appropriate flexibilities in the light of the CA-driven human development. In this regard, the people-centered notion of sustainable development can draw on the normative framework of human development to inform copyright and higher education systems.

To this end, the HDCA proves useful to recalibrate and re-orient the respective objectives towards sustainable human development. The approach is also helpful to integrate into the policy and statutory frameworks both human rights and other pertinent dimensions. Indeed, human rights and constitutional law regimes offer a relevant legal framework and policy guidance to articulate and incorporate the appropriate flexibilities. Once incorporated, the flexibilities will have the role to interconnect copyright and higher education for sustainable human development. For an optimal utilization of relevant development-enhancing flexibilities, there should be a better coherence and collaboration among the relevant policy, legal, and institutional frameworks in a manner that facilitate their joint contributions for human development. In a broader context, this task requires reforming the existing regimes and forging appropriate coherence. In effect, the coherence will promote the collaborative realization of the underpinning development objectives. Hence, it is imperative to rethink the development orientation and alignment in the policy, legal, and institutional regimes towards a sustainable human development.

7.4.2 Rethinking and re-integrating copyright flexibilities

Within the framework of general flexibilities that involve constitutional and human rights aspects, it is crucial to rethink and ensure a complete integration of the relevant copyright flexibilities elaborated in this book. To this effect, as emphasized time and again, the HDCA is apt for its integrative and comprehensive approach to accommodate both development policy and the emerging users' rights approaches to copyright flexibilities. This integrative normative approach offers a broader room with maximum flexibilities in order to address the national development priorities and realities. From the general flexibilities, the guiding elements include the public interest–related constitutional flexibilities and the human rights-related flexibilities that are useful to strike an appropriate balance between creators and users' interests/rights. In particular, relevant constitutional and human rights aspects should be integrated into or recognized in the national copyright laws. Further, the constitutional and human rights norms should be regarded as a set of overarching principles for rethinking and guiding the integration, interpretation and application of the various copyright-related flexibilities for the advancement of human development.

From the international norms of development flexibilities, both the policy and legislative reforms should take the utmost advantage of the flexibilities inherent in arts. 7 & 8 of the TRIPs Agreement. In effect, the flexibilities can be used to entrench a balance between the twin aspects of the public interest—protection and access—that that underlie a robust copyright system. In line with the provisions, an explicit recognition of education at all levels and in all modes should be made to underscore its role as a '*sector of vital importance*' and *an instrument* of sustainable human development. As enshrined in the WTO Agreement, the principle of sustainable development and the flexibilities envisaged in the WIPO DA can be used in the national policy formulation and legislative-norm setting process to reflect a nation's level of development and context.[30]

In revisiting the existing copyright system, it is critical to eliminate the TRIPs-plus approach often adopted for the expansive scope of exclusive rights, the narrow L&Es and the stringent enforcement measures. In particular, the wholesale criminalization of acts of infringement and the prescribed severe penalties should be avoided to insulate legitimate uses made for non-commercial purposes. For most LDCs, it is also important to consider an equitable remuneration scheme for use of works relevant for education.[31] Pertinent are the proper integration and judicial interpretation of general flexibilities inherent in the expressions/idea distinction and conditions of protection. For the L&Es, an *appropriate* integration of the three-step test is vital to serve as a general rule of copyright flexibilities. In compliance with the TRIPs Agreement and relevant copyright treaties, a member-state should take a strategic and proactive measure to integrate the test in light of its human rights obligations and sustainable human development objectives.

In their critique of the test for its vagueness and double-edged effect,[32] scholars have suggested a number of approaches for its adoption and application at national levels. From the ranges of proposed approaches such as a reverse reading of the steps,[33] a holistic approach with an overall assessment of the steps[34] and the infusion of the test with the open-ended US fair-use doctrine,[35] the adoption of the last approach in the light of the HDCA is useful to offer a concrete and flexible balancing framework to mediate between the public and private interests. For a nation to optimize the relevant copyright flexibilities, its adoption, interpretation and application of the three-step test should take a holistic approach.

In order to improve the sustainable human development of their peoples, countries such as the LDCs should to take appropriate policy and legal reforms. Tailored reforms are important to facilitate comprehensive and coherent integration of the flexibilities, including the open access licensing models. For the specific flexibilities, a set of broad and mandatory L&Es should be designed for private use, quotation, teaching, scientific research, libraries, and archives as well as for persons with disabilities. As emphasized in this book, the flexibilities are critical for higher education and creative innovation that advance the formation of human capabilities. In the same vein, the scope of compulsory license should be extended while an international exhaustion should be adopted to facilitate affordable or bulk access to copyrighted materials. Informed by the human rights and constitutional dimensions, the flexibilities should better be reframed as users' rights. Further, these flexibilities need to be insulated from criminalization, digital locks, and contractual overrides.

7.5 Exploring licensing models as flexibilities: embracing OA

As noted in the preceding chapter, both blanket licensing and ECL models are important to facilitate access to learning materials. In particular, the ECL is considered to promote an access to a broader repertoire. In addition to the limits, their benefits are still contingent upon an effective and a well-organized operation of CMOs. As a regime of private ordering, a more decentralized and collaborative OA model can offer a better access to digital contents for educational purposes. Given its potential to facilitate access, OA is enjoying an increasing traction among educators, researchers, libraries, and academic publishers.

In this sense, an OA model holds a great promise for a free access to relevant digital learning materials such as scientific journals, books, software products, course packs, data, and research reports. Indeed, several public and private initiatives have been taken both in developed and developing nations to adopt OA mechanisms to promote collaborative creation, sharing, and dissemination of digital contents. The OA mechanism has the potential to complement the existing flexibilities and mitigate the impediments against access to learning materials in developing and LDCs. It is instrumental to facilitate a trans-border access to relevant knowledge housed in other countries.

It is true that OA has enormous benefits to promote creative innovation and higher education through improved access to knowledge. Yet, the legal, financial, technical, and social factors constitute critical challenges for the effective exploitation of the potentials of the OA models. In order to address the challenges and harness the benefits of OA, appropriate steps should be taken. First, an unawareness creation about OA should be made along with investments in the necessary infrastructure. Second, policy and legal reforms are needed to integrate OA into the broad framework of copyright-related flexibilities to promote access to creative works. An OA policy operating in isolation will be ineffective to promote access to learning materials. As suggested for other flexibilities, the HDCA is useful to facilitate its integration and role in promoting users' rights.

From the emerging variants of the models, the licensing models such as GNU/GPL for open source software and CC licenses for OA journals are instrumental to promote access to digital contents.[36] In the implementation of the policy and legal reforms, an institutional mandate or funders' contractual requirement is vital to facilitate scholars' embrace of OA for public-funded research.[37] In sum, it is important to harness the potential of OA for enhanced freedoms of access, learning and collaborative innovation to facilitate the expansion of human capabilities. As it is not a sole means of access, OA serves to complement other access models.

7.6 Conclusion

For all nations—in particular for the LDCs, advancing sustainable human development is critical both for its realization as a human right and the enlargement of human capabilities. In this regard, creative innovation and higher education should be regarded as essential components of sustainable human development. In order to promote the complementarities between copyright protection and higher education, there need to be coherent and appropriate linkages in the policy, legal, and institutional frameworks. The integration of copyright-related flexibilities is vital to strengthen the linkages and promote the complementarities to advance a sustainable human development. The integrative and more inclusive HDCA is thus useful to incorporate and align relevant development-oriented flexibilities.

In so doing, the formulation of robust and comprehensive copyright and educational policies should incorporate both the exiting international copyright-related flexibilities and the emerging open access models. Such an integrative approach will offer more choices to facilitate enhanced access to knowledge in general and learning materials in particular at national levels. To this end, the following measures need to be taken. First, it is essential to consider the differences in the national contexts and levels of development in order to free up more policy space for sustainable human development. Second, the necessary alignment should be made across relevant laws in order to realize constitutional and human rights to sustainable human development.

Third, the significance of reframing or incorporating legal flexibilities as users' rights must be underlined to empower users and promote the expansion of human capabilities. Fourth, appropriate institutional coherence and collaboration must be forged. Indeed, the proper integration and effective utilization of copyright-related flexibilities require strong, robust and collaborative institutions. Further, promoting institutional collaboration and capacity building is instrumental to strengthen complementarities and mainstream sustainable human development in the institutional practices.

Notes

1 UNDP, *Human Development Report 1990* (New York & Oxford: UNDP & Oxford University Press, 1990) at 9.

2 See Paul Goldstein, *International Copyright: Principles, Law and Practice* (New York: Oxford University Press, 2001) at 3 [Goldstein, *International Copyright*].

3 *Ibid* at 4.

4 *Ibid.*

5 See Ruth L. Okediji, "The International Copyright System: Limitations, Exceptions and Public Interest Considerations for Developing Countries" (2006) UNCTAD-ICTSD Issue Paper No. 15 at 8 & 31–32 [Okediji, The International Copyright System].

6 *African Charter on Human and Peoples' Rights*, art. 22, 27 June 1981, 21 ILM 58 (entered into force on 21 October 1986) at art. 17 (1) [African *Charter*].

7 Michael Spence, *Innovation and Prosperity in an Age of Transition: Foreword*, at xiii, Rohinton P. Medhora, *New Thinking on Innovation: Introduction*, Center for International Innovation Governance, Special Report 2017 ("[P]eople as [the] most important investable resource … are the source of innovation, creativity and dynamism.").

8 See Rohinton P. Medhora, *New Thinking on Innovation: Introduction*, Center for International Innovation Governance, Special Report 2017, at 5 & 8.

9 See Peter Drahos, *A Philosophy of Intellectual Property* (Aldershot: Ashgate, 1996) at 29–46 [Drahos, *A Philosophy of IP*].

10 *Ibid* at 47–50. See Justin Hughes, "The Philosophy of Intellectual Property" (1988) 77 Geo L J 287 at 297–298 & 314–316 [Hughes, *The Philosophy of IP*]; Wendy J. Gordon, "A Property Right in Self-Expression: Equality and Individualism in the Natural Law of Intellectual Property" (1993) 102 Yale LJ 1533 at 1544–1570 [Gordon, "A Property Right in Self-Expression"]; see Jeremy Waldron, *The Right to Private Property* (Clarendon Press, 1988) at 184–252 (critiquing Lock's theory).

11 Hughes, "The Philosophy of IP," *supra* note 10 at 310–311; Drahos, *A Philosophy of IP, supra* note 9 at 85–106. Waldron, *supra* note 10 at 347–378.

12 Chidi Oguamanam, "Beyond Theories: Intellectual Property Dynamics in the Global Knowledge Economy" (2009) 9:2 Wake Forest Intell Prop LJ 105 at 112–116.

13 See generally Alina Ng, "The Social Contract and Authorship: Allocating Entitlements in the Copyright System" (2008) 19:2 Fordham IP Med & Ent L J 414.

14 William Fisher, "Theories of Intellectual Property," in Stephen Munzer, ed, *New Essays in the Legal and Political Theory of Property* (Cambridge University Press, 2001) 168 at 172–194.

15 See generally Jack Donnelly, "Human Rights as Natural Rights" (1982) 4:3 Hum Rts Q 391.

16 See generally Charles Beitz, "Human Rights and Social Justice," in Peter G. Brown & Douglas Maclean, *Human Rights and U.S Foreign Policy* (Massachusetts: Lexington Books, 1979) [Beitz, "Human Rights and Social Justice"]; Charles Beitz, The *Idea of Human Rights* (Oxford: Oxford University Press, 2009) at 136 [Beitz, *The Idea of Human Rights*].

17 John Dewey, *Democracy and Education: An Introduction to Philosophy of Education* (New York: Macmillan Company, 1916) at 94–108.

18 Gary Becker, "Human Capital Revisited," in Becker, *Human Capital: A Theoretical Analysis with Special Reference to Education* (The University of Chicago Press, 1994) 15 at 17–25; Lucas, "On the Mechanics," supra note 361 at 17–41.

19 See generally Melanie Walker, "Framing Social Justice: What Does the 'Capabilities' Approach Offer?" (2003) 51:2 Br J Educ Stud 168; Madoka Saito, "Amartya Sen's Capability Approach to Education: A Critical Exploration" (2003) 37:1 J Philos Educ 17.

20 Tristan McCowan, *Education as a Human Right: Principles for a Universal Entitlement to Learning* (London, UK: Bloomsbury, 2013) at 120–125.

21 See generally Paul Romer, The Origins of Endogenous Growth (1994) 8:1 J Econ Perspect 3–22; Robert E. Lucas, "Ideas and Growth" (2009) 76 Economica 1 (underscoring the contribution of knowledge of individuals for economic growth).

22 See generally Amartya Sen, *Development as Freedom* (New York: Anchor Books, 1999).

23 See United Nations World Commission on Environment and Development, *Our Common Future: World Commission on Environment and Development* (Oxford: Oxford University Press, 1987) at 48.

24 Ruth Okediji, "Reframing International Copyright Limitations and Exceptions as Development Policy," in *Copyright Law in an Age of Limitations and Exceptions* (Cambridge: Cambridge University, 2017) 429 at 475 & 482–489 [Okediji, "Reframing International Copyright"]; Agreement on Trade-Related Aspects of Intellectual Property Rights, 15 April 1994, Marrakesh Agreement Establishing the World Trade Organization, Preamble, paras 6 & 7 *cum* art. 8, Annex 1C, 33 ILM1125 (1994) [TRIPS Agreement]; Carlos M. Correa, *Trade Related Aspects of Intellectual Property Rights: A Commentary on the TRIPS Agreement* (Oxford: Oxford University Press, 2007) at 104–107 [Correa, *Trade Related Aspects*]; David Vaver, "Copyright Defenses as User Rights" (2013) 60:4 J Copyr Soc USA 661 at 672.

25 See generally Janewa Osei-Tutu, "Human Development as An Intellectual Property Metric" (2016) 90 St. John's L Rev 711; As Osei-Tutu notes, "human development is an implicit objective of patent and copyright law and policy because these laws regulate innovation, creativity, and the production of goods that promote human flourishing." *Ibid* at 743. Janewa Osei-Tutu, "Human Development as a Core Objective of Global Intellectual Property" (2016) 105 Ky LJ 1.

26 See generally Okediji, "Reframing International Copyright," *supra* note 24.

27 *Marrakesh Agreement Establishing the World Trade Organization* 33 ILM1125 (1994), Preamble, para 1. See Henning Grosse Ruse-Khan, "Sustainable Development in International Intellectual Property Law-A New Approaches From EU Economic Partnership Agreements?" (2010) ICTSD Program on Intellectual Property and Sustainable Development, Issues Paper No. 29 at 1–3. As Ruse-Khan observes, [s] ustainable development as a treaty objective is well equipped to guide and direct the utilization of [state's] discretion towards a reconciliation of all relevant economic, social and environmental concerns in domestic decision-making processes. He further notes that "[t]reaty objectives that focus on overreaching and inclusive goals such as sustainable development and a balance of all interests involved can re-shape the interpretation and implementation of specific IP provisions." *Ibid* at viii.

28 *Ibid* at viii & 1–3.

29 See Christophe Geiger, "The Social Function of Intellectual Property Rights, or how Ethics can Influence the Shape and Use of IP Law," in Graeme Dinwoodie, ed, *Intellectual Property Law: Methods and Perspectives* (Cheltenham, UK: Edward Elgar, 2014).

30 The WIPO DA acknowledges taking due account of the level of development in norm-setting process for flexibilities. WIPO Development Agenda (2007), Recommendation No. 13.

31 Several jurisdictions have adopted an equitable remuneration scheme for works that are relevant for educational purposes. See Jane Ginsburg, "Fair Use for Free, Permitted-but-Paid?" (2014) 29 BTLJ 1383 at 417–432.

32 Daniel Gervais, *(Re)structuring Copyright: A Comprehensive Path to International Copyright Reform* (Cheltenham: Edward Elgar, 2017) at 84; Ruth L. Okediji, "The International Copyright System: Limitations, Exceptions and Public Interest Considerations for Developing Countries" (2006) UNCTAD-ICTSD Issue Paper No. 15 at 13–14 [Okediji, The International Copyright System].

33 See generally Daniel Gervais, "Towards a New Core International Copyright Norm: The Reverse Three-Step Test," (2005) 9 Marq Intell Prop L Rev 1 at 18–19 (2005).
34 See generally Christophe Geiger et al., "Towards a Balanced Interpretation of the 'Three-Step Test' for Copyright Exceptions" (2008) Eur IP Rev 489.
35 See generally Martin Senftleben, "The International Three-Step Test: A model Provision for EC Fair Use Legislation" (2010) 1 JIPIT 67; Ruth Okediji, Towards International Fair Use Doctrine (2000) 39 Colum J Transnat'l L 75.
36 Jerome Reichman & Ruth Okediji, "When Copyright Law and Science Collide: Empowering Digitally Integrated Research Methods on a Global Scale" (2012) 96 Minn L Rev 1362 at 1470.
37 *Ibid* at 1466–1467 & 1469–1470; Eric Priest, "Copyright and the Harvard Open Access Mandate," (2012) 10:7 Nw J Tech & Intell Prop 377 at 394–395.

Index

For Product Safety Concerns and Information please contact our EU representative GPSR@taylorandfrancis.com
Taylor & Francis Verlag GmbH, Kaufingerstraße 24, 80331 München, Germany

www.ingramcontent.com/pod-product-compliance
Ingram Content Group UK Ltd.
Pitfield, Milton Keynes, MK11 3LW, UK
UKHW020008200926
475702UK00015B/2544
* 9 7 8 1 0 3 2 1 0 2 2 4 5 *